THE GEORGIANS AT HOME

*

The Author:

Born in Cairo, Elizabeth Burton grew up in Windsor,
Ontario, and later studied privately in Rome where her
main interests were music and history. Returning to
Canada she made a career for herself in radio and advertising until, in 1936, she decided to settle in England.
She has been a reporter, a foreign correspondent, and,
under another name, has written six novels. Now, at
her home in Oxfordshire, she concentrates solely on
history, and in addition to *The Georgians at Home*, is
the author of *The Elizabethans at Home* (also available
in Arrow Books), *The Jacobeans at Home*, and *The Early
Victorians at Home*. She is currently at work on further
additions to her extensive study of English domestic life.

The Illustrator:

Felix Kelly, one of our leading topographical painters,
was born in New Zealand and came to London shortly
before the war. While serving with the R.A.F. he
started to paint seriously in his spare time, and first
exhibited in 1943 at the Lefevre Gallery. Since then he
has exhibited in the United States and, in this country,
at the Leicester Gallery, the Arthur Jeffress Gallery, and
at Arthur Tooth & Sons. *Paintings by Felix Kelly*, with
an Introduction by Sir Herbert Read, was published in
1948. Felix Kelly has also designed stage sets which
include Sir John Gielgud's production of *A Day by the
Sea*, *The Last Joke* and the opera *Nelson*.

Elizabeth Burton

The Georgians at Home

illustrated by
FELIX KELLY

ARROW BOOKS

ARROW BOOKS LTD
3 Fitzroy Square, London W1

AN IMPRINT OF THE  HUTCHINSON GROUP

London Melbourne Sydney Auckland
Wellington Johannesburg Cape Town
and agencies throughout the world

First published by
Longmans, Green & Co. Ltd 1967
First paperback edition
Arrow Books 1973

*Made and printed in Great Britain by
C. Nicholls & Company Ltd
The Philips Park Press
Manchester*

ISBN 0 09 907480 X

It is by studying little things that we attain to the great art of having as little misery and as much happiness as possible.

DR SAMUEL JOHNSON

CONTENTS

ACKNOWLEDGEMENTS

I am deeply grateful to His Grace the Duke of Devonshire and the Trustees of the Chatsworth Settlement for permission to read and to quote from the Family Papers and Accounts of the Cavendish Family, preserved at Chatsworth; I am also vastly indebted to Mr T. S. Wragg, M.B.E., T.D., Curator of the Devonshire Collections, who has for years given me his assistance and advice.

I am also grateful to His Grace the Duke of Marlborough for allowing me to quote from certain letters written to the first Duchess; and to Mr David B. Green, Blenheim's Historian, who, among other kindnesses, let me read, in manuscript, certain relevant portions of his biography *Sarah, Duchess of Marlborough*.

Once again, my sincere thanks to Professor Donald F. Bond, of the University of Chicago, who has, with such patience and fortitude, endured and answered the many questions I have put to him. To Dr Peter Willis, A.R.I.B.A., Dumbarton Oaks, Washington D.C., I am most grateful for generous information concerning Charles Bridgeman—on whom he is an authority—and for his thoughtfulness in providing me with the necessary references which saved me time and anxiety. Mr William A. Billington, Curator of the Wedgwood Museum, was enormously helpful on many points and particularly on the production of the great dinner service made for the Empress Catherine the Great. My thanks also go to Mr F. G. Emmison, M.B.E., County Archivist of the Essex Record Office; to the Keeper of the Public Record Office, and to Mr Reginald Williams, Research Assistant of the Department of Prints and Drawings, British Museum.

As the reader will see at a glance, this book owes much to Mr Felix Kelly's enchanting and beautiful illustrations, but I owe him even more for his constant encouragement and for the help and advice he gave me with Chapter Two.

Acknowledgements

Dr Margaret B. Noble, M.R.C.O.G., most kindly read Chapter Six for me, while certain friends and even strangers allowed me to see and examine closely many eighteenth-century 'treasures'. They also loaned me rare books and pamphlets from their libraries. For obvious reasons they prefer to remain anonymous.

I am greatly indebted to the Librarian and staff of the London Library for their unfailing courtesy and assistance; as I am to the Librarian and staff of the Bodleian—especially Mr R. G. Chapman; to the excellent Oxfordshire County Library—particularly to Mrs Wheeler of the Witney Branch; and to the Librarian and staff of the Royal Zoological Society of London.

In view of the assistance and kindness I have received from so many people who are experts in their own fields, I must, in fairness, state that any errors of fact, any mistaken judgments are entirely my own.

Hailey, Oxon   E. B.
September 1966

CHAPTER ONE

Of Georgian England

It all went off rather better than expected. There was little rioting
in London's streets, only one duke missing from the Abbey,
and if Lady Nottingham made rather an exhibition of herself by
the theatrical way in which she indicated her High Church Tory
tendencies it is doubtful if the chief actor, born a Lutheran, even
noticed. What was important to him and to the country, on this
bright, fine twentieth day of October 1714, was that he, George
Lewis of Brunswick-Lüneberg, hereditary lay Bishop of Osna-
brück, Elector of Hanover and a great grandson of James I,
was now, if not entirely by the Grace of God, at least by the Act
of Settlement, crowned King, and our 'Liberties and Properties',
no less than 'our holy Religion', were 'thus preserved'.[1]

This frog-eyed, corpulent, unpleasant little man of fifty-four
was the first of the four Georges. His wife, Sophia Dorothea of
Zell, was not present on this or any other occasion. He had
divorced her on a trumped-up charge in 1694, then locked her
up for life in the fortress castle of Dahlen. Their only son, thirty-
one-year-old George Augustus, who loved his mother and hated
his father, was there, however—a temporary 'hanging up of
hatchets' had been effected for the great ceremony. What seems
a trifle negligent is, the new King had known for many years
that England, with luck, would be his (he had once even wooed
his cousin the late Queen Anne) but he could not speak a word of
the beastly language of this very foreign country over which he
was now ruler. So there he stood amid the traditional ceremony,
the music, the age-old but refurbished ritual of the coronation,

our first Hanoverian sovereign; the end product of the Glorious Revolution of 1688, and of a good deal of skirmishing, bitterness and intrigue in between. Here, personified, was the triumph of the Whigs; the disaster of the Tories.

Lady Mary Wortley Montagu who had met him in Hanover called him 'an honest blockhead'.[2] She was wrong on both counts. George's rapacity and dullness was exceeded only by that of his stupendously ugly mistresses, but he was no blockhead. He knew on which side his bread was buttered, and so did the Whigs. Quite simply, they could not do without George; he could not do without them. And if many loyal Hanoverian subjects had expressed alarm at their Elector going off to a barbarous country where he might have his head chopped off, George Lewis had no qualms. 'I have nothing to fear,' he told them, 'for the king-killers are all my friends.'[3]

So began the long ascendancy of the Whigs, the wanderings in the wilderness of the Tories. Ironically, it had been a Tory major-ity which had passed the Act of Settlement in 1701.

This England over which the first George came to rule was as foreign to him then as it is to us now. The new King stood at that very last moment in our history when the age-old balance between countryside and town still held. For the Georgian era began on horseback and ended in a railway carriage. That the new King disliked England and its people is neither here nor there. England was still beautiful and still essentially rural. It is true the barrister, Jethro Tull, had already invented his new seed drill and horse-hoe—probably the first real advance in the mechanization of agriculture since the days of Pliny—and was propounding new and improved methods of husbandry on his farm near Hunger-ford, Berkshire, but only great landowners, agricultural 'scien-tists' and the intellectual *élite* were, or could afford to be, interested. Small squires, tenant farmers, yeomen, the agricultural labourer with his strip of common still broadcast seed and hoed by hand. Not yet had 'John Kay of Bury in our county of Lancaster, Reedmaker'[4] invented the fly shuttle, nor Richard Arkwright, 'the father of the factory system', his loom. Industry, particularly the textile industry, was still in the main domestic, carried on in cottages. And if Newton had already answered the great question '*Come son fisse/Le stelle in cielo*', only mathematicians and philosophers could understand that, basically the answer meant a universe which worked independent of a spiritual or supernatural order and into which a revealed religion had somehow, rather awkwardly, to be fitted. The average countryman still knew, if not by instruction at least by oral tradition, who bound 'the sweet influence of the Pleiades' and guided 'Arcturus with his sons':[5] Arcturus ploughing the heavens at dusk in early spring, Arcturus, the 'churl's wain', out at dawn in autumn to carry the harvest home.*

As to the countryside, where the vast majority of England's five and a half to six million lived, although enclosures were by no means new, they had not yet affected the overall pattern of the country. It was not until the reign of George III, when the great enclosure Acts were speeded up so enormously, that the 'look' of England began to change radically and a new pattern was superimposed upon the old.

The old, save in the extreme south-east and some western counties, was still to a great extent a country of champion fields, sprawling common, waste and woodland. Fen drainage had begun in Cromwell's time, but there were still vast marshlands alive with waterfowl, to say nothing of that strange bit of country in Cleveland which 'if wild geese attempt to fly over, they fall down dead'.[6] Even more 'dismal and frightening',[7] to humans if not to geese, were bogs like those near Black Barnsley, thin of houses and people and near the treacherous moors into which posts were driven to show the infrequent and terrified traveller how to pick his lonely way in comparative safety. There were vanishing fields such as those near Hedon, so long fretted by the Humber that they were 'quite eaten up';[8] while some small

---

* Arcturus, once a constellation and not, as now, one of the brightest stars in Boötes, has been known as the plough, the bear, the dipper, the wagon and 'Charles's wain'. The last derives, possibly, from Charlemagne or perhaps from 'churl's' (peasant's) wain. For spring and autumn tasks on the land associated with Arcturus, see Hesiod, *Works and Days*.

villages in the Holderness peninsula, so people said, truthfully as it happens, had been entirely consumed.* In the Midlands and some parts of East Anglia, corn was still produced by the open-field method as it had been since medieval times. In the vast East Riding of Yorkshire, black cattle and the finest horses in the world were bred. But as England straitened to the north, the poverty of the soil, the impassability of the mountains, the scarcity of the population, were such that Defoe describes Westmorland as a 'country eminent only for being the wildest, most barren and frightful of any that I have passed over in England'.9

Although many towns were expanding and there was a slight shift of population northward, the largest unit in the average countryman's life was the village with small farms clustering around it. There was a true relationship between tiny community and countryside. They were interdependent. Isolated and cut off, for even the best roads were vile, a man might spend his whole life and never go farther than the nearest village market. In those days markets were not chiefly affairs of country towns, many a village had a tiny one of its own. Here too was the church, still the centre of village life and which, apart from its spiritual function, was the place where documents were kept (and some-times arms) where records were stored and proclamations read. The church had always been a stronghold for man in times of material as well as spiritual trouble, its tower a lookout, its bell to sound a tocsin as in the Jacobite risings of 1715 and 1745.

After mid-century, the speeding up of enclosures altered all this and imposed upon the countryside that 'chequerboard' pattern still recognizable today. Fields, it is true, were of various shapes and sizes; some followed the boundaries of the old strips, others were rectangles newly incised in unbroken land, but all were delineated by walls, fences and quickset hedges. This delineation went deeper than mere surface pattern. Apart from those dis-possessed of their rights to the common,† enclosure Acts were a

---

* Ravenspur, the port where Bolingbroke, later Edward IV, landed, was one of these.

† See Chapter Five.

major instrument in creating a new kind of landed interest. As the possession of land had always conferred upon its possessors certain political rights and social status, the increasingly rich commercial classes of the eighteenth century were hungry for the privileges land brought. In addition, owners of great estates always wanted to add a bit more to what they had. This inflated land values, and the small squire or landowner with a few hundred acres or less who could neither afford to add to his holding nor increase production had great inducement to sell. Thus, over a period of time a large number of small squires and landowners sold out. Some used their capital to go into industry or commerce, a few perhaps made fortunes. Others sought fortunes by buying themselves commissions in the army or navy. They ploughed with the sword and the keel. Sometimes the harvest was good, more often they left their blood to fertilize foreign fields or their bones to be picked clean by tropical fish. Some went out to India, like Warren Hastings, whose family had fallen into poverty and whose early education was as a Charity school boy. Some set out for the thirteen Colonies or the West Indies. Others rotted away at home with nothing to live on but bitter memories and reduced means. The already weakened yeoman fared worse. If lucky he became a tenant farmer; if unlucky a farm labourer; and if utterly damned drifted to the towns and cities to find work, if he could, at any sort of job. By the end of the eighteenth century there were virtually no small squires and certainly no yeomen, in the old sense of the word, left in England. The England of the first two Georges is far more remote from us than that of the last two.

As to its people? 'You do not know what a difficult task you set me', the Swiss protestant César de Saussure writes in 1727, when asked to describe the character, habits and customs of the English. Nevertheless, he tackles us bravely enough with 'I do not think there is a people more prejudiced in their own favour. . . . They look on foreigners in general with contempt and think nothing is as well done elsewhere as in their own country.' This comment was neither original nor new. Foreigners had been saying the same thing for centuries. But at least Saussure attempts to give a reason for our odious self-satisfaction and smugness. 'Certainly many more things contribute to keep up this good opinion of themselves,' he continues 'their love for their nation, its wealth, its plenty and liberty.'[10]

And with that word 'liberty', he touches upon what was once —and perhaps still is—the nerve centre, the core, the mainspring of the English character. Continental monarchs for centuries had tended towards absolute rule, but we, for both good and bad reasons, had always attempted to curb monarchal power by parliamentary institutions. This is the great outstanding and distinguishing fact of English history; and in the eighteenth century —which did indeed 'preserve our liberties'—our political institutions, ramshackle, inadequate and corrupt though they look to us, were the envy and admiration of liberal minded European philosophers and thinkers.

Voltaire,* after a short spell in the Bastille, where he had been thrown for daring to challenge a nobleman, came and lived in England from about 1726 to 1729. He moved in rather grander circles than Saussure but was no less astonished by our freedom. We were allowed to say and publish what we liked without fear of prison or exile. There was no such thing as torture or arbitrary imprisonment. Noblemen and priests were not exempt from certain taxes; 'it was the poor who enjoyed exemption from taxation in England, in France it was the rich'.[11] Religious sects were allowed to flourish, even that odd one called 'Quakers' which went so far as to denounce war as un-Christian! Montesquieu, who lived here from 1729 to 1731, was even more impressed. 'England', he writes in his *Travel Notes*, 'is the freest country in the world. I make exception of no republic. And I call it free because the sovereign, whose person is controlled and limited, is unable to inflict any harm on anyone'.

Another fact in our favour, as the less sophisticated Saussure discovered when he attended a levee at St James's, was that the king was not hedged round by pseudo-divinity. When people

---

* He later became an enthusiastic disciple of Tull's method of farming and practised it at Ferney.

Greenwich Hospital

bowed to George I he acknowledged this by inclining his head. 'The English do not consider their king to be so very much above them that they dare not salute him as in France',[12] he writes in utter astonishment. He can have known little of our history. Even our worst monarchs have rarely failed in that common civility which is the courtesy of kings. Rickety old St James's surprised him too—it was far from impressive as a great king's palace—even if it did have a 20-foot-long whale's skeleton clamped to the wall in the first court. Indeed, most foreign visitors thought us mad as we lodged our 'beggars' in beautiful buildings at Greenwich and Chelsea and our kings in what looked like almshouses! Even madder, many an English merchant was far richer than many a sovereign prince of Germany or Italy, while positively lunatic was the ambition of almost every merchant to make a fortune so that he could buy land in the country, build himself a fine house which couldn't even be *seen* from the road, and live the life of an English country gentleman.

Saussure's London, then as now, was a city of contrasts. If not the most beautiful of cities, travellers reported it to be the largest and most populous in Europe. Stretching for ten miles along the

Thames from Millbank to Blackwall, it was three miles across from Southwark to Moorfields,[13] and its population was estimated by some to be a million. This was a traveller's tale, the population was possibly around 650,000. But London, by now, had some new long straight streets and beautiful squares where the ground on either side was paved, not with gold as so many believed, but with 'flat stones so that you can walk without danger of being knocked down by coaches and horses'.[14]

Pavements were convenient for pedestrians but, needless to say, roadways were still bogs in winter, rutted and dusty in summer, and generally so bad that it was better not to trust one's self to a hackney. It was safer to walk on the pavement or go, when possible, by river. Once off the broad streets, once out of the Strand or Piccadilly or Hanover Square, London still consisted of a maze of narrow twisted streets and alleyways which stank abominably and where rotting dwellings and tenements housed the unfortunate. Some of these ancient houses were the shored-up relics of Tudor times, some had been jerry-built after the great fire of 1666, some were newer but were equally badly, if not worse, built—despite building regulations. Houses often fell down without warning, burying the luckless inhabitants and injuring passers-by. Fires were frequent, but London was so smoky that a Swedish traveller reported, when 100 houses were burned down near the Royal Exchange, Londoners didn't know about it until they read it in the papers the following day.[15]

Despite the fact that parts of London were, by continental and provincial standards, well lit by lamps shaped like frying pans, it was certainly very unsafe to go out alone or unarmed after dark. Gangs prowled the streets to rob, beat up, gouge out the eyes of their hapless victims. Thieves and robbers, according to Dr Tobias Smollett's *History of England*, were more desperate and savage than at any other time in the history of civilization. Every generation it seems has felt the same. It is true that in early Georgian times there were watchmen and constables, but they were of small use. Drawn largely from those who were physically or otherwise incapable of any other sort of job and armed only with poles, they naturally preferred to seek their own safety by staying indoors—chiefly in beer shops. It wasn't until around 1750 that Sir John Fielding, the blind Bow Street magistrate with his half-brother the great novelist and magistrate, Henry Fielding, began a 'police' system of picked men and placed them under the direct control of Bow Street magistrates. So the famous Bow Street Runners came into being.

London, as the twenty-nine-year-old, relatively unknown, Samuel Johnson put it, was a place where

> . . . . malice, rapine, accident conspire.
> And now a rabble rages, now a fire;
> Their ambush here relentless ruffians lay,
> And here a fell attorney prowls for prey;
> Here falling houses thunder on your head,
> And here a female Atheist talks you dead.[16]

Better it seems, and one can barely disagree, to be ambushed by thugs, diddled by lawyers, buried under rubble than talked to death. Yet it was the great Dr Johnson, that inveterate Londoner, who said nearly forty years later: 'Walking in the streets of London, which is really to me high entertainment of itself, I see a vast museum of all objects and I think with a kind of wonder that I see it for nothing.'[17]

Certainly there were few visitors, native or foreign, or even Londoners, who would have disagreed with this at any time during the whole era. London was full of things to do and see, of people, of excitement; it was at the heart of affairs great and small. Mobs overturned coaches of foreign ambassadors, or insulted Members of Parliament, or rioted at the cry of almost any rabble-rouser, or gathered in hordes to gawp and stare at the beautiful, the famous or infamous as they passed by. For a price there were theatres, balls, assemblies, wax works, taverns, gardens, thousands of grog shops, bawdy houses from the fashionable bagnios of Covent Garden, like that run by Mrs Cole* whose

---

* Mrs Cole, the procuress, is supposed to be Mother Douglas of the Piazza. She was very well known. Hogarth introduced her into several prints, and she was also impersonated on the stage.

young ladies included Fanny Hill, to the cheap cat-houses of London's underworld. London catered to every taste and pocket. Shops were fascinating, full of every imaginable and unimaginable thing brought from the four corners of the earth—save when several corners were at war with each other, which was not uncommon. Shop signs, beautifully painted and gilded, swung over the streets like stiffened, triumphal banners. In early Georgian London, the medieval walls still surrounded the city, and the supposed head of Cromwell, together with other malefactors, still embossed Temple Bar.* St Paul's was, as yet, brand new and glittering and considered to be one of the three most beautiful churches in the world—a statement of Saussure's with which one cannot quarrel.

The view from the top was magnificent, smoke permitting, which it rarely did. From here London and its environs were spread below like a gigantic piece of stump-work. Over there was the charming little village of Kensington with its houses, gardens and 'extremely smooth lawns'.[18] To reach it one drove along a beautiful road 'perfectly straight and so wide that three or four coaches can drive abreast'.[19] To the north was the village of Marybone with its public gardens and open fields—the last near the Oxford Road. Here, one James Figg, a famous fighter, was proprietor of a 'boarded-house' where he showed off his own prowess and arranged matches. Those between women were particularly popular, and the most celebrated female prize-fighter was a Mrs Stokes. She was at the top of her form in 1725 and attracted enormous crowds.[20] We loved fighting, all foreign visitors commented on this, and when two members of the 'brutal lower populace'—the words are Saussure's—fought it out in the street, a crowd quickly collected and began laying bets. Brutal though they may have been, the antagonists, in their English way, always shook hands before slogging it out.

Farther away was the tiny village of Paddington. And two miles off the market town of Islington with its famous Sadler's Wells.

* We were still at it in 1745 when we used the heads of the leaders of 'the '45' as bosses.

The new St Paul's. Sir Christopher Wren, 1632–1723

But the roving eye returning from distant prospects looked straight down from Wren's triumph on to 'the foster mother of London',[21] the Thames, 'everywhere wide and beautiful'. Everywhere full of excitement, interest and colour. London's lifeline and her greatest highway. Above the only bridge which spanned it, London Bridge, where a rising tide roared and rushed like rapids under its arches, the river was 'covered with craft of every sort' and there were, in addition to the gaily coloured gilded barges of the rich and of various livery companies, at least '15,000 small boats for the transport of persons'. Below the bridge the river was 'almost hidden by merchant vessels from every country . . . anchored in rows'.[22] These formed streets with open water in between the rows to allow free passage. One 'street' was entirely of French ships, another of Dutch, another of

Spanish and so on. In a sense the Thames was sectionalized into foreign quarters. But there were also sections for native coastal vessels which brought goods and commodities to the capital. Chief among these were those which carried coal from Newcastle. Opposite old Somerset House the famous barge and bawdy house *The Folly* lay. On the first floor—or deck—'water nymphs' ate and drank with 'tritons' while a band played popular music of the day. On the second floor were many small and convenient rooms to which 'nymphs and tritons' retired, 'when tired of the world'.[23] The euphemisms are Saussure's, not mine.

London was less easy to see on foot. Nevertheless, there was Westminster Abbey, without the two towers on its west front, which weren't built until 1734.* Saussure was not impressed with the Abbey, and though he thought the Henry VII Chapel splendid, he notes that 'on all the wooden seats intended for canons' there were 'carvings of a very immodest design'.† His eyesight must have been positively microscopic for in the next breath he tells us that these immodest figures are so small 'they generally pass unperceived'.[24] Nor was he much impressed with that other mecca for sightseers, the Tower of London, and notes only that the king's menagerie was a rather small, poor, dusty affair containing ten lions, one panther, two tigers, four leopards, a large monkey from Sumatra (it perished of cold during the following winter) and 'a great quantity of curious birds'.[25]

But London changed, grew and spread with the century. As new industries moved in, it became smokier and smokier, more and more populous, more and more congested with wheeled traffic to say nothing of the great droves of cattle driven through the streets to Smithfield to keep Londoners supplied with fresh meat. By 1756 traffic had become so appalling that it was decided to build a new road—called just that—to run in a curved line north of the city. This was, very probably, our first ring road,

* Nicholas Hawksmoor designed these to Wren's plan in 1725, but work was not begun until 1734 and not completed until 1740. We now regard the towers with affection but at the time many were very dubious about them.
† Having carefully examined the carvings on the misericords, I can only conclude Saussure was a prude.

though it was only half a ring. Forty foot wide and right out in the country, it passed over fields and farm land so that the most thickly populated areas could be avoided. But the New Road did not long remain in the country, for the surrounding country rapidly became a built-up area. Other changes took place too. By 1760 London's medieval walls were demolished and the traditional gates removed, a new bridge spanned the river at Westminster (not the present one) while the old, tumbled-down clutter of houses on London Bridge had been torn down to help relieve the traffic problem. By this time, it had been decided that the Lord Mayor should have a special house in which to live and not, as formerly, occupy his own house. So the Mansion House was built (1739–53). Here London lagged behind the capital of the north, York; its beautiful Mansion House was built in 1728.

In 1782 when the disastrous American War was ending, another visitor, Pastor Moritz, a Swiss like Saussure, visited London to begin that unheard of thing, a walking tour of England. He first glimpsed London 'enveloped in thick smoke',[26] and though London houses struck him as being 'prodigiously great and majestic', they were also 'dark and gloomy'. There were not so many fine streets as in Berlin and these not-so-fine streets were always crowded with 'a tumult of people'. But at least it is a comfort to know he thought us a good deal better looking than Berliners. He, too, notices the shop signs, but by now few swung over the streets; they had been replaced by lettered boards affixed to doors and windows. It was not uncommon 'to see on doors in one continuous succession, *children educated here; Shoes mended here; foreign spiritous liquors sold here; Funerals furnished here*'.[27] The commonest of the lot was the spirituous liquors one, and the drinking of brandy and gin, he notes, was carried to excess by the common people. Saussure had also noted our piggy drinking habits, but in his day, the chief tipple of the 'common people' had been beer at a penny a pot. Water existed in abundance but 'would you believe it', he writes, '. . . absolutely none is drunk'.[28] It was perhaps just as well. There were enough diseases to carry us off in droves without drinking contaminated water.

Standing on Westminster Bridge and looking towards the new Blackfriars Bridge (opened 1770) Pastor Moritz was also enchanted by the river and notes particularly that 'on the left side of the Thames are delightful terraces, planted with trees and those new tasteful buildings called the Adelphi'.[29] But ceasing to contemplate the beauties of the river and hieing himself on foot through London he found nothing more disgusting than the butcher's shops, especially those near the Tower where 'Guts and all nastiness are thrown into the streets and causes an insupportable stench'. St James's was 'one of the meanest public buildings in London;' St Paul's was a work of art but not a church and much too closely surrounded by houses. The Abbey failed to move him, bar the Poet's Corner; and Westminster Hall he calls 'an enormous gothick building' which he passed through en route to the Strangers' Gallery in the House of Commons where he bribed his way in with a bottle of wine. The Commons was pretty 'mean looking', the benches covered with green cloth, the speaker elderly and almost eclipsed by an enormous wig. More surprisingly, Members of Parliament wore no special dress, in fact they came in boots and greatcoats and kept their hats on. Many a M.P. lay prone upon a bench eating oranges or cracking nuts during a debate. Bad speakers were laughed out, but good ones were heard in 'perfect silence' and were approved by calls of 'hear him'. Moritz was also struck (and perhaps horrified) by the downright 'open abuse' and the rude remarks members indulged in. But he saw and heard both Fox and Burke, and of his visit to Parliament he has this to say; 'Had I seen nothing else in England but that, I should have thought my journey thither amply rewarded.' He also says this of England and the English: 'In this happy country, the lowest and meanest members of society . . . testifies the interest which he takes in everything of a public nature . . . high and low, rich and poor . . . a carter, a common tar or a scavenger is still a man, nay an Englishman; and as such has his rights and privileges defined and known as exactly and as well as his king, or as his king's ministers.'[30]

Poor Moritz, although he didn't know it when he arrived, was

Kensington Palace in neglect

also in for something equally English, 'one of the most deplorably wet summers'[31] Horace Walpole (1717–97) could ever remember. And Horace's memory went a long way back. He had kissed the hand of George I, when a boy of ten, just before the king departed for his beloved Hanover for the last time, and he did not die until that year when we stood absolutely alone in the war with France —and won the battle of Cape St Vincent. But in 1791 Horace at last succeeded to his great father's diminished estates and title and became 4th Earl of Orford.* The Rev. Daniel Lysons (1762–1834), who became his chaplain, wrote the fascinating books, *The Environs of London.*

Kensington, as in Saussure's time, was still a village with some pleasant pastures and fields, but it also now contained about

* Gossip had it that Horace, the fourth son of Sir Robert Walpole, 1st Earl, was really the son of Carr, Lord Hervey. Certainly Horace was not big boned and fleshy like the Walpoles and his wit (particularly when leavened with malice), and eccentricities seem more Herveian than Walpolian. But the rumour is discounted by R. W. Ketton-Cremer in his biography, *Horace Walpole* (Faber, second edn., 1946).

230 market gardens and some 1,240 houses. At Earl's Court, the famous Dr John Hunter had a villa and a 'valuable menagerie of foreign animals'. As for Kensington Palace, so frequently inhabited by King William, Queen Anne and the first two Georges (all of whom except George I died there) it was 'entirely forsaken'.[32] Marybone, a parish of 8¾ miles in circumference, had a new church near the Tybourne and was about one-third built over; plans for more extensive building were already well in hand. The famous gardens once occupying the present site of Beaumont Street, parts of Devonshire Street and Devonshire Place, were no more. But Marybone now contained many splendid mansions. Manchester House, Foley House, Harcourt House, Chandos House, to say nothing of 'Mrs Montagu's very elegant mansion in Portman Square'.[33] The district also contained the Middlesex Hospital, instituted in 1745, for sick and lying-in married women—the unmarried could, presumably, lie in the gutter—which had just received a gift from an anonymous donor to provide an 'establishment' for those 'afflicted with cancer', a plan which had been suggested by John Howard, the great prison reformer.

Paddington was still a village scarce a mile from Tybourne turnpike on the Edgware Road, but there was a fine house on the east of Paddington Green, and the 'messauge' (now Westbourne Place) once the property of Isaac Ware, the architect, was extremely pleasant and so 'uncommonly retired' that it was as good as living in the country. Emma Hart, before she went out to visit Sir William Hamilton in Naples in 1786, lived in Paddington. The parish was, however, chiefly church land and there had been little increase in building until 1788 when about 100 small cottages were built and let chiefly to journeymen and artificers who worked in London. These cottages, which housed about six souls each, were let at from £7 to £12 per annum. One might have expected the church to see that some sort of education was provided for the children of the parish—but no. There wasn't even a Charity School, although there was a Sunday School supported entirely by voluntary contributions.

The parish of Islington was still almost wholly pasture and meadow and contained about 1,200 houses to its 3,000 acres. Islington provided some of London's milk and butter and the cow population, half of which belonged to a Mr West, numbered 1,200 to 1,500. The Rev. Mr Lysons lived to see even greater changes than those which had occurred in the seventy-five odd years between Saussure's description of the environs of London and his own. London went on spreading, its environs linked hands and joined together in a sprawling mass, while the population rose to over a million in 1801 and, increasing by an average of fourteen per cent every decade, was around 1½ million in 1831, the year following the death of the last Hanoverian George. Lysons may not have seen, but was certainly alive when the first horse omnibus in London began running in 1829 from Paddington Green to the Bank of England, carrying a load of eighteen passengers. For Paddington had become populous and full of good houses standing cheek by jowl with its slums. The 'city gents' who went by omnibus were provided by the proprietors with newspapers and books to while away the long journey. But if the distance was not great London's traffic was appalling. It vexed and tormented everyone. Sad to say this was, and is, nothing new. As far back as 1598 when coaches were first intro-duced into England, John Stow had grumbled that 'the world runs on wheels' and the clumsy, heavy vehicles of that time obstructed London's streets. London's traffic problem will soon celebrate its four hundredth anniversary.

The growth of London was matched in other urban centres. In the first edition of Defoe's *A Tour Through England and Wales*, written in 1725, Defoe dismisses Birmingham* in four words. In the eighth edition of the work 'as revised in 1778 by a Gentleman of Eminence in the Literary World', Birmingham is already noted as 'a large and save for some narrow streets, handsome

---

* This is interesting for even in Leyland's day, Birmingham—or Bremischam as he calls it—was a good market town and famous for its smiths, lorimers and 'naylors'; but see, Leyland's *Itineraries* (1535-43) edited by Lucy Toulmin Smith, Part v, Bk. ii, pp. 96-7.

town' with a pleasure garden and full of lively, gay people. It was also a positive hive of industry (the shift in population towards the midlands and north was by now very apparent). Birmingham's 'navigable cut' of 1760 had made this industry possible by supplying the town with good cheap coal; an extension of the cut also linked Birmingham to the Severn and thus to Gloucester and the great port of Bristol. A further link with Liverpool, via the Mersey, was already planned.

Bristol in 1723 was 'the best port of trade in Great Britain London only excepted'.³⁴ The city was 'close built' but the 'obstinacy' of the inhabitants who, incidentally, had done some pretty rioting at the coronation of the first George,* prevented anyone trading there unless he were a freeman of the city. This meant that in one part where 'the liberties did not extend' many new streets and houses were being built. By 1778 Bristol was the second city in Great Britain; its trade had grown enormously. Great fleets of merchant ships from Holland, Hamburg, Norway and Russia, from the cold coasts of Newfoundland and the warm waters of the Mediterranean, anchored there near the great new docks. Freedom of the city could now be bought for a small sum and since Defoe's first visit 4,000 houses had been built; there was also a new Parade and a theatre, 'a perfect model of elegance'.³⁵

As for Liverpool, Defoe visited it three times in 1680, 1690 and 1723, and on each occasion found it greatly grown. It had more than doubled, he says, between 1690 (when the population was about 6,000) and 1723, and there was a great increase in wealth, people, business and buildings. 'There is no town in England, London excepted, that can equal Liverpool in the fineness of the streets and the beauty of buildings', and, he adds, 'what it may grow to in time, I know not.'³⁶ By 1788 Liverpool rivalled

---

* This was followed at Norwich, Reading, Birmingham, Bedford. London took to rioting too and the Riot Act, still in force, was passed in June 1715. Disgruntled and anti-Hanoverian Tories went in for low libels of George I and the Whigs, and stirred up mobs to embarrass the government. But Whigs and Tories also went for each other in newspapers, broadsheets and ballads of a most scurrilous nature.

Bristol as a port but had become so over-crowded that 'No place . . . except London and Edinburgh' contained 'so many inhabitants in so small a compass'. The buildings were no longer beautiful and the streets too narrow for 'convenience or health'.[37] Manchester had jumped from being the 'greatest meer village in England'[38] to one of the greatest textile centres, for cottons and silks no less than 'velverets'—a type of fustian with a velvet surface. Even so, great, populous and thriving Manchester still had no parliamentary representation. Newcastle had doubled its population since the turn of the century and was now almost as smoky as London. Sheffield flourished, and the dark, narrow streets of the old town were encompassed by new, handsome ones; a new beautiful Assembly Room had been built and 'a large commodious theatre'[39] seating 800.

The growth of towns and villages was due to a number of things. Transport was one. Roads did improve slightly, particularly the turnpike trust roads nearer the larger towns, but the majority remained 'as God left them after the flood'.[40] This is not strictly true. Roads were worse than in the immediate post-diluvian years, for if the Lord created the horse, it was man who created the vehicles for horses to draw, and these cut the bad surfaces into dangerously deep ruts and pot-holes. By the time of George II there were so many different kinds of conveyance that the Pelham Government in 1747 imposed an excise duty of £4 per annum 'for every Coach, Berlin, Landau, Chariot, Calash with four wheels, Chaise, Marine, Chaise with four wheels and Caravan* or by what name such Carriages now are or hereafter may be called or known'.[41] Still, no one had to pay the tax on more than five vehicles, which seems to indicate that the really rich must have owned a variety, each designed for a different purpose. Just what the government used the money for is anybody's guess, as it is today, but it certainly was not for the improvement of roads. Arthur Young, who made several tours of England on horseback, gives us an excellent picture of the state of the roads. For example, to take only his *Six Months Tour*

* A covered wagon or cart, now shortened to our word 'van'.

Through the North of England, he covered, he says, some 2,500 miles and traversed 123 different roads. Separating out his comments on these 123, one finds 59 were good or fairly good; 64 are labelled 'indifferent', 'middling', 'vile' and 'execrable'.[42] The road to Asrig was 'fit only for a goat to travel', as for the turnpike at Warrington, 'any person would imagine the people of the country had made it with a view to immediate destruction'.[43] On the other hand, there was an 'astonishingly good road' from Bedford to Biggleswade, 'due to the efforts of a gentleman who gave £50 to assist'.*[44]

The world did, indeed, move on wheels but faster than ever. Stage coaches and mail coaches now ran between London and all large towns; people travelled a good deal more despite the chronic overturning of carriages, bogging down of coaches, and the depredations of innumerable highwaymen. So news of London now reached the provinces more rapidly than ever before. At the beginning of the Georgian period people who lived in remote parts of England, were almost as strange in manners, fashions, customs—compared, that is, with those who lived in London— as if they lived in a foreign country. But with improved transport and the regular operation of much swifter coaches provincial centres were brought into much more rapid contact with the capital, and emulated its ways. Manners, fashions in dress, furniture, architecture, food, ornaments, spread out from London as they always had done, but the time-lag was now almost negligible, whereas in the previous century it had been estimated —a trifle sarcastically one feels—to have been about fifty years.

And, like the rich London merchant who had long since ceased to live above his shop, the rich provincial merchant now followed suit and built himself a neat villa in whatever was the prevailing fashion, outside the town in which he carried on his business. This continual moving outward enlarged towns at the perimeter but often left appalling slum conditions in the centre.

---

* It was not until 1827 that J. L. McAdam (1756–1836), a Scot, was appointed Surveyor of Roads and had a good number 'macadamized' that is, properly drained and surfaced with broken stone.

Canals: new waterways in the sky

Another kind of transport had an even greater effect upon the growth of many towns and on industry. This was an inland waterway system of canals which linked navigable rivers together and provided better transport for goods. Hitherto, goods bound to or from centres which were neither on the coast nor on a navigable river had been transported by broad wheeled covered wagons or by trains of pack-horses. If the greatest speed at which a man could travel was on horseback—and we bred fleet riding horses—so the greatest quantity of goods which could be carried overland was limited and controlled by the strength and number of horses (or even bullocks) used. But in 1761 Francis Egerton, third and last Duke of Bridgewater, with that great engineer James Brindley, completed his famous canal* from Worsley, his estate 'abounding with coal mines',45 to Manchester. Upon this cheap and swift supply of coal Manchester's new prosperity was founded. Arthur

* I suppose the Roman fosse Dyke was our first artificial canal. Camden (*Britannia*) says it was deepened in 1121 and to some extent made renavigable. A few very small canals were built in the seventeenth century too.

Young went by barge from Manchester to Worsley in 1766 and thoroughly enjoyed it. He was full of wonder and admiration for the way the canal was carried 'Roman aqueduct' fashion on arches over the Irwell and across a large valley. Further, the canal ended up—or began—in the heart of the coal mine itself. This not only provided transport at the immediate source of supply, but the canal also kept the mine drained. The canal was subsequently carried to Liverpool, which even as late as 1760 had no carriage road, and the Duke's 'experiment' was such a success that it started a boom in canal building.

The Grand Trunk Canal (now the Trent and Mersey), instituted by Josiah Wedgwood, supplied the potteries with special clay previously brought from the south by sea or up the Severn to Chester and from there transported by pack horse. Canals now carried the raw materials to the site of manufacture and the finished product from the site back to distribution centres. John Wesley, in 1781, thought that canals had changed the face of the country in a mere twenty years, particularly in the potteries, where villages and towns had sprung up and turned the wilderness into a fruitful field. But the cutting of canals was an enormous engineering project and the 'navigators' (hence our word navvy) who worked on them invaded the countryside in hordes and often rather disrupted village life. Further, the wages they were paid drew so many labourers from agriculture that by 1793, a Bill was introduced prohibiting work on canals during harvest for fear shortage of labour in the fields would mean a shortage of bread. As we were then engaged in a desperate war with France, we needed every ear of wheat we could produce. Even so, the price of bread soared catastrophically and if it hadn't been for the general improvement in agriculture, due in a large measure to enclosures which made improvement possible, we might have been defeated.

The building of canals created an entirely new profession, that of the civil engineer. Such men as Telford, Smeaton, Brindley, Jessop, Whitworth and Cubitt made their names—and their profession—through canal building. This was not a simple job like digging a ditch over flat land. Tunnels, bridges and aqueducts had to be built by manpower alone, while a clever system of alternative locks had to be devised to overcome rises in levels.

Early canals were built at small cost. The Duke of Bridge-water's cost only £200,000 and by 1792 was bringing in a neat £80,000 per annum from freight. No wonder there was a boom, and most canals built between 1760 and 1790 did well for their owners. But those who built canals after then and during the Napoleonic wars were caught by the rising costs of labour and materials.* Then, too, many were built solely as speculative ventures and ran through purely agricultural areas, the speculators hoping thereby to create enough trade to make them profitable. But it was the coming of the railways which finally ended the great canal era.

Railways were, of course, not new. Coal and minerals, since the seventeenth century and probably before, had been carried from mine to nearest waterway by means of wagons, often with flanged wooden wheels. These were drawn along wooden or sometimes metal-faced rails by men or horses. When coal mines near waterways became exhausted, these wooden lines were extended inland and posed as many problems for engineers as canals did later on. It is something of a shock to learn that the very first railway bridge—the Tanfield Arch in Co. Durham— was built at the end of the reign of George I (in 1726 to be precise) by a local mason, Ralph Woods. While the stone used to build beautiful Georgian Bath was carried from the Combe Hill quarries as early as 1730, along a railway laid down by Ralph Allen of Prior Park who, incidentally, is the model for good Squire Allworthy in Henry Fielding's *Tom Jones*.

Railways as we know them were, however, impossible until steam power could be properly harnessed. In the seventeenth century the Marquis of Worcester had invented a steam engine for pumping water,† and this had been vastly improved upon by such men as Savery and Newcomen. But it was not until James

* Wholesale prices increased by about ninety per cent between 1790 and 1810.
† See *The Jacobeans at Home*, Chapter VII.

Newcomen's atmospheric engine, 1717

Watt, a Scot, discovered when repairing a Newcomen engine, how, by means of a separate condenser, to make it far more powerful and efficient, and cheaper to operate, that steam began to replace water power in certain industries. These early engines were stationary, but as Erasmus Darwin, grandfather of Charles, prophesied in regrettable verse,

> Soon shall thy arm, Unconquer'd Steam, afar
> Drag the slow barge, or drive the rapid car.[46]

The rapid car came first when in 1801[*] the Cornishman, Richard Trevithick (1771–1833), made the first full-sized steam

---

[*] The steam barge appeared the following year when the *Charlotte Dundas*, the first practical steamship, invented by Symington, was tried on the Forth and Clyde canal. She was a paddle-wheel steamer with a double-acting condensing engine made by Watt. When in 1822 George IV visited Scotland, his yacht the *Royal George* was attached by hawser to the *Comet*, a steam packet.

road carriage.* And in 1804 produced the very first true locomotive in the world. It began working on the Pen-y-darran
railway on February 13th and one week later transported ten
tons of bar iron and about five tons of excited sightseers (that is
seventy people) from the Pen-y-darran works to the Glamorgan-
shire Canal, a distance of nine miles. Trevithick, the true father of
the locomotive, was an erratic genius and not very businesslike.
After adventures in many parts of the world, he returned to
England, petitioned a deaf government for aid, and died penni-
less. He was buried, at the expense of the workmen of Hall's
factory, in Dartford churchyard.

Trevithick was followed by others, and this invalidates the
common belief that George Stephenson invented the locomotive.
But it does not denigrate the splendid work of Stephenson, a
brilliant engineer. He worked on our first public railway—the
important word is public—the Stockton and Darlington which
opened in 1825. This railway was designed for locomotives *and*
horses. Goods were drawn by engine, passengers by horse. The
first public railway where goods and passengers were drawn by
the new iron horse was the Liverpool and Manchester, built to
compete with the Bridgewater Canal which by now was inadequate for its purpose and so charged very high carriage rates.
The building of the L. and M. met with every sort of opposition
from all sorts of interests. Those with money in the turnpikes
or canals; coach builders and proprietors of coaches; makers of
saddle and harnesses; landowners who believed this terrible
monster would lower land values and ruin their farms by scaring
cattle; blacksmiths and ironmongers who thought that iron
rails would so increase the price of iron they would be put out of
business . . . all these and others protested loud and long. George
Stephenson was, however, put in charge of the L. and M. in
1826 and was responsible for laying the line and for its locomotive power. The directors, undecided at first whether to use

* Models of machines which moved had been made around 1784 by James
Murdoch. Even earlier, in 1769, a Frenchman, Nicholas Cugnot had built a
'steam carriage' in Paris but this came to nothing.

stationary engines which would pull the wagons along by ropes, or to be brave and try locomotives, agreed to offer a prize of £500 for an improved locomotive. There were, in all, five entries, one of which, a 'Cyclopede', was powered by a horse working a sort of treadmill on a flat car. Another was George Stephenson's famous 'Rocket'. It could reach the unheard of speed of thirty miles per hour!

On June 26th 1830 the last of the four Georges died. Ninety-one days later, on September 15th, the London and Manchester was officially opened. It was a great occasion. The Prime Minister, the Duke of Wellington, was on hand (with lesser notables) and travelled in an open railway carriage of the greatest elegance, complete with Grecian scrolls, gilded balustrade, massy handrails and draperies of rich, crimson silk, the whole topped by a coronet. Alas, the great event was tragically marred by the first railway accident ever. William Huskisson, a progressive Tory statesman and M.P. for Liverpool in succession to Canning, had certainly not seen eye to eye with the reactionary Duke. Nevertheless, he descended from his carriage to go and shake the Prime Minister's hand and was run down by an engine which was merely showing off its speed on another line. This event, wrote Mr Creevey, 'must be followed by important political consequences. The Canning faction* has lost its cornerstone, and the Duke's government one of its most formidable opponents.'47 Two months after Huskisson's death the Tory administration came to an end, and the Whigs after many years of political exile, assumed office.

It is odd that the term 'Whig oligarchy' always springs to mind when one attempts to unravel the politics of the Hanoverian period because, in truth, this oligarchy ceased with the accession of George III. It took the new King ten trying years to learn the political ropes. But this he did, and so ably that in 1770 Lord

---

* The brilliant George Canning (1770–1827) had died, after a very short tenure as P.M., three years before. A Tory who did not hold with many of the reactionary Tory tenets he had a number of like-minded M.P.s on his side. Thus the 'Canning faction' persisted within the Tory party even after his death.

North (1732–92)* could form a powerful Tory ministry, though he always refused to be called Prime Minister. It is true Tory domination was broken for a few months in 1782, due to the American War—the King's War as many American sympathizers in this country called it—but after an ineffective coalition ministry the Tory party was subsequently entrenched more firmly than ever. It became as powerful, though possibly more broadly based and less oligarchical, as the famous Whig oligarchy or 'Robinocracy' as the Walpole haters called it; and it did not lose power until after the death of George IV. 'Naught's permanent among the human race', said Byron, bitterly, 'Except the Whigs NOT getting into place.'⁴⁸ Thus the Hanoverian era, politically, falls into two halves—Whig and Tory, with what might be called a parliamentary interregnum between 1760–70. If one translates this into virtually continuous years of power from the Stanhope† ministry to that of the Iron Duke‡ it will be found that the Whigs had a run of forty-six years, the Tories sixty-two. So the Tories, who under the younger Pitt became the really progressive party, win by several lengths !§

* In 1754 Banbury, where Benjamin Franklin's father came from, elected twenty-two-year-old Frederick North, M.P. His father was High Steward of Banbury. Franklin's was a dyer. Franklin, one of the truly great men and geniuses of his time, was, until the Revolution, a good friend of Great Britain. Had his advice, together with that of Chatham and Burke, been taken, there would have been no American War of Independence—at least not at the time it happened. The war, in the very nature of things was, I think, inevitable.

† James, 1st Earl Stanhope (1673–1721), took a leading part in securing Hanoverian succession and making it acceptable to the country. He was unjustly charged by Walpole and Townshend with treachery to colleagues. Walpole the great Whig who succeeded him, actually joined with the Tories in 1717 to protest against a standing army.

‡ He was not a progressive Tory and resigned in 1830 rather than accept parliamentary reform.

§ It was customary to call opposing parties Whig and Tory; neither were political parties as we know them but were largely made up of personal groups, each wanting power, but held together by ties of friendship, intermarriage and patronage rather than clear policies. Governments did not necessarily fall with the fall of a chief minister. Walpole was a Whig, so was the elder Pitt (Chatham) but he was an anti-Walpole Whig. The younger Pitt began life as a Whig, so did Canning,

This is of course no way to look at it. There are those who maintained then, as now, that the Whigs and George I saved us from Stuart absolutism, popery and bloody civil war. Others held—as some still do—an opposite view. They were strong for the 'legitimate' succession and drank to it with a toast worded 'to three pounds, fourteen and five pence' (James III, Lewis XIV, and Philip V). But if it is not by now perfectly clear that this book in no way purports to be a standard history, an economic history, a constitutional history or a social history, but merely a domestic history which concerns people and things of the age, then this point must be stressed.

Here, save in the briefest terms, is little concerning the momentous events of Georgian times. Perhaps it is better put this way; the immensely rich Duke of Newcastle was, in a sense, the cabinet maker of the early Georgian era, as George III was later on* but there were other kinds of cabinet makers—Chippendale, Hepplewhite, and Sheraton. Sir Robert Walpole was, some say, our most brilliant Prime Minister, but it is his son Horace who (pace Lord Macaulay) left us the richer for his brilliant, amusing, witty, malicious letters. Thus, broadly speaking, it is the Chippendales and the Horace Walpoles who chiefly concern us. Yet politics plays its part even in minor aspects of history. The great architect James Gibbs was a Tory and suspected of Roman Catholic leanings. When the Whigs with George I came to power, Gibbs was dismissed from his Surveyorship to the Church Building Commission. Robert Adam was more fortunate. He was a Tory, lived in the time of George III, and became architect to the king from 1762 to 1768. He was also M.P. for Kinross-shire! In short,

both ended as progressive Tories. Tories were often more progressive than Whigs. Coats were turned frequently, either out of conviction or sheer opportunism. Political parties were no more rigid than the class system, and to be a 'doctrinaire' anything would have been considered stupid.

* The Duke of Newcastle (1693–1768), twice Prime Minister, is said to have been the greatest corrupter of his time, yet he remained uncorrupted. The same may be said of George III. Both men had vast sums at their disposal and could outbribe almost any opponent. In the 1780 election George III complained that his expenses were double that of any previous election.

great architects, cabinet makers, artists, musicians and writers could not live without patrons and their influence. Patronage and influence also happen to be the key words of the politics of the time; without them no government, Whig or Tory, could have functioned. For if the power of the crown had been limited by the revolutionary settlement, and if the court also ceased to set a standard for culture, there were still innumerable offices—secular, ecclesiastical, and in the King's household*—in the gift of the crown.

These offices, or the disposal of them, were lucrative prizes for those loyal to the crown. Since George I had, understandably, chosen his whole cabinet—even before he arrived in England— from the Whig faction, the Whig Ministers had his ear and could promote their own party and personal interests by filling every office down to that of a customs man at a minor port with a loyal Whig.† Civil service posts, military, naval and colonial appointments; church preferment, sinecures of all sorts opened a broad field in which a political party could operate and in this field the Whigs operated splendidly. They would have been fools not to. They created a network of Whig power which spread from top to bottom. In addition, there were great Whig nobles and landlords who could and did make Whig dynastic marriages for themselves and their children, and who controlled votes by bribes, threats or because they owned various boroughs. They could find sinecures for younger sons, places for poor relations. The rich Whig merchant-prince could do the same (money talked) and most rich merchants, like the Puritans before them, represented the commercial interests of the country. Puritanism makes good business men, or did, and the commercial interests were to a

---

* Members of the sovereign's household were still in the process of being metamorphosed into ministers of state. For example Lord Bute, Groom of the Stole to George III when Prince of Wales, was one of the major influences on the King's early life (a father figure perhaps) and in 1762 became Prime Minister and a thoroughly detested one too.

† The so-called Whig Bible is the second edition of the Geneva Bible where, due to a printer's error, Matt. 5:9 reads: 'Blessed are the place makers, for they shall be called the children of God'.

large extent nonconformist, while the Tories were thought, often unjustly, to be tainted with Jacobitism and near-popery. The Tories were the country and 'Church' party. The Whigs had the city behind them. It is an interesting fact that few sovereigns and later few governments could survive without the backing of the city.*

Of course, the commercial theory of the time was not ours. It was believed no commerce could be of real advantage unless the value of exports exceeded the value of imports. Although we say we believe this, it is obvious we do not. But in those days money alone, that is hard cash, was considered real wealth, and the sole purpose of trade and commerce was to get as large a share as possible of precious metals. If the value of exports exceeded that of imports and the plus paid for in precious metal that was good. If, however, the plus were paid for in goods, it was not a plus at all, it was a positive evil as it diminished the supply of gold and silver.

One of the great achievements of Walpole† was that, like Queen Elizabeth I, he realized when he attained power, that England, after the protracted continental wars, needed a long period of peace to restore stability and balance the economy. It was Walpole who sorted out the mess left by the South Sea Bubble when it burst. He had warned against it—and judiciously made money by it. But this greatest of all bubbles was by no means the only one of the get-rich-quick schemes which, since the gambling instinct is one of the most deeply ingrained characteristics of the English, attracted a host of speculators great and small. One scheme, which we in our time should appreciate, was a method for making 'Salt Water Fresh'. Then there were

* During Queen Anne's last illness, stocks fluctuated with her condition. They rose when she was reported worse, and fell if she were reported better. Anne was a Tory.
† Since it is often said that we jail leaders of 'recalcitrant' parties in emergent countries and later have to treat with them when they become prime ministers of those countries, it is as well to remember that we imprisoned Walpole in the Tower before he became P.M. Since he is often called our first prime minister, this is not without significance!

Building Westminster Bridge, 1738–56 (demolished 1860)

companies formed for 'Extracting Silver from Lead'; 'Transmuting Quick Silver into a Malleable Fine Metal' (even King Charles II had been interested in this); 'Trading in Human Hair'; 'Fishing up Wrecks on the Irish Coast'; 'A Wheel for Perpetual Motion' and even a scheme for 'Importing Jackasses from Spain', which seems hardly necessary as there were obviously so many at home. Public lotteries were more popular than ever. Westminster Bridge was chiefly financed by lotteries, and in 1753 lotteries were used to help buy the Sloane, Harleian and Cottonian collections.

By 1753, however, Walpole was dead, though the Whigs under the elder Pitt (Lord Chatham) were still in power. Walpole had resigned in 1742 after a vain endeavour to stop the popular clamour for war against Spain and although in 1743 George II pleaded for his advice, it was too late. Walpole, by then Lord Orford, died vastly in debt in 1745. But the second George had not always sought Walpole's advice. In fact on the death of the first George, the second sacked Sir Robert—which is what everyone expected would happen. One of the things which bedevilled and perhaps even controlled the Georgian political scene is that all the Georges were at loggerheads with their sons. All the reigning sovereigns loathed their heirs apparent. This meant that disgruntled Whigs who hadn't got what they wanted, 'Hanoverian' Tories, and various other dissatisfied people, plus a number of the *nouveau riche* (money was always useful to the heir), collected round each Prince of Wales and formed a sort of opposition party in the hope that when it came to the cry 'the king is dead, long live the king', they would be given power and preferment by the new monarch. That Walpole would be sacked was a foregone conclusion. That he was swiftly recalled to office was a great surprise, and was due to a good deal of clever and tactful foot-work on the part of the new King's wife, that extremely able, patient, intelligent and beautiful woman, Caroline of Anspach. She pointed out to her husband that, among other things, Sir Robert was brilliant at finance—which was true— and he would probably be far better able to keep the King's coffers full than anyone else because of his masterly control of the Commons.

Could Walpole have managed without Queen Caroline? One doubts it. The Queen, in her quiet way, controlled the King but was wise enough and feminine enough not to show it. The King for his part treated her abominably; he was rude, snubbed her constantly, fell into vile rages with her, expected her to treat his mistresses who—like those of his father—were dead bores, with great civility (which she did). Yet no one who reads the moving and terrible story of Caroline's death can doubt that George loved her and, what is more, trusted her. George II may not have been a good king, but fortunately there was Caroline of Anspach behind the throne, and that coarse-grained man, Robert Walpole, the first minister since the Restoration to make a real study of finance and commerce, as chief of a small 'efficient' cabinet. Its meetings were rarely attended by the first two Georges, who by their non-attendance set a precedent which contributed to the

growth of cabinet government and the ultimate downfall of George III's attempt at what is often called 'personal rule'.*
And what of society both with a capital and a small 's' during this long period which stretched from 1714 to 1830? Perhaps if one belonged to the capital S brand or were rich, or belonged to the still rising and prospering middle classes it would not have mattered much where between those two dates one's life lay. But were one poor, it would have been better to have died before 1770, or best not to have been born at all. Seventeen-seventy is possibly an arbitrary date, for although much is known about the grand and the rich in almost every century, little is known about the poor, save through the poor rate, until well on in the eighteenth century. The poor held no offices, important or minor; being illiterate they wrote no letters, journals or diaries; they kept no household accounts; they did not have their portraits painted, though Hogarth and Gilray depict them. They are the anonymous, faceless ones and they made up probably seventy-five per cent of the population. Paupers appear in parish overseers' accounts and in workhouse records, so about the completely destitute we know a few things—such as what clothes they wore, what they ate and how much such things cost. But about the poor as people, as human beings, we know nearly nothing. They do not, for they could not, tell us themselves what they felt and suffered. Others had to speak for them—and others began to do so.

Poverty is perhaps less hard to bear in a primarily rural society, just as it is possibly easier to endure in a warm climate. But by 1770 England, for better or for worse, was well into what is

---

* George III was stubborn, obstinate and like Charles I, a good man but a bad king. Yet his attempt at 'personal rule' was certainly not unconstitutional. Both William III and Anne had believed that a mixed cabinet, in which neither party had complete ascendancy, and which was responsible to the crown and able to transmit the crown's wishes to parliament, was the best form of government. Political parties were thought of as 'factions' to be reconciled. The first two Georges by non-attendance at cabinet meetings and fully favouring the Whigs set a precedent. Such a thing would have been unthinkable in William and Anne's day, and George III found it unthinkable too.

usually called the 'Industrial Revolution'.* That is to say, we were developing from an age-old collection of small, self-supporting, rural communities into an industrial society with national and international communications. Our national communications had been improved by swifter transport and canals as they were later improved by railways. For international communications we had our sailing ships and later our steam packets. When Abraham Derby—the first of three Abraham Derbys—discovered and pioneered a method of smelting iron from coke instead of from charcoal (even though the method was kept secret for years), England became the birthplace of the iron and steel industry. This caused such a demand for coal, even in early Georgian times, that great landowners were by no means averse to prospecting for it on their estates. If they found the precious stuff under a lawn, parterre or new plantation, up it came and to the devil with the landscape so carefully created by a master gardener to set off the new, beautiful Palladian house. When James Watt in 1761 improved the stationary steam-engine, a greater source of power became available, even though the production of engines was slow work as each had to be hand-built, and there were no spare parts instantly available for they had to be hand-built too.

The changes which took place in the textile industry† are too well known to need retelling. Kay's fly shuttle came early and caused alarm and riots among workers. Hargreaves' spinning jenny—a multi-spindle machine perfected in 1765—could be hired out and used in workers' cottages. But in 1769 when Arkwright patented his spinning frame and erected the first practical cotton mill in the world, the factory system, necessarily, had to come into being. This sounded the death knell of the cottage textile industry. Apart from weavers and their families

---

* The phrase, invented by a Frenchman, is a convenient misnomer. We had been evolving industrially over a long period. The Revolution was a speeded up phase of evolution.

† Demand had begun to exceed supply so greatly that necessity here, in one of our essential exports, was invention's mother.

who devoted their whole time to cottage industry, many an agrarian labourer's wife and children had added to the minute family income by spinning, when the labourer himself, due partly to the agrarian revolution and the speeding up of enclosures, had reached the depths of poverty. The problem of the rural poor was not new and had long since become a burden too heavy for individual parishes to bear.* In 1723 Parliament permitted certain parishes to combine and erect 'Union' workhouses. Often these Union houses were let to a manufacturer who, provided he kept the inhabitants alive, had a good supply of cheap labour. Workhouse children if they tried to run away were often manacled. Rural poverty, the fear of the terrible workhouse—for by the 1723 Act if you did not go into the workhouse you were not eligible for relief—drove many of the country poor to seek what they hoped would be a better life in the rich and expanding towns. It was not. Later, the Act of 1782 once again allowed outdoor relief. This was indiscriminately applied after the spread of the Speenhamland System. The result was an ever increasing rate burden and such a great demoralization of the poor that it led to the much resented Poor Law Amendment Act of 1834.

Towns and cities had their own poor and they feared, for many reasons, the influx of the country labourer. In certain circles it was believed that this influx would depopulate the countryside and spell ruin for landowners and farmers. To induce the agrarian labourer to stay on the land, higher wages would have to be paid, and if the farmer had to pay higher wages he might be unable to pay his rent. Nevertheless, the rural poor went to the towns and cities in the hope of better pay and there, unable to get parish relief, they lived in tenements, in the old shored up houses

---

* In the Tudor period the onus of responsibility for the poor was placed on the parish and when parish poor funds—provided by private benefactors—could no longer meet the demands, a compulsory rate was introduced (1572). In 1576, materials were provided to set the poor to work. This together with the relief of the helpless poor and an apprentice scheme for pauper children were incorporated in the Act of 1598. Inadequate though it may have been at the time, it was the first Act of its kind in the world and far in advance of anything seen on the Continent.

darkened by the window tax, subdivided and re-subdivided by the owners, so that one large family lived in one small room. Or, if in work and homeless, they stayed for a penny or tuppence a night in common lodging houses sleeping, without covering, on the floor, twenty to a room.

The small master, particularly in the woollen trade, was also destroyed by the rise of the factory system. He had hitherto worked in his own house employing, perhaps, a dozen apprentices and journeymen who lived and worked with him under his careful—and sometimes even paternal—eye. But now he had not the capital necessary to start even a small factory, set up machines and produce more. He could not compete, so he too went to the wall. His apprentices and journeymen, no less than the agrarian labourer, had to go into the factories to work under appalling conditions for wages upon which they could barely subsist. Children, in particular, were favoured for factory work. New machines required less physical force. No need to pay a man for what a child could do. In addition to drawing ample supplies of child labour from workhouses, manufacturers could generally count on a good supply from poverty-stricken parents who contracted their children out from the age of five or six. So these wretched infants were sent off to spend the rest of their short lives working twelve to fifteen hours a day—which means all day and half the night. Undernourished, uncared for, uneducated and unwanted, they died like flies, sometimes standing at their looms. But the poor were prolific and there were so many of them that there was always a plentiful supply of children. If the famous judgment of Lord Mansfield in 1772 abolished slavery in England, what need had we of slaves? We had children to make the finished Manchester cottons* from the raw products grown by the Negro slaves in America.

The first Factory Act was not passed until 1802, when the elder Sir Robert Peel,† himself a manufacturer, tried to regulate the

---

* But see Dr Aiken's *Description of the Country around Manchester* (1795).

† The son of Robert Peel, founder of the calico printing industry. He himself

employment of pauper children in cotton mills, and then Parliament began to recognize that it had a limited responsibility for the protection of child labour. The second Act of 1819,* dealt with all children and provided that no child under the age of nine was to be employed, and those between the ages of nine and sixteen for not more than twelve hours a day—no night work permitted. Both Acts were easily evaded because enforcement was the duty of the local magistrate, who may have been a factory owner or the friend of one, or who simply did not care and thought it all a lot of silly nonsense. The abject misery of the poor in lean years became unendurable; there were riots and looting, burnings and mob violence put down by the militia. Offenders or instigators, when caught, were hanged or transported. Many preferred to be hanged.

So in the Georgian era the rich got richer, the poor poorer. Looking back on it even now one finds the 'case histories' contained in Eden's *The State of the Poor*, agonizing reading. How could we have permitted such things to happen? How could we have allowed such poverty, such riches, to exist side by side? How could we have produced so many beautiful things and yet been such blind barbarians? Here is Georgiana, the beautiful Duchess of Devonshire, always in debt, always borrowing, always gambling. There is Mary Wotton, apprenticed by the parish to a Mrs John Easton. It must have been an unhappy domestic-service apprenticeship and worse than the workhouse, for one day Mary ran away, taking with her twenty-seven of Mrs Easton's golden guineas. Mary was caught and sentenced to death. She was just nine years old.[49] It is true Mary's tragedy happened in 1735, but even as late as 1801 Andrew Brenning was publicly hanged for breaking into a house and stealing a spoon. Andrew was all of thirteen. And in 1808 a girl of seven was hanged at Lynne.[50]

applied the inventions of Arkwright and Hargreaves in his own business. His son, the second baronet, became Prime Minister for the first time in 1834.

* This Act was largely due to the efforts of that remarkable man and philanthropist, Robert Owen (1771–1858). He is called 'the father of socialism'.

The Adelphi, 1769. Adam brothers

Yet no matter how sick and angry this makes us, it is to read history backwards. It is to illuminate the sharp contrasts between our own age and theirs. It does not show the development, the growth of the social conscience throughout the century. To be fair one must not, for example, skip the last pages of Eden's monumental work, for there one finds listed the books, the pamphlets, the speeches made by those who concerned themselves with the poor, and it is a very long list indeed. Apart from our terrible predilection for hanging—and we went on hanging more and more people for increasingly trivial offences—there were many rich and not so rich who were deeply concerned with the state of the poor, the miserable, the wretched. There were truly benevolent private individuals, public bodies and religious leaders who attempted to, and did, help. Only a few individuals can be listed here. Dorset born Thomas Coram (1668?–1751) who became a shipbuilder at Taunton, Massachusetts, and later a prosperous London merchant. He was so appalled at the number

38

of children left exposed in the streets to die that he worked for seventeen solid years before he was allowed to establish his Foundling Hospital. He got government support in 1739, also the support of many titled women, and subscriptions poured in. After his death further government help was required, and given —on condition that the hospital took in children from everywhere. The hospital was then besieged by the living, dead, and dying. They were even sent in from the country in wagons and carts; many died en route.

There was James Oglethorpe (1696–1785) who saw a friend imprisoned for debt in the Fleet. The friend, unable to pay the usual fee to the warder, was confined to a house where smallpox raged, caught it and died. Oglethorpe thus knew the dreadful conditions of the debtors' prison at firsthand and tried to help in various ways. One was by obtaining a charter (1732) for the settlement of Georgia as a refuge for debtors (after imprisonment) and for the poor and needy—and also as a barrier for the British Colonies against Spanish aggression from Florida. As Governor, he encountered much opposition in Georgia because he prohibited Negro slavery and rum.

Then there was the great philanthropist and prison reformer, John Howard (1726?–90) who visited city and country gaols and bridewells, wrote his book *State of the Prisons* (1777), and managed to get legislation passed to abolish gaolers' fees,* and for the improvement of sanitary conditions. There was also a Dr George Armstrong, about whom we know very little, who set up the first dispensary ever for 'The Relief of the Infant Poor'. This

---

* Gaolers and governors made a good living out of their work by extracting money from those who had it, or who had rich friends and relatives. The wardenship of the Fleet (and other prisons) was regularly put up for sale. It had been bought by John Huggins from Lord Clarendon for £5,000, and Huggins sold it to Bambridge for the same amount in 1728. There were large and regular emoluments from the office and heavy fees charged those who could pay for accommodation and extra luxuries. Those unwilling or unable to pay were treated with the utmost brutality; manacles and thumb-screws were used. As the dungeons were above the common sewer, gaol fever was rampant. Starvation was the usual lot of those who could not pay.

dispensary in Red Lion Square, London, opened in 1769* and the idea led to the establishment of many other dispensaries in London and provincial centres. Here for the first time the poor could come for medical treatment and free medicine, while those too ill to come were visited in their homes. Hitherto physicians had been only for the fee-paying rich and so they knew only the diseases of the rich. Now they began to learn about the diseases of the poor, brought on in too many cases by filth, squalor, undernourishment, and drink. And as they learned from these poor patients they also tried to teach them the rudiments of hygiene and cleanliness. That they were successful is shown by the drop in the incidence of typhus which began to be apparent around the turn of the century.

The drop in typhus must also have been due to cheaper, washable cotton clothing, and to various citizens who showed what we call 'civic pride'. It was a body of private citizens who banded together in the 1760s and, by a private Act of Parliament, obtained the right to levy a house rate out of which the paving and lighting of Westminster was paid. Birmingham swiftly followed suit, and soon many citizens of many cities and towns obtained the right to run social services in their own areas. Paving, lighting and, above all, sanitation was improved and, strangely enough considering the era, on these committees there was no distinction of race or creed. Anglicans, Dissenters, Roman Catholics and Jews worked together for the civic good. This is how and where local authorities began. It is one of the major developments of the Georgian era and it made English cities and towns the envy of the Continent.

There were also various societies such as that for *Bettering the Condition of the Poor*. This particular one was not set up until 1796 when people began to discover, uneasily, that poverty was not always the result of idleness, but could be due to miserable wages. Much earlier were the Friendly Societies formed for mutual

* A centre for the inoculation of the poor against smallpox had been set up in St Pancras in 1746. Inoculation should not be confused with vaccination, but see Chapter Six.

assurance against sickness and old age. They had begun, rather tentatively, in the seventeenth century but during the eighteenth their numbers and membership increased enormously and they became an alternative to parish relief; for there were many wage earners 'who preferred to be indebted for relief', should they need it, 'to their own industry and frugality'.[51] By late century there were some 7,000 societies with, in 1797, a membership of about 650,000. Many societies failed, due to lack of contributions (it is difficult to support a family and spare sixpence out of a weekly wage of 8s.), to lack of legal standing, and also to mis-appropriation of funds.* Nor were these societies concerned solely with the relief of those living within the parish. In Norwich, for example, the Scots Society was formed to relieve poor Scots who came to Norwich in distress; for by English law 'a stranger coming into England and not having obtained a parish settle-ment' was 'not entitled to parish relief'.[52] No one had any obligation to relieve him. He was entitled only to starve to death in his own fashion.

This Norwich Society is unusual because the Scots were any-thing but popular in England. For two centuries they had been our enemies, more or less, and twice in the Georgian era they had supported Stuart rebellions. Furthermore, they were thought to flock to England and take jobs away from Englishmen. Flock they did, as they had done under the Stuarts, but they were a poor, proud, industrious people—perhaps it is this last we found un-forgivable. Lord Bute, a Scot, was a most unpopular Prime Minister, and because of his early friendship for, and influence upon, George III it was thought the court favoured the Scots, who had no real interest in English affairs. 'Their venality', says

---

* A modicum of protection and recognition of these societies was given by the Friendly Society Acts of 1793 and 1795, and the movement grew rapidly. Sub-sequent Acts throughout the nineteenth and twentieth centuries provided greater security and protection, and the National Insurance Act of 1911 used the frame-work of the Societies in the form of 'approved societies'. The Approved Society system was abolished by the National Insurance Act of 1946. Though Friendly Societies still exist, they are fewer in number and in membership.

Lecky unkindly, 'was notorious.'[53] So the Norwich Society was already ahead of its time when it took on the Scots. It moved even farther ahead and into our own era when, in 1778, it decided to extend its charity to 'all distressed subjects of Great Britain, and the natives of foreign countries residing in England'.[54] Enlarging its aim it enlarged its name to *The Society of Universal Good-will*. Between 1778 and 1784 it had already relieved the need of 111 Scots, 29 Irish, 1 Frenchman, 14 Americans, 5 Germans, 8 Italians, 2 Turks, 2 Prussians, 2 Barbaries, 1 Norwegian, 1 Hungarian, 1 Swede and 2 Jewesses, plus 4 others who could not say positively quite where they had come from. This is an interesting, if tiny, sidelight on the foreign-born poor who lived here. One longs to know how and why these Turks and Barbaries had come? And, even more in view of the date, what those fourteen Americans were doing in Norwich. Obviously the Man in the Moon* knew what he was doing, and it is a pity he was misdirected.

Nevertheless, despite the good work done by private individuals and public bodies, 'Disease, poverty, fear, malnutrition . . . was the common lot of our ancestors, and all the restless energies of the "improvers" could not save them from it'.[55]

Nor, apparently, could God—at least not God as interpreted by the Church of England. The Church, after years of sectarian warfare, was now safely Established and fell into a slumber occasionally punctuated by a gentle snore. This, in a way, was a good thing as in the long run it made for a much-needed tolerance; but, since ecclesiastical preferment was in the gift of the crown, as Queen Anne's Tory bishops died off they were, wherever possible, replaced by faithful Whigs who could express their devotion to the Ministry—the political one—by regular attendance at the Lords and in managing the electoral interests of their diocese. This caused rather a rat-race among bishops since some Sees were far more valuable than others. Minor ones brought in as little as

---

* Although the Man in the Moon has had many different applications in our folk-song history, it is perhaps interesting to note that the particular rhyme in which Norwich is mentioned seems to have appeared in print for the first time in 1784, although it is probable that it was orally transmitted earlier.

£300 p.a. but bishoprics such as London, Winchester, and Durham were worth around £3,000. One did not wish to blight the prospect of being improved by translation to a richer See by even a murmur of disagreement with government policy. This is not to suggest that this was true of all bishops. Secker nearly ruined his career by disagreeing on a minor point. Bishop Butler was probably the greatest thinker of his age, and that devoted and saintly Bishop of Sodor and Man, Thomas Wilson, made his diocese a model for those on the mainland. But bishops were not free from the venality of the age and few were raised to the Episcopate for reasons other than their services to political parties, patrons or, fortunately, to scholarship.

So low down on the ladder of preferment as to be almost sunk in the mud was the parson or curate, who was lucky to get a stipend of from £30 to £50. A great economic, intellectual, and social chasm yawned between him and his bishop (most bishops were related to the aristocracy). Often ill-educated and of humble birth, he was frequently treated abominably by his lay patron or 'socially' superior parishoner.

The majority of parsons were, and had been for a long time, like Mr Salteena, 'not quite'. But gradually and chiefly due to the rise in value of tithes and glebe farms (in turn due to improvements in agriculture) those gentlemen who had livings in their gift began to regard such livings as suitable 'places' for younger sons, tiresome brothers, impoverished ex-tutors, or impecunious relatives—all the better if the living were plural. This may be materialism at its worst, but in the end it did mean that the parson rose in the economic, educational and social scale, and the lowest echelon of ecclesiastical preferment became a respectable profession.* Towards the middle of the era one may contrast the plight of that Greek scholar, innocent and good man Parson Adams with the mean and worldly 'parson on Sundays', Mr Trulliber. By the end of the era there are Edmund Bertram, Mr Collins and hundreds of others. By then the parson had become a

---

* This applies in the main to endowed livings. Even as late as George III there were thousands of poverty-stricken, half-educated parsons all over the country.

Somerset House, 1775. Sir William Chambers

common ingredient of English fiction, which shows that the profession of a clergyman had become a part of English life.★ The parson could hunt with the squire, get drunk or gamble with the gentry, farm his glebe, indulge his hobbies—intellectual or otherwise—or take his parish duties seriously, whichever course suited him best. Certainly we are the richer for Parson Woodforde and his *Diary* and for Gilbert White and his enchanting *Natural History of Selborne*. White is, perhaps, our first field naturalist.

But if the Established Church slept, so too did our two Universities—open to Anglicans only—and the standard of scholarship, learning and discipline fell to a dispiritingly low level. Penal laws against Roman Catholics had been passed under Queen Anne—fortunately they were rarely strictly observed—and under the Test and Corporation Acts neither Roman Catholics nor

★ One does not forget Goldsmith's *The Vicar of Wakefield* (published 1766), but curiously enough this delightful book was not popular at the time. It was not until the Victorian age that it became a best seller.

nonconformists could go up to Oxford or Cambridge. The Test and Corporation Acts were, however, chiefly directed against nonconformists and assured that no one could hold any office, no matter how minor, under the crown without first receiving Holy Communion according to the rites of the Church of England.* Throughout the century there were attempts to have the Acts repealed and in 1780 the matter was put into the hands of an Anglican, Henry Beaufoy, M.P. As he so rightly put it, 'The Saviour of the World instituted the Eucharist in commemoration of his death, an event so tremendous that afflicted Nature hid herself in darkness; but the British legislature has made it a qualification for gauging beer barrels, and soap boilers tubs, for writing Custom's House dockets and debentures, and seizing smuggled tea'.[56] The motion was defeated as were similar motions in 1787 and 1789. Repeal was not effected until 1828.†

In the meantime dissenters wanted their children to receive an education, so they set up their own Academies, to which all were admitted. Here much broader based curricula were followed; the outlook was liberal and the spirit of enquiry rather than the dead hand of scholasticism animated tutors and students. At one of these academies a young man could be taught, in addition to the usual things, that very new subject, geography, to say nothing of mathematics, science, mechanics, hydrostatics, physics, astronomy and anatomy—subjects which rarely if ever stirred the quiet waters of the Cam or the Isis. These academies gave far and away the best education in the England of the time.‡

---

* The Toleration Act of 1689 allowed all Protestant nonconformists their own places of worship, their own teachers etc., subject to swearing certain oaths and declarations. The odious Occasional Conformity Act was repealed in 1719 but the almost equally repugnant Test and Corporation Acts remained.
† Roman Catholic emancipation was finally allowed in 1829. It should be remembered that George III objected strongly and sincerely to this because he genuinely believed it violated the Coronation oath. Jews gained relief by Acts of 1846 and 1858 but atheists had to wait until 1888 before being admitted to Parliament.
‡Probably the most famous was that at Warrington which led in placing mathematics and science high on the list. Later it moved to Manchester, and Manchester College, Oxford, is its lineal descendant. Warrington was due to be torn down in

They were not, or at least the more modern ones were not, in the least against literature, the arts or the theatre; the old let's-not-let-anyone-enjoy-anything strain of Puritanism was also becoming more tolerant.

Alive and active as the Academies were, and because dissenters were excluded from every branch of civil government, they also became fertile soil for philosophic radicalism. Those who, like the Rev. Dr Priestley, called themselves 'radical Dissenters' took a critical interest in the abuses of government* and in the rights of the individual. Those great abstractions, Freedom, Liberty, Reason, Rights, were the four cornerstones upon which a better world could be built. This is all very splendid, but it must also be said that this kind of dissenter, intellectually engaged in larger issues, sometimes overlooked the immediate needs of the people. The poor laws, they thought, only feather-bedded the poor† and made for idleness, as did alehouses, while their morals needed continuous supervision. (Incidentally, those of the *ton* were far worse.)

But help came in another way. Paradoxically it sprang from stupefied and stultifying Oxford in the person of John Wesley (1703-91). Wesley, his brother Charles and a dozen like-minded friends were so dissatisfied with the sleepy, apathetic and lax methods of the Established Church that around 1729 they formed a group which went in for rigorous church observance and tried, by prayer and fasting, to lead spiritual and practical Christian lives. This group of 'methodists', of which George Whitefield

1965 to make room for a road. It was granted a reprieve—for how long one does not know.

* They linked with small groups which since 1769 had met in the provinces and London for the purpose of reforming and controlling Parliament from without. They attempted to make M.P.s subservient to their constituencies. One famous group was the Society for the Supporters of the Bill of Rights, founded to help Wilkes in his battle against king and parliament. Wilkes was a rogue, but parliament had behaved unconstitutionally.

† The well intentioned Speenhamland System certainly did this. For full details the reader may care to consult *The Village Labourer* by J. L. and Barbara Hammond.

was one, were High Churchmen.* On the practical side they visited the sick and imprisoned and gave to the poor. John Wesley refused flatly to have his hair dressed fashionably so that he could give more. Although he became noted for abstinence and gloomy views, was credulous, believed in witchcraft and demonic possession and was undoubtedly difficult—as many with enormous will-power, energy and intellect are—he made religion the core and object of his life and his deep piety and self-renunciation are unquestionable. He and his brother did a brief stint as missionaries in Georgia, at General Oglethorpe's invitation, and John was one of the earliest and strongest opponents of slavery. But it was under the influence of the Moravian Brotherhood that he experienced, at 8.45 p.m. on May 24th 1738, 'conversion'; that is to say, a metamorphosis of the spirit by which he realized the enormous importance of 'justification by faith'. From then on Wesley laid emphasis on the missionary spirit, on the preaching of the gospel to quicken men's faith and transform their lives. In other words he was Evangelical.

The average Church of England ecclesiastic from parson to bishop was certainly not this. The parson, when well educated, delivered as his sermon a logical, reasonable little theological essay, spoken in a perfectly level tone and often excessively boring. Miracles had to be got over somehow, they were rather awkward material in an age which believed that reason was the point at which God touched man, and one had to be rather careful too about a 'revealed' religion. If one raised one's voice to emphasize a point one might be accused of 'enthusiasm' which, after the banging about due to the violent sectarianism of the seventeenth century, was definitely and understandably out. But such sermons were totally meaningless to the poor and un-educated, many of whom, particularly in the expanding cities,

* One of the great influences in Wesley's life was his conversations with the High Churchman and near non-juror, William Law, author of *A Practical Treatise upon Christian Perfection* and *A Serious Call to a Devout and Holy Life*; the latter first caused Samuel Johnson to think seriously about religion. Law later came under the influence of Jacob Boehme the Moravian peasant who may, perhaps, be considered the founder of modern mysticism.

never set foot in a church. So if the poor would not come to church, the Church in the person of John Wesley and George Whitefield went to them. Before Wesley died at the age of eighty-seven he calculated that in the half century of his itinerant life he had travelled 250,000 miles on foot, horseback and by boat and preached above 400,000 sermons. Before his death he also said, 'I live and die a member of the Church of England and no one who regards my judgment or advice will ever separate from it'.[57]

That other early great Evangelical, Revivalist or Enthusiast, George Whitefield, was born in 1714 and his soul 'was taken to Emmanuel's bosom on the 30th of September 1770' but his body 'lay in the silent grave at Newbury Port, near Boston in New England'.[58] Whitefield, zealous from an early age, unlike Wesley was given to cards and novel reading, and had a positive passion for fruit and cakes. He had a poor time of it at Oxford as a servitor but joined the Wesley brothers' group where he was given to fits of 'morbid devotions'. He too, went to Georgia,* returned, was ordained priest in 1739, and was in this year denied a pulpit at Bristol. It was a denial which changed the lives of thousands. Whitefield, undaunted, decided to go out and speak to the colliers at nearby Kingswood. There on a hillside he stood looking down on his first audience of some 200 tough, brutal, savage and illiterate men. He took as his text the first words of the Sermon on the Mount. The effect was electric. No one had ever spoken to these poor, miserable, brutalized creatures with such passionate conviction, using such homely, easily understood words and such vivid images. His sincere and consuming desire to save their souls moved them to tears. In their misery, in their poverty, in their degradation, a voice had spoken directly to them. The voice of someone who cared. It is true Whitefield had a splendid, powerful voice and great histrionic ability and was, himself,

---

* He made seven voyages to America; founded an orphanage at Savannah in 1740 in which he took a lifelong interest. It was later converted into Bethesda College but was burned down in 1773. Not to be confused with the great American Naval Hospital in Maryland.

frequently moved to tears while preaching, but soon thousands
were coming to hear him, many out of sheer curiosity, and
hundreds were 'converted'. It all sounds rather commonplace
and over dramatic to us and we, I think, would call Whitefield a
hot-gospeller, but he did bring comfort and help to many, and
he did begin field preaching in England. Revivalist preaching,
undoubtedly, produced a good deal of hysteria which had little
permanent value and was often dangerous. And, equally, Mrs
Siddons could produce almost the same kind of frenzy and swoon-
ing when she shrieked or moaned as Lady Macbeth. But the
lasting value of the Revivalists lay in the Evangelical Movement
within the Church which, after 1780, became a powerful force
and attracted such people as Hannah More, Zachary Macaulay
and others of the famous 'Clapham Sect', so called because in
1807 a group of evangelicals formed around John Venn, rector of
Clapham.

But Whitefield's Evangelism, unlike Wesley's, was Calvinist.
This ultimately led to a schism between the two (although they
remained good friends all their lives) which in turn, split 'methodism' into two sects. One of Whitefield's earliest Calvinistic
supporters was Selina, Countess of Huntingdon (1707–91). Mrs
Delany remarks upon an extraordinary dress worn by the
Countess at the Prince's birthday court in January 1738/9.*
A black velvet petticoat embroidered with chenille 'the pattern of
a *large stone vase* filled with ramping flowers' all embossed in
between with gold. Over this a white satin gown with gold
ornaments 'no *vases* on the sleeve, but *two or three on the tail*—
a most laboured piece of finery, the pattern much properer for a
stucco staircase than for a lady'.[59] Nevertheless, it was in 1739
that the Countess became a member of the first Methodist society
in Fetter Lane. Highly intelligent, deeply concerned with religion;
frail, iron-willed, she was also a splendid organizer, which
Whitefield was not. After the death of her husband, the 9th Earl,

---

* The new year still began on March 25th. We did not adopt the new style
calendar until 1752; by then we were eleven days behind most continental
countries.

in 1746, she devoted her life and fortune to Methodism, building chapels,* helping the poor—not only with spiritual but with physical nourishment. She opened her London drawing-room to Methodist preachers, for as she was socially impeccable, she wished to convert the noble and fashionable too. George III, though noble, was certainly not fashionable, but he was an intensely pious man and thought very highly of her, as had his unlucky father, Frederick, Prince of Wales. The great Edmund Burke encouraged her fight against 'Atheism', and she literally bullied the rich and noble into her drawing-room. When White-field preached there, among his auditors were the sophisticated Chesterfield and the sceptical Bolingbroke. Neither was converted, but both thought Whitefield remarkable. Not so the Duchess of Buckingham, a natural daughter of James II. She found it all 'highly offensive and insulting', and she writes to the Countess 'I cannot but wonder that your ladyship should relish any sentiments so much at variance with high rank and good breeding'.[60]

High rank and good breeding, however, were scared out of their wits and into the churches by the French Revolution of which, in its early days of 'aristocratic' revolt and reform, many had approved; but when it descended to the bloody chaos of the reign of terror it filled everyone with panic, horror and a terrible fear. Atheism and a total disregard for the rights of property had led to this. What would happen if the poor of England, stirred up or led by rational Dissenters, or those dreadful little 'republican' clubs so keen on reform, took it into their heads to behave in a similar fashion? That the poor in England did not, some claim, was largely due to the Evangelical Revival and Methodism. It would be difficult to disprove this. It would be even more

* 'Lady Huntingdon's Connexion' consisted of some seventy chapels. She used her right as a peeress to choose her chaplains and thus strongly promoted Calvinistic Methodism. But the original Wesleyan chapel, which is the one the Countess first attended, had been in use since 1739. These Wesleyan chapels were never intended to be distinct, separate or opposed to the C. of E., but supplementary to it.

Charlotte Dundas 1801. Built by William Symington

difficult to disprove that the immediate and ultimate effect of the French Revolution and the Napoleonic Wars was to set back liberal thought in England and upon the Continent for a good half century. The struggle to obtain rights for the poor, better education, a more representative (and annual!) parliament, a wider franchise, better working conditions and pay for agrarian and factory labour was regarded with suspicion, mistrust and fear. Peterloo★ followed hard on the heels of Waterloo.

Although it has become a rather tedious commonplace to think of the Georgian era as one of the most materialistic in our history,

★ Great economic distress followed the Napoleonic wars. There were bread riots and much desire for economic and parliamentary reform. On August 16th 1819 about 60,000 perfectly peaceable and unarmed people of Manchester—men women and children—marched to St Peter's Fields waving banners, to hear the reformer Hunt, speak. The magistrates thought this unarmed gathering signified insurrection, had the local yeomanry arrest Hunt and called on the 15th Hussars to disperse the crowd. Eleven people were killed and 400 injured. 'Peterloo' is the ironic name given to this tragic event.

it was, as we have already seen, a period of great and genuine philanthropy. Benefactors are, however, by their very nature less colourful than rogues. Napoleon has more biographers than William Wilberforce, and even Satan emerges as the hero of *Paradise Lost*. But charity was enjoined upon all Christians, and if it were performed sometimes out of a sense of duty or hope of heavenly reward, rather than out of love, it nevertheless existed in abundance and expressed itself in many ways. We find the idea of 'Lady Bountiful' with her bread, soup, homemade homilies and shawls odious and patronizing, but to many a below subsistence level Georgian family she was what the word 'lady' means. The loaf-maker. The giver of bread.

There was more to be done than alleviating the lot of the poor through meeting their material needs. They lacked other things too; chiefly religious education, and this could best be achieved by organization. Organization and stock-jobbing were something the Georgians knew about and both were needed. Hence, whilst education mouldered away at the two Universities and the number of undergraduates declined, and while the boys at Eton, Harrow, and Winchester frequently rioted because the schools were so ill run, there was, throughout the whole of the era, a movement towards providing a free, primary education for poor children.* This movement had begun late in the previous century with the Society for the Promotion of Christian Knowledge, the Society for the Propagation of the Gospel and the Society for the Reformation of Manners, all of which were concerned with moral, that is, Christian education. The Charity School movement of the eighteenth century, chiefly organized and supported by voluntary subscriptions from the middling sort, was wider in scope. 'If the present Age is more laudable than those

---

* The endowed grammar schools could not provide this; they were too few and far between, besides grammar school curricula were based on Latin—of small use to the boy whose father was, say, an illiterate agrarian labourer, or later, a mill hand. What was needed was an education in the vernacular, and the Charity Schools did this. For a full account the interested reader should consult *Charity Schools in the Eighteenth Century* by M. A. Jones.

which have gone before it in any singular Particular; it is in that generous care which several well disposed Persons have taken in the education of poor Children',[61] Eustace Budgell* writes. And from Robert Nelson (1666–1715) to Hannah More (1745–1833) there stretches a long chain of men and women who, though they differed in religious views and social standing, were linked together in their efforts to educate poor children and to raise money for Charity Schools.

Such an education, these reformers and their supporters believed, was now a dire necessity. The condition of poor children was appalling, particularly in overcrowded cities, and nowhere worse than in London. Pauper children went to the workhouse, but poor children lived huggermugger in dark, squalid overcrowded rooms, in foetid and filthy alleyways. These ragged, miniature, underfed savages roamed the streets in gangs and at a very tender age became thieves, disturbers of the peace, destroyers of property, gin-swilling and blaspheming beggars. They were without religion and without discipline. Only schooling could provide both. Certainly neither could come from the 'home' background. Teach them to read from the Bible, inculcate the moral precepts of Protestant Christianity, this alone would help them. Besides, if one did not—Oh dreadful thought—*Rome* might get them, but on this point Anglicans and Dissenters agreed.† 'Serious Christians', said Wesley, 'must learn to read, and must be provided with suitably edifying reading material.'[62]

---

* Budgell (1688–1737) a cousin of Addison and a contributor to *The Spectator* lost all, including his reason, when the South Sea Bubble burst. He drowned himself in 1737.

† This fear of Rome was largely due to a fear that the Stuarts might return and bring with them what we always had detested, 'clerical rule'. One might have expected this fear to be finally laid after the last, abortive rebellion of 1745. Yet as late as 1780 the dreadful Gordon Riots occurred as a result of Savile's very moderate Act for R.C. relief. But one must remember that mob violence was common throughout the era, and was often used by politicians for its nuisance and intimidation value. The Gordon Riots at least taught politicians the grievous dangers of appealing to the mob.

There was, as usual, much opposition to Charity Schools from various quarters, but the greatest objections were raised in cities and towns by mercantile interests, and, in the country, by farming interests. Poverty and illiteracy provided the cheap labour so necessary to a mercantile economy. To push exports at an attractive price required economy at home, and the only way the Georgians knew how to regulate this was by keeping labour costs low. To educate the poor, so the argument ran, was to unfit them to be hewers of wood and drawers of water; poverty alone could supply a large enough pool of cheap labour. Middle-class farming interests took the same view. Cheap agrarian labour was essential. To teach the illiterate children of poor illiterate agrarian labourers to read and write and even cast accounts was sheer folly; it would deprive the farmer of cheap labour and the child's parents of his earnings. It would educate children (and many feared this) 'out of their place'. They would become dissatisfied with that station in life into which it had pleased God to call them. The plain fact was, however, that it was never the object of the Charity Schools to do this. The knowledge and practice of religion was the ground upon which they based themselves. To teach a child to read, to learn the catechism, to give him a Bible to read from, to teach him the moral precepts of Christianity, was to set him on the right path for his own salvation. Where possible, the child might be taught to write and even given a smattering of arithmetic, but the three R's were of secondary importance and often only the first R was taught, particularly to girls. Girls, however, of all classes were 'educated in the grossest ignorance', as Lady Mary Wortley Montagu—herself largely self-educated—said. Most schools also attempted to give instruction in various handicrafts and to teach the virtues of thrift and hard work. As to being educated 'out of one's station'! 'Make me temperate, chaste, meek and patient, true in all my dealings and *content and industrious in my station*'[63] (my italics) was the opening hymn sung by the girls of a Sheffield Charity School. Children fed and instructed by charity ought to be robed in humility and sing incessant praises to their benefactors; this was the precept constantly banged into their small heads. Revolting as this appears to us, there was nothing repellent about it in the eighteenth century, either to those on the dispensing or to those on the receiving end of the line. One has only to read, for example, Fanny Burney's *Cecilia* to realize this. The one truly curious thing to us now is that it seems quite clear few Christian benefactors can have read Matthew 6: 1–4 with any real understanding. Nor even the secular and handsomely bound copies of *The Spectator*⋆ which went through innumerable editions during the century and long remained favourite middle-class reading.

Despite opposition and the rather mixed motives of some benefactors, despite failures due to bad management and often, regrettably, to the falling away of subscribers, the movement grew and spread and, supported by voluntary contributions, provided 'tens of thousands of children with their only means of instruction'.[64]

So too did the Sunday Schools. There had been sporadic Sunday Schools before Robert Raikes (1735–1811) began his in Gloucester in 1780. Raikes, a printer and owner of the *Gloucester Journal* was able to attract widespread notice for Sunday schools and enlist voluntary support. Although he was not a man who in other circumstances Fanny Burney, who met him in Gloucester in 1788, 'should have greatly admired', being somewhat 'too flourishing . . . forward and voluble', he was, she knew, 'worthy, benevolent, good natured and good hearted' and one had, therefore, to allow for his 'delighted vanity'.[65]

Sunday Schools, which spread rapidly, did not differ in their teaching from Charity Schools; they differed in that they operated on one day a week only. In a society now rapidly becoming highly industrialized, more children than ever were needed to mind machines and to work in coal mines while many parents, since prices were rising and wages were not, were even less able than before to do without their children's earnings. Sunday was the only free day the children had. And these children, too,

⋆ See particularly, No. 294, Wed., February 6th 1712.

must be saved from godlessness, savagery, vice and profanity—Evangelicals, Methodists and Dissenters agreed.* One of the most touching things in the whole of our history is that these children really seem to have wanted to be rescued from ignorance. Worn out from a six-day week's work, no matter how vile the weather, they flocked regularly to the Sunday Schools, which opened at eight in the morning and closed at six or seven in the evening. They attended church or chapel twice a day; the rest of the time they were given religious instruction, taught to read and write, taught to keep themselves clean and to sing hymns—and they loved hymn singing. Admittedly, pressure to attend Sunday Schools was applied by the clergy, by employers and parents—it kept the children off the streets, or out of the house, and it prevented property damage. Admittedly, too, the children probably loved to be given a Bible as a prize, and enjoyed showing off their knowledge, and perhaps even enjoyed the brief security the schools offered. But this still does not explain away the children's genuine enthusiasm. It almost seems as if an army of zealous children was on the march, led by equally zealous clergymen, philanthropists, voluntary workers and teachers; and this children's crusade set out, not to liberate Jerusalem but to slay the Goliath Ignorance.

Later on the Mutual or Monitorial System (we would call it the pupil-teacher system) of education, invented by Bell and Lancaster, came into being and spread general education. How successful this was is indicated by a note in Greville's diary for 1829. He writes, apropos of the republication of the works of Sir Walter Scott, that this would 'produce him [Scott] an enormous fortune' as 'a new class of reader is produced by the Bell and Lancaster schools, and this is the cause of the prodigious and

* The Sunday School Society, set up in 1785, was undenominational in membership, as were many charity schools. Its aim was to unite all persons of whatever Protestant denomination. This grand idea of unity fell apart in late century because of political unrest due to the French Revolution and because Dissenters were suspected of being inclined to sedition and to favour the Jacobins. The Church of England then instructed its clergy to withdraw from the Society and begin their own strictly Anglican schools.

extensive sale of cheap publications'.[66] But it was not until three years after the death of George IV that a reluctant House of Commons, after acrimonious debate, grudgingly granted a paltry £20,000—the first grant for educational purposes.*

With the great public schools no less than the universities in such a decayed state, the wonder is that the Georgian era is so rich in brilliant men—and in women too, who were far worse educated and rarely had the advantages of the Grand Tour as had their brothers. The answer seems to lie in the fact that the great spirit of enquiry set moving in the seventeenth century, persisted and grew throughout the next century. If it is true that disinterested intellectual curiosity is the life blood of any civilization then the brilliance of the Georgian era in so many spheres may,

* Laggard as usual in such matters, elementary education (free in cases of need, only) and compulsory attendance were not made law until the Acts of 1876 and 1880, although there had been some sort of free and compulsory education in Prussia as early as 1717; and a good deal in pre-Revolutionary America too.

The Rocket, 1829. George Stephenson

perhaps, be explained in these terms. Curiosity—intellectual or otherwise—the desire to know and more, the need to set down what one had discovered or knew about a variety of things— agriculture, breeding monkeys, astronomy, cookery, chemistry, cosmetics, physics, waterproof boots, philosophy, curl papers, the making of houses, furniture, gardens, trouble or love; the meaning of words, Roman antiquities, and of who said what to whom, was a positive passion with literate Georgians. The era is full of books, manuscripts, and countless pamphlets upon every conceivable and some quite inconceivable subjects, from the great controversy between Newton and Leibniz which went on from 1704 to 1735, to fumble-fisted works concerning the awful effects tea drinking had upon fertility (it was really thought to be, by some cranks, an oral contraceptive!).

The period is also so full of letters, diaries, journals, memoirs kept, with but few exceptions, by the upper and middling classes, that it is possible to get a much richer and more detailed picture of how people lived than ever before and, as a concomitant, a better idea of what people were like. Some of these diaries, letters and memoirs were thought to be so scandalous that by the time of George IV—who created a fair number of scandals himself— publication was suppressed or memoirs and diaries so edited that only a pallid shadow of the robust, the racy, the gossipy remains.* Victorianism did not begin with Victoria. It is not without significance that the proto-Victorian Mrs Grundy, an off-stage character of whom all were in awe, appeared in 1798 in *Speed the Plough* by Tom Morton, or that by 1818 Dr Thomas Bowdler had added a new word to our language. 'We know of no spectacle

---

*When old Creevey died in 1838, leaving a 'copious journal', there was panic in Mayfair and elsewhere, and by some means the papers were suppressed. On the other hand, Dr Burney left, it appears, a complete Memoir of his life. His daughter Mme d'Arblay, perhaps in an attempt to deify her father, suppressed bits, burned others, snipped out this and that and produced the *Memoirs of Dr Burney*, a quite unreadable and badly distorted book. Why Fanny did this one does not know. There seems to have been little in her father's life to warrant this mutilation, unless relatively humble origins, love of a lord, a rather unsatisfactory son, great ambition and hard work are unworthy attributes of a demi-god!

so ridiculous as the British public in one of its periodical fits of morality,'[67] Lord Macaulay thundered six years before Victoria became Queen. It was of little use. The cleaning up process, the turning of one's relatives or friends into saints, the passing of judgment had begun. And, six years after Victoria became Queen, Horace Walpole, of all people, is referred to as 'the cynical voluptuary of Strawberry Hill'.[68]

Nevertheless, and thanks to disinterested curiosity, many things have subsequently come to light on the human side. Although we are short of diaries and journals relating to the reign of the first George, the Georgian era gets off to a typical start with an entry in the diary of an obscure curate of Rothbury, who notes in 1717, 'Charles told me a story of a strange young gent. in Northumberland that courted and married a lady near Hexham and was afterwards found to be a woman'.[69] This curate, later rector of Glenfield, who prided himself on his sermons and kept a weather eye out for a woman of fortune for a wife, was curious about all sorts of things, consequential and inconsequential. His diary notes love affairs, horrid practical jokes, the height of the Nile, ravished women. He gives information, or misinformation, about the natives of Virginia, rattlesnakes, dolphins, whales and sharks, plus some very rude stories about James I—dead nearly a century. The past was mined not only for Roman and Druidical ruins but for *chroniques scandaleuses* as well.

There was little need to dig up the past for this sort of thing. There never is. 'Lady Delorain has at last brought forth a dead child,' Lady Elizabeth Finch scribbles to the Countess of Burlington in 1735, 'as soon as she was delivered,' the letter continues, 'her Majesty desir'd to see it and 'twas accordingly sent her up upon a silver plate to inspect.'[70] This macabre little item seems merely ghoulish unless one knows that Lady Deloraine, governess to the royal princesses, was the king's most recent mistress and that the infant was stillborn at six months. Queen Caroline's curiosity, intelligent though she was, was not, one feels on this occasion, either disinterested or scientific.* Even so this

* It was believed with good reason that the king had become the lady's lover in

minor incident helps illuminate the age—and the Queen.

No less illuminating is a sentence contained in a purely political letter from Henry Pelham to the Duke of Devonshire.* 'When I troubled you last,' he writes, 'I was in expectation of an addition to my family, it might have been as I thought, of the best sort, but my luck is bad, and it prov'd a Girl.'[71] The upper classes, less fortunate in such things than the lower, could hardly get rid of a girl by exposing it in the streets or popping her into the parish workhouse. They had to leave this sort of thing to nature, which often obliged with diphtheria, measles, scarlet fever and smallpox. Nature, however, unable in this case to distinguish between the sexes, in November of the same year quietly removed the two young male Pelhams within two days of each other by means of what was first thought to be 'only a common cold with a Sore Throat'.[72]

There are hundreds of accounts in letters and diaries of the accession of George II's grandson, George William Frederick, and of the excellent impression the new King 'who gloried in the name of Briton' (which certainly the first two Georges did not) made upon everyone. No monarch since the Restoration of Charles II had been greeted with such popular enthusiasm, and the countless published panegyrics, no less than the unpublished private ones, seem perfectly genuine. Yet one rather likes the laconic remarks of the Duchess of Northumberland† who heard the first speech made by the new King. 'Went to the House of Lords, much crowded to hear ye King's speech. The Crown like to fall, sat down on his nose and misbecame him greatly. He faulter'd a little at first but afterwards spoke like an Angel.'[73] Never one to waste words, the Duchess noted on May 6th of the

the late summer of the previous year. If the child had arrived full-term, it could not have been the King's. The Queen seems to have been anxious to find out—from inquiries she made—just how premature the child was.

* William Cavendish, who became 4th Duke in 1755.

† The Duchess (1716–76) wife of the 1st Duke (3rd creation) became one of the Ladies of the Bedchamber to Queen Charlotte which suggests she bore an unimpeachable reputation.

same year: 'Went home; voided a large Stone. Tired to Death. Went to Ball; tired to Death. A Bad Supper. Miss Townshend drunk.'[74] And there is the Duchess. Brief, indomitable and forthright. A painful calculus, fatigue, yet up she gets and goes to a Ball, notes the inferior food and the behaviour of Miss Townshend which, in that era, must have been rather more than deplorable even to warrant a comment.

And what about the christening in 1778 of Georgina Charlotte, infant daughter of the Duke and Duchess of Chandos? George III and Queen Charlotte were the sponsors and were 'very gracious' while the Archbishop of Canterbury* observed genially that he had 'never christened a more quiet child'. This is not surprising. The infant was dead 'it expir'd under a load of lace' just as the candles were being lit. Its mother, despite this mishap, was 'determined that the ceremony should proceed, and it did proceed'.[75] Presumably such a grand christening with Royalty as sponsors couldn't possibly be ruined by the ill-timed death of the principal agent. Yet somehow one feels the Archbishop cannot have been very observant—or perhaps he was just being tactful.

The third George reigned for sixty years, which is a very long time. It carries us with major and minor vicissitudes from mideighteenth century to the third decade of the nineteenth. And it was in the year of accession that John Carrington (1726–1810), erstwhile gardener and later working farmer, went up to see the coronation in 'Mr Warren's Shaisse'—'Espences 0.10s.0.', married Elizabeth Waple, and settled down at Bacon's Farm (belonging to Lord Cowper) at Bramhill near Hertford. John, although he made sporadic notes on odd scraps of paper over a period of time, seems not to have kept a comparatively consecutive account of what was going on until after his wife's death in 1797. The record is a mass of information on John, on village life, people, customs, prices of corn, good and bad harvests, and the joys, sorrows, and frustrations of the ordinary farmer and countryman. John, too, had

---

* The Hon Frederick Cornwallis (1713–83), particularly noted for his hospitality at Lambeth Palace.

curiosity about people, things and events and, obviously, some education. His diary or journal,* is all the more interesting because it tells us what a working farmer of humble origins thought, and this kind of opinion is very rare. 'Still at War with the French', he jots in 1804, 'and the latter end of this year the Great Boniparte was made Emperor of France . . . and our Millitia and Armey of Reserve and other forces are all on the Coast round the Kingdom to prevent their Landing, and our Shipping looking out at Sea, and the inland Associations and Yeomendry, so plenty of Soldiers, Seamen, Shipping and loaded with Taxes.' Two years later, 'Bonipart still at war with us, and the Prussians and Russians has got into Poland to Burlin and Warsaw, and his Beat the Prussians & now the Russians are coming with a Great Armey. . . . Taxes still increeseing.' By the end of 1808, 'still at Warr, Bonipart is conquering Spain and we have sent 40 Thousand men and money to help the Spaniards & a Sad Disturbance in Spain and Portugall all a Seat of Warr. Some times we have good news, some times bad and Taxes Encreeseing.' Back in 1805 John had noted 'the Great Battle by Sea, of Trafalgar Near the Straits of Giberalter', and Admiral Lord Nelson's body 'brought home and landed at Grinwish Hospital' and 'Buried at St Pauls London with Great Solemnity indeed, aged about 55'.† John did not live to see the triumph of Waterloo. He died on May 22nd 1810, and the last note he made is on May 10th. It reads: 'At Home all Day.'

In the autumn of the same year another death took place, that of George III's favourite daughter, the Princess Amelia, and shortly afterwards, the poor sad King entered the lonely twilight of the last decade of his reign. No one, least of all his eldest son who in February 1811—the year of the first Luddite riots‡—

---

* I must state at once that I have not myself examined this 'diary' and have drawn my information exclusively from that excellent book *The Carrington Diary*, compiled, with such exemplary patience, by W. Branch-Johnson.

† John was certainly right about increasing taxation, perhaps this led him to increase Lord Nelson's age by eight years.

‡ March 1811 to Jan. 1813; caused by great distress due to unemployment and reduction of wages in the textile industry and increased food prices. Began in

became Regent (subject to certain limitations) expected the sick old King to last for more than a few months. But the greatest shock was sustained by the Whigs who never for one moment suspected the Prince, the 'patron' of Whig politics, would not send his father's servants and ministers packing and form a ministry of his old Whig friends. The Prince did nothing of the sort, and so a parcel of disgruntled Whigs, who had hitherto not hesitated to roister with the heir apparent at Carlton House or the Pavilion, now discovered, for the first time it seems, the utter profligacy of the Prince. In a very minor way this is reminiscent of the relationship between Falstaff and Hal before and after that Prince became Henry V.

The ubiquitous Mr Creevey, M.P. (but not for long), often a guest of the Prince, opens his heart to his wife on this first 'betrayal' in a letter dated July 20th 1811. 'Prinney's attachment to the present Ministers,' he wails, 'his supporting of their Bank Note Bill and his dining with them must give them all hope of being continued. . . . The folly and villany of this Prinney is certainly beyond anything.'

In February 1812 the regency restrictions expired and the Prince became Prince Regent, king in all but name. Again the Whigs were mighty hopeful. 'Lord Moira sent for, Whigs coming in at last',[76] a contemporary diarist notes late in May. The next entry is even more brief, 'Whigs not coming in'.[77] They were, in fact, a sadly divided party. The brief coalition of Foxite Whigs under Lord Grenville's leadership had long since expired, there was dissent within the party and a good deal of jockeying for power on lower levels. Perhaps too the Whigs had forgotten, when Charles James Fox died in 1806, the Prince had then said that he was no longer a 'party' man. This forgetfulness is quite excusable as the Prince often said things, political and personal, which his actions belied. Then too the big Whigs, Lords Grey and Grenville, had offended the Prince, never a very safe thing to do.

Nottingham, where disciplined bands destroyed knitting frames. Later much other new machinery destroyed in northern counties. Government adopted policy of severe repression; destroying frames was made a capital offence.

On the other hand, the Prince had no great love for the Tories, but he had recently fallen in love again with the forty-seven year-old Lady Hertford. She and her husband, the second Marquis (2nd creation) who became lord-chamberlain of the household in 1812, were arch-Tories.

The Prince from all accounts, now rushed about asking advice from everyone—Whig or Tory—as to what to do, and it is said it was Lady Hertford's advice which influenced him in favour of the Tories. But here, I feel, one must be a little cautious. The Prince probably still had vague and unrealistic hopes that a coalition might be achieved. He had hoped it perhaps in 1811 when he asked Lords Grey and Grenville to join a government on terms which they refused. Now George Augustus Frederick had a great many faults and was certainly unpopular with the people, but weak, vacillating, self-indulgent, eaten away by vanity and foolish as, undeniably, he often was, he was not the fool he is frequently made out to be. Leaving Lady Hertford aside, in fairness, two things at least might be considered here. First, we had been at war with France for twenty years and in July 1812, after Salamanca despite great losses, for the first time the tide of war seemed to be turning in our favour. Also by 1812 it was fairly certain that America would come in on the side of France and, apart from the damage done to our shipping, would attack Canada.* The Whigs, particularly the Foxite ones, had always been the anti-war party, so it is quite possible that early in 1812, they would have been prepared to treat with Napoleon—busy though he must have been with his plans to invade Russia. But surely no one but an utter fool would have risked changing horses at this stage in our affairs.

Second, it is perfectly possible that the Prince's Whiggery had been much more for the sake of opposing his father—the usual King versus heir-apparent pattern common to all the Georges—than a matter of true political conviction. With the 'good old King', which is now what the people called George III, no longer

---

* War was declared on June 18th, 1812. It was due chiefly to Henry Clay and his 'War Hawks'. New York and the New England States were dead against it.

capable of frustrating his detested son, there was no need for the
Prince Regent to oppose him. Very often, and quite unexpectedly,
when one loses a lifelong personal opponent one is for a time
far more lost than relieved. In the Prince Regent's case since his
life-opponent had been his father, the King, it may be that he
discovered in himself certain fundamental characteristics which
he and his father shared and which had been obscured by hatred.
Certainly the Prince was no liberal and, equally, like his father,
he was against the emancipation of Roman Catholics. This was
now less a religious issue than a constitutional one. The Protes-
tants had 'given' the Hanoverians the throne of England, and one
of the oaths each sovereign had to swear was to uphold the
protestant religion. If the Prince Regent's 'wife',* the Roman
Catholic Mrs Fitzherbert, had ever attempted to influence the
Prince on this question—and there is not the smallest shred of
evidence that she ever did—she was certainly unsuccessful. Thus
there are various factors, political, constitutional and psycho-
logical, which should be taken into account before attempting to
assess the Prince Regent's conduct.

Nevertheless, for whatever reasons, the Prince, with some
reluctance, supported the Tories when he became Regent. Later
in the year they returned triumphant from the polls, and the
Regent earned the undying hatred of the Whigs. He had, it is
often said by Whiggish historians, jettisoned the Whigs. Yet he
had certainly made overtures to them which they had found unacceptable. As to that word 'jettison'! The Prince had often done
this to a person when that person ceased to amuse or be useful to
him, so the only surprising thing is the acute astonishment of the
Whigs. They should, perhaps, have known better.

In opposition, a section of the Whig party (not that headed by
Grey, Grenville or Holland) led by that rather gadfly personality,

---

* The Prince had, as we now know, married Mrs Fitzherbert in 1785. This
offended against the Act of Settlement and also against the Royal Marriage Act
and could, among other things, have put him out of the line of succession. He
never acknowledged this marriage and when pressed had Fox deny it in the House.
His subsequent marriage, at his father's request and on a promise to help him pay
his debts, to the Princess Caroline took place in 1795.

Brougham, could think of little better to do than become the partisans of the Prince's wife and cousin, the eccentric, not very clean, garrulous and possibly slightly mad, Caroline of Brunswick.

In 1820 the Prince Regent at long last became King, and the King's wife Caroline, Princess of Wales, mob-supported and with the dubious Alderman Wood as her champion, returned from the continent where she had been racketing around for years, hoping to be crowned Queen. The scandal which was revealed during the King's attempt to have his marriage dissolved rocked society and even the foundations of the monarchy, and is too well known to bear repetition. It is sufficient to say that Caroline never became Queen Consort. The last Hanoverian George, theatrical and resplendent in fantastic robes of his own designing, was crowned, like the first George, alone in July 1821, while his wife rushed round outside the Abbey vainly seeking admittance at every door. The mob, which had so often cheered her, now jeered at her. She died the following month.

Nine years later at 'ten minutes past three'[78] in the morning at Windsor Castle the fourth George clasped his physician's hand and said, 'My boy, this is death'. And so it was.

It was death for the Tories too who, like the Whigs in the time of the first two Georges, had held power for so long. It was also death for the already decayed Georgian era, once so beautiful, so brutal, so splendid, so squalid that it might with some justice be called our own particular and peculiarly English Renaissance.

But 'certainly nobody ever was less regretted than the late King'.[79] The era, as well as the King, was swiftly forgotten. Few grieved for either. 'I saw nothing like grief or joy', a friend of the late Lord Byron observed, walking home from the Commons on the afternoon of the King's death, 'only a bustle in the streets.'[80]

CHAPTER TWO

Of Stately Homes, Houses, and Hovels

Wearing a grey poplin semi-soutane, girdled by a black silver-spangled sash, and with purple stockings covering his gouty legs, Frederick Augustus Hervey sat in the Neapolitan sunshine writing to his daughter. 'Dearest Elizabeth' he wrote '. . . You beg me on your knees that Ickworth house may be built of white stone brick. . . . What, child, build my house of a *brick* that looks sick, pale, *jaundiced* red brick and to which I am certain our posterity will give a little rouge as essential to its health and beauty? . . . my dear, I shall follow dear, impeccable Palladio's rule, and . . . shall cover house, pillars and pilasters with Palladio's stucco which has now lasted 270 years.'[1]

Commonplace as the letter seems, it is interesting for a number of reasons. Its writer was the son of Lord John Hervey who had been the confidant of Caroline, Queen consort of George II. He also happened to be 4th Earl of Bristol,* no less than that rich and eccentric Bishop of Derry who spent most of his time on the continent. Hence his curious costume, invented by himself and thought by Italians to be that of an Irish Bishop. Hence, too, innumerable continental hotels named after him. The daughter to whom he wrote was Lady Elizabeth Foster, 'so alluring' that 'it was the opinion of Mr Gibbon no man could withstand her'.[2] She was one of the three angles in that notorious *ménage à trois*

---

* Second creation. Third son of Lord John Hervey, he succeeded two brothers to the title in 1779.

of which the 5th Duke of Devonshire and his first Duchess, Georgiana, were the other two. Finally, and more germane to our present purpose, the letter is dated March 6th 1796. This is really odd because by this time true Palladian architecture was as dead as the first two Georges. The lighter, more graceful neo-classical architecture, sired by the Adam brothers, was as good as out. Henry Holland and James Wyatt, neo-classical romanticists, had only a few years to live. John Soane was well established and John Nash was just at the beginning of his brilliant, not to say flamboyant, career.

The Earl-Bishop (1730–1803) had been born too late. He should have belonged to the 'Burlington Circle', for Ickworth (begun 1794) although as interesting and eccentric as the Bishop himself (he is said to have designed it*) certainly does not follow any of 'dear, impeccable Palladio's rules', either as enunciated by Palladio himself, or as Englished by Inigo Jones in the seventeenth century and revived by Colen Campbell, William Kent and their great patron Roger Boyle, 3rd Earl of Burlington.

Yet not fifty miles north of Ickworth, and long finished by the time the Bishop started his house, stood—as it still does—Holkham Hall, and Holkham with its estate is probably the best single example of the rich Whig outlook on life as expressed through Palladian architecture. These very rich second generation Whigs, who dominated the early Georgian scene, believed their party had evolved a *modus operandi* which had, at last, reduced political chaos to something ordered, reasonable, fixed and, if they had their way, eternal. They had evolved or created this formula and were also the powerful, if corrupt, force which kept it in operation. They were, therefore, masters if not of the universe at least of England—which comes to the same thing. There were, they felt, few problems incapable of solution; there were, however, other rather minor chaoses to which they fortunately applied their philosophy with equal assurance, unlimited capital and disciplined energy. There were waste areas to be transformed into acres of

* It is also said to have been designed by Francis Sandys.

beauty and profit. There were malodorous marshes to be drained and turned into arable fields—a by-product of this was a reduction of mosquitos and malaria and a consequent increase in population, but of this the improvers were unaware. There were melancholy, unproductive stretches of shifting sand-dunes on the coast of Norfolk and elsewhere to be reclaimed, if possible; and there were new houses to be built on newly saved or newly acquired land. Further, there were still a number of old-fashioned and vulgar Elizabethan and Jacobean mansions—so exuberant, so enthusiastic, so lacking in good manners and taste—to be pulled down or completely disguised.

And here we must back-track for a moment and enquire, with our greatest architect Sir Christopher Wren alive until 1723, why architecture did not develop in the English vernacular so beautifully spoken by him? The answer is twofold. First, Wren had been court architect under the wrong monarchs. Furthermore, court patronage died with the Stuarts (never to revive) and had passed into the hands of the new lawmakers and of private Whig Maecenases. Anyone or anything connected with the old monarchy was tainted and suspect. So the Whigs, shamefully, removed Wren as Surveyor-General and for years filled his office with a numbness of nonenties who were mere political place holders.* No more would Wren—coarse and awkward—ruin noble public buildings which, according to the ultra-Whig Earl of Shaftesbury who hated Hampton Court and St Paul's, had miscarried 'under the Hand of one single Court-Architect through several reigns'.[3]

The second reason is, post-Restoration very rich nobility—Whig or Tory—had never taken whole-heartedly to Wren (his influence lay elsewhere). The less rich followed Anglo-Dutch styles, the very rich turned chiefly to France and Italy for inspiration.

Thus Wren was 'out', partly for political reasons and partly

---

* The office of Surveyor General held neither prestige nor lustre until 1782 when Sir William Chambers was appointed.

because, in a narrower social sense, he had never been 'in'. So here were these rich, reasonable Whigs faced with the need to express themselves in new, suitable terms: unable to accept Wren, unwilling any longer, to accept cross-channel architecture because 'modern' continental architecture was impossible. The sinuous curving baroque, the gay, light-hearted rococo might be fit enough for decadent, corrupt, non-puritanical peoples; for absolute monarchies and papal states but not for us. We were none of these things—thanks to 1688. We were, or so we fondly thought, nearer in spirit to ancient Rome. That we were, briefly, to replace the Roman Empire at a later period in our history was probably not in the minds of our early Georgian ancestors. But certainly they were imbued with the Roman classical spirit. The education enjoyed by the rich was wholly classical. Every young man made a Grand Tour and spent much time in Italy. It was, of course, an aristocratic spirit and outlook. Beginning at the top, it gradually spread out, seeped down and was, as we shall see, responsible for our most beautiful phase of town planning.

It is hardly surprising, then, that Palladian architecture should chime so well with the rational spirit of the age. Deriving from Palladio, and his seminal source Vitruvius, whose prophet Inigo Jones (1573–1652) had not yet been greatly honoured in his own country, it had the triple advantage of being Classical, English— and New. Furthermore, Palladio's villas were of a size to suit the taste of an English country gentleman—very unlike the English Baroque palaces of Blenheim, Castle Howard and Seaton Delaval, so massive and theatrical. But if the true subtleties of Palladio's harmonics in building escaped the English Palladian architects (and they did) his less complex rules of, and formulae for, proportion—particularly in rooms—were lovingly followed. Externally, the level 'panoramic' look achieved by horizontal lines, the balanced alternation of plain wall and openings, the great pillared portico with a heavy pediment, like the front of a Roman temple, is typical English-palladian. Such houses are also nearly always set on a rusticated base or podium, with the *piano nobile* on the first floor, which raises state rooms above the common level. Doors and windows are often heavily pedimented, or are framed by a moulding with superimposed blocked quoins. Or there are round-headed Venetian windows, like a triptych, set (by Burlington anyway) within a relieving arch. All windows at this period had thick glazing bars (they grow thinner as the era advances) and many a beautiful Palladian house is now spoiled because the bars have been removed. These, very briefly, are the chief features of Palladian architecture by which we can today distinguish some of the most beautiful 'stately homes' and smaller houses ever built.

It is never easy to say when ideas first become solid, but for our purpose perhaps we could put the beginning of the Palladian revival at 1715, with the publication of Colen Campbell's first volume of *Vitruvius Britannicus or the British Architect*. A magnificent book with 100 engravings; these, which already reflected national taste, probably had more influence on architecture than the text. Among the engravings was that of Campbell's Palladian Wanstead House. This book, together with Leoni's on Palladio, seems to have triggered off the Earl of Burlington's interest in pure Palladian architecture. Although he had only just returned from Italy, he hared straight back and went to Vicenza to study Palladio first hand. On his return he brought with him the Yorkshire artist and one time coach-painter, William Kent. While in Italy in 1716 Burlington met seventeen-year-old Thomas Coke* who had been there for some years, knew Kent, and was himself studying architecture with Signor Giacomo. Coke was heir to an enormous estate in Norfolk—some forty thousand acres—much of it meagre land, marshy and looking bleakly across sandy wastes to the North Sea. This was Coke's challenge. He met it by reclaiming land, laying out pictorially designed parks and gardens in 1729 and then building Holkham Hall.

* Thomas Coke was a descendant of Lord Chief Justice Coke. He became Lord Lovell in 1728 and Earl of Leicester in 1744, died 1759 leaving no son. Holkham passed to his nephew Wenman Roberts who took the surname Coke. It was Wenman's son (1776–1842) who became the celebrated Coke of Norfolk, a rabid Whig, devoted to George Washington, and, possibly the best-known agricultural pioneer in the world.

Chiswick House, 1725

It is probable that the designs for Holkham were first worked out by Burlington, Kent, and Coke when they were all in Italy but, as the house was not begun until 1734, doubtless plans were changed many times between that early meeting in Italy and the beginning of the building. Holkham is not Palladian in the style represented by Campbell's Mereworth or Burlington's Chiswick House; these are rather heavy variations (some call them charming adaptations) of Palladio's famous Villa La Rotonda (Villa Capra) near Vicenza. Nor does it resemble Campbell's triumph, Wanstead House (1715-20) with its huge hexastyle portico—the first in England, Campbell claimed. We cannot see Wanstead (it was destroyed in 1822) but we can still see Holkham, the work of the chief evangelist of the Palladian movement, Burlington, and of its greatest apostle, William Kent. Kent, who was nearly fifty when he began Holkham, was an indifferent painter, a great pictorial designer of parks and gardens, an incomparable interior architect and designer of furniture. He was, in fact, the first in our history to combine a ministry of these consanguineous talents in one person. This, which imposed a homogeneity on disparate yet related parts, was new to the Georgian era and became typical of it. Kent's influence can be traced throughout the whole period. That he was also one of our greatest architects is proved by the Horse Guards in Whitehall.

Whitehall is immediately appealing. Holkham is not. But to understand the building itself and the relation of its parts to the whole, one should look at a ground plan, which shews that the house is laid out as what I can only call a quincunx;* that is, its separate units are so placed that four occupy the corners and the fifth (and largest) the centre of a great rectangular area. In other words, and very simply, the five units are arranged in the same pattern or order as are the pips on the five of any suit of playing cards—an unusual and difficult arrangement.

At ground level this five unit plan is not noticeable. Viewed straight on, the house on both fronts presents to the eye the more usual three unit façade—a large rectangular central block flanked on east and west by a service wing, each wing attached to the main mass by a low short corridor. The whole effect is of length rather than height. It is a horizontal house and, with its unimaginatively rusticated ground floor, sits tight to the ground. Although its triple-pedimented wings, each the size of an ordinary house, stand well forward and effectively recess the main mass, Holkham does not embrace the landscape as winged houses with curving linked corridors seem to do.

The central block has, on the north or entrance front, a slightly extruded pedimented entrance.† All corners are also extruded but rise in low, shallow-roofed towers slightly above roof level. The overall effect is one of flatness and mathematical precision which

---

* I do not mean to suggest that the quincunx had any esoteric meaning for Kent as it had for Sir Thomas Browne (d. 1682)—also a Norfolk man—and others. The quincuncial plan is interesting, though, because more usually houses are of three units. This is of five, giving the impression of three.

† The one storey ante-entrance room was added in the mid-nineteenth century.

seems rather bleak. This is not greatly assisted by the fenestration, for there seems to be no thematic link here. On this front windows are chiefly Venetian and seem to be stylistically isolated. This, and the rather cold look of the north front, is due, I believe, to the fact that the original thick glazing bars have been removed and all windows are glazed with sheets of plate glass. Originally, sash frames and glazing bars were gilded and this must have added liveliness to an otherwise very serious face.*

The south front is more effective because here a great Corinthian pillared and pedimented portico stands well forward and carries the eye upward. This gives both lightness and grandeur to the façade. The windows too are more satisfactorily arranged. The south front is altogether more successful, more Palladian (although possibly neither Palladio nor Inigo Jones would have thought so) and it is not surprising that when Arthur Young saw the house in the 1760s he was disappointed that this was not the entrance front. There were no stairs to this portico 'in fine taste' and this was 'a disappointment and fault in the building'.[4]

Some years earlier than this, Mrs Lybbe Powys on one of her jaunts describes Holkham as 'a stone building esteemed the most elegant of its kind in England' and although 'not yet completed [this was 1756] when that era arrives it will be magnificent indeed'.[5] So even before it was finished Holkham was, as it still is, one of the sights to be seen, a part of one's education. But Mrs Lybbe Powys was wrong about the stone; the house is yellow brick—this may have been why the Earl-Bishop detested it—and it is said the decision to use this colour was taken because a yellow brick was found in a consignment of antiquities Thomas Coke had had shipped home from Rome. Kent experimented and discovered that brick of this colour could be made locally—and how one wishes he had not! Nevertheless, Holkham† in its own

* As late as 1803, Humphry Repton says, 'In palaces and houses of the highest description, the sash frame should be gilt as at Holkham and Wentworth.' Sashes of gentlemen's houses, he says, should be white, and those of cottages green. Repton, incidentally, would like to have seen the Dome of St Paul's gilded.[6]
† Matthew Brettingham Sr, a not very original architect, was Kent's assistant. After Kent's death in 1748, he completed Holkham.

Holkham. William Kent, 1685–1748

way is magnificent. It is Kent's biggest private house and very
grand indeed, particularly inside. Furthermore, it is definitely
Burlington-Kent Palladian. And if here Palladio's serenity has
been translated into a selfconscious solemnity, not to say grim-
ness, which suggests Burlington's chill, correct hand rather than
Kent's warmer one, this characteristic is possessed to a greater or
lesser degree by many Palladian houses in England. Beautiful,
symmetrical, correctly proportioned and highly civilized though
they are, some are aloof and some are sober almost to the point of
pomposity. This may be due to the Whig outlook. It may be due
to the differences in light and climate which undeniably exist
between England and Italy—or it may be just another aspect of
the Englishness of the English.

While Holkham was being thought about and built—the
process covers nearly half a century and the whole of the early
Georgian period—much grand building was going on elsewhere.

Sir Robert Walpole built Houghton Hall, Norfolk. The design by Colen Campbell, was carried out by Thomas Ripley (d. 1758). Ripley, an ex-carpenter and protégé of Walpole, built the Admiralty. Sir Robert's youngest son Horatio, or Horace, thought it 'a most ugly edifice'.[7] It is fortunate he cannot see its utterly repulsive wartime extension. Houghton, Lord John Hervey thought 'had all the beauties of regularity without the inconveniences'.[8] But Mrs Lybbe Powys felt it 'had rather a too heavy appearance'.[9] She vastly preferred Eastbury,* the seat of the Rt. Hon. George Bubb Dodington (later Baron Melcombe). 'The building', she says, 'may be styl'd an elegant fabrick; tis of stone, extending in length 570 feet, of which the main body of the house takes up only 144; the rest is arcades and offices. Having ascended a grand flight of steps, you come under a Doric portico whose pediment extends 62 feet, with pillars 46 feet high.'[10] Houghton is also of stone, Portland stone, and this, a young French visitor remarks, was 'by itself a matter of great expense . . . I do not know how many miles it travelled to get here'.[11] Only the enormously rich could afford to bring Portland stone such a distance by sea. This is why, until other forms of transport were developed, more modest houses were usually built of local materials.

Up in Yorkshire on April 30th 1728, a north country diarist tells us that old Wentworth Woodhouse, 'built about sixty years ago', began to be 'pulled down'[12] to make room for the largest house in England. This was begun half a dozen years later by Lord Malton (Marquis of Rockingham) whose architect was the not very original Henry Flitcroft, a Burlington protégé. Wentworth Woodhouse is a monster of mechanical Palladianism with an endless 600 foot façade. Flitcroft, known to intimates as 'Burlington Harry', also built part of Woburn Abbey for the Duke of Bedford around 1747.

Just about this time Lord Chesterfield, who wrote the much admired utterly cynical and, therefore, very useful letters to his

---

* A late period Vanbrugh.

illegitimate son, was employing Isaac Ware (d. 1766) to build
Chesterfield house (demolished 1934). Ware, reputedly a chimney
sweep with a talent for drawing, had come under the aegis of
William Kent and held various offices in the Works, as did
Flitcroft. He also built Wrotham Park, Middlesex, with its
characteristic portico and flanking wings, for the ill-fated Admiral
Byng. Wrotham is Kent-Palladian, at one remove so to speak,
and a bit dull, but Ware was rather better at other things.

It is obviously impossible to give details of all the architects
who were influenced by, or who stemmed from the Burlington-
Kent coterie. But mention should be made of another building
Earl who had great influence too. This was Henry Herbert, 9th
Earl of Pembroke (1693–1751), public spirited, honest and hot
tempered but 'so blasphemous at tennis that the primate of
Ireland was forced to leave off playing with him'.[13] He was a
friend of Burlington and also a patron of Colen Campbell. It is
believed that Pembroke did several designs himself, but unfortunately we do not know because one of his protégés was
Roger Morris (d. 1749), and as they worked together it is impossible to tell what is Pembroke and what Morris. One thing we
know for sure is that Pembroke and Morris built that most
exquisite Palladian bridge at Wilton; another is that the Earl
promoted Westminster bridge (c. 1705–62), the first classical
bridge (though not Palladian) of its size in England. Since Roman
times there had been but one bridge over the Thames at London;
this was the second and forerunner of many others.

Pembroke and Morris are Campbell-Palladian, and one or the
other—perhaps both—built Marble Hill, Twickenham, for one of
George II's mistresses, the Countess of Suffolk. It is a small,
smooth, urbane house, beautifully sited and has perfect manners,
which cannot be said of that *enfant gaté*[14] the King. Morris, too,
is thought to have had a hand in the alteration and modernization
of Lydiard Tregoze, Wiltshire (between 1743 and 1749). This is
not a grand house—nor is Marble Hill—but it is crisply informa-
tive of the Palladian manner.

If we know less about Pembroke than Burlington, it must be

Palladian bridge, Wilton. Roger Morris, 1695–1749

remembered that in those days Earls still had great influence. Two dire and dreary German monarchs, whose bad taste in the arts (bar music) was exceeded only by their taste in women, set no standard or example to be followed. The nobility set the standard now, created the fashions in this and that and were followed at a greater or less distance by the less exalted. So if we recognize Burlington's rather puritanical hand in architecture more clearly and more often than Pembroke's, it does not mean, necessarily, that Pembroke had less influence. Indeed in the long run he may have had more. His protégé Roger Morris had a relative, Robert (who was also his pupil), and Robert wrote numerous books on architecture which had a very wide circulation indeed. One of them, *Select Architecture* (1755), even crossed the Atlantic and provided some of the inspiration for Monticello, the magnificent house built by the great liberal Francophile, writer and signer of the Declaration of Independence and third President of the United States, Thomas Jefferson (1743–1826).

Books on and about architecture were flooding the market by this time, and were carrying the gospel to all parts of England. Most great architects wrote about their work and their theories, so did some of the less great, like Isaac Ware whose *Complete Body of Architecture* (1756) was one of the handiest compendiums of the day on every aspect of the building trade. Probably the most prolific producer of 'pattern-books' was the notoriously unsuccessful architect Batty Langley (1696–1751) who produced some twenty-one books on the subject. That he was not a successful practitioner is not to say he was not a successful designer, or interpreter—the best pianoforte coach I ever knew could barely stumble through *The Merry Peasant*—and Langley's books had a wide sale and were very useful in spreading detailed knowledge of the new standard in taste.

Yet there were still outsiders. Still those who went their own way. There was, for example, old-fashioned William Winde (d. 1722), working away at Buckingham House (*c.* 1705) for John Sheffield, Duke of Buckingham (2nd creation) whose third and last wife was a natural daughter of James II by Catherine Sedley. She was half-sister to the Old Pretender and a rabid Jacobite. Today, as Buckingham Palace after many alterations, it is neither political nor beautiful, but its contemporaneous, smaller and very near replica still stands in Buckinghamshire at Wotton Underwood.

The greatest 'outsider' of all and to some the greatest architect of the early Georgian era, was James Gibbs (1682–1754) who, living at a time when the Palladian had become a cult, created some of the most beautiful buildings in England. Gibbs was neither irrevocably wedded to the strict proportion of the English Palladian style, nor was he an idiosyncratic innovator. His style is beautiful and very individual. Like Campbell, he was a Scot; like most celebrated architects he studied in Rome (1703?–9). He was also a Tory, may have had Jacobite leanings, and is said to have been a Roman Catholic. This was a triple disadvantage to anyone wanting a career in Whig, Hanoverian, Protestant England. Although Gibbs makes free use of the Palladian manner,

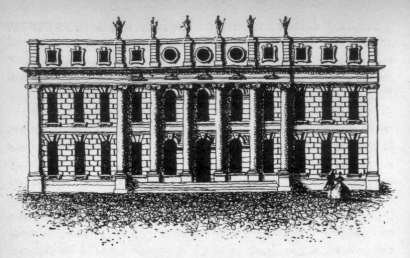

Canons Park. James Gibbs, 1682–1754

he seems to have more in common with Roger Pratt* and with the Rome of Carlo Fontana† than with the Burlington Circle or the Augustan Rome seen by Vitruvius and interpreted by Palladio.

His most noble achievement, according to Defoe, was 'Cannons' near 'Edgeworth' (Edgware) built for James Brydges, ninth Baron and first Duke of Chandos. It was built before Holkham and was 'the most magnificent house in England'. Lofty, majestic 'built of free stone' with 'the pilasters running flush up to the cornish and architrave . . . the windows very high with all possible ornament' and 'the whole structure . . . built with such a profusion of expence and all finished with such brightness of fancy (and) goodness of judgment' that 'not Italy itself can shew such a building rais'd from the common surface by one private hand'.[15] This wonderful house, which cost

---

* See *The Jacobeans at Home*, Chapter Two.
† Gibbs studied with Carlo Fontana (1634–1714) and Fontana is responsible for much of the Rome we know today. He had been a pupil of Bernini and was probably the first of what Professor Wittkower calls 'late Baroque Classicist architects'.

£230,000,* did not long survive. The Duke lost his money and in 1747, a few years after his death, Canons was pulled down and sold for its building material which fetched £11,000. In its place 'Mr Hallet, an upholsterer in London' built 'a small but neat and Elegant villa'.[16]

Fortunately for us one of Gibbs's most beautiful houses—perhaps it is one of the most beautiful eighteenth-century houses in England—still survives.† This is Ditchley Park, Oxon., built *c.* 1720 for the 2nd Earl of Lichfield. Dignified, truly elegant (an overworked word of the period for Holkham is not what we should term elegant) and beautifully proportioned, the main block has a slightly projecting entrance and its corners also extrude slightly. All quoins and doorways are rusticated and the two service wings, both with tilt roofs surmounted by delicate clock towers, are linked to the main building by curved quadrant corridors. The windows would shock a strict devotee of Palladio —not a pedimented or a Venetian one anywhere. On ground and first floors they are rectangles of the same size, the attic floor windows are square. All have architraval keystones. Some find this dull, others regard Ditchley as having the finest fenestration in England. It is often said, too, that Gibbs is cold and aloof and that his work suffers from 'a paucity . . . of external decoration'.[17] This can be a matter of personal taste only. Yet there must be many who feel with Gibbs himself, that 'It is not the Bulk of a Fabrick, the Richness and Quality of Materials, the Multiplicity of Lines, nor the Grandeur of the Funishings, that give Grace and Beauty and Grandeur to a Building; but the Proportion of the Parts to one another and to the whole, whether entirely

---

* This is the Rev. Dr Stukeley's figure but the Rev. Daniel Lysons says it cost £200,000 and that 'James of Greenwich' was the architect; i.e. John James (1672?–1746) who held various posts in The Works. He designed St George's, Hanover Square, and may possibly have had some part in designing Canons.[18]

† In the non-domestic field Gibbs, among other things, built St Martin-in-the-Fields and St Mary le Strand, London; All Saints (now the cathedral), Derby; the Radcliffe Camera, Oxford; the Senate House and Fellows' Lodge, King's College, Cambridge, and the Tower of St Clement Danes, London.

plain or enriched with a few Ornaments properly disposed'.[19]

James Gibbs died in 1754. So did a man called John Wood (b. 1704). And with John Wood, the Elder, we are at once transferred from the stately homes of the Palladian Paladins to towns, cities and the urban houses of the middling sort.

Cities and towns, as we know, began to expand with great rapidity. Most of the rich aristocracy, in addition to their country estates, had town houses with a good deal of property surrounding them. In London and York, in Bristol and Norwich, in Bath and Newcastle, as populations and industries grew, urban property became more valuable. A town house with a large garden and fields near it was all very well, but gardens, park and fields could be turned into a handsome profit if developed.

The idea of developing town property was not new to the century. The Piazza (Covent Garden) and the first London square to be called a square (Bloomsbury); the first street of regularly built houses (Queen Street); the first speculative builder on a large scale (the rogue Nicholas Barebone)—all belong to the previous century. But these efforts, separate and sporadic though they were, first exemplified a certain discipline, a desire for order, a regularity in architecture, a planning of streets, squares, crescents and terraces which the Georgian era was to make peculiarly and beautifully its own. The key word is 'beautifully'. We have been planning ever since but neither very well nor very beautifully.

Speculative building still goes on and in our own day has fallen into bad odour. But in the eighteenth century, the speculative builder could be, and often was, anyone from a duke to a building craftsman. The difference between then and now is that both duke and craftsman had taste. A noble landowner might want to develop the land himself, lay it out in streets or squares with his own new town house, never very large, as the central feature. He might have a hand in, or oversee, the design or he might, and often did, prefer to let his land on 42, 60, 61 or 64 year leases— the 99 year lease did not become customary until the end of the eighteenth century. When the lease fell in, so did the buildings— sometimes quite literally. But the original landlord, or more often, his descendants, still owned the land and the buildings, no matter how many times the lease had changed hands or the buildings been altered.

Any one with money, flair, or a knowledge of building could rent land, build on it and hope to derive a pretty profit. Sometimes the speculative builders were carpenters, or masons, or bricklayers, or plumbers accustomed to building. Sometimes they were architects who designed and planned but let the actual building out to subcontractors. Sometimes they made a fortune like John Wood. Sometimes they did not, like the Adam brothers, who came such a cropper over the Adelphi that the debt was a burden all their lives. But, profitable or not, town building boomed.

Happily by now there was a new, accepted standard of good taste in architecture, and the standard was, in many instances Palladian. Its uniformity, its regularity, its proportions, its use of central pediment meant that a whole street of houses could be designed as an architectural whole. Could, in fact, be made to resemble one great house. A rusticated ground floor with as many regularly spaced separate entrances as required; above this, a first floor with long pedimented windows; the second floor with smaller ones with mouldings; engaged columns or pilasters to support the great central pediment of the façade; corners at each end of the street, extruded and rising above roof level—and there, for example, is the north side of Queen Square, Bath, built by Wood the Elder from about 1729 and fortunately still extant.

Wood began his career in London where he did some work for the Duke of Chandos in Cavendish Square. But as lease-holder, architect and builder he, together with his son, John Wood the younger, who invented or introduced the crescent into street planning, is largely responsible for Georgian Bath. There is still enough of Georgian Bath left to make us feel with Mrs Lybbe Powys that it is 'a city, in my opinion, more worth seeing than any I was ever at, the great Metropolis excepted'. This was in 1759 and she had been at Bath on two previous occasions, but now she finds it 'infinitely improv'd by the building of the circus and the whole street by which 'tis approach'd from the square'. Although only nine houses were as yet built in this street they gave Mrs Lybbe Powys 'an idea of the elegance of the whole, they being in magnificent taste in the Doric, Ionic and Corinthian orders'.[20]

In the Metropolis by this time much had happened. London was spreading to the north and west, a great rectangle of land had already been laid out in a square with adjacent streets named in honour of the new King from Hanover. The Palladian Earl of Burlington rebuilt Burlington House (little remains) and let out the land behind it on building lease. Colen Campbell built himself a house in Old Burlington Street, William Kent did the same in Savile Row, while 'Burlington Harry' Flitcroft preferred Sackville Street. Berkeley House had been burned down and was replaced by Devonshire House (demolished 1924), and in the fields north of Piccadilly, where a famous cattle fair was held every May, streets increased in number and houses were occupied by persons of quality. The group of fields of the Grosvenor estate was planned, probably as a complete unit, and was intended to be the largest and architecturally the most important square in London. Colen Campbell made a design for this but it was not used. All the sites seem to have been leased to a builder, John Simmons, who it is believed designed the east side, while Edward Shepherd is said to have done the north side so Grosvenor square emerged looking as if it had a single continuous building on each of these sides but, of course, this architectural whole contained many individual houses. People liked living in Grosvenor square, even if it was rather far out, for the air was healthy due to the large garden in the middle. Here it should be pointed out, that not all streets of contiguous houses were built in the grand Palladian manner, numbers of them were very definitely in the Wren or Queen Anne style; red, brown or grey brick with stone quoins, parapeted roof and short flights of steps leading to canopied doorways. Simple, unaffected and very beautiful in their own very different way.

The Cavendish-Harley estate was also developed, and Marylebone fields as well, by a group of rich Tory landowners most of

The Royal Crescent, Bath, 1767–75. John Wood II

whose names survive today in the street names of this area. Harley, a Queen Anne Tory, employed James Gibbs to supervise the architecture of Cavendish Square where Wood worked, but the square was a long time a-building,* because by about 1730 the steam had gone out of the boom in London, and John Wood deserted it for Bath (*c.* 1727). By mid-century Bath had become nearly as important as London as a centre of artistic leadership; the influence of its type of building and the new layout of its streets was felt elsewhere. The Crescent at Buxton, Derbyshire, built (1779–84) by the Duke of Devonshire to the designs of John Carr of York (he built Harewood House), is a direct, important, and delightful adaptation of the Bath Crescent. By the end of the Georgian era the Bath type crescent, in the hands of various

* 'The failure of the South-Sea year put a stop to the improvements', says Lysons.

architects, had moved out to the coast and became a favourite feature of seaside towns. Georgian houses, Georgian streets all over England—and throughout the whole of the period—owe as much to Bath as they do to London. But all Georgian streets, terraces and crescents were originally laid out so that there were vistas of masonry terminating in clumps of trees and gardens centred in squares or circuses.

All contiguous houses occupying newly laid out squares, terraces and crescents were generally smallish and, with few exceptions, were let to middling people. But in addition to rented town houses, middling people (as and when they made money, which a great many of them did) leased land in the suburbs and bought or built small but elegant villas like that erected by the famous upholsterer, Mr Hallet. 'I had before discovered that there was nowhere but in England the distinction of *middling* people', Walpole writes on his return from the continent in 1741. 'I perceive now, that there is peculiar to us *middling houses*: how snug they are!'²¹ Sometimes these new small suburban villas showed the Palladian influence. Often they exhibited a sturdy or graceful development of the Wren house—square, rosy-brick houses with hipped roofs, dormers, regularly spaced sash-windows and doorways with canopies, fanlights or both; they are charming, strong, placid, no frippery, *j'y suis, j'y reste* houses. They, too, are Georgian and set a style which has been revived, not too happily, in our own century where for obvious reasons, it is known as 'post-office' or 'municipal Georgian'.

But not everyone in England was rich or even moderately so. There were millions and millions who were not. How and where did they live? Amid the beauty, the splendour, the good taste, the elegance of the new accepted standard of architecture, they lived like rats in cellars and tenements. They froze and starved in dreadful huts and broken cottages in the countryside. They lived in such squalor, such misery, such despair, filth and want that even today one cannot bear the thought with equanimity.

In rapidly growing cities as local industries developed apace and new ones were started up the rich moved out of their houses in the centres of the towns and built new houses farther out where it was less crowded. Their old houses rapidly decayed into tenements. Those who lived in the basements lived herded together with their pigs, domestic fowl and even horses. In squalid alleyways, ramshackle, weather-boarded one- or two-room hovels stood back to back, holding their overplus of the miserable and the hopeless. There was no sanitary system. Streets for the most part in these older sections were narrow and unpaved and served as the communal dustbin. Everyone, including tradesmen and butchers, threw his refuse and offal into the streets. In fast growing Manchester, it was not uncommon for ten people to be living in one room. There was often no furniture at all. The occupiers 'slept close together on shavings for warmth'.[22] Death was their constant companion and friend.

In country districts there were many good cottages but there were also appalling ones which increased in number as the era progressed. 'Hovels, made of mud and of straw; bits of glass, or of old off-cast windows, without frames or hinges, frequently, but merely stuck in the mud walls ... bits of chairs or stools; wretched boards tacked together to serve for a table; the floor of pebble, broken brick, or of bare ground; ... a thing called a bed ... and ... rags on the backs of the wretched inhabitants.'[23] This is the way the majority lived in Georgian England. The age of reason and enlightenment was also the age of wretchedness. The magnificence of the few was overmatched by the misery of the many.

Misery continued and increased in the second half of the era, so did grand building. But by the time the third of the four Georges came to the throne, in 1760, the original Palladians— Kent, Campbell Leoni, Burlington, Morris, Pembroke were dead. The inheritors of the tradition—and it is a tradition which persisted well into the nineteenth century—were men like Robert Taylor (1714–88), James Paine (1716–89), and William Chambers (1723–96). It is said that in the 1760s, Taylor and Paine 'divided the whole practice of architecture between them'. Taylor began as a sculptor (he did the carved pediment of the first

George Dance's unappealing Mansion House in 1744) and then became an architect, principally in London, where he worked on a number of public buildings. His most splendid country house was Hevingham,* Suffolk, (c. 1782) which he did in the traditional Palladian manner, enriched with a French touch, as the great central block of the north front has four grand figures standing before the pilasters of the upper storey. Unlike the Italians, the French, or the ancient Greeks, we rarely seem to feel that sculpture and architecture should be perfectly correlated. Taylor, being both sculptor and architect, understood this correlation. His figures belong to the building and do not look as if they had been put there as an afterthought or to conceal some shortcoming or defect. Taylor, who became a Sheriff of London, also built part of the Stone Building, Lincoln's Inn (c. 1775), Maidenhead Bridge and, by no means incidentally, he made a great deal of money. He died in 1788 and left his fortune to found an institute of modern languages. So his name still lives in Oxford, quite unconnected there with either architecture or sculpture, in the 'Taylorian'.

James Paine, Taylor's junior by two years, was the leading mid-Georgian country house architect, and one of his stately homes is Kedleston, Derbyshire (1761). As at Holkham the original plan called for four wings, but only two were built and these are attached to the main block by curving corridors. The north front and two wings are by Paine; the south front, to which we shall return later, is by Robert Adam. Paine's front is unmistakably Palladian with a heavily rusticated basement, arches, a most beautiful Corinthian portico and a great pediment surmounted by terminal figures. It is said that both Taylor and Paine were the first architects to take pupils, possibly articled, into their offices. Thus they turned architecture into a profession. In other words, although working masons, carpenters, builders and even designing earls still became architects, either through practical knowledge of building or through interest and 'flair', Taylor and Paine had

* Later remodelled by Wyatt.

architect's offices as we now know them, where young men were trained to become architects.

William Chambers, younger than Taylor and Paine, at one time had been architectural tutor to the future George III. Chambers built arches, stables, gateways and houses for men of title but we know him best by his masterpiece, Somerset House, Strand. Built on the site of a centuries old Royal Palace, Somerset House retained its old name but had a new function. It was built for government offices, and with it Chambers quite altered the conception of bureaucratic building. Somerset House might be a very grand house indeed, one of those smallish palazzi which still grace Italian and French cities. It is firmly but broadly Palladian, and the Strand block has 'a rustic arcade basement, a Corinthian order of columns and pilasters enriched windows, balustrades, statues, masks (and) medallions'.[24] It is very beautiful and with its sculptured figures set in front of a high attic it, like Taylor's Hevingham, has a slightly French feeling. The terrace front overlooking the Thames must have been much more lovely and dramatic when the water lapped against its massive stonework— there was no embankment then—and arches, water-gates and bridges served their original purpose in a majestic way.

These three then, Taylor, Paine, and Chambers, together with John Carr of York (who built numbers of great Midland houses) were the last to build in the great Palladian tradition. But much 'Palladian-type' building went on in a dreary mechanical style, and the end result was much as Alexander Pope had foreseen when he addressed his brilliant and satirical epistle to the Earl of Burlington*

> Yet shall (my lord) your just your noble rules
> Fill half the land with Imitating Fools;
> Who random drawings from your sheets shall take,
> And of one beauty many blunders make;
> . . .

* Pope was a Tory, a Roman Catholic and a friend of James Gibbs who built his house, but he was also a friend of Burlington.

Reverse your Ornaments, and hang them all
On some patch'd dog-hole ek'd with ends of wall;
Then clap four slices of Pilaster on't,
That, lac'd with bits of rustic, make a Front.[25]

But if many were imitating fools a good proportion were not.
Alongside the traditional good and the mechanical bad Palladian,
a fierce battle was now going on between those who believed in
the superiority of Greek over Roman architecture and vice versa.
This is now commonly known as 'the battle of the styles' and it
raged all over Europe. The ammunition in the beginning was, as
it had been in the first half of the era, books: illustrated books.
These were produced, first, by travelling architects, draughtsmen
and dilettanti who, since Turkish power was decaying rapidly,
found the eastern Mediterranean no longer so difficult nor
dangerous of access. The intrepid and the interested were now
better able to visit Greece and Syria; and the English, quick
enough off the mark on such occasions, were among the first to
get there. Robert Wood (1717?–71) traveller, politician, member
of the Society of Dilettanti and later M.P. for Brackley, visited
Coele Syria in 1751 and, in 1753, published *The Ruins of Palmyra,**
concerning that late classic and once fabulously rich city where
Rome overlaid Greece and which had such splendidly ornate
tombs. In 1757 Wood published *The Ruins of Balbec*. Fortunately
he saw it when he did, Baalbec, always subject to earthquakes,
suffered a devastating one in 1759. This further ruined those
ruins which are, today, world famous.† Here, then, was ancient
architecture not overlaid by the Italian Renaissance.

In the same year Wood visited Syria, James Stuart (1713–88)
painter, architect, member of the Society of Dilettanti, set off for
Greece with a draughtsman, Nicholas Revett. Upon his return he
built a pure Doric Temple at Hagley Park, Worcestershire

---

* Palmyra first became rather vaguely known to Europe through a visit made in
1671 by Dr William Halifax of Aleppo.
† European attention was first drawn to Baalbec by Baumgarten in 1507 and by
Belon du Mans in 1553.

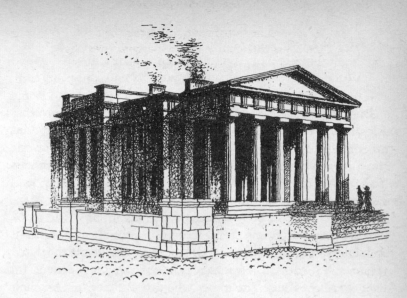

House in the Doric style, *circa* 1810

(1758), for, being English, we naturally try out our architectural innovations and our bits of nonsense in our gardens. This temple, still extant, is the first neo-classical building in the pure or severe Doric style, a style which shocked William Chambers to the core. He thought it absolutely barbarous with its short, thick columns rising straight from the stylobate without benefit of base, and supporting a heavy entablature and pediment. The Doric order, according to Palladio's interpretation of Vitruvius, had taller, more slender fluted columns, lighter capitals, a much lighter entablature and pediment and, furthermore, columns had a moulded base. So here, on the one hand was Palladian Doric (we now call it Roman) and on the other was the real thing— straight from ancient Athens! James Stuart added further fuel to the flames when, in 1762 with Nicholas Revett, he published the first of his volumes on *The Antiquities of Athens*. He immediately became the recognized authority on the pure Greek style and was for ever after known as 'Athenian' Stuart. Unfortunately, for ever after he also drank too much and rather went to pieces as few Athenians have done.

In the meantime, in 1754, the year in which James Gibbs and John Wood the elder died, and Horace Walpole became M.P. for Castle Rising, Norfolk, a young Scots architect went to Rome to study. His name was Robert Adam (1728–92), the son of an architect and one of four brothers, of whom James became his associate. Robert saw antique Rome, no less than Renaissance Rome, the Bernini-Fontana and eighteenth-century Rome— a palimpsest city. And ancient Rome, during Adam's stay, was also being presented to the world through a series of magnificent engravings (nearly 2,000 of them) by his friend, Piranesi.* Piranesi's antique Rome was accurate enough in detail but absolutely vast in conception: a Brobdingnagian Rome inhabited by a race of Gullivers. So massive, masculine, magnificent and overpowering a Rome, that those who saw the city first through Piranesi's engravings found it meagre and disappointing when they got there and used their own eyes. To offset Piranesi's wide-screen, imaginative and visionary Rome, there were the buried cities of Herculaneum,† about which books began to appear in 1751, and Pompeii,‡ where the architecture showed the transition from the Greek to Roman styles, with a good admixture of Etruscan. As opposed to the vast remains of Imperial Rome, here was domestic architecture. People had lived in these small, beautifully decorated houses. Much use was made of stucco, both for facing and ornament; walls were painted with scenes and arabesques, and all sorts of delicate ornamentation was used. In addition, there were Raphael's 'grotesques' to be studied at the Villa Madama and the Loggia of the Vatican. These were imitations and interpretations of paintings found in ancient tunnels and grottos (hence grotto-esque). Across the Adriatic, at Spalatro

---

* Giovanni Battista Piranesi (1720–78), a Venetian architect and more artist than archaeologist, began publishing his plates in 1756. His first book, *Le Antichità Romane* (4 vols) had a wide European influence.
† Discovered 1719; excavations begun, 1738.
‡ Discovered 1748; systematic excavations begun, 1763.

(now Split) was the villa or palace built by Diocletian in the third century A.D., to which, after resigning the imperial purple, he retired to grow cabbages and write infuriatingly smug letters to his restless, ex co-Augustus, Maximian. Young Robert Adam went off to Spalatro too, and although mistaken for a spy he managed in a few weeks to take measurements and draw pictures of the villa. He was so thorough that he even comments on the climate, soil and crops. This venture resulted in the publication of yet another book, *The Ruins of the Palace of the Emperor Diocletian at Spalatro* (1764). But Adam had returned to England earlier, and by the time this book was published he was already a quite fashionable and famous architect.

His style, eclectic and delicate, is basically a *mélange* of various classic styles—Greek, Roman, Graeco-Roman, Pompeiian, Etruscan, Renaissance Italian. This does not mean he was not original. He was. In architecture anyone can learn the rules just as in music anyone can learn to write counterpoint, but in both arts it takes genius to compose. So out of these diverse but related elements, Adam created his own style. Like that of James Gibbs, which it does not resemble in the least, it was highly personal and individual. Unlike Gibbs's style it caught on very quickly.

Adam is regarded as the father of the neo-classical movement in architecture, and here, perhaps, it is best to define our terms as briefly as possible. Classic, I suggest, means perfection in any field of endeavour at any period in time. In architecture, for example, the Parthenon at Athens, the Pantheon at Rome, are separated in time by five hundred years. Each is a classic of its own epoch. The classical style, on the other hand, is that which for its inspiration returns to, imitates or bases itself upon the ancient classic style; or uses the ancient classic as a springboard or point of departure. Playwrights have been doing this sort of thing for centuries. By this definition Palladian architecture is classical because it is based on the work of the sixteenth-century Italian architect Andrea Palladio who, in turn, based his work on the translations he made of the books of architecture written by the Roman Vitruvius, perhaps in the time of Augustus. Since Vitruvius's books were not illustrated, Palladio did illustrations for them, basing his drawings on the proportions and references to ancient buildings given verbally in the text.* Thus, in England, the Palladian is a classical style at one remove so to speak. Whereas the classical style of the second half of the Georgian era is based on direct observation; on measurements and surveys of ancient buildings and ruins which still existed. So it is useful and helpful to refer to this as 'neo-classicism'.

Greek classic architecture, or what remains of it, is almost wholly temple architecture, noble and slender (apart from the severe Doric). It is a matter of verticals standing upon and supporting horizontals. Domes and arches are not typical, but sculpture is used as an integral part of architecture. In Athens there is much marble, but the Greeks had no cement. They had to use cramps, dowels and hot lead to hold their masonry together. This meant that all blocks of marble masonry, all segments of columns and so on, had to be made with perfect accuracy and exquisite finish.

Roman architecture is much more municipal—or rather what could be seen of it in the eighteenth century was—fora, baths, basilicae (originally basilicae were meeting places and assembly rooms). Romans liked to put domes on circular walls. They used much tunnel vaulting, cross vaulting and hemispherical coffered ceilings. Their sculpture was set in niches or on pedestals. As much of it was booty from conquered countries it was decorative —triumphal not architectural. But one basic difference between Greek and Roman architecture is that the Roman was firmly based, in both senses of the word, on pozzolana—and with pozzolana, or cement, many structural innovations are possible. So the core of Roman building could be brick, stone or rubble, and marble could be used for facing, like a veneer. This is why Augustus found Rome a city of brick but could turn it into a city of marble. Walls, because of this could be, and were, immensely thick so that deep niches left in them for sculpture presented no problem. Cement foundations can bear enormous weights. Thus,

---

* Others before and since Palladio, have made illustrations for Vitruvius.

fewer columns are required to span greater spaces. Indeed, in ancient Rome columns began to lose their structural significance. They no longer had to be free standing and closely spaced like Greek columns, they could be engaged or turned into decorative piers or pilasters. With cement, ancient Rome could build the skyscraper of the day, the immense Colosseum. Pozzolana was to ancient Rome what ferroconcrete is to us.

Significantly, the development of newer and better cements belongs to the later Georgian period. Various districts in England had always had reputations for cements of differing qualities and this, to a certain extent, conditioned building. But just about the time George III came to the throne, the engineer, John Smeaton (1724–92), busy on the third edition of the Eddystone lighthouse, began to try to discover why some cements hardened better under water than others. He experimented and discovered the best 'hydraulic limes' were of limestone containing a good deal of clay, and he thought that the cement he evolved from this 'would equal the best merchantable Portland Stone in solidity and durability'.[26] So our neo-classical architecture came at a time when we had, after a thousand years, improved on a building material unknown to the Athenians and which enabled us, as it had enabled the Romans, to go in for new structural innovations and to speed up building, as later on we did.* We also took to using stucco, a kind of cement, but not the same kind as used by 'dear impeccable Palladio'. With stucco (and its use became lavish as the era aged) housefronts could be plastered, columns fluted, and pediments ornamented in double quick time.

It may be that Robert Adam introduced the new use of stucco, no one seems quite sure of this, but he held the patent for a 'new' stucco invented by Mr Liardet, a Swiss clergyman. We also began to use an artificial stone, sometime during the late sixties or early seventies. It was put out from a Lambeth factory by a Mrs Eleanor

---

* In 1796 Parker invented 'Roman Cement' which set in twenty minutes, in or out of water. Aspidin produced what he called 'Portland Cement' (not the same as that in use today) in 1822. Ferroconcrete was developed by the French in 1868.

Coade and was known as 'Coade Stone'. It was a very fine artificial material and no one today knows its exact formula, but it
could be used for quoining, for ornaments and for sculpture. Real
stone was terribly expensive and as a London building Act of
1774 had banned all but the minimum use of wood—a cheap and
inexpensive material then—for structure or ornament because of
the fire hazard, 'Coade's Artificial Stone'* came just at the right
time. It surrounded doorways, made ornamental keystones and
fine churchyard tombs, it could be, and was, used for sculptured
figures and for all sorts of ornament. Today Coade stone can be
found unaffected by time, weather and even fire. Beautiful
examples are the stags and urns surmounting the gateway to what
is now Towcester race track. Thus new building materials
influenced architecture in the later Georgian era as they always
have and always will.

But to return to Robert Adam. It may be he owed his introduction into the exalted world which employed him to the
detested Lord Bute, for in 1758 Lady Mary Wortley Montagu
writes from Venice to her daughter: 'I saw some months ago a
countryman of yours (Mr Adam) who desires to be introduced to
you. He seems to me, in one short visit, to be a man of genius and
I have heard his knowledge of architecture much applauded.'[28]
Lady Mary's daughter was the Countess of Bute. Her husband was
then tutor to the future George III and the favourite of George's
very bossy and tiresome mother, Augusta, the widowed Princess
of Wales. Architect and Earl met in May 1758 and the meeting
was a resounding failure. But somehow things were mended,
Bute became Adam's patron and he was taken up by those who
were bored to death by the Palladian style and by the increasingly
stereotyped use of orders—inside and out. Adam and his brother
are best known now for their interiors, but one of Adam's earliest
'outdoor' works, before he fully developed his own style, is the

* Discovered or invented *c.* 1722, but it did not flourish until Mrs Coade, daughter
of the inventor, took over the business. Horace Walpole, writing in 1780, says
Batty Langley 'invented an artificial stone of which he made figures; an art
lately brought to perfection'.[27]

Admiralty archway (not to be confused with the Admiralty Arch) a screen of Doric columns with sculpture by Michael Spang, which successfully corrected the excessive wing projections of poor, dull Ripley's deadly Admiralty Building. Probably his best-known exterior today is what is left of Kenwood, London. But, possibly, Kedleston Hall, illustrates most clearly the difference between the 'classical' Palladian and the 'neo-classical'. Paine's north front is beautiful, perfect of its kind and quite still. Adam's south front is full of movement* (and movement was the thing he strove for). The outward curve of the dome is contrasted with the concave curve of the double flight of entrance steps. The projecting entablature below the dome is like a Roman triumphal arch and is supported by disengaged columns. The pedimented door is set within a shallow arched recess, which becomes typical of Adam's later work. All the elements are classical but there is nothing static here, it is three-dimensional not flat-faced architecture; all parts advance, recede, flow into each other. This is the grand manner. A manner enunciated in the Grecian (not Roman) portico at Osterley and alas, no longer to be seen in the delicate bow-shaped portico of Luton Hoo, built for Lord Bute and now vastly altered inside and out.

In London the brothers Adam went in for speculative building and, taking a ninety-nine-year lease from the Duke of St Albans, laid out and built the Adelphi (celebrating their brotherhood in its name) on the site of old Durham House. Nothing could have been more different in character than the Adelphi (begun 1772) and Somerset House. Both on the site of ancient houses. Both right in the heart of London. The one Palladian, the other, on its river side with its great arched storage vaults and wharfs echoing the palace of Diocletian, while high above, on this manmade cliff of masonry, rose a magnificent terrace of brick houses delicately ornamented with pilasters decorated with honeysuckle; and where, at either end, detached, projecting buildings had roof

* He defines movement as 'meant to express, the rise and fall, the advance and recess, with other diversity of form, in the different parts of a building' (*Works:* Vol. 1, Preface (A)).

House in the Adam style

pediments ornamented with wreaths and swags. Streets behind the terrace were also laid out. But very few of the original houses survive to delight us.

The Adam brothers did other work in London. Between 1776 and 1780, James produced Portland Place now, due to chronic rebuilding, altered beyond recognition. Robert built houses in Portman Square, one of which, Home House, is now the Courtauld Institute. He also designed the east and south sides of Fitzroy Square, but only the façades survive. This was much later work and by this time the Adam 'style' was well known all over the country because as early as 1773 the brothers had begun to issue their fine series of folio engravings, *Works in Architecture*; like all such books, it was avidly read, used and copied. The lightness, freshness, delicacy of style; the use of graceful ornaments—swags, wreaths, vases, medallions, paterae; the typical recessed arches for windows, the adaptation of the Venetian window—all were enthusiastically taken up, copied and, in the end, run to death. Adam and Chambers were two great architects of the first thirty years of the long reign of George III. Totally dissimilar, both classical in entirely different ways, they not unnaturally despised each other's work. And there were other and younger architects who, around the 1790s, with equal fervour despised snippety old Adam and rigid old Chambers.

They too were neo-classicists—and rather strict ones—but we can deal with only a few here. One was Henry Holland. Born in the year which saw the death of Sir Robert Walpole (Lord Orford) and Jonathan Swift, and the last Stuart uprising, Holland died with Fox and Pitt in 1806. He was an anti-Adamite who vastly preferred the simplified Greek Ionic style (much reduced) to any other. The son of a mason-builder, Holland married Bridget, daughter of the famous landscape gardener, Capability Brown,* and perhaps moved from designing garden houses to designing stately homes—Whig ones, for Holland worked exclusively for the Whig aristocracy (the Whig Club, Brooks's 1776 is his). By now the Whigs, out of office, moved in concentric and sycophantic circles around Charles James Fox and his dear friend George, Prince of Wales. The prince loathed and detested his Tory father. When in 1783 he attained his majority and a separate establishment he decided to have Whig Holland alter this establishment Carlton House—an old fashioned mouldering place built in 1709—into a suitable residence for the 'first gentleman of Europe'.

Holland metamorphosed Carlton House, which stood where the Athenaeum and York place now are, both inside and out; and he did it in a strictly neo-classical manner. The Pall Mall façade, long, low and lightly rusticated from eaves to ground, had a central portico deep enough to act as a *porte cochère*. A colonnade of coupled Ionic columns with entries at each end screened the

---

* Brown and Henry Holland Sr were great friends and worked together on various buildings. Holland's son, the architect, it is said, was introduced to a rich clientele by Brown.

house from the gaze of the vulgar—but as nothing could ever screen the behaviour of the Prince, Londoners seemed to find this screen simply silly or, perhaps, ironic. Outside and in, Carlton House was undoubtedly very beautiful. More reserved, more austere, much purer and more splendid than Adam's later work which, undeniably, had become over-elaborate and bitty. Horace Walpole still going strong at seventy, still tetchy, malicious and diverting, is much impressed with the 'taste and propriety' of Carlton House. 'How sick one shall be, after this chaste palace of Mr Adam's gingerbread and sippets of embroidery',[29] he writes from Strawberry Hill. Those who regarded Horace's Gothic Strawberry Hill as an affair of gilded gingerbread and flim-flam must have been astonished by his condemnation of Adam. But no one could have been surprised that Horace should wonder how Carlton House could ever be paid for, 'where the money is to come from I conceive not—all the tin mines in Cornwall would not pay for a quarter'.[30] And indeed, the cost of Carlton House was very great and added to the Prince's already not inconsider-able debts. Beautiful and expensive Carlton House, which set a turn of the century fashion for the Greek Ionic, was destroyed in 1826, but its columns were rescued and now make up the central portico of the National Gallery.

A contemporary of Holland was James Wyatt (1747–1813)—anti-Palladian, anti-Adam, extremely versatile and capable of building in any style. But he seems to have been given to wine, women and architecture; roughly, in that order. When at twenty-five he returned from Rome he astonished fashionable London with his design for the Pantheon Assembly Rooms in the Oxford Road, a 'winter Ranelagh' erected 'at the expense of sixty thousand pounds'.[31] From then on he never looked back. Although he left little impression on London he did build some good country houses. Generally speaking when he stuck to the neo-classical, he preferred simplified masses to which he often gave bow-windowed bays rising through two storeys, and these bow-windowed bays later became characteristic of the smaller Regency house—although what we call Regency began long before 1811. Heaton Park, Manchester, which Wyatt built for the first Earl of Wilton, has a semicircular bay as a feature of its south front, with engaged columns (they have cast iron capitals) running from a very low podium to the entablature. The central block is linked to octagonal, rather 'Tower of the Winds'* shaped pavilions by a very simple pillared loggia. Dodington Park, Chipping Sodbury, is Wyatt's outstanding neo-classical work. The west front has an enormous but simple Roman portico; round the corner the south front has a raised attic storey with pilasters running up to it; round the corner again, the east front has two protruding bows. The three quite different faces are yet allied and if the conception is daring and dangerous it also 'comes off'. Wyatt was so popular that he took on more work than he could handle and often drove his client to despair by his dilatory and unbusinesslike methods. But Dodington was his last house. Returning to London from there on September 4th 1813, the carriage in which he and the owner were driving overturned, no unusual occurrence, and Wyatt was instantly killed.

Already he had a successor or, rather, two. John Nash (1752–1835) and John Soane (1753–1837), a pupil of Holland. They are very dissimilar these two, and it is Soane who really stands out of the main stream. Although many experts feel he is not a classicist, he seems to me to be a classicist of the most scholarly and imaginative kind. Structurally and superficially he pares away detail until only the essentials are emphasized—and this is rather like Euclid. His attenuated and characteristic arches are often without benefit of supporting pillars, pilasters, piers or columns, and rise, like elegantly elongated Edwardian croquet hoops, straight from the ground. Or when they do rest on pillars they rest on their points. His finish is Greek in elegance and perfection. Tyringham, Buckinghamshire, is his (the Dome is a later addition), and the gateway shows his austerity in the handling of simple masses. His own house in Lincoln's Inn Fields is very different. Here one notices that its projecting stucco frontispiece has attenuated

---

* Wyatt used an almost exact replica of the Tower of the Winds at Athens for the Radcliffe Observatory, Oxford.

arches, flat pilasters with incised line decoration and key pattern ornament above the windows. The roof balustrade has small thin arches with acroterions. The house is now the Soane Museum.*

Soane, who studied in Italy—where he was enthusiastically taken up by the Earl-Bishop of Derry, who made him many fair promises of patronage and forgot them all—was an intense individualist and not much appreciated by the Victorians; perhaps they found his work too disembodied. Yet it seems to me—and this is a personal view—that Soane goes back in time to early Greece and also to the perspective painting of Piero della Francesca (1416–98); more specifically, to a fresco of perspective architecture by Francesca in the Palazzo Ducale at Urbino. Then too, Soane seems to move into the future and can be found in the architecture of the paintings of Giogrio de Chirico (b. 1888). This makes him, possibly, the first of the moderns; like Inigo Jones, he was a good century ahead of his time.

John Nash is an entirely different *chaudière de poisson*. At one time he worked in Robert Taylor's office and later with another landscape gardner, Humphry Repton. Extroverted, slapdash, rather perfunctory in his use of classical detail, and heartily loathed by many a modern architect, he was, among other things, a brilliant 'town planner'. He gave us Regent's Park as we know it, but not as originally planned and designed by him. He turned Regent Street (now no longer) into a Royal Mile from Carlton House to the Park. He had a passion for stucco, which when painted is charming, and an even greater passion for dramatic effects—considered by some to be stagey and therefore bogus. But architecture has always owed much to the theatre and to painting. And Nash's Cumberland Terrace, Regent's Park—to take only one of his terraces—is a stupendous theatro-architectural panorama. It is perfectly true that behind this triumphant and triumphal façade lie inconveniently planned houses, just as behind all the grand and middling building in England; behind all the new

---

* Although not a domestic building, Soane's major and greatest work was designing the Bank of England. It was subsequently greatly altered.

Cumberland Terrace, 1826. John Nash

streets, crescents, terraces, circuses and squares going up in Hove,
Brighton, Cheltenham and elsewhere, lay the hideous slums of an
England now enduring the horrors of the French wars abroad, and
the desperate misery brought about by the so called Industrial
Revolution at home. But apart from the moral implication, what
a triumph Cumberland Terrace is, with its gigantic central pediment containing grouped terra-cotta figures of Britannia attended
—a little incongruously now—by the Arts and Sciences. The wings
on each side are deeply recessed, and the great porticos and triumphal arches at both ends lead into those buildings from which, as
Swift would have thought, the Houyhnhnms have long since
been driven by the Yahoos.

And then, of course, Nash produced the Royal Pavilion at
Brighton. And how, one may well inquire, after a century or
more of classical architecture of one kind and another, did such
an utterly bewildering, divergent and glorious thing so suddenly

Regency villa, *circa* 1820

happen? It happened perhaps because too much reason generally brings about a reaction, and the reaction is generally romantic. Nor was this reaction sudden. It did not, by any means, begin with the Brighton Pavilion. In a special way it ended there. And almost from the beginning of the Georgian era the romantic was with us, running, as it were, underground before it surfaced.

The Rev. Dr William Stukeley (1687–1765), mad keen on Roman and 'Druidical' ruins, shared a taste for antiquities, old furniture, buildings, painted glass and 'Gothick architecture' with John, second Duke of Montagu (Marlborough's son-in-law), and this taste for the past was for the English, or the northern, past, not the Greek, Roman or Mediterranean past. In 1744 Dr Stukeley says he designed a 'Gothick bridge' for Montagu 'of 3 arches and a temple in the middle'.[32] He does not say that one of Batty Langley's innumerable books *Gothick Architecture Improved* may have influenced him, and perhaps it did not; though Langley had

Castellated Gothic. Second half of the eighteenth century

'invented five orders for that style' and even designed a 'temple with Gothic orders'[33]—a delightful contradiction in terms and orders. But Langley's book indicates there must have been a fairly widespread interest in the Gothic for some time before this. And indeed there was. Gothic bridges, temples, garden houses and ruins ornamented many a garden and park long, long before Horace Walpole built his miniature rococo-Gothic castle, Strawberry Hill. But Gothic is only one aspect of the romantic break away from the classical—although surely the classical itself with its nostalgia for the past is at bottom just as romantic.* Sir William Chambers, that well-known Palladian, was architect to Frederick,

* From about 1815 architecture split into two main camps known to us now as 'Greek Revival' and 'Gothic Revival'. William Wilkins (1778–1839) and Robert Smirke (1781–1867) were great 'Greek' exponents and built many public and semi-public buildings.

Prince of Wales, grandfather of George IV. And Frederick, for all his faults, certainly had a romantic and fantastic taste in architecture which his grandson inherited.

Sir William, who had been to Canton, built for Frederick the Chinese pagoda at Kew. This survives although the quasi-Moorish, Hindu and Gothic buildings there have long since disappeared. Chambers even wrote a book, *Designs for Chinese Buildings* (1757) but even earlier (1750–53) William Halfpenny, alias Michael Hoare, had brought out *New Designs for Chinese and Gothic Architecture*. Both the Chinese and Gothic were much favoured as incidental architecture and for decoration and furniture.

Now China had always seemed a romantic fairyland to us ever since the previous century (and even earlier) when we had started to import, on a quite generous scale, Chinese *objets d'art*—or what we fondly thought were Chinese *objets d'art* for much of the stuff was specially made in China for the western trade. But when Warren Hastings (1732–1818) went to India in 1750 and later, in 1772, became Governor of Bengal, interest in Indian art and architecture was aroused in England. Again, much of this interest was due to travellers and the books they produced. William Hodges (1744–97) who was once one of Captain Cook's draughtsmen, painted many pictures of India under Hastings's patronage, although he did not publish his travels until 1793. Thomas Daniell (1749–1840) and his nephew William (1769–1837) were both landscape painters, both went to India and returned to publish books showing Indian architecture and scenery which seized the imagination of the English. The palaces, the temples, the mosques, the minarets, the pagodas—all provided another springboard, another point of departure for architecture. And so, in a typically English and pastoral part of Gloucestershire, in 1806, the first Hindu palace, Sezincote, arose.

But the romantic reaction was not just rococo-Gothic, like Strawberry Hill; nor the light-hearted Chinoiserie of the Kew Pagoda, or the free interpretation of the Indian, like Sezincote. It developed too, in other, more massive directions and James Wyatt, that anti-Adam neo-classicist, was the chief protagonist of the massive; that is the massive medieval Gothic. His most gigantic Gothic work was Fonthill 'Abbey', Wilts. This he designed for the fabulously rich and equally odd William Beckford, who inherited millions at the age of nine, was given music lessons by Mozart, wrote an oriental fantasy *Vathek* in French, and was suspected of indulging in Black Mass orgies.

Fonthill, first conceived as a rather minor Gothic ruin containing an apartment for its owner, ended up as a cross between Salisbury Cathedral (which Wyatt had 'ruined' some claimed) and Westminster. Yet it was a private house which would have put most medieval abbeys to shame—provided one didn't investigate too closely its detail and workmanship. The great central tower soared 278 feet into the peaceful air of Wiltshire, already sky-pierced by the 404 foot spire of Salisbury's Cathedral. Due to bad construction Fonthill's tower collapsed some years later, leaving Salisbury unrivalled. The house covered six acres and contained, in addition to the usual rooms, a vast long gallery, a choir, octagon rooms, dining-rooms. It took eighty-seven servants to run it; its owner burned perfumed coal in the fireplaces, and once entertained Lord Nelson and a pregnant Lady Hamilton. Fonthill was almost as fantastic as Brighton pavilion. It cost £273,000 to build this Gothic fantasy which lasted only a quarter of a century. Ashridge is another of Wyatt's giant Gothic buildings (it was finished by his nephew Jeffry) and has a great hall large enough to stable a dozen railway engines. It is terribly solid and slightly absurd. Solid and not a bit absurd are the alterations which Wyatt's nephew Jeffry Wyatt (he later added 'ville' to the Wyatt to make it sound more medieval) carried out at Windsor Castle, then a mouldering old ruin. Inconvenient, shabby, and good enough for George III but not for George IV, the alterations which make Windsor Castle what it is today are entirely due to George IV who, as we can now see, was as given to liking various types of architecture as was his age. And here we owe this George a great deal, Gothic-medieval Windsor, Regent's Park and finally —the Brighton Pavilion.

The latter which might easily have been put up by Kubla

Khan, was begun by John Nash in Waterloo year, around the core of an old house which had already been altered for the Prince by Holland. The Pavilion, the complete and absolute antithesis of the classical, is the apogee of non-gloomy romantic—of light-hearted fantasy. It is the happy admixture of the dreamlike irrational coupled with flights of imagination and inspiration which so rarely happens, but when it does produces sheer magic. Bulblike domes from which exotic and hitherto unknown lilies might emerge at any moment are contrasted with high thin minarets made for no mortal muezzin. Exterior ground-floor arches are Moorish, their smaller curves echoing in minature those of the domes. Nothing of this is English, save the actual doing of it. Only the English would be silly, imaginative, and poetic enough to produce such a thing. An oriental fantasy overlooking the English Channel!

It seems a very long way from that other great house overlooking the north sea, the severe Holkham Hall. A long way from William Kent and the Earl of Burlington to John Nash and the Prince Regent. A great distance from the original Palladians to the Romantic, via the neo-classical, the picturesque, the *cottage orné* (invented by Nash) the Gothic, which were to take such a firm hold on the Victorians. But perhaps it is really not so very far after all. William Kent himself is now credited with inventing the 'Georgian Gothic'—a light and amusing interpretation of the true medieval Gothic—when, in 1729, he embellished the Tudor Gatehouse at Esher Place (now destroyed) with quatrefoil and ogee-arched windows. And the ogee arch is surely reminiscent of the Moorish. Then too, Kent was a poetic and romantic landscape gardener and the gothic, the poetic, the picturesque, the neo-classical appeared first in follies, temples, bridges, ruins, garden houses, *cottages ornés* and lodges which were built in great parks and middling gardens.

In a sense this is what the Pavilion is. It is summer architecture, built for pleasure, for diversion, for enchantment. It succeeds. And like some strange exotic butterfly it is poised upon the golden flower of our finest period of architecture.

CHAPTER THREE

Of Furniture and Interior Decoration

Raby Castle like many an ancient house had been ruined by 'spruced-up' taste—or so Colonel the Hon. John Byng* thought when he visited it in 1792. The 'whiten'd, ill fancied Gothic buildings in the park'; the 'mean' plantation; the porter's lodge with a wooden portcullis and a 'vile gate', these displayed the 'fancy of a citizen' not the 'grandeur of a northern baron'.[1]

Inside Raby, things were even fancier; few past splendours remained to stir the heart of this touring colonel and minor official in the Stamp Office who dearly loved the English countryside, the old things, the old ways of England, and who frankly admits that he wishes he had lived in the time of Charles I. Raby, alas, had been altered in 1765† and its now 'Frenchifi'd' apartments were 'deal floor'd' and had 'modernly glazed'[2] windows. In the drawing-room, the traveller recalls later with uncooled indignation, 'instead of large chairs rolling upon casters there is nothing to be seen but little light French chairs while 'French linen festoonings' replaced thick, welt lined damask or velvet curtains. Most contemptible of all, breakfast, dining and writing-tables were no longer 'substantial and immovable'. They had been banished in favour of 'little skuttling tables', easily moved to a strategic position in front of what, in these degenerate days, passed for a fireplace, a 'little low dug hole . . . surrounded by a

---

* Nephew of Admiral Byng, and later, 5th Viscount Torrington.
† Altered many times before this date and certainly altered again in the nineteenth century. But no visitor must be put off seeing Raby by the Hon. John's strictures.

slip of marble'. It gave no real, roaring warmth and the marble merely served as an elaborate shin toaster for a 'genteel people'.[3]

Accustomed as we are to thinking of the years between 1760 and, perhaps, 1810 as the really great period for English furniture, Mr Byng's criticisms sound positively heretical. Curiously enough, the year he visited Raby—and he was a great visitor of country houses—was that in which Robert Adam died, and Robert with his brother had made the English interior a unique specimen of English art. Even more curiously, Byng's life overlapped the lives of all the great-name cabinet makers of the Georgian period. He was five when William Kent died and he outlived Sheraton by seven years.

What is puzzling is Byng's seeming unawareness of the 'unmeasurably ponderous'[4] work of William Kent which, for weight alone, might have satisfied his longing for solidity and size. And, as interior decorator and furniture designer for grand houses, most of which were open to the travelling public of the day, William Kent is undoubtedly the outstanding figure of the early Georgian era. His belief that each room should be a separate individual work of art was new to England. Moreover, he was the first architect in our history to regard furniture as an essential part of interior decoration and this influenced the whole of the Georgian period.

In rooms of Palladian proportions, using the fashionable classical Roman motifs of the day, Kent constructed—for a few very rich men—interiors of superlative opulence. Carved, coffered, honeycombed, hemispherical, coved or flat ceilings are painted, gilded and married to damasked or stuccoed walls (niched to hold statues) by elaborately carved painted and gilded cornices. Important doorways are triumphal arches where columns support pediments with entablatures and tympana carved with festoons of flowers, fruit, foliage, masks and husks. Sometimes the pediment is broken to contain within the break a bust or fully modelled putti. Windows are thematically linked to doors and have pediments and carved architraves with heavily looped

Settee, mirror and stool, *circa* 1730 (in the manner of William Kent)

velvet to curtain them. Even mirrors and pictures are framed to carry out the architectural style of the room. In a Kent room, 'little skuttling tables' and 'light French chairs' would have been as incongruous as an Elizabethan cup-and-cover legged table, or a Tudor box chair. But Kent's treatment of furniture is as bold, as massive, as rich, as ornate, as architectural as his treatment of interiors.

His interiors were often criticized by the next generation for being too heavy—he had brought external architecture indoors. His 'constant introduction of pediments and the members of architecture over doors and within rooms' was 'disproportioned and cumbr'ous'.[5] It is quite usual for one generation to dislike, decry and criticize the taste of its immediate predecessor—which is why things become 'dated' before they become 'period'—but without Kent, the English interior might have remained an uncoordinated hodge-podge and a good deal less magnificent to boot. The Marble Hall at Holkham, for example, must be one of the most striking of private entrance halls in Europe, and the sober exterior of the house, perhaps deliberately, gives small indication of the splendours within.*

The Marble Hall is like a Roman basilica. In shape it is apsidal but the main portion of the hall is narrowed by low, marble-faced walls, behind which lie galleries with walls niched for statues. On the galleries purple and white veined columns of Derbyshire alabaster support a glorious cove, coffered to the painted ceiling. From ground level, and at the far end of the hall, a flight of steps leads up into a gallery-level exedra. From the exedra a discreet door leads into the saloon. Thus the *piano nobile* or first floor, where all state rooms are situated, is reached by interior steps. This is far from usual. Great Palladian houses, generally, have exterior steps leading to the grand portico or entrance. This looks and is very splendid, but in our climate it is hardly convenient. To arrive at a great Palladian house on a wild wet summer's day or a wilder, wetter one in winter; to be set down by a coach at the foot of the steps; to have to toil up them and reach the top wet to the skin and blown to bits (umbrellas did not come into popular use until after 1780) can have improved neither the appearance nor the temper of the visitor. So the opulence of Holkham's Marble Hall is matched by its convenience. Its architectural structure serves a practical purpose.

Yet, in general, Palladian interior planning is not what we should call convenient. All state or reception rooms were arranged to open out of each other and doors were so placed that when opened there would be 'vistos' running the whole length of the *piano nobile*. Naturally, to achieve this impressive effect all rooms had to be square or rectangular with exactly opposing doors— and in Palladian houses all rooms were rectangles set within the greater rectangle of the house.

Another astonishing room at Holkham, the Statue Gallery, was 'most superbly elegant . . . but the whole house deserves that distinction' Mrs Lybbe Powys says. The gallery was painted 'dead

* Most of the Holkham interiors were designed by Kent or carried out, after his death, to his designs, by Brettingham.

white with ornaments of gilding'[6] and, with its octagon tribunes at each end, was, as Arthur Young tells us years later, 'one of the most beautiful rooms I have ever seen'; the 'dimensions . . . proportion itself'. The ceiling was the only plain one in the house, all others are 'gilt fret-work and mosaic'[7]—hardly an adequate description of some of the richest ceilings in England. But Young was too occupied with the statues to describe much else. Perhaps this is not surprising, he seems to have admired particularly 'a Venus in wet drapery' where 'nothing [could] exceed the manner in which the form of the limbs (is) seen thro' the cloathing'.[8]

Splendour, sumptuousness, rich colours, carving and gilding are the chief ingredients of early Georgian grand interiors, and no one could surpass William Kent at this sort of thing. At Houghton, Mrs Lybbe Powys found 'the fitting up and furniture' of Kent's rooms 'very superb and the cornishes and mouldings of all the apartments being gilt, it makes the whole what I call magnificently glaringly, more especially as the rooms are, instead of white, painted dark green olive'.[9] There were sixteen 'magnificently glaringly' rooms on this floor, two wings and a 'famed' picture gallery '75 feet long' holding paintings esteemed 'the best collection we have in England'.[10] *

Every great house now had to have a picture gallery, to house the notable collections of paintings, marbles, bronzes every rich man collected (often collections were begun on the Grand Tour). This gallery quite replaced the old-fashioned long gallery which had been considered essential ever since the time of Queen Elizabeth. Every great house, also, had to have a library—middling houses often had them too. The rather eccentric, rich, scholar-bachelor Mr Spilman, who built an off-beat house not far from Holkham, had a saloon-library in which he grudgingly received guests wearing 'a jockey-cap and white, stiff dog's gloves'.[11] His house, like his appearance, was unusual. It was all on one floor; offices and servants' quarters were underground while the front door of this early equivalent of the basement bungalow was

---

* Sold in 1779 to the Empress Catherine of Russia by George, 3rd Earl of Orford, Horace Walpole's nephew (whom he succeeded) to pay his debts.

reached by a flight of twenty-one steps so steep as to be virtually perpendicular. In addition to the saloon-library, the single floor contained a Hall 90 by 18 feet—no Palladian proportion here—two 'parlours' and three bedchambers. All doors were of solid walnut, all floors of Ketton stone, all chimney pieces and table tops of imported green marble.

The profuse use of marble is one of the characteristics of this period; even Lady Leicester's dairy at Holkham was of marble. The rich had no need to dream they dwelt in marble halls, they literally did so—although few halls can have been as splendid as the saloon of now vanished Brandenburg House, Hammersmith, where the columns were of Sicilian jasper and the door cases of lapis lazuli. Fireplaces were of marble and if the operative bit containing the fire had shrunk, the superstructure, particularly in state rooms and libraries, had again become as important a feature as it had been in Elizabethan days. But now it was architectural, restrained and formal—which Elizabethan ones were not. Usually two-storeyed, the lower half was marble with engaged columns, pilasters or full bosomed caryatids—the latter often in profile—supporting a narrow marble mantelshelf which, in turn, supported the second storey. This, frequently of marble but sometimes of wood or stucco, also had pillars or pilasters supporting a triangular pediment where, as at Ditchley Park, modelled or sculptured figures reclined rather unhappily on converging sloped cornices*. Or columns and pediment made a frame for a picture, a looking-glass, or for a *basso-relievo* showing a classical, mythological or a hunting scene. The upper storeys of grand, early Georgian fireplaces, particularly those where such reliefs, are used, resemble those sepulchral monuments so beloved by the Greeks and Romans which were built in the form of *aediculae*.

The simple fireplace was considered best for smaller rooms and for less grand houses. This too had a marble surround and a mantel-shelf held up by pilasters, a bracket or a long, S shaped scroll. Hearth stones were also of marble. But not all marble was marble, as Henry Purefoy discovered to his sorrow when he 'did

* At Ditchley, Gibbs, Kent and Flitcroft all worked on the interior.

up' several old-fashioned fireplaces at Shalstone Manor, Bucks. In October 1739 he opens a correspondence with a certain Mr Palmer, stone-cutter of Bedford Row, London. 'I want a very handsome red and white marble mantle peice & slob', he writes, giving the dimensions required—these were simple fireplaces— and asking also for another 'black marble slob' for another 'chimney' (i.e. fireplace). A few days later he orders yet another in purple marble which, he warns, 'had need to be very good and well matcht at 7s. a foot'.[12] But things did not go at all well. In December Henry complains to Mr Palmer that 'the black marble slob is not so beautifully veined as I expected'; worse, 'the purple marble seems cract in some places & as though it had bitts of something put into it artificially'. Further, it seemed to Henry, it would be apt to 'peell and fly'. Despite Mr Palmer's assurances that this wouldn't happen, it did. In fact, the purple marble turned out to be a 'Counterfiet'. It 'blisters & rises up', Henry complains, and when trodden on broke off so that underneath he could see 'a course stone like freestone'.[13] Since his near neighbour, Lord Cobham, had several 'purple mantle pieces & slobs' which wore well and did not peel, Henry feels there must be some good purple marble to be had and, after much wearing correspondence, Mr Palmer replaces the faulty purple slab. Alas, this too had cracks in it into which Henry could, and doubtless did, 'thrust a pin'.

All this trouble and nonsense is as maddeningly familiar to us as it was to poor Henry, but if a purple marble 'slob' is not to everyone's taste, one wonders just what the 'Counterfiet' was. The blisters make it sound as if it were some composition, perhaps of plaster mixed with glue and colouring matter which would be highly unsuited to a hearth stone, as would Scagliola—a mixture of cement, isinglass and colouring. Scagliola, a manmade 'marble', existed in its own right and was much used instead of marble, particularly for table tops. Sometimes it was plain, sometimes it had designs made of marble chips pressed into it, but no stately home was complete without a number of tables topped with marble, pietra dura, or with incised and polished gesso. Not all were so fortunate as the Duke of Northumberland,* the 'mosaic

* Second Duke: 3rd creation (1742–1817).

work' of the tables in his drawing room at Syon House 'was found in Titus's Baths and purchased for the Duke out of the Abbé Furetti's collection at Rome'.[14]

William Kent was particularly addicted to marble tables and such tables require massive frames, or perhaps it is the other way round. Great side tables with double scroll, eagle, or mermaid legs carved, gilded and standing on plinth feet, had apron pieces descending almost to the ankles. Apron pieces were elaborate; often a huge shell or a lion mask was the central motif, and this was linked to the upper curl, the eagle beak or the mermaid head of the legs by heavy festoons of carved fruit, leaves or flowers. Kent also designed slimmer, lighter console tables—console tables were most fashionable—with rectangular legs, but probably the single-eagle console, or clap-table, is best known to us as 'typically Kent'. Here a great fierce, solitary gilded eagle, gripping a rock set on a plinth base, bears on outstretched wings a heavy marble semicircular top. Such tables were screwed to the wall with a framed looking glass above. Sometimes the frames were crested with an eagle, sometimes with an owl or a shell. Often pedimented, they were of carved and gilded wood or of gesso work, And this was the great age of English gilding and of gesso, gilt. Gesso, a mixture of calcined gypsum and size, was applied to carcasses of soft wood in successive layers; when hard, a relief pattern could be cut by working away the ground. Once carved the whole piece was then gilded—more rarely silvered. Gesso was used mainly on mirrors, console tables and chairs.

Kent's chairs, in fact most of his seat furniture, show a distinct Venetian baroque influence with ornate carving and gilding. Fabulous or mythological creatures are often a part of the design. Furniture such as this, usually upholstered in Italian velvet, would not be out of place in a Doge's palace, and this is another reason Kent's furniture, when seen divorced from its proper background, seems too massive; conceived on too grand a scale or even, 'unmeasurably ponderous'. His furniture—and that of his followers should not be judged out of its context or setting, and its setting was a great state room. As ceilings in these rooms were often twenty feet high* compared with our average eight foot six inches, furniture had to be proportionate in size while its ornamental detail had to suit the rich background.

Kent's cabinet furniture is also massive, but it is not Venetian. It is architectural. His bookcases, for instance, made for the new libraries—and furniture designed especially for libraries was a feature of the time—often stand above eight foot. A Kent bookcase is a Roman triumphal arch, or perhaps it is like the façade of a Palladian house designed for a pygmy prince. These bookcases sit on podiums (cupboards or drawers) and usually have three glass compartments above—the middle one tallest and heavily pedimented. Made in natural wood, carved or often painted and gilded, the ornamentation—that is the detail of carving or ormolu mountings—matches that of seat furniture. (This is also true of library tables.) In this way a thematic link is achieved between Roman-Palladian architectural cabinet furniture and Venetian baroque seat furniture.

The architectural quality of Kent's furniture had far-reaching effects on cabinet makers of the time. By 1740 the indefatigable Batty Langley with his brother Thomas, produced a pattern book *The City and Country Builder's and Workman's Treasury of Design*. Its chief concern was with architecture, but in one section the Kent style was translated into less massive furniture suitable for use in middling or smaller houses.

Middling and smaller houses increased in number. The plan of a London house remained much the same as in the previous century. Deep, with a narrow frontage and rising three or four storeys, it had a room front and back on each floor and a passage and staircase on one side. All but the poorest houses had shallow basements. The back basement room at ground level looked on to the garden, but the front basement room looked into an area because roadways were built up above natural ground level. As the outer wall of the area was the retaining wall of the roadway, storage space was provided under the

---

* The ceiling of the Marble Hall, at Holkham, is fifty feet high.

road—a plan so common that most of us are still familiar with it.

At the back of the house, if the property were long enough, there was a garden and, if longer still, a coach-house or stables. Sanitation was excessively simple. There were few if any bathrooms and bathing was not much indulged in. Under the house ran a brick drain attached to the public sewer. If there were no sewer it ran into a cesspool. The privy, called politely 'the Necessary House' and impolitely various other names, was placed at the back of the house or at the end of the garden with its circular pit hopefully attached to the drain. Very occasionally water was laid on, and this rather feebly swilled out the receptacle, but the trap water closet remained unknown until the end of the century. There was only one inside closet at vast Holkham, a two-seater in a tiny, windowless room. At Luton Hoo, however, Robert Adam, more modernly, allotted four. Cold water at very low pressure was supplied at stated hours, for a quarterly sum, by the New River Company, and later by the even newer Chelsea Water Works. It ran sluggishly through wooden pipes into cisterns often situated in the basement areas. In better houses, water was sometimes raised to a roof cistern by means of a hand pump, from there gravity took it through a pipe, usually to a kitchen. Most kitchens had a cold water tap and a stone sink or trough; all water had to be heated over the kitchen fire.

Central heating was unknown. Fires were woefully inadequate. Most of the heat went up the chimney and, if lucky, some of the smoke did too. London lay under a perpetual pall of smoke. Foreigners from the colder parts of the continent simply could not understand why we did not keep cleaner and warmer by using stoves, as they sensibly did. A Swedish visitor staying with a London merchant in 1748 brought his thermometer with him and noted, with undisguised astonishment, that in his host's house in February the drawing-room temperature never rose above 50° F. More often it was nearer 45° F. In the country, it was even worse, and the visitor remarks that many of his countrymen 'would . . . not be able to imagine that English cottages are colder (in winter) than Swedish', even though 'the English farm labourer and peasant' burned as much, if not more, wood than his Swedish counterpart. It is 'as cold indoors as outdoors'[15] he says, feelingly.

It was just as bleak in other ways too, for in the cottages and tenements of the poor there was practically no furniture. Perhaps a rough table tacked together from boards, a straw mattress, a few old pots and pans, a broken chair, and blocks of wood for children to sit on. Increasing opulence on the one hand was matched by increasing distress on the other. Even the not-so-poor were ill-provided with household goods. When John Day a carpenter of Writtle died in 1725, his furniture was valued at £9 16s 0d. He lived in a four-roomed house which boasted a 'Buttre and a Brewhouse'. Among his effects were a long table and '6 jount stools', four old chairs, a 'worming pan' and 'in the Parler . . . one ondeferent bed and bedsted', a chest of drawers, a 'press cubard', a small table, and '2 sorry old chairs'. In the chamber above the parlour was another sorry bed with a 'linciwolcy teeke', and there were two other 'very mean'[16] beds elsewhere. Much of John's furniture had probably been handed down from parents and grandparents, this would apply particularly to beds, which were always expensive. Some of it might have drifted down to him from the lumber rooms of grander houses; the description of a few pieces—long table, joynt stools, press cupboard—suggests furniture of earlier eras. Since John was a carpenter it seems surprising his furniture was in such a sorry state. But John is no exception to the vast majority. Inventories of the day prove a great corrective to any idea that the golden age for furniture and architecture was golden for everyone.

In addition to the new houses being built, people were also altering and modernizing old houses. One way of giving an old house a new look was to put in sash windows. Sash windows had been replacing old-fashioned casement ones in London and nearby counties ever since the end of the previous century. But it took time for such innovations to reach remoter areas. Up at Dodsworth Green, near Barnsley, John Hobson notes in 1726, 'Guest (a glazier) put glass into the sash windows in the buttery, being the first that ever was in this town'.[17] This John Guest was an old man who had stood with a weeping crowd when the Scots delivered Charles I to Cromwell.

Putting in sash windows was by no means all. Old-fashioned wainscotting needed repairing, or tearing out. A tasteful arch thrown over the stairs gave a modern look. So did painting the woodwork: the Georgians, unlike their predecessors, nearly always painted and gilded woodwork. Mrs Purefoy, Henry's mother, who owned leasehold property in Cursitor Street (let at £40 p.a.) found it necessary to alter and repair the house for a new tenant. Among many other things roof and chimneys needed repairing; lines and beads for twenty-nine sash windows and pulleys for those in the 'fore Parlor' were required. A new kitchen stair had to be put in; wainscotting and panelling provided for 'an Elcove' in the garden. Painters did '1120 yards of inside painting clear, cold & finished at 3*d*. a yard'.[18] Outside, 58 yards were painted 'twice in oyle' at 5*d*. a yard. The total painting bill came to £18 18*s* 2*d*, according to Henry, but he is 2*s*. 6*d* out. Plastering was done and colour-washed; glaziers cleaned thirty sash windows (so this was not a very small house)* and supplied crown glass where necessary. The total bill for all work done from roof to basement came to £42 17*s* 0½*d* by Henry's reckoning. But Henry although undeniably cold-blooded, was no adder—the amount should be £43 17*s* 0½*d*. Workmen were maddeningly dilatory; it took them three whole weeks to do the job and when done the house was let at ten guineas a quarter. So the cost of the repairs and improvements, which seem ridiculously low to us, really amounted to above a year's rent.

There is no indication that Mrs Purefoy's house was let furnished. But many houses were, because people often came to town (to London and York particularly) and took lodgings or furnished houses for a season. Yet in all houses, great, middling or small, new, old or modernized, certainly not all furniture was new. Indeed in new great houses only state or public rooms were new

---

* One suspects, perhaps wrongly, that this means fifteen windows with double sashes. They cannot all have been casement sashes because of the mention of pulleys.

furnished, old furniture was used elsewhere in the house. The same thing applied on a minor scale to middling houses. A new piece of furniture might replace an old piece in saloon or 'eating' room, but the 'style' of the room was probably a mixture ranging from elaborate Charles II to plain Queen Anne, with perhaps an inherited white elephant in the shape of an Elizabethan or Jacobean stool or chest. 'The Duchess of Portland has new painted her dressing room', Mrs Delany says, 'hung it with green, and turned out the lumbering chest of drawers'.[19] Lumber meant a disused article of furniture or any other useless thing—which is why we have lumber rooms. Perhaps the Duchess's old-fashioned chest fetched up in Elizabeth Elstob's rooms. Miss Elstob was governess to the Duchess's girls. This was fortunate for Miss Elstob.*

* Elizabeth Elstob (1683–1756) produced among other works an Anglo-Saxon grammar (1715) and an edition of Aelfric's homily on the birthday of St Gregory.

Walnut bureau, candlestand, mirror and stool, George I

Although she was a famous Anglo-Saxon scholar and medievalist, she also happened to be a single woman of no fortune and would otherwise have starved to death. She was considered a pure scholar in her day and Queen Caroline gave her £100. She opened a school at Evesham which failed because she could not teach sewing and spinning.

It was not easy to tell new furniture from old in the first quarter of the eighteenth century. Apart from its newness, furniture design in general during the reign of George I remained much the same as in Queen Anne's day, so today it is often difficult to distinguish one period from the other. Design in both reigns is characterized by good proportion and restraint; the most favoured wood is walnut. Important or big pieces 'were nearly always made of imported yellow deal suitably prepared to take veneers', and 'veneering showed off walnut to perfection'.[20] The cabriole leg remained a favourite but it became shorter, heavier, sturdier in the time of George I and, between 1710 and 1720—so this could be either Anne or George I—it became usual to decorate legs and seat rails of chairs with the scallop shell. Claw and ball, and lion-paw feet were still popular, but the club foot was not discarded. This period also very probably saw the introduction of the tripod table. Standing on short cabriole legs, it had a plain or carved stem and the top was a reproduction in wood of a silver salver with plain or gadrooned edge.

In 1720 and 1721 two things happened which, in time, influenced furniture greatly. First, the French placed an embargo on walnut. Second, the British Government, requiring more wood for ship building abolished the heavy duty on woods from the colonies in America and the West Indies. The French embargo was not so serious as is often thought, but the abolition of duty was a boon since it considerably reduced the price of wood. Cabinet makers began importing larger quantities of the tight-grained, darker Virginian walnut, and also small quantities of West Indian mahogany. London, the greatest port, the most populous and richest city, was then famous for new ideas of all kinds, and attracted craftsmen of every sort. Eminent furniture makers set up shops and manufactories and profited greatly. One very successful 'upholsterer' or cabinet maker was that Mr Hallet who was able to build his 'neat villa' where the Duke of Chandos's magnificent house had once stood.

In addition to the many makers with their own craftsmen and workshops, the number of retail furniture shops—hitherto known but rather rare—increased greatly. Retailers or vendors simply bought furniture (all handmade) for resale and employed no craftsmen themselves. There was a boom in furniture because of new building and also because by this time people were using more furniture than ever before. Yet it is a mistake to think it was all mahogany, or that the 'age of mahogany' began with a bang the minute duty was abolished. This is not so. Between 1722 and 1750, it was perfectly possible to buy exactly similar pieces in either wood. The total value of mahogany imported in 1722 was but £277; fifteen years later it was still only £6,430; not until 1750 did it reach £30,000. So it was not until mid-century that mahogany really supplanted walnut as the favourite wood. Cabinet makers were slow to realize that in a number of ways mahogany was more useful than walnut. True, it was not easily used in veneering, but it was very hard, resisted worm (worm loves European walnut veneering); it was a rich red colour and would take a wonderful polish. Its hardness made it ideal for carving, while the size of the actual tree meant that board width was greater than that of walnut or oak.

Board width was important in cabinet doors and table tops. The gate-legged table, so popular in Anne and George I's day, had always presented a problem to joiners because each of the three sections making its oval top had to be made of several joined planks. The greater width of mahogany solved this problem. At first large gate-legged tables continued to be made in mahogany, then someone had the clever idea that gate-legs and flap were not really necessary to enlarge a table. A square or rectangular table could be enlarged by adding a pair of tables with square flap tops as, and when, required. When not required these extensions could do duty as side tables. It was only a short step from this to the invention of the table which could be enlarged by leaves—and so the vast Victorian dining table of the future began here.

In other furniture, mahogany also affected construction. As it was hard it could be curved and carved and, following French and Dutch fashions, surfaces could be serpentine, bow, or hollowed rather than flat. The bow-fronted chair and small table, the serpentine fronted side table, the shaped front and drawers to a desk, all became popular. The sinuous baroque curve crept in with mahogany. Chair backs became rather lower; square rather than rectangular. Uprights were straight or curved to meet a bow toprail crested with carving. Splat backs, veneered when in walnut, were pierced or carved in mahogany. The arms of armchairs were often scrolled and terminated in an eagle's head with a sharp savage beak. Where legs were hipped—the hip is an extension of the cabriole leg above the seat rail and is usual in fine chairs and settees—the hipping was finely carved. Chief motifs in use, apart from leaves, were the lion, the satyr or human mask, the cabochon. With lion masks feet were, correctly, lion's paws; with satyr masks, the cloven foot was natural; the cabochon and leaf required a scroll foot.

Stools were still much used, their cabriole legs enriched with carving, their seats upholstered in rich velvets or needlework. Producing exquisite needlework was an occupation of the leisured woman as was playing cards and gaming. But gaming was so common to both sexes and increased so greatly that even today Georgian card tables are relatively easy to find. All had folding tops often dished to hold candlesticks or counters. Many had back legs which moved out to hold the flap, rather on the gate-leg principal, but at some point—possibly even in the later years of Queen Anne's reign—the card table with the hinged folding framework for both back legs was conceived, and the 'concertina' table was born. The grandfather wing chair and the ladderback chair came into being too. The pole screen replaced the old fashioned 'horse'—or *cheval*—fire screen, and its adjustable panel gave women another excellent opportunity to display needlework.

Women were by now using very small three-drawer dressing tables with table mirrors. Kneehole dressing tables also came in. The top drawer, compartmented for cosmetics and those odd bits and pieces which women collect, was fitted with a hinged toilet glass. Dressing tables with table mirrors were often draped in soft silks from mirror top to table toe. *Torchères* grew taller, as did pedestal stands used for heavy candelabra or to display busts and bronzes; their stems were twisted. Sometime about 1740 the mahogany pedestal stand with a tripod base (a tripod is much the safest base on an unlevel floor or in a crowded room) was introduced. These often had galleried tops. Pedestal library tables became positively monumental. Furniture made especially for libraries was a new idea and was usually heavy. It is thought that this heaviness was the necessity which mothered the invention of the caster, upon which the Hon. John Byng reflected with such nostalgia.

It is difficult to say with any accuracy just when metal casters first came in, usually their introduction is placed in the fourth decade of the eighteenth century. Yet in 1735 the Purefoys order from London, a new, low bedstead 'that takes all to pieces & goes on 4 swivell wheels to draw about'. And in July 1740 Mrs Purefoy writes to her London agent and asks for '4 pullies to go on swivells every way to put on the bottom of an easy chair'. These, she says, 'are to be had at Mr Parkins & Sitwell at White Horse, in ffoster lane, Cheapside', and, she adds, 'pray see they be strong enough'. These 'swivells' are undoubtedly an early form of—or perhaps only an early name for—casters which must have been known in London long before Mrs Purefoy ordered them.*

In country districts, local carpenters and joiners for the most

* In the accounts of the Early Warm Blanket Co.,Witney, there is an item of 4s for 'A Sett of Brass Casters for the Master Weaver's Chair of the Company of Blanket Weavers'. The date is 1765 and the casters, still extant with the chair, are small brass cylinders on iron swivels. But much heavier metal casters were used on invalid chairs certainly as early as 1710.

part went on making furniture of first-rate craftsmanship and traditional design. Walnut veneers were used for the more important and more expensive pieces, while pearwood, alder, ash, birch, elm, plane and yew were favoured for cheaper furniture. The parts of the Windsor chair—new to the early Georgian era— were often of different woods. The seat, elm; spindles, beech; arms and top rail, yew. Easy to make and comfortable to sit on, the Windsor chair was in a class by itself and lent itself to numerous variations. Its top rail could be round, flat or pointed like a Gothic arch. It could have a wheel, comb, braced-comb or pierced splat back, and it was the only chair with a saddle seat. Legs were cabriole, straight or turned, with either an H or cow's-horn stretcher, and they jutted out. The Windsor chair, although we do not know exactly when invented, soon became a great favourite, particularly in coffee-houses, taverns, inns and pleasure gardens, and by 1730 'All sorts of Windsor Garden Chairs of all sizes, painted Green' could be bought at 'John Brown's* at the Three Chairs and Walnut-Tree in St Paul's Churchyard near the School'.[21]

Polite society took to the Windsor chair and this homely cottage chair sometimes became quite resplendent. The Duke of Chandos had several of them japanned; Frederick, Prince of Wales, had a number made in mahogany for his library at St James's. But it is rather doubtful if the chair, even when made in expensive wood, was used in the State apartments of Palladian houses. Against walls with their recessed panels set within heavy carved borders, or of plaster lavishly ornamented with masks, trophies, festoons and sculptured figures in very bold relief, or even against those plainer walls hung with imported velvets and damask, or papered with most expensive block-printed papers, one cannot see the Windsor chair fitting in. It would have been uneasy mixed with Kent furniture too. Nor, indeed, can the chair have looked well in the transitional period, which came about mid-century, when the stucco ornamentation of walls was becoming

* John Brown was a cabinet maker in the time of George II, his trade sign 'The Three Cover'd Chairs and Walnut-Tree'.

Chinese style chair, *circa* 1765. Upholstered chair, *circa* 1740. Windsor chair, *circa* 1770

much lighter and gayer, and continuously interlaced scrolls, amusing and fanciful, made frames for plaster panels. For at this time the decorative repertoire of the fashionable moved away from the classical to the contemporary French *rocaille*—we call it rococo—an intoxicating and fantastic mixture of rocks, shells, flowers, foliage with balanced asymmetry as its key note. High fashion had become just as tired of Palladian interiors and the almost inflexible use of the five orders as it was of Palladian exteriors.

Closely related to rococo, at that time called 'the modern taste', were the 'Chinese taste' and the 'Gothic taste'. There was a revival of interest in japanned furniture and screens, which had enjoyed a great vogue fifty years before, and also for what we imagined were Chinese motifs: pagodas, waterfalls, strange elongated birds, icicles, dragons and lattice work. These motifs were adapted to nearly everything and were mixed freely with rococo. Chinese scenic wallpapers were imported (later made here), and the scenes were planned to continue around the whole room. At

Eastbury, 'the Managareth' a 'Chinese bedroom and dressing room', was the show piece of the attic storey in an otherwise classical house. It was 'excessively droll and pretty, furnish'd exactly as in China, the bed of an uncommon size, seven feet wide by six long'.[22] Droll and pretty though it was, we can be absolutely certain it was not 'furnish'd ... as in China'. Nor is that most exquisite and remarkable rococo-Chinese room (still to be seen) at Claydon House, Bucks. Here a pagodalike alcove of carved wood riotously covers nearly the whole of one wall, and Chinese heads feature on door jambs and chimney pieces. By the middle of the 1760s the vogue for Chinese taste went into a decline and did not recover until the time of George IV and the Brighton Pavilion.

The Gothic style, on the other hand, was not foreign. It was native. We adapted this too with the same, light-hearted disregard for medieval art as we had adapted the Chinese. About the Chinese we knew very little. About the Gothic we knew a great deal because medieval Gothic was still with us: Horace Walpole took up Gothic with passionate enthusiasm. Beginning in 1743, he transformed his small house at Strawberry Hill into a miniature Gothic castle, and was a prey forever after to hordes of curious visitors. But this is rococo-Gothic. Gothic was the springboard for Horace's imagination and even he admits that his Strawberry Hill Gothic is more fanciful than imitative.

Thus, by mid-century, heavy interiors were on the way out, and with them, Kent-style and traditional (i.e. Queen Anne and early Georgian) furniture. So when in 1754 Thomas Chippendale (1718–79), a Yorkshire cabinet maker who set up and prospered in London, brought out *The Gentleman's and Cabinet-Maker's Director*, all the new, modern styles could be seen together and compared. The *Director* is a landmark in English furniture. It was the first completely comprehensive pattern book ever published to deal only with furniture. It was the first book ever written by a practising cabinet maker. As its very long title says, in part, it was 'calculated to improve and refine the present Taste and suited to the Fancy and Circumstances of Persons in all Degrees of Life'. It also contained 'a large collection of the most Elegant and Useful Designs of Household Furniture in the Gothic, Chinese and Modern Taste'. By the third edition (1762) Gothic and Chinese do not appear in the title while taste, no doubt sufficiently improved and refined, has become 'the Most Fashionable Taste'.

There is some question whether Chippendale originated all the designs himself. Matthias Lock, a pioneer of rocaille ornament, brought out his first book of a 'modern' design as early as 1740, while H. Copland produced his in 1746. Together these carvers produced a joint effort in 1752. Both men, although older, knew and were friends of Chippendale and it has been suggested that 'all the designs for carver's pieces in the first edition . . . were made by Copland. The designs for . . . basic forms of chairs . . . of case pieces were made by a cabinet maker (perhaps Chippendale himself)' and that Lock was used for any 'other items of carver's work commissioned . . . on behalf of clients'.[23] But whatever the genesis of the book with its numerous copper-plate engravings, it had a wide circulation among cabinet makers and rich subscribers (it cost £2 8s 0d, a vast sum) and its influence was great. It was, in fact, the finest 'trade' catalogue ever published.

The *Director*, with its great reputation, has made Chippendale's name better known to us than the names of his contemporaries and near contemporaries such as Kent's pupil, Matthew Brettingham, or Benjamin Goodison (d. 1767), one of the leading cabinet makers in the reign of George II, or William Ince and Thomas Mayhew, partners in the firm of Ince and Mayhew. These were far better known than Chippendale. As was the firm of Vile and Cobb, undoubtedly the foremost makers between 1755 and 1765. Able, brilliant craftsman though Chippendale was, first rate at organizing workshops, clever when it came to business, nevertheless his workshop could not possibly be responsible for all the extant furniture called Chippendale. Popularly believed to be responsible for the best mahogany furniture of his period, it is surely significant that the first edition of the *Director* does not even mention mahogany. The riband-back chair may or may not

Chairs in the Sheraton, Chippendale and Hepplewhite styles

be his. 'Chinese Chippendale' is neither Chinese nor his invention, nor is 'Chippendale Gothic'. But what Chippendale *did* do was to English the new styles.

Even more important, the publication of this first furniture pattern book meant that to possess the most fashionable and best in furniture—and in those fortunate days the words 'best' and 'fashionable' when descriptive of anything other than morals were synonymous—was no longer the prerogative of the well educated, the well travelled, the highly cultured section of society. Smaller cabinet makers in country towns, like eminent ones in London, could look at the *Director* and produce either exact copies of, or their own variations upon, its designs. Thus there emerged in furniture, as in architecture, a standard of taste which, due to its educated origins, was very high. The standard was maintained throughout the remainder of the Georgian era by other architects, designers and cabinet makers some of whom, following Chippendale's lead, also issued design and pattern books. Curiously enough, Chippendale's finest work was done under the direction of Robert Adam, and here he ranks as the great exponent of the neo-classical style in furniture. This style is the direct antithesis of the styles shown in the first *Director*.

Robert Adam, like William Kent, believed that an interior

should be homogenous right down to the last detail. Like Kent, he did not design for general production but only for patrons, and his patrons included members of the Royal Family, the nobility and landed gentry. But here the resemblance ends. Adam's style bears no relation to that of Kent and Kent's followers, nor to the mid-century fashionable *mélange* of rococo, Chinese and Gothic. In fact it is quite likely that Robert and his brother James saved us from a Palladian style,* now becoming debased by overdiscipline and mechanical repetition into mere 'Palladianism', no less than from the wild formless excesses which could easily proceed from undisciplined rococo.

So the rich, opulent, 'glaringly magnificent' and weighty 'Roman' interiors of the early era became *démodé*, and Robert Adam's neo-classical became the rage. Colour is delicate. Ornamentation though classical is eclectic, deriving from Greece, Rome, Pompeii and from Italian Renaissance grotesques and arabesques. Although he and his brother admired the use of orders, when properly applied, they did not believe they should be used for every room in a house. 'Nothing', they say, 'can be more sterile and disgustful than to see for ever the dull repetition of Dorick, Ionick and Corinthian entablatures . . . reigning round every apartment',[24] no matter what the size or height of a room. This had led to dreadful mutilations. Architraves and friezes, perforce, had been left out and replaced by ponderous cornices of 'ample dimensions' more 'fit for the temple of Jupiter Tonans' than for an English gentleman's house. What they actually did was 'to seize . . . the beautiful spirit of antiquity, and to transfuse it, with novelty and variety', through all their 'numerous works'.[25]

This beautiful spirit was altogether lighter and more graceful. It was a social not a senatorial spirit—gay, charming, witty, elegant. Rooms took on stimulating shapes, round, square or rectangular; surprised by arcades, divided by screens of columns, curved with apsidal ends or *exedrae*. Such diversification in Adam's

---

* Adam's father, William, was the outstanding Palladian architect in Scotland.

expert hands meant there were seldom two rooms of similar shape in any single house. At Luton House (now Luton Hoo), which Adam began to alter for his patron, Lord Bute, in 1767, he achieved a triumph of diversification in one single room—the Library. Mrs Delany (1700–88), there on a four-day visit with the Dowager Duchess of Portland, describes it as 'in effect, three or five rooms; one very large one, well proportioned in the middle; each end divided off by pillars, in which recesses (i.e. the divisions made by the pillars) are chimneys'. Beyond each division was a large, square room closed off by doors, but 'when the doors are thrown open it makes it appear like one large room or gallery. I never saw so magnificent and so pleasant a library, extremely well lighted, and nobly furnished with everything that can inform men of learning and virtü'.[26] Lord Bute, one is happy to record, was 'very civil'. But who, other than her arrogant, selfish snob of a brother, Bernard, to whom she wrote the description, could have failed in civility to the accomplished, artistic, charming, tactful, sensible, intelligent, affectionate Mary Delany?

The whole of Luton House, although not completed, she found impressive and, since her own taste was excellent, she is a reliable guide. The five complete bedroom apartments were 'very commodious', each with a bedchamber and two dressing-rooms with furniture 'well suited to all. The beds, damask and rich sattin, green, blue and crimson, mine was white sattin. The rooms hung with plain paper, suited to ye colour of ye beds, except mine which was pea-green . . . the curtains, chairs and sophas are all plain sattin, every room fitted with pictures; many capital ones. . . . The chimney pieces in good taste; no extravagance or fancy; indeed throughout the whole house that is avoided. Fine frames to the pictures, but very little guilding besides, and the cielings elegant and not loaded with ornament.'[27]

What Mrs Delany means by elegant and relatively unornamented ceilings is that Adam had revolutionized them. He did away with the heavy compartmented, thick ribbed ones, beloved by the early Georgians and with which Mrs Delany was so familiar, as well as with those crick-in-the-neck ceilings which were usually just one vast and generally apotheosistic painting. In their places, he put ceilings as delicate and varied—though certainly ornamented—as they were beautiful. Ceilings are, perhaps, Adam's highest achievement.* Light mouldings form compartments, lunettes, squares, circles and ovals which are often filled with arabesques and grotesques in very shallow relief, or painted with small scale scenes by artists such as Angelica Kauffman, her husband Zucchi, Cipriani and Bonomi. Square ceilings have concentric ornaments; oblong ones often have a central square panel with small oblongs at ends and sides. The radiating fan treatment is used in rooms with apsidal or rounded ends. Frequently certain panels are filled with shallow, flat modelled or cast medallions, or with nymphs dancing, or with Graces, happily transformed from those lumpy girls so favoured in mid-seventeenth century into charming, graceful, Grecian figures. Winged sphinxes, gryphons, fantastic foliated beasts are also used while the flowing lines of the favourite bell-flower husk fill the interstices. 'Light tints of pink and green, so as to take off the glare of white, so common in every cieling, till of late' create 'a harmony between cieling and sidewals with their hangings, pictures and other decorations'.[28]

Walls were damask, brocade, silk or paper hung; or of plaster with medallions, trophies, urns and so on in typical Adam flat relief, and set within panels framed by very light mouldings. Sometimes they were completely painted as in the Etruscan room at Osterley. Shallow pilasters often enriched with arabesques grotesque or honeysuckle—painted or in stucco work—frequently divide walls into sections niched for statues or recessed or built-in bookshelves.† Engaged columns serve the same purpose. Apses and *exedrae* are screened by free-standing columns. Fluted Corinthian

---

* Since this is neither a book nor even a chapter on Adam, I deal, necessarily, with only his best period. His early ceilings were rather heavy. His later ones often became prolix and fussy.

† The drawing room of Adam's Lansdowne House with its beautifully painted pilasters may now be seen in the Philadelphia Museum of Art. Similarly the niched 'eating-room' may be looked at in the Metropolitan Museum of Art, New York. The Americans had enough aesthetic sensibility to buy up what we, to our eternal shame, destroyed in 1929.

ones have delicately enriched capitals, as in that supreme Adam achievement, the library at Ken Wood.* Ionic columns, 'which ought to be used in gay and slight buildings'²⁹ stand in the vestibule at Syon house; and the more simple Doric column is displayed in the entrance hall at Shardeloes.

Important doorways leading into important rooms are pedimented, but pediment cornices are much thinner and lighter and there is a good deal less overhang. Less important doorways—and by now there are fewer of these leading into rooms and consequently less draught—are of deal painted, perhaps white, with architrave, frieze and a straight cornice, the latter supported by ancones (carved scrolls). Windows are as temperate as doors and glazing bars are thinner. Fan lights of outer doors are enchanting. Paintings are often commissioned with subject matter and size of canvas specified to suit the decor and to fit into an exact space in a room. Fireplaces are much more subdued. Two storeys are rare, but the chimneybreasts are beautifully ornamented, often with a chaste classical, urn-topped mirror above the mantelshelf or a specially painted picture. Fireplaces in great state rooms are of marble, delicately carved; sometimes inlaid with coloured marbles, or the marble is painted. Mrs Delany made wonderful *trompe l'oeil* fireplaces by cutting out delicate 'Etruscan' designs in coloured paper and pasting them on a black background. Later in the century, 'carved' fireplaces of Coade stone were much used. Fire grates and fire irons carry out the classical theme and are decorated with urns, rosettes and finial figures. No detail was too small for Mr Adam, everything, right down to door furniture, comes under his designing eye. He had, in fact, the genius's infinite capacity for taking pains.

Floors in entrance halls are of marble or scagliola and, in some state rooms, carpets were designed and specially woven to repeat

---

* 'Hampstead is risen from a little village, almost to a city . . . on the north-east side . . . is Caen-Wood, the noble seat of the Earl of Mansfield. . . . The house has been greatly improved and enriched and contains . . . a drawing room of which novel design and elegant decorations, are a credit to the taste of Mr. *Adam* . . . and his noble employer.' (Defoe's *Tour:* 1778 ed.)

Upholstered settee and pole screen, *circa* 1775. Adam style. Regency sofa and lamp table, *circa* 1810

or reflect the main design of the ceiling. And here it is interesting to note that around mid-century a new type of floor covering came into relatively common use. Known as 'Oil Floor-Cloths', it was made of resin, pitch, Spanish brown, beeswax and linseed oil, melted and rolled into canvas under pressure.* This is the true ancestor of our present-day linoleum—an English invention. But when it came to cleaning this new material the wretched servants must have had a terrible time. Nothing so simple as brushing over with tea leaves—guaranteed to preserve colour and pile of the

* A certain Nathan Smith began to manufacture these cloths at Knightsbridge in 1754, but the earliest patent for 'Painting with oyle cullers upon woollen cloath' was taken out in 1636. It cannot have been durable and was probably used for hangings. In 1751 India rubber and gum lastic were used; doubtless more expensive than Smith's cloth. In 1844 an expensive material of cork dust and rubber was used, but in 1860 F. Walton invented a process of oxydizing linseed oil and this made a cheap, rubber substitute, and so linoleum was born.

best carpets—would do. Oil floor-cloths had to be cleaned with milk and polished until dry because 'mopping spoils them and wears them out soon besides making their sides turn up'.[30] To prevent turned up sides, the covering had to be turned over every week, although 'Wires fix'd so as to be drawn will answer better'.[31] This piece of advice cannot have been so meaningless as it now sounds and one can only hope, whatever it may mean, it *did* answer better.

It is probable that such floor-cloths were not used at first in grander rooms, but by 1796 they had improved considerably in colour and design. One gathers this from Horace Walpole who, recommending them to Lord Holland's attention, says: 'Mr Lysons is having some beautiful carpets made of very large dimensions from the Roman pavements he has discovered in Gloucestershire.'[32] Later he adds 'Give me leave to correct a blunder . . . I mentioned *carpets* made from Mr Lysons's Mosaic pavements* I ought to have said *oil-cloths* which cost a good deal less.'[33] We may, I think, assume that this oil floor-cloth was designed after the great 'Orpheus' pavement of the Roman villa at Woodchester which Samuel Lysons, the antiquarian, considered 'undoubtedly superior to anything of the same kind found in this country'.[34]

But what a business it must have been removing the furniture every blessed week so that oil floor-cloths could be milk-polished and turned. Fortunately furniture had by now become a good deal lighter—although more of it was used than in the days of George I and II—and was considerably easier to move, to rearrange or regroup as the owner wished. We do not know whether Mr Adam insisted on his furniture remaining where he ordered it put, he may easily have done so, but we do know that furniture

---

* In 1793 Samuel Lysons (brother of Daniel) commenced his extensive excavations at Woodchester. The great pavement which was found buried beneath the graveyard of the church has no protective building over it and must be covered deeply with earth to protect it from frost, etc. It is therefore rarely to be seen and has been 'undug' only four times in the present century: 1926, 1935, 1951, 1963. Those fortunate enough to have seen it will certainly not quarrel with Mr Lysons's view of the superiority of the pavement.

designed by him and made by contemporary cabinet makers such as Chippendale and the firm of France and Beckwith, gave rise to the 'Adam style',* long popular and often revived. Since it is impossible to deal with individual pieces here, we may say, speaking very generally, that apart from his earliest furniture—which is a bit on the florid side—a classical austerity informs all Adam's work, although it is an austerity enriched by low relief and linear and flat decoration.

Specifically, the long-favoured cabriole, the massive carved and the flim-flam leg, is out. The straight, slim, square or circular tapered leg—fluted, reeded and with occasional decoration in chased brass—comes in. Often at leg tops there are panels containing carved, moulded, marquetry, or ormolu *paterae*, and the *patera*† is typical Adam. Chairs have oval or shield-shaped backs and, when padded, if the shield is at any height above seat level it is often supported by winged female sphinxes. The bell-husk and the bay-leaf garland are used on framing; cresting often takes the form of a small wreath. Dining-room chairs—seat padded only—have splat backs in various designs and the lyre back with brass stringing is often attributed to Adam.

Furniture was frequently mahogany (dust the carving with a paint brush and remove spots with stale beer is the advice of the day), but it was also very often made of cheaper wood painted a light colour and ornamented with painted designs to harmonize with the décor of the room. Other pieces were japanned in black or in soft shades of slate and green, with gilt or painted decoration. Marquetry returned to favour; various delicately coloured woods

---

* The Adam style is rare in the United States, although Chippendale is not. The reason seems to be that when Adam was at his height, so was the Revolution. Afterwards Hepplewhite and Sheraton styles arrived together, and one finds charming Sheraton-Hepplewhite furniture there.

† A *patera* was originally a small flat saucer-like vessel of earthenware, bronze, silver or gold used to receive the wine with which libation was made. It was ornamented on the inside chiefly with a single rosettelike flower banded by a bay leaf garland—perhaps because sacrificial beasts were similarly garlanded. Many *paterae* were found in Pompeii and their decorative value must have been realized by the Adam brothers.

were laid in classical designs—urns, swags, *paterae*, etc.—against satinwood or harewood (sycamore). Free-standing book cases— and there are many more books printed now than hitherto— are architectural but much lighter, with straight cornice, pediment and curved glazing bars. Servants are warned not to 'meddle' with the books but 'they may be dusted as far as a goose wing will go'.[35] Below are cupboards and drawers, marquetry ornamented. Grand tables have marquetry, painted, inlaid, marble or scagliola tops. Sometime during the 1770s the Pembroke table came in. Made in mahogany or satinwood, or even japanned, it had slim tapered legs and two hinged side flaps to the rectangular top. The similar but larger 'Sopha table' was also introduced. Sofas, not to be confused with settees, were relatively new and had developed from the long-known daybed. They were generally used for that purpose. Reclining gracefully upon 'th'accomplish'd SOFA'[36] became an art carried to its highest pitch by Mme Recamier, and by elegant gentlemen too. The Hon. Mr Listless spent most of his time lying 'supine on the sofa'.[37] Another and later introduction

Tripod table, *circa* 1750. Satinwood dropside table, painted decoration
circa 1790

was the circular top table—excellent for the centre of the room, an apsidal end or a bow window. Even later this became the monopodium with a heavy three-sided pedestal inlaid with ivory and ebony, standing upon paw feet. Stools continued to be popular, as they had been since furniture was first invented, their seats upholstered or, and this was new, caned; their unstretchered legs following current patterns. The window stool, backless and with out-curving arms, was in great vogue.

Although Adam is not credited with inventing any of the few new pieces mentioned above, he is very probably the father of the sideboard. Side tables had long been used to hold plates of food, silver, napkins, urns and knife boxes. Adam designed, *en suite*, a side table to fit between two pedestal cupboards, each surmounted by a metal-lined urn. So the first sideboard was what we should call a three-piece unit. One metal urn was for iced drinking water, the other for hot water with which to wash up the flat silver. Silver knives and forks were still not nearly so plentiful as courses (sixteen dishes each) or guests. Kitchens were rarely sited near dining-rooms, so silver had to be washed in the dining-room between courses and re-used. One pedestal, presumably below the hot urn, was a warming cupboard; the other served as a cellarette, or as a place to keep the chamber-pot, a most necessary utensil in eating-rooms where gentlemen sat long over their wine after the ladies had withdrawn. The table between the pedestals had a brass gallery and supported silver and knife boxes. Later on, the three-piece sideboard was made in one piece and drawers replaced pedestals. This was obviously a retrograde step. Large single sideboards were difficult to move and, since it was advisable to place a hand behind anything to be set against a wall because 'for want of this trifling attention great pieces are often knocked out of the stucco',[38] the single, heavy sideboard must have bashed knuckles and stucco with equal indifference.

Adam's designs were copied, adapted and freely interpreted by others, but he was not the only designer of the 'Adam period'. Thomas Shearer, George Seddon, John Linnell and Robert Gillow were all cabinet makers and designers of the time. But probably the best known to us today are two of Adam's younger contemporaries, George Hepplewhite and Thomas Sheraton. Since Hepplewhite appears to have made no furniture for important patrons, although it is believed he made some for Adam, we know singularly little about him, and it is likely that his name is much better known to us than it was when he was alive. Once an apprentice to Robert Gillow of Lancashire, who had opened a branch in Oxford Street, London, sometime before 1760, Hepplewhite opened his own business in Cripplegate and died in 1786 leaving his widow, Alice, to carry on the firm. His fame was posthumously achieved when his book *Cabinet-Maker and Upholsterer's Guide* appeared in 1788.

The *Guide's* expressed and laudable aim was 'to unite elegance and utility'; to produce a work 'useful to the mechanic [i.e. craftsman] and serviceable to the gentleman', and to show what the taste in English furniture was really like. Strange as it may seem 'English Taste and Workmanship' had 'of late years been much sought for by surrounding nations'. This service to foreigners was also intended to be of use to 'our own Countrymen and Artizans whose distance from the metropolis' made even an imperfect knowledge of its improvements difficult to acquire without 'much trouble and expence'. The book, meant to be more or less a plain man's guide, therefore eschewed articles of 'mere novelty' produced by 'whim' or 'caprice' while at the same time it followed 'the latest or most prevailing fashion'.[39]

In other words, Hepplewhite was a conservative designer (the term is relative) and translated the high, neo-classical language of Adam and his imitators into the English idiom: bold, vigorous, without extravagance and well suited to the less rarefied type of domestic atmosphere. Although commonly credited with having introduced the shield back no less than the splat back with Prince of Wales feathers, we know he did not create the first and have no real evidence that he devised the second. But he is responsible for what we call the Hepplewhite style, so the term Hepplewhite is used in a generic sense.

Hepplewhite shield backs are of great variety. He used all kinds of interlaced ornamental lines, as well as urns with dependent swags; the famous feathers, or ornamented splats radiate from shield point. Square backs are equally varied, and the square back was now fashionable as opposed to the long narrow rectangular or spoon-back of the early era. Bow-fronted or serpentine sideboards, dressing tables, bureaux bookcases and tallboys were made in mahogany (walnut was quite out) and ornamented discreetly with inlaid bands or carving in light relief. Japanning was recommended as being 'new'—which it was not—and satinwood was still popular. It remained so until the turn of the century when it suffered a twenty year eclipse. The 'confidante', a new piece, was introduced and became very popular. This was a padded seat with a 'Barjia' (*bergere*?) chair set at an angle at each end of the middle bit. Whoever sat in the end chairs could hardly confide without raising the voice well above confidence pitch. Possibly the Barjias served as eavesdropper's or blackmailer's chairs★ used for the purpose of overhearing what was said by the occupants of the settee. Nevertheless, no elegant, modern drawing-room was complete without a confidante—or so the *Guide* says.

Apart from reclining on sofas, settees and possibly even on confidantes, the fashionable, although quite intemperate nighthawks did go to bed for at least half the day—

> Till noon they sleep, from noon till night they dress
> From night till morn they game it more or less,[40]

and they slept until midday in such beautiful beds. Grand beds were now of extreme elegance and were, as they had always been, highly prized, expensive pieces of furniture. But they had changed a good deal since the first half of the century. They were not nearly so massive, nor did they expose clumping lion paw or plinth feet. Frieze, cornice and bed-posts were no longer entirely silk covered. Bed-posts, usually mahogany, were left bare,

★ The dumb waiter had been invented *circa* 1740 to do away with the presence of servants who, overhearing certain kinds of conversation, were prone to indulge in blackmail.

State bed, *circa* 1770

delicately carved, and tapered to the top, where they supported a frieze or cornice, sometimes plain carved, or carved and gilded, or japanned. The cornice acted as a frame for the tester which was flat, curved or, often, deliciously domed. Domes were surmounted by carved armorial bearings, trophies, urns, Roman lamps, turtle doves, feathers or a miniature gallery. Urns, gryphons, sphinxes and lamps also marked the four corners of the tester and acted as finials for the bed-posts. Valances hid legs and feet. They were full, loose, and had overdrapings of tasselled swags in contrasting materials. Furnishings—that is curtains, counterpanes, valances, pelmets and testers—were of rich silks, satins, damask, woven materials and, not so richly, of cottons or linen. Beautiful and complicated as beds were they were also desperately difficult to keep clean; 'set open the windows of the Bedchambers and uncover the beds to sweeten and air them;

which will be of great help against Bugs and Fleas'. If this didn't work, and it rarely did, to 'infallibly kill and destroy them' all furnishings and framework should be frequently brushed or 'spunged over' with a mixture of 'Spirits of Wine, Spirit of Turpentine and Camphire.'[41] Advice and laments upon this chronic problem appear with horrifyingly monotonous regularity in the household books and journals of this age of taste and elegance.

More simple, less expensive, and more commonly in use was the tent-bed, so called because when the hangings were drawn the contraption looked just like a gabled tent. The beautiful, newly married Countess of Coventry refused a tent-bed in Calais, kindly offered by Lord Downe who feared the Inn beds were infested. 'Oh,' said she 'I had rather be bit to death than lie one night from my dear Cov.'[42] The couch-bed, a transitional piece halfway between the old fashioned stump bed and our relatively modern divan, was even simpler. It had wooden head and foot boards, very low sides and cushions replaced the mattress. The very low truckle-bed which when not in use was pushed under the great bed, was now fitted with casters and changed its name from 'truckle' to 'trundle'. Portable chair-beds were also known, and were carried about by the travelling rich. There were also press beds which folded back into a press cupboard, obviously the ancestor of the Murphy bed. But beds, as yet, were unsprung, even though some sort of metal springing for chair seats and settees seem to have been known from around mid-century.

And it was in mid-century, 1751 to be precise, that Thomas Sheraton was born at Stockton-upon-Tees. Though 'bred to the cabinet business' he was probably never master of a workshop and we do not know of a single piece of furniture made by him. He lived 'by his exertions as an author',[43] poor pickings it appears, as he is reputed to have died in poverty. But his *Cabinet-Maker's and Upholsterer's Drawing Book* (1791–94) was very popular, served as a guide to others and set a style. So the term Sheraton must also be used in a generic sense.

This furniture happily combines reticence and ingenuity.

Chimneypiece, *circa* 1730 (in the manner of William Kent)

French styles are much in evidence and furniture is yet lighter—
hence the Hon. John Byng's scorn of 'skuttling tables' and
French furnishings. (We were, of course at war with France when
the book appeared but such things did not much hinder the inter-
change of fashions between the two countries.) Satinwood,
decorated with paintings, and mahogany are the favourite woods;
occasionally tulip wood is used and the newer rosewood which in
the early nineteenth century ousted satinwood. Japanning was still
very much to the fore. Handles, now usually oval in shape, were
sometimes in silver, sometimes in Sheffield plate. Ovals, a
favourite motif, were much used in inlay. Chairs of this time have
their seats caned, and caning is used, often in squares, between the
splats. A new type of leg is introduced—a concave curve the
opposite of cabriole—which frequently tapers to no foot at all.

Chimneypiece, *circa* 1775, designed by Sir Robert Taylor

Cresting rails are also slightly concave to fit the sitter's back and are sometimes turned.

Sheraton is credited perhaps rightly, with inventing the kidney-shaped table, but he is probably best known to us for introducing the six-legged sideboard. Made usually in mahogany inlaid with satinwood and various other woods, these sideboards have four legs in front and two at the back. Unlike Hepplewhite, he seemed to like intricate pieces and although he did not invent the Harlequin Pembroke table, it appears with all its tricky mechanism exposed in his book. This was a table 'of many parts' in both senses of the phrase. It was a writing, working, breakfast table with foldover flaps, and had a drawer as well as a 'till' of small drawers and pigeon holes which could be raised or lowered at will. An equally versatile piece was the cylindrical desk cum bookcase. Press shelves were enclosed by doors in its base, the desk bit enclosed by a tambour front, and the recessed upper stage for books was glazed and surmounted by a swan neck pediment. Even more compartmented was the 'Secretary'. It boasted a writing desk (at which one stood to write) and a sunk writing well in the middle backed by drawers and pigeon holes, four cupboards (one for a pot and slippers) two large drawers and a slide candlestand. The fitted work-table, known to Hepplewhite, becomes with Sheraton a pouch-table fitted with drawers and with a well or pouch of fabric suspended from it, in which everything could, did, and still does, get into a muddle, as in the handbag of a giantess.

Thomas Sheraton died in 1806; so did the younger Pitt, Charles James Fox, and the beautiful and gay Georgiana, Duchess of Devonshire. So did Henry Holland the architect. By this time the long period stretching back to the reign of Queen Anne which had produced such beautiful English furniture, was drawing to a close. Yet the twilight was also beautiful in its very different way. And its very different way was due to the much more severe neo-classical style developed by Henry Holland, Nash and others. The 'august simplicity' of Holland's Carlton House which 'charmed' and 'astonished' Horace Walpole, was due he says, 'to its taste and propriety', to its 'delicate and new' ornamentation which was 'rather classic than French'.[44]

Holland is always restrained while a meticulous care in interpreting classical forms, both in large and in little, is characteristic of his work. In the round drawing-room of Carlton House, the ceiling was painted as the sky. Scagliola columns of his favourite Ionic order, painted to look like porphyry, supported, with silvered capitals, a silver cornice on a lavender background. Recessed doors and windows were hung with Roman tent draperies, and low Roman couch-settees with chimerae legs carried out the theme. Admittedly, it is difficult to imagine what the excessively corpulent Prince Regent looked like on a Roman settee, but the room must have been very beautiful indeed. Although we should probably call it splendid and magnificent rather than simple, compared with Adam's work it must have seemed austere and august. Holland swept away all the accretions, the fussy nonsense with which Adam's followers too frequently loaded their work. He swept well and he garnished too, but discreetly.

Holland and Sheraton form the link between the eighteenth and nineteenth centuries in that they both foreshadow the Regency Style. There are hints of it in Sheraton's *Cabinet Dictionary* of 1803, and certainly more than a hint in the interior and furniture of Southill, Bedfordshire, which Holland designed in 1795 for Samuel Whitbread. For Regency, when it comes to architecture, interiors and furniture, is not chronologically coincident with the 'political' Regency of 1811–20. It begins a decade earlier and ends a decade later. It was not called Regency—that is our word for it—it was for a long time known as 'English Empire'. Empire is now a rude word so we fear to use it, although the French do not. And it was France which contributed largely to our Regency style.

French Empire interiors and furniture—and *'le style Empire est caractérisé surtout par la sobriété et la sévérité des lignes'*[45]—were based upon a much closer than hitherto study of Greek and Roman remains, and also upon the brand new study of Egyptian antiquities. Napoleon, after Nelson* defeated him at the battle of the Nile (1798), hurried home and ordered Egyptian motifs to be used in the furniture and furnishings of his private apartments,† which seems rather a salt-in-the-wound thing to do. Already the purer Greek and Roman styles were favoured in France and to these was added the Egyptian. So English Regency is based first, on French Empire adapted for English use and taste; and second, upon a strong English antiquarian spirit which had persisted in one way or another for over a hundred years. There was much

---

* After Nelson's victory at Trafalgar, the rope motif became a popular decorative touch in England, and the so called Trafalgar chair much favoured.

† Baron Denon, the archaeologist who accompanied Buonaparte to Egypt produced his *Voyages dans la Basse et Haute Egypte*, 1802. It speedily became a source book for English design, though popular interest had been aroused by Nelson's victory.

fresh studying of Greek vase paintings, of sculptural monuments, of Egyptian hieroglyphics; and it was discovered that Greeks and Romans, particularly the earlier ones, had not always tricked things out in great ornamental detail. Both civilizations had had more simple periods belonging to their early history, while the Egyptian civilization was older than both. What emerged from this fresh study was the knowledge that lines were simple, contours bold, surfaces plain. Colours were pure and 'primitive'; crimson, black, terra cotta, ochre and citron, rather than blue, green and pink. But, since vase paintings, monuments and hiero-glyphics tend to depict only a minimum of necessary furniture (beds, chairs, stools, tables and couches) even though used by gods, goddesses and pharaohs, designers were faced with a problem of creating furniture in the new style for which there was no ancient prototype. Sideboards, tea-poys, commodes, Carlton House and Harlequin tables, fitted wash-stands, wardrobes, bureaux, and hundreds of other furnishings are noticeably absent in antiquity. So designers had to work out what they thought the ancients would have done had their world known such refinements.

In this they were greatly assisted by a book produced in 1807 by Thomas Hope, banker, scholar, amateur architect, author* and traveller. The book *Household Furniture and Decoration* was a record of furniture made to his own design for his house at Deepdene, Surrey. Hope, of Dutch origin and a friend and admirer of the work of the French architect–designer Percier, had, in his travels, collected a great number of Greek, Roman and Egyptian antiquities, and had studied the remains of these civiliza-tions at first hand. So his rooms at Deepdene were designed to show off his collections in the 'correct' setting. Much interest must have been shown in this for Hope claimed that even before his book appeared his designs were known all over London.

His rooms for housing his Egyptian collection were in the

---

* He wrote an immensely popular novel, *Anastasius*, and a metaphysical work, *An Essay on the Origin and Prospects of Man*, which Carlyle in his downright way calls 'a shameful Abortion'.

Armchair, *circa* 1805. Sideboard, *circa* 1760. Stool, settee, chair and work table, *circa* 1800 (in the style of Thomas Hope)

Egyptian style, a style which did not long persist* but which gave us, for a brief space, interiors with papyrus and lotus columns, splay and torus mouldings, and beam architraves. Linear designs of twining lily and papyrus stems, sometimes in *cavo-relievo*, sometimes in brass inlay, ran riot. Rooms had friezes painted with figures representing pharaohs and Egyptian deities; Sekhmet, Horus, Bast, Sebek, Hathor, Nekhebet, Thoth, Anubis—respectively, lion, hawk, bull, cat, crocodile, cow, vulture, ibis and jackal headed. Nothing could have been more novel, less Greek, or more unsuitable for England. In furniture, tables are supported by Egyptian figures or lion monopodia. The

* It produced, in architecture, the famous Egyptian Hall, Piccadilly (destroyed 1904) another at Penzance and an Egyptian public library at Plymouth which stood almost next door to Plymouth's Greek town hall! Much earlier Burlington designed an 'Egyptian Hall' for the York Assembly rooms but this, based on Vitruvius, is Roman.

lion and ring mask—the archaic Sumerian or Egyptian lion not the shaggy British one—were used as applied ornaments wherever possible and impossible. Truncated, sphinx-topped pyramids, obelisks;* and lotus bowl chandeliers became commonplace; scarabs and crocodiles crawled everywhere. So novel was it all, so new, that the style spread very quickly and equally quickly degenerated into what a good many thought farcical, if not vulgar. By 1812 Mr Soho the upholsterer is already informing Lady Clanbrony that although she can have 'the *Egyptian hieroglyphic* paper with the *ibis border* to match' it would be most unwise as one sees it everywhere. It is 'quite antediluvian' and worse, 'has gone to the hotels even'.[46] When it came to furniture, a sphinx supported sofa could be a charming piece but a couch in the shape of a crocodile, undoubtedly, went too far.

The same is not true of the 'new' Greek furniture. Hope's book is full of captivating designs and the Greek influence persisted strongly until the unlamented death of George IV. Speaking broadly, the characteristic Greek chair had legs and back in a continuous curve balanced by out-curving front legs (the sabre leg). The top rail, overrunning the uprights, was a wide board shaped to the shoulder curve. Stools revert to their original x-shape cross frame with lion feet, but the awkward pigeon-toed look of Greek and Roman stools was avoided by turning the feet out instead of in—even if 'in' is more sensible. Couches had a rolled end, or ends, and claw feet. Pillars with claws supported large, sectional dining tables which could be bolted together and, as families were large and guests numerous, these became enormous and very un-Greek: Greeks and Romans preferred small tables. But small tables proliferated too, and it ecame fashionable to have several occasional tables scattered about a drawing-room (we were beginning to overfurnish by this time). Little sets of three and four tables known as 'trios' and 'quartettos' were also in great demand.

About large pieces of furniture, such as bookcases, little could be done. There was no classical precedent for such things, so

* It should be noted that obelisks were favourites of the Elizabethans too.

bookcases remained firmly and traditionally in two stages but Greek and Egyptian motifs could be, and were, used for ornamentation. It was not unusual for the anthemion and lotus to be used together—inlaid usually in brass. Thomas Hope designed a bookcase with carved sphinxes' heads on the pilasters separating the doors. But the fact that the ancients had little furniture while we had a great deal did not deter designers from inventing still more. The dwarf bookcase was introduced, its door glazed or brass trellised, and was much used in smaller houses, now called villas.* The square or circular revolving bookcase was also small and new to the Regency. But in great houses with great libraries there was still need of library steps and these became very ingenious indeed; they folded into chairs, stools or tables and are all delightful. The davenport† was invented, another very small and useful piece. The huge, monopodium library table was much used. Hope had a Greek one with its three-sided pedestal inlaid with ivory and ebony. The Regency chiffonier stopped being the French chiffonnière—a case of drawers on legs—and became a low cupboard with shelves at each end for those books in constant use, the middle section being enclosed by a glazed or brass trellis door, silk-backed. Shortly after 1800 the circular convex mirror became vastly fashionable (it had been popular in France for fifty years). The hollow moulding of the frame filled with gilt balls, the outer edge reeded and topped by a carved eagle or a clutch of acanthus leaves. Reeding was also used on the legs of chairs and tables, and spiral reeding also came in. Another piece new to this period was the supper Canterbury,‡ a partitioned tray to hold knives and forks with a round end for plates. It stood on four legs and was a rather tippy adjunct to the dining-room.

Since lines and forms were bold and surfaces plain, designers achieved variation by using new veneers and woods. Mahogany

---

* The villa had been reduced in size and meaning from the large Palladian to almost any separate house between cottage and mansion.
† A small writing-desk with a swivel top; the word is also used, especially in America, for a large sofa.
‡ A Canterbury is also a small music stand.

came first but dark streaked rosewood (easily faked) ran it a close second, and boldly figured woods such as calamander, zebra-wood and amboyna were also very popular. Light-coloured woods were definitely out, and when wood was painted it was usually black with touches of gold. French polishing came in—one wishes it had not. Those who hoped to keep abreast of the times took to having old furniture stripped. Off came the lovely patina produced by years of hand polishing; on went the new mixture of shellac dissolved in spirit which transformed the old piece into something bright, glossy and often deliberately darkened by the addition of colouring matter.

Yet clear as the neo-classical and even the Egyptian quality of Regency furniture seems to us today, the whole period is noted for its constant search for new forms, for novelty. The classical pattern, with all its infinite variations on Greek and Roman themes, was breaking up along with the traditional pattern of English society. Changes in taste were so rapid, the search for something 'new' so feverish, that around 1820 one cabinet maker felt that it would soon be necessary to publish furniture designs, like ladies' fashions, every month. Etruscan and French styles were re-explored with an overwhelming paucity of ideas, and there was also a brief Chinese revival as well as a Gothic one. But the Gothic was no longer the rococo-Gothic of the mid-eighteenth century. It was a part of the fashionable Picturesque or Romantic movement, and lovers of Gothic were split into two camps. There were those who preferred the Perpendicular—thought to be the purer—and those who preferred the 'Elizabethan' or English-Renaissance Gothic. By now, too, so many machines for turning out furniture had been invented, so many designers were producing what Hope called 'extravagant caricatures' that the end of the English furniture craftsman was at hand; and when architects gave up designing furniture, which they did, the twilight of the golden era tipped into darkness.

Back in 1757 Mrs Lybbe Powys had visited the Elizabethan prodigy house, Hardwick Hall, Derbyshire. 'Of course it is antique', she says, 'and render'd extremely curious to the present age, as all the furniture is co-eval with the edifice. Our ancestors' taste for substantialness in every piece makes *us* now smile; they too would, could they see our delicateness in the same articles, smile at us, and I am certain, if any one was to compare three or four hundred years hence a chair from the dining room of Queen Elizabeth's days and of the light French ones of George II, it would never be possible to suppose them to belong to the same race of people, as the one is altogether gigantic, the other quite lilliputian.'[47]

Caroline Lybbe Powys was, of course, wrong. She could neither know nor guess that less than a century after her visit to Hardwick, we were already moving into a period where size, heaviness, and a dark, brooding, vulgar Germanic taste would vie with a new, revived, massive and nearly as vulgar Elizabethan style for supremacy in English interior decoration and furniture.

But then, neither could she know that the Victorians, like the Elizabethans, would produce giants too, albeit of an entirely different order.

CHAPTER FOUR

Of China, Glass, and Little Things

On the face of it, the year 1729 does not appear to be of vast importance in our annals. The twenty-two-year-old son of George II, Frederick Louis (1707-51), who had 'a much weaker understanding and, if possible, a more obstinate temper than his father',[1] was created Prince of Wales with an income of around £50,000 a year. He regarded it as a pittance.* Robert Walpole concluded the Treaty of Seville with the reluctant assent of his confrère and brother-in-law, Charles, 2nd Viscount Townshend, who quickly retired to his Norfolk estate and devoted himself to agriculture—chiefly turnips.

At Oxford John Wesley became leader of that society jeeringly nicknamed 'methodists'. It was rumoured that ambitious William Hogarth had furthered his ambitions by a clandestine marriage to the daughter of the famous and rich painter Sir James Thornhill. The rumour was true. The final curtain fell for William Congreve and left Henrietta, Duchess of Marlborough,† so bereft that she had him reproduced in wax and frequently dined with the effigy. In London, Thomas Newcomen, inventor of the 'atmospheric steam-engine', died at sixty-six. In Birmingham, the infant Matthew Boulton celebrated his first birthday. In Dublin, the

---

* In fairness, it should be noted that George II had received £100,000 a year when Prince of Wales, but refused his hated son the same allowance.

† Lady Henrietta Churchill, m. Francis Godolphin (later 2nd Earl) in 1698. Since her father's peerage could descend in the female line, she became Duchess of Marlborough upon his death in 1722.

Roman Catholic wife of one Burke, a Protestant attorney, gave
birth to a boy. They christened him Edmund.

The well-known Palladian architect, Colen Campbell, exchanged the marble halls of this world for those of the next; as
did the unknown Widow Haward who had probably never
entered a marble hall in all her mortal life. She seems to have kept,
or lived over, a shop at Writtle and the post-mortem valuation
of her household effects came to £136. 18s. 3d.—rather a far
cry from the annual allowance allotted to Frederick Louis. Yet
Margaret Haward's inventory can tell us something of importance, that is if one holds with Dr Johnson, 'it is by studying
little things that we attain to the great art of having as little
misery and as much happiness as possible'.[2]

Certainly nothing could be much smaller than a valuation of
5s. 6d. set upon the lately defunct Widow Haward's 'two punch
bowls, six slap basons and sugar pot, glasses, tea potts & cups'.[3]
But the significance lies not in the value—which seems very low
—but in the articles themselves, the slop basins, six of them; the
sugar pot and, more particularly, the tea pots and cups. Here, for
the first time in these mid-Essex inventories which date back to
1635, cups are mentioned specifically as tea cups.* And there is
one thing we know—or rather we can guess with some hope of
accuracy—about these long vanished, saucerless cups, tea pots,
basins, sugar pot and even the punch bowls: that is, unless
given her by a rich friend, they cannot have been made of china.
They must have been pottery,† possibly green or brown
earthenware. A widow whose total effects were valued at only
£136 odd, could hardly have afforded either porcelain or china,‡
which was imported by the rich at great price, either from

---

* Tea was not introduced into England until the 1650s and was then only a rich
man's drink.
† My reason for assuming the punch bowls were pottery and not metal is that any
metal object in the inventory, even the tin coffee pot is listed as such. It was customary to list metal articles, and often when of pewter, brass, etc., by weight.
‡ China is the common name for porcelain, originally imported from China.
Today the word porcelain seems to be used almost exclusively for hard-paste ware
while 'china' is used for soft-paste. Strictly speaking both are porcelain.

the continent or from the Far East via the East India Company.

'My sister,' Lady Elizabeth Finch tells the Countess of Burlington in 1735, 'is become China Mad, frequents all the shops in town in order to gett either old or Dresden China, the first purchases she made of that sort of Ware were yellow & green tea Cups variously and most hideously intermingled as like Delf as ever was seen, but They told her 'twas old China and that was inducement enough to her to buy 'em however they are now exchang'd for a sett of Dresden.'[4]

Indeed, we came late into the field of china making and did not really begin manufacturing it until the middle of the eighteenth century. The Italians, under the patronage of false and despotic Francesco dei Medici, had begun to imitate Chinese porcelain, not very successfully, from about 1580. The French followed a bare century later with manufactories at Rouen and St Cloud. But the imitations produced by each country were soft-paste porcelain; that is, made of some glassy substance stiffened with white clay. Tea-table ware of this soft-paste stuff had an unhappy knack of flying to pieces when filled with hot liquid. It was not until 1709 that true, hard-paste porcelain was achieved at Meissen, near Dresden, and Saxony was saved from bankruptcy.

The story is that Augustus the Strong, Elector of Saxony, King of Poland and a rather excessive personality, had two great passions—women and oriental porcelain. The first passion produced 352 illegitimate children; the second reduced the Royal Exchequer by 100,000 thalers in the first year of his reign. Augustus, always pressed for money, also had an alchemist, J. F. Böttger, working phrenetically in an attempt to discover how to transmute base metals into gold. At this he failed lamentably, but, luckily for him, he did discover how to make true hard-paste porcelain out of kaolin and petunste. As early as 1713, this first European hard-paste ware was exhibited at the Leipzig Fair. It immediately became the rage and, although Augustus tried to keep the process secret, rival factories sprang up at Bayreuth, Berlin and Vienna.

In England, since we did not know we had any kaolin available, we were experimenting with various materials trying to produce hard-paste and, as early as 1716, a pamphlet relates that it was possible to make china in England 'as good as ever was brought from India'. The process was simplicity itself, merely grind up the real thing (imported) mix with gum and lime and carry on as usual. This must have been as impracticable as it was expensive, although a very similar idea proved of great worth in making glass.

Nevertheless by 1745,* and probably for some years before, there was a factory at Chelsea working in the soft-paste tradition

Chelsea asparagus tureen, *circa* 1756 and Bristol vase, white enamelled glass, *circa* 1780

* The earliest piece of English china we have is a Chelsea jug dated 1745, but our early china is ill-documented and it is always possible an earlier piece, or documentary evidence of earlier china, may still come to light. The mystery is, where did Chelsea get its kaolin from? (It was not discovered here until 1750.) It may have been imported by the E.I.C., or perhaps from America. In Virginia the Cherokee Indians used kaolin—they called it unaker—and we do know that porcelain was being made in Savannah, Ga., by Andrew Duché, perhaps as early as 1738. This is seven years earlier than our first date for Chelsea.

of France. At Chelsea, French designs were usually followed since the first two proprietor-managers were French. The second of these, Nicholas Sprimont, began life as a silversmith, so it is not surprising that Chelsea followed current patterns in silver ware. As this was the rococo period for silver, Chelsea tureens come in the form of animals, birds, and vegetables. There is a very fine example of a rabbit tureen (*c.* 1755) painted in colours in the Victoria and Albert Museum, and Chelsea asparagus tureens still turn up at sales. One, a naturalistic coloured bundle of asparagus tied at each end with brown raffia, was sold at Sotheby's in 1962 for £950.

Chelsea ware (1745-84) was very highly thought of at the time, and indeed it is probably the finest English porcelain of the eighteenth century. Designers, modellers and painters were original and excellent. Flower-painting developed from the rather stiff formality of European designs (excluding Meissen which was never stiff), and from a free copying of Japanese designs, to large scale paintings of flowers taken from actual botanical examples found in the albums of dried flowers, or *horti sicci*, of the day. To contemporaries these flower paintings were known as 'Sir Hans Sloane's Plants', as he had a fine collection of dried botanical specimens. But probably Chelsea became best known to most people of the era for its production of 'toys'; that is tiny, exquisitely made and painted etuis, scent bottles, seal hafts, bonbonnières and patch boxes, all much used for love tokens. Hence, a miniscule cupid drums on a pair of breasts; minute amorini busy themselves at a scent-flask forge with a gold flame stopper and a base inscribed *Mon feu ne peut s'eteindre.*★ A seal has a bee-size nun on a rock inscribed *Amour Spirituele*— which is an unlikely label for the age. Another inch-tall cupid with a tiger is boldly labelled *Amour Dompte Tout*, which is equally unlikely. A very rare bonbonnière, only two-and-half inches high, has a meek British lion devouring a thoroughly un-appetizing Gallic cock. This was a non-love token for the French.

★ One of these sold in 1959 for 310 gns. In 1963, a single 'Hans Sloane' plate fetched £200, while in 1966 a pair of 'Hans Sloane' vases went for £3,000.

These toys were made in such quantity that they can still be found today in fair numbers—for a price.

Rivalling Chelsea in date is Bow, and Bow may be even earlier since its patent goes back to 1744, but we have no specimens dating from that year. None the less, it was at Bow, possibly in 1748, that a discovery was made which turned out to be England's most notable contribution to the chemistry of porcelain. This was the adding of bone-ash to soft-paste, an ingredient which greatly reduced the risk of collapse in the kiln, and produced a soft-paste ware which for hardness, whiteness, translucence and resonance when lightly struck, rivalled hard-paste. Thus, the famous English bone-china was born. The use of calcined and powdered bones is an exclusively English development and it distinguished English from Continental china in the eighteenth century as it does today.

At Bristol, around 1749, another new ingredient was introduced; this was soap-rock, a natural mixture of china-clay and steatite which occurs in that part of the world. This too gave the porcelain body, as does bone-ash, and a much greater resistance to changes in temperature, a particularly useful characteristic since we were by this time chronic tea drinkers. And here it should be noted that English china began as, and continued to be, soft-paste ware. We did for a period of some fifty years make a true, hard-paste porcelain at Plymouth, at Bristol and at New Hall* successively; this was due to the independent discovery of kaolin and petuntse (china-stone) in Cornwall in 1750, by a Quaker, William Cookworthy (1705–80). Yet hard-paste does not figure in the real development of the English china industry—probably due to the discovery of bone-ash which was readily available in all parts of the country.

But if we were late comers to china manufactory (we had always made pottery) we soon made up for lost time, and by the 1750s soft-paste ware was being made at Derby,† Worcester,

---

* New Hall gave up making hard-paste porcelain in 1810 and turned to manufacturing a rather glassy bone-china.

† Dr Johnson and James Boswell visited the Derby works in 1777. They found

Liverpool, Longton Hall, Lowestoft and elsewhere. In the 1790s Pinxton added porcelain to its pottery making, as did Minton. Spode added it around 1800. Wedgwood bone-china was first produced in 1812, and shortlived Rockingham around 1820. But the only factory existing continuously from the early years of English porcelain making to the present day is the Worcester Royal Porcelain Company which celebrated its second centenary in 1951. In 1757 Worcester employed Robert Hancock, who had previously worked at the Battersea Enamel Works where transfer printing was either developed or perfected, because Hancock was the most important practitioner of transfer printing. Thus Worcester was the earliest to use transfer printing on china; this, incidentally, is also a purely English invention. It was also a one-time Worcester apprentice, Thomas Turner, who took over the Caughley pottery and turned it to soft-paste in 1772. Turner is said to have invented the still popular Willow pattern, though the invention is also claimed for Thomas Minton, then apprenticed to Turner. We shall probably never know the answer, but Willow is absolute 'chinoiserie'; that is, it has no Chinese proto-type whatsoever, either in fact or fiction. Willow pattern is a purely English invention.

Among other little things for which the era is famous, are china and earthenware figures. 'Unpaper the curtains, take the civers off the couch and chairs, and put the china figures on the mantel-piece immediately',[5] Mrs Heidelberg orders the parlourmaid. Such figures were the rage among those of any degree of *ton*, as well as among those who had no such pretensions. They were a development of the ivory, wax, marzipan or sugar figures long popular as table decorations and used to make up elaborate little scenes at grand dinner parties. Mythological and allegorical subjects, river gods, the personification of the continents, the seasons, the arts—all these made much sought after groups: so did birds and animals. Princesses disguised as shepherdesses against fabulously floral backgrounds, were wooed by the most

the china exquisitely beautiful but Johnson 'justly observed . . . he could have vessels of silver, of the same size, as cheap'.[6]

elegant shepherds, while in 1751 disconsolate Britannia mourns the death of Frederick, Prince of Wales. A lady of unbelievable fairness and delicacy, attended by a blackamoor page, sits in an ornate chair with an infinitesimal tea table complete with chocolate-pot and cups by her side. Famous actors and actresses— Quinn as Falstaff, Garrick as Tancred, Mrs Cibber as a Vivandière —found much favour. So did characters from the Italian Comedy —Harlequin, Columbine, Pantaloon, the Doctor, Punchinello, Pierrot and the Advocate. All these graced tables, mantelpieces and cabinets. Figures were highly valued and were not left about, at least not among the *nouveau riche* like horrid Mrs Heidelberg and her boring and pretentious brother, Mr Sterling.

Both porcelain and pottery makers produced these figures. If porcelain ones were expensive, pottery ones must have been almost equally so, as the 'fine productions of Staffordshire' shown at Christie's in 1771 were certainly superb, but they also bore 'a price only for those who have superfluous money'.[7] Those lacking such a welcome superfluity no doubt made do with plaster figurines. Parson Woodforde whose income was, perhaps, £400 a year (on which he lived very well indeed) paid an Italian sixpence for two figures in 'Plaister of Paris, one of the King of Prussia & another of the present Duke of York, both on horse-back and colored'.[8]

Porcelain, of the hard- or soft-paste variety, is one thing, stone-ware and earthenware are another. Yet they could be, and were, superbly made and glazed, and so fine that even translucence was achieved. Most porcelain works in England had begun with earthen and stoneware and added porcelain to their already rich and varied repertoires. Many potteries did not go in for porcelain at all but continued to improve methods of making, glazing and modelling, and to add to the range of articles produced. Leeds, for example, founded *c.* 1760 by the brothers Green, never made soft-paste ware, yet its exquisitely enamelled cream-coloured earthenware, with delicately pierced patterns or enchanting feather mouldings, rivals porcelain in its beauty. Wedgwood too, apart from a brief period in the nineteenth century, stuck to

Wedgwood coffee pot, *circa* 1783, Worcester vase, *circa* 1775 and Staffordshire jug, *circa* 1770

earthenware; and if Worcester is the oldest continuing name in the history of English porcelain, Wedgwood is certainly the oldest name in pottery; the family name in the Potteries dates back to the seventeenth century. 'I am just returned from viewing the Wedgwood-ware that is to be sent to the Empress of Russia',[9] Mrs Delany writes in 1774. This dinner service she says, consisted of 'as many pieces as there are days in the year, if not hours'. The ground was 'pale brimstone, the drawings in purple, the borders a wreath of leaves, the middle of each piece a particular view of all the remarkable places in the King's dominions neatly executed. I suppose it will come to a princely price.' And, she adds, she is very glad if it does, for the 'ingenuity and industry' of the manufacturers 'deserves encouragement'.

Josiah Wedgwood's ingenuity and industry had been displaying itself ever since 1754 when he entered into partnership with James Wheildon who, from 1740 to 1780, was one of the foremost makers of pottery of the day. In 1759 Wedgwood set up for himself at Burslem and, being a man who, with unusual felicity, combined foresight, business acumen, and a knowledge of the related arts and crafts, with a love of antiquity, he became the greatest and best known potter of his time. Quick to see that a large potential market existed for an earthenware which did not have the disadvantage of salt glaze, he set about refining and improving the cream coloured ware developed by Wheildon and others, and produced such beautiful earthenware that in 1765 he became Royal Potter to Queen Charlotte and was allowed to call his cream-ware 'Queens Ware'.

The Imperial Russian Service* was of Queen's Ware and (pace Mrs Delany) it consisted of 952 pieces. The 'princely price' was not less than £3,000—an average, say, of a little more than £3 a piece. The cost of producing the service itself is estimated at only £51 8s 4d., but the decoration is thought to have cost £2,400 at the very lowest.

Queens Ware was followed by a pink lustre and a white one; the latter, known as Pearl Ware, was much used for table services. But it is in an unglazed stoneware, locally known as Egyptian Black, which Wedgwood refined, improved and called 'Black Basalte' that we really see how much he was influenced by a love of antiquity, and what a part the classical movement played in his work. In 1769, in partnership with Thomas Bentley, Wedgwood opened another famous pottery just outside Burslem (he called it 'Etruria') for making ornamental pieces and some domestic ware of great beauty and variety—urns, sculptured figures, *tazze* and so on. In addition to large pieces there were lesser ones, such as relief medallions made for those who could not afford to collect the real thing—the collecting of cabinets of medallions was a very fashionable pastime. In fact in the production of unglazed stoneware of all kinds, Wedgwood surpassed everyone else. There is his variegated ware; a cream base with surface streaking to represent marble, agate and granite. His terra cotta ware—cane, bamboo and chocolate coloured—frequently ornamented with

---

* Also known as the Frog Service, as it was to be used at the palace of La Gre-nouille near St Petersburg. So on the border of each piece a little green frog is painted.

reliefs of black. And a fine white 'semi-porcelain' stoneware, first used for the plinths of vases and later for smaller things such as cameos and medallions.

A further instance of Wedgwood's love of the antique was his reproduction of the Barberini Vase, brought to England by Sir William Hamilton and sold to that unfairly named 'convenient cypher' the third Duke of Portland* in 1786 (Mrs Delany says it was 1784). It took Wedgwood three years to reproduce what Sir Joshua Reynolds called 'a correct and faithful imitation' of what is today known as the 'Portland Vase' now in the British Museum,† repaired after being shattered by a madman.

Possibly the most successful and best known of all Wedgwood ware was, and still is, his jasper ware: a dense, hard stoneware

* His mother, *née* Lady Henrietta Cavendish Holles Harley, was Mrs Delany's great friend.
† A Wedgwood copy was sold at Christie's in 1964 for 2,900 guineas.

Candelabrum. Ormolu mounts by Matthew Boulton

first coloured throughout by metallic oxides and produced with relief ornaments, usually in white. Jasper ware insets for furniture were much used by Robert Adam, and Wedgwood employed artists, such as John Flaxman, James Tassie and other notable modellers to make the models for his relief designs. About 1780, 'jasper dip' was invented, a solution into which jasper ware was dipped so that only its surface was coloured. The colour range was extended; light and dark blue, sage and olive green, lavender, lilac, black and, very occasionally, yellow, were the colours used. In addition to the more usual things made in jasper dip, a host of little objects was produced—rings, etui cases, boxes, bell-pulls, door handles and even buttons. Chatelaines were sent off to Messrs Boulton and Watt to be set in ormolu or cut steel, as were bracelets and combs. Chess sets were made—Flaxman designed the first one ever made in jasper ware. The opposing sides were blue and white and the pieces represented contemporary actors playing Macbeth. Charles Kemble as Duncan and Mrs Siddons as Lady Macbeth were the royals. These sets were very popular and sold for five guineas. In 1964 one of them sold for £620.

Inevitably and naturally, since Wedgwood had created new kinds of pottery both in materials and design, a host of potters followed him. Leeds, for example, produced a perfectly plain cream coloured ware and was particularly successful with staggering dessert centre-pieces, some of which stood four foot high. Many potters produced jasper ware in quantity, and it is pleasant to note that even the great continental manufactories of Meissen and Sèvres bowed to Josiah Wedgwood and began producing jasper ware too! Yet all this beautiful and fine work could be afforded only by the well-to-do. For poorer people various potters turned out brightly coloured earthenware, and there was much gay and not too expensive rural pottery which pedlars took from door to door. The Woods, brothers and sons, produced many inexpensive coloured figures as well as the more usual domestic ware—although the name, Wood, is today remembered almost solely in connexion with the introduction of the Toby Jug, sometime in the 1760s. These rather grotesque jugs, representing all sorts of figures, found immediate favour as ornaments in farm houses and cottages. Other potters took to making them too, and the Toby Jug has continued to be popular ever since, and to be produced with steadily diminishing merit.

The rise of a flourishing porcelain and pottery industry in Georgian times was matched by a similar flourishing of the glass industry. With the discovery of flint (lead) glass by Ravenscroft in the previous century, glass had been given an hitherto unprecedented durability and clarity. Durability makes for economy, so glass, formerly a prerogative of the rich, was brought within the reach of the not so rich. By the beginning of the eighteenth century, good and relatively inexpensive glassware was being made for household use as well as for export. It is therefore not at all surprising to find 'glasses' listed in the effects of Widow Haward in 1729, although less than fifty years earlier it would have been unheard of. These glasses may have been flint glass or they may have been of soda glass—an utility glass for the use of poorer people and the more frugal type of housewife. We do not know, of course, what type of glasses they were—wine, ale, or sturdy goblet but, I feel, there is one thing of which we may be quite confident—these glasses were neither etched nor cut. Etched glass had been long known and was very expensive, but the cutting of glass in England was entirely new to the Georgians.*

It is said that in elegant Hanoverian circles—if Hanoverian Society was ever elegant which one rather doubts—cut glass was much used. Shortly after the accession of George I, German craftsmen began coming into England and sometime, perhaps around 1719–20, English cut glass tableware made its first appearance. Little is known about this English cut glass in the reign of George I, but we do know from an advertisement that 'Glass Shandeliers'[10] and George arrived on the scene almost simultaneously, though the chandeliers had a slight edge on George as the

---

* We had imported cut glass from Germany from *c.* 1709, to the great annoyance of the Glass Sellers Company. It was very expensive. But English lead glass proved ideal for cutting because it is easily worked and has a high refractive index. This is why eighteenth-century cut glass is superb.

advertisement, which seems to be the earliest notice we have of glass chandeliers, appeared in April 1714 and the king did not appear until September. These early chandeliers followed the plain brass or silver Palladian style, with bowl and 'S' shaped branches and were not cut. But, naturally, chandeliers followed current styles of interior decoration throughout the period. Branches were soon flat cut, smooth drops were faceted. The rococo style chandelier, elaborate and sparkling, had richly cut canopies in the Chinese taste, hung with innumerable drops cut in a variety of shapes. High points of branches and canopies were set with glass spires or wands, star topped; or with fleurs-de-lis. Rococo was followed by the Adam or neo-classical chandelier, where the old-fashioned globular or bowl centre gave way to an urn shape. Neo-classical austerity also stripped off many of the more fanciful trappings and substituted a brilliant cut, pear-shaped drop. Strung on wire and hung in swags from branch to branch and round the canopy, these multiplied to such an extent they soon obscured the design of stem and branches, so that the formerly ornamented stem became unimportant while arms or branches became quite plain.

The end of the era saw the fabulous chandeliers of the Brighton Pavilion. There were five in the Banqueting room alone (there still are). The vast central one which weighs nearly a ton and cost £5,613 9s. hangs from the claws of a silvered dragon. Below, six smaller dragons hold lotus flowers of tinted glass in their mouths, while cascades of brilliants fall down the vertical stem and hang in deep swags below the dragons. These dragons really did breathe fire, as the chandelier was designed for that very new method of lighting—gas. Hence in October 1818, slightly more than a century after the arrival of the first George and the first glass chandelier, that ageing Florizel, who shortly afterwards became the fourth George, met John Nash at the Pavilion to see these fantastic chandeliers lit up for the first time.

Chandeliers, and there are no more beautiful ones than those of the middle to end of the eighteenth century, were usually called 'lustres'. William Watkinson, a 'Chinaman' selling off his stock in trade in 1727, advertised 'all sorts of drinking Glasses, Sweet-Meat Glasses, Jelly Glasses, Salvers, Decanters and all other sorts of Glass Wares' as well as 'curious Cut Glass and Fire Lustres'.[11] Fire lustres were chandeliers; and a better name for them, too, as the beauty, the sparkle, the shimmering rainbow and jewel-like colours of the chandelier are now largely lost in the steady, un-wavering light of the electric bulb. The real glory and brilliance of a fire lustre can only be seen in the tenative, flickering flames of innumerable candles.

Cut glass fire lustres, girandoles with drops, decanters, and similar things were strictly for the rich. As was cut glass table-ware such as double cut jelly glasses with bell-shaped bowls and domed feet. These, when set on a glass salver or on tiered salvers, diminishing in circumference as they grew in height and topped, triumphantly, by a tall stemmed sweet-meat glass, made a pyramidal centre-piece much in vogue at dinner parties. Glass epergnes with little glass baskets were also greatly favoured. The less rich made do with more modest table ware; instead of fire lustres and girandoles they had perhaps a glass candlestick or two. These were a good deal easier to keep clean than were silver, pewter or brass, although they did require more careful handling. In even humbler, tallow-candle homes, there might be one or two glass float-wick lamps or glass taper lamps with a fixed central wick, or a peg lamp—a glass bulb with a neck designed to fit into a candle socket. These burned train oil and emitted more smell and smoke than light, as their wicks were fat and round. Not until 1780 was this overcome, when someone invented the flat ribbon wick. As for the desperately poor, if they had any light at all it came from the old rush-dip.

Although the rich used them, lamps really did not begin to oust wax candles until the Argand lamp with its air-burner was intro-duced late in the century. These lamps with ornamental hollow-ground glass globe tops, decoratively painted, burned spermaceti or colza seed oil. The Argand principle was retained for use in gas chandeliers and wall brackets, both of which came in during the reign of George IV.

Argand brass lamp, *circa* 1815–1830

Most small glass articles followed very closely similar articles made of china; just as china at first followed silver patterns (and sometimes the other way round) so scent bottles, smelling bottles, 'casting' bottles, toddy glasses, bowls, dishes, epergnes, ewers, flasks, ginger and honey jars, ladles, patch stands shaped like tiny *tazze*, medicine phials, tea and coffee pots, salt cellars, trays, urns, vases, toys and *verroterie*, were turned out in breakable profusion. Not all were of clear glass (and we should not have thought clear glass all that clear anyway), some were opaque, some painted, some enamelled or gilded—and gilded glass was at one time relatively inexpensive. White enamelled glass, known as 'white japanned glass' was in use from the late 1720s, and coloured enamels were used from about 1760. The brother and sister team of William and Mary Beilby (*fl.* 1762–8) who worked at

Newcastle—a great glass centre—are the most celebrated glass enamellers of the period. Beginning simply enough with designs of flowers and leaves in greyish enamel veined with a needle, they later and more ambitiously took to enamelling goblets, and decanters in colours, with armorial bearings, pastoral scenes, and the inevitable classical ruin. Beilby's best work is signed with his name and his mark. Appropriately enough, his mark is a butterfly.

Glass was also used, and by one man only, for the production of what can only be called for lack of a better name, *objets de vertu*. The producer of these objects was a Scot, James Tassie (1735–99), who once worked for Wedgwood. He began life as a stone mason, studied drawing and modelling, went to Ireland, learned about porcelain and glass, and came to London in 1767 to seek his fortune, as so many Scots did. Tassie had evolved, discovered, or invented a secret process known only to himself and his nephew, William, whereby he could make jewels, medallions and cameo portraits out of a certain kind of easily fusible, powdered glass. His reproductions of antique, engraved gems became enormously popular and were collected for their own sake as works of art, or were set by jewellers into rings and seals. He then turned to medallions and cameos and was so highly successful that by 1775, only nine years after his first appearance in London, he issued his first catalogue, which listed more than 3,000 items. His glass-paste gems were so beautiful and so novel that Catherine of Russia ordered a collection of them; his glass medallions and portraits became equally famous. These were usually entirely moulded of opaque white glass, or the relief was of glass-paste mounted on glass and framed like a miniature. Tassie seems to have produced some 500 portraits including those of such widely differing personalities as George III and Benjamin Franklin.*

Although the sixteenth-century alchemists' dream of making glass malleable had not come true, glass, limited only by its frangibility had become even in the early part of the century, a

---

* Tassie's work can be seen at the Victoria and Albert Museum and at the Scottish National Portrait Gallery.

very versatile material. On November 10th 1738, when the Prince and Princess of Wales—Frederick and Augusta—visited Bristol and made a Royal progress through that busy and thriving port, they were attended by the City Companies 'in their formalities, marching two by two' and 'preceding the Corporation and the royal Guests'.[12] Leading the grand procession was the Company of Glassmen, mounted and dressed in Holland linen. Some carried swords, others held crowns, still others sceptres, all glistened and sparkled wonderfully, for all these emblems of loyalty and royalty were made of glass.

Indeed the Georgian era until around 1780, witnessed the heyday of Bristol glass, a flourishing and inspired industry which had begun about the middle of the previous century by manufacturing bottles when bottles began to replace pottery for wine. Bristol changed the long necked, onion-bulb bottle to the cylindrical, shouldered bottle with a glass ring at the neck to strengthen it for stoppering. That these new, narrow bottles should stand firmly, the base was pushed very slightly upward, an excellent idea which unfortunately went too far and produced the prodigious 'kick-up' we know today—an odious device which makes a bottle appear to hold more than it does. But there was certainly a genie in the early Bristol bottle—or rather, there were geniuses among Bristol glass makers and Bristol soon branched out and became famous for its ornamental glass ware. It is not known when the extremely fragile, opaque, white glass decorated with enamel was first made at Bristol but during the second half of the Georgian era, candlesticks, tea-caddies, ornamental bottles, bodkin cases, all beautifully decorated with flowers and fruit, came from Bristol. The famous Bristol blue glass was used for a variety of things too, but fashionable women around 1760 found it bewitching for trinket cases, scent bottles, patch boxes and other small articles, particularly when decorated with chinoiserie enamel painting.

Near Bristol was Nailsea, and just about the time Bristol glass began to go into a decline a beverage maker, John Robert Lucas, began to manufacture brownish-green bottles for use in his then

more important beverage business—this was *c.* 1778. His bottle
business soon began to flourish as cider making was a great west
country industry and cider makers bought Lucas's bottles in
quantity. When war with France broke out in 1793, and higher
taxes were imposed which crippled the glass industry, Lucas
had the bright idea of legally evading the tax on glass by making
table and ornamental ware in his bottle glass. Bottle glass did not
attract tax. Here it should be noted that taxation was always
affecting industry. The only thing any industry had to do to be
stopped dead in its tracks by government taxation was to be
successful. The case is not much altered. Even earlier, after the
rebellion of 1745, an excise tax had been levied on glass (1746)
which amounted to 1*d* per pound by weight on the raw materials
used, and the raw materials of glass weigh heavy. This led to a
reduction in size and weight of all glass ware and seriously
interfered with the development of cutting. A thin wine glass

Wine glasses, *circa* 1725, 1760, 1770

cannot be cut but its thicker stem can, and this is how stem-cutting came about. As eighteenth-century wine glasses were generally held by the foot, ornamental stems—and the century is notable for this—were very important. But the new tax on glass was evaded in another way too. Glass makers bought up all the broken glass they could find. Broken glass was not a raw material so it escaped tax and could be re-melted and re-made.

But to return to clever Mr Lucas and his perfectly legal tax evasion: green bottle glass, roughly ornamented and flecked with white, was popular and profitable but required some skill, and there was a great deal of unused skill lying about Bristol. Each glass blower had his own collection of fantastic objects, clear or coloured by metallic oxides, blown by himself either to show his own skill or merely as an amusement. Glass blowers often made extra money on the side by selling these fancy objects to visitors. Lucas, who by now had a partner William Chance, realized that such highly skilled blowers could be used to produce purely ornamental glassware in really gay colours, for Bristol had always excelled at coloured glass. Thus, by putting skill, fantasy and colour together, Nailsea glass came into being. Red and white striated glass flasks and violet-blue ones decorated with white, to be used for toilet waters were among the first Nailsea glass products in the late eighteenth and early nineteenth centuries; so were curiously shaped, long-stemmed and quite useless tobacco pipes decorated with pink, blue and opaque white. By about 1810, glass walking sticks with coloured twists were being made, and glass bells with a ruby red body, clear clapper and opal handle topped with a blob of peacock blue, were being used to summon servants—although in fairness, it must be said that such bells had been made at Bristol as early as 1755. To ornament walls in the 1820s were dress swords, daggers, enormous coaching horns, all in glass; and 'watch' balls which reflected the whole room in miniature were hung from ceilings or in window niches. There was, too, the traditional glass rolling pin, which for years had been made of bottle glass and used as a salt container. These were hung in kitchen fire-places to keep the precious, tax-burdened

salt dry. But by Waterloo year glass rolling pins became ornamental as well as useful (they *were* used for pastry-making) and
in clear or striped glass were sold filled with tea, sugar, or comfits.
This was the high-grade packaging of the day. Soon such rolling
pins were inscribed with suitable mottos such as:

> This roller round it is for you
> If you'll be constant, I'll be true

and were just the sort of present sailors gave their wives and sweet-
hearts. They also took them abroad for their every-port women.
But, since the pins were hollow and were filled with water to
give them weight, many of them returned to England again
filled with untaxed gin.

These colourful glass trifles first made at Nailsea (later Nailsea
was made at Birmingham) were also produced at other places
such as Tyneside and Stourbridge, and glass had been made at
Stourbridge since the early seventeenth century. In Georgian
times Stourbridge gained a great reputation for hand-made and
domestic glassware—a reputation it has maintained ever since.
Yet in 1757 when a Mr Postlethwaite produced his *Dictionary
of Trade and Commerce* he notes simply that 'Stourbridge has been
much enriched by iron and glass houses; there is about half a
score of glass works near it where glass bottles and window-glass
are made'.

But in the furnaces, dog-houses and glory-holes* of Stourbridge, and in the many glass houses elsewhere in England, all
sorts of new things were being produced in glass. Glass salt
cellars came in *c.* 1724 and finger bowls around 1760. The bowls,
known as finger glasses or finger cups until the middle of the
nineteenth century, were a more elegant variation of the silver or
pewter bowl in which polite society had, for centuries, rinsed its
mouth after dinner. Wine-glass coolers—small bowls with one or
two lips—were introduced around 1750, and the sham dram,
much used by innkeepers because the thick bowl magnified

---

* A dog-house is a small annex to the main furnace; a glory-hole is a supplementary furnace used for elaborate work.

capacity, about 1775. The toddy lifter, a large pipette with a bulbous body (not unlike modern oven-glass basters) and gold-fish bowls were all new to the era. And throughout, shapes changed according to the dictates of fashion. Cutting, painting and enamelling developed and the British Plate Glass Man-factory, using the French method of casting plate glass, was established in 1773. Ten years later the famous Irish Waterford Glass Works was set up by John Hill, a glass maker of Stour-bridge; and the era just escaped, by a few years, the making of pressed glass which was first pioneered in the United States and introduced at Newcastle in 1833.

But if it is a long way from heavy green glass wine bottles to the British Plate Glass Company or to the fantasies of Nailsea; or from the plain glass candlestick to the fabulous chandeliers of the Brighton Pavilion, it is still a much longer way from making buttons to making steam-engines. This, however, is what the infant Matthew Boulton did when he grew up.

Buttons, though small, were used in enormous numbers in Georgian England, particularly by men who, buttoned or un-buttoned (for buttons were in many instances purely ornamental), rarely used less than five dozen of them on coat and waistcoat, to say nothing of the buttons used on their favourite hat, the tricorne. Buttons were also a status symbol. At the Birthday Ball given for Queen Caroline in March 1728/9, King George II wore blue velvet with diamond buttons and his hat was 'buttoned up with prodigious fine diamonds'.[13] The Prince of Wales, who had 'a great deal of spirit' and danced well, wore 'mouse-coloured velvet turned up with scarlet and very richly embroidered with silver'.[14] His buttons are not mentioned but among the jewels listed as belonging to his father are forty coat buttons, valued at £4,000—or £100 each; thirty-six waistcoat buttons, value £1,000 and six loops and buttons for sleeves.[15] Jewelled buttons were common for state wear if one were rich enough and many men were. For less stately occasions the really rich wore gold or silver buttons, and the loss of such a button, whether for show or use was a serious affair. Henry Purefoy lost one off his shirt in

August 1739 and had to send to his goldsmith, Mr John Chabbert in Holborn, to have another made to match 'exactly sized'.[16] And devotees of Smollett will remember that the glorious Captain Hawser Trunnion at his wedding wore 'his best coat of blue broad-cloth . . . trimmed with five dozen of brass buttons, large and small'.[17] So it was metal buttons for the not so rich and heaven knows what for the poor.

This class distinction in buttons might have continued had it not been for a minor accident which happened in 1743 in an attic workroom in Sycamore Street, Sheffield. Here Thomas Boulsover, a cutler, while engaged in repairing the silver haft of a knife, wedged it into his vice with a copper penny and then found that the heat he'd applied to make the repair had fused the copper to the silver—or so tradition has it.* Yet no matter how this new method of plating came about, it was certainly Thomas Boulsover's discovery. Other methods of plating, such as close-plating and French plating, where silver was applied by various methods to an already completed article, were now superseded by the entirely new and different method of Sheffield plating. First called copper-rolled plate or fused plate (and later Old Sheffield Plate), the secret lay in fusing a sheet of silver to a copper block in a furnace. Since silver has a lower melting point than copper, it became fluid just when the copper was softening. When cool the two metals united as one and, as both were ductile and malleable, the material could be rolled and worked as silver. Thus, articles could be made straight off from Sheffield plate, they didn't have to be made first of some other base metal and then laboriously plated afterwards.

Realizing, but only partially, the potentialities of this new material, Boulsover began to make buttons of it. Such buttons were very much cheaper than silver ones, yet they looked exactly like silver. So Sheffield plate, an English discovery of the Georgian period, began life as a button.

---

* The reader is warned that this old and pleasant story is given no credence by the Sheffield City Museum.

Silver candlesticks, *circa* 1780, 1770, 1785

It was Joseph Hancock who first saw the enormous possibilities of this new, compound material and in 1751 he set up his Copper Rolled Plate factory in Sheffield where he began producing candle sticks, table ware, jugs, coffee pots and other articles of the same design as sterling silver and at a fraction of the cost. There were naturally various snags to be overcome before perfection was reached. How were the copper edges to be hidden? At first they were either coated with a very hard solder, a tedious job, or were turned over to form a double edge. This second method gave strength where most needed and led to the development, *c.* 1768, of applying silver-plated wire to the edges. Next, what about the inside of articles like coffee pots, or the bottom of things like trays and salvers where the basic copper would show? Sometimes the exposed copper was coated with tin, sometimes two sheets of Sheffield plate were soldered back to back before rolling, so that each side would have a silver surface. This wearying process, which also made for great heaviness, went on until 1765 when someone had the bright idea of producing a single copper sheet plated on both sides. Engraving posed a problem too, so shields, bands or plates of very heavily plated copper were let into the article or soldered to its surface; then the family crest could be perfectly engraved with no tell-tale squiggles of copper to show that the article was not sterling. Next, there was piercing, so popular in silver work—pierced cake baskets, fish slices, cruet stands and coasters were very fashionable—but pierced Sheffield Plate would show its copper base. So in 1760 a clever punching machine was invented which dragged a thin skin of silver over the holes as they were being punched. This hid the raw edges of copper which otherwise would have been exposed. By such means Old Sheffield plate could, and did, rival silver.

In nearby Birmingham, which Edmund Burke called 'the Toy-Shop of Europe', a successful young manufacturer of 'artistic' metal-work, including silver and gold, decided that Sheffield Plate was a coming thing, went to Sheffield, mastered the technique, returned to Birmingham and began to produce Sheffield Plate at his works at Soho* in 1762. The young man was Matthew Boulton. He obtained a monopoly and swiftly became the largest single manufacturer of Sheffield plate, producing articles of an exceptionally high quality—buttons, snuff boxes, trinket holders and finally every article which had formerly been made in silver and some which had not. Much was exported to Europe and although the French tried to produce Sheffield Plate, nothing Europe produced could touch the quality of that produced in England.

Boulton continued in his large way—he was a remarkable man, a kind of Leonardo among industrialists—monopolizing output until around 1770, when others stepped into the field. But by this time Boulton had other fish to fry. He was making beautiful 'or-mulu . . . greatly admired by the nobility and gentry'.[18] Whether native and foreign nobility and gentry admired the oil paintings his factory produced by mechanical means is another

* Soho Hill, Handsworth Parish, was one of the show places of the area.

matter, but Messrs Boulton and Fothergill were as enterprising
as they were efficient. They employed 1,000 men and had
'availed themselves . . . of many ingenious contrivances'[19]
such as water mills, to save time and labour. In 1798 they were
the first to experiment with gas lighting for factory illumination.

The largest of all Boulton's fish—a positive whale—came
in 1772* when a Dr John Roebuck, unable to repay a loan of
£1,200, gave Boulton in lieu of payment the two-thirds share of
the interest he, Dr Roebuck, held in a patent. The patent was for
James Watt's steam engine. Three years later, in 1775, Boulton
and Watt entered into that famous partnership which put
England ahead of every manufacturing country in the world;
for as Boulton remarked with commendable candour to James
Boswell in 1776: 'I sell here, Sir, what all the world desires to
have—POWER.'[20] Boswell 'contemplated' Boulton as an '*iron
chieftain*' who was nevertheless 'a father to his tribe of work
people'. So only a baker's dozen years lay between Boulton's
buttons and his steam engine. Such a great oak from such a little
acorn in so short a time, illustrates the kind of Georgian initiative,
enterprise and industry which, in the next century, turned us
into the richest and most powerful nation in the world.

Not far from Boulton's factory was another where a Mr Henry
Clay was also busily engaged in turning out nearly everything
from buttons to coach panels in another new-to-the-century
material, papier-mâché.† 'To 11. Dozen Buttons Coat & Waistcoat, some Italian, some Clay's paper ones, all black at Baker's
(of Norwich) pd. 0. 9. 6',[21] Parson Woodforde notes in his
painstaking way. An earlier and more distinguished patron of
Clay's buttons was King George III, who when young had
delighted in 'turning and button making'. So when Mr Clay,

---

* The year Boulton began to fight for an Assay office for Birmingham and
Sheffield, as all gold or silver had to be sent to London or Chester to be assayed
and marked. The fight was won in 1773 and it is suggested that as most of the
Parliamentary business concerning the Assay Bill was transacted at the Crown
and Anchor Tavern, Strand, London, this gave Boulton the idea of choosing the
Crown mark for Sheffield and the Anchor for Birmingham.
† Papier-mâché, like porcelain, had long been known in the East.

after years of experiment, produced his new button the king said to him 'Send me several sets of buttons, for as I am called George the button-maker, I must give a lift to our trade'.[22]

It was in 1772 that Mr Clay patented his own process for making papier-mâché. This consisted of specially made sheets of paper, soaked in a strong size of glue and paste, stuck together, then pressed into the required moulds. It was then stove dried, hardened with an oil dip, and suitably decorated.*

A visitor to Birmingham in 1778 noted the work produced by Mr Clay was 'curious, ingenious and deserving of both praise and encouragement' and that his 'manufactory for japanning' turned out 'paper cases, stands, waiters, tea-boards, coach-pannels, &c. all of paper finely varnished and painted'.[23] In this same year, Mr Bailey, a member of the Society for Promoting Arts and Commerce, wrote a treatise on *The Utility of Work Houses*. The problem he sought to solve was how to provide diversified and gainful occupation for the poor lodged in work-houses. He lists a variety of things which, as they occupy little space and require 'only a very small stock of money and materials', are suitable for this purpose. The list is long and is chiefly concerned with things needed by weavers, lace, and glove makers, and with the making of straw and chip hats for women: most of the things formerly common to cottage industry. But among less common things, he suggests 'all sorts of wicker ware . . . matches and mops . . . door mats' and 'the making of *papier maché*' (his italics). I do not know if papier-mâché articles were produced in workhouses, but it is interesting to see how swiftly this new substance became popular, and how great the demand for it must have been. 'My buckles and box are in exquisite taste', says Mr Simkin Blunderhead preparing an assault upon the heart of Miss Toser, 'The one is of paper, the other of paste.'[24] Apart from its obviously ornamental uses, papier-mâché became almost the

---

* This made the strongest of papier-mâchés. Anyone interested can make a very bogus papier-mâché of shredded newspapers soaked first in water, squeezed out and re-soaked in a strong size. This can be moulded by hand or pressed into moulds, dried, painted and varnished. It is not durable but it is fun to do.

'plastic' of the age; there seemed little it could not do* and its popularity and purposes increased and multiplied as time went on; and as time went on it also became more elaborately decorated. Tea tables, work tables, chairs, desk-topped chess tables—scrolled, painted, gilded and, later still, inlaid with mother-of-pearl, were Regency and early Victorian favourites. Papier-mâché of the highest quality continued to be made until the 1850s and sixties when the two-hundred-year-old taste for japan ware declined.

Earlier and much less versatile than papier-mâché, although it could withstand both fire and water which papier-mâché could not, were flat articles made of japanned iron. These were known, to an inconsiderable extent, as early as the reign of George I. As iron had a smallpocked surface it had to be tinned before japanning, but the japan had a habit of peeling off with an almost gleeful facility. This problem was solved by two discoveries made almost simultaneously in the early 1730s. Edward Allgood, a Northamptonshire Quaker, discovered a heat-resistant, very hard, colourful varnish which when applied in successive layers, each layer separately stove-dried and hand polished, produced a wonderfully smooth surface for decoration. Then, at Pontypool in Monmouthshire, a method was discovered of dipping iron plate into tin so that the tin completely penetrated the iron.†

One of the executives of Hanbury's Pontypool Iron Works, where a small amount of tin-plate was also produced, was Allgood's son, also called Edward. This younger Edward, obviously a far-seeing man, realized the possibilities of bringing together tin-plate and his father's 'secret' varnish. So in 1736 he set up for himself at Trosnant, a suburb of Pontypool, and called his small

* I have heard that it was so hard, durable and cheap, it was once suggested it could be used for making wheels of railway carriages—but I have been unable to verify this.

† This was the beginning of the Welsh tin-plate industry and Pontypool became a generic name for this kind of ware made elsewhere. After Edward Allgood's death his sons quarrelled. Thomas remained at Pontypool but Edward number three and John removed to Usk. The making of Pontypool ware at Pontypool died out *c.* 1820. Usk lingered until about 1860. A fine collection of both can be seen in the National Museum of Wales.

manufactory 'The Pontypool Japan Works'. Since he employed only his brothers and their wives and children in japanning, his process remained a family secret, although 'Pontypool ware' was soon made elsewhere particularly in the Midlands. It, too, quickly became famous for its brilliance and its almost everlasting quality.

At first Allgood confined production to tea trays and waiters which were immediately successful because the japanning was so hard and so tough that boiling hot kettles and tea pots left no mark upon it. An outcome of this welcome advantage was the production of tea pots, coffee pots, coffee urns (with charcoal burners in their bases) and, since English porcelain at this date could not stand up to hot liquids, Pontypool hollow-ware became immensely successful too. Soon all sorts of things were being made of Pontypool ware for the domestic and the European market—tea cannisters, candlesticks, snuffers, toast racks, cheese-cradles, argyles, urn-shaped vases, cake baskets and many similar things, as well as small articles like patch and snuff boxes (often

Pontypool japanned iron teapot, *circa* 1810

these were of japanned copper). Pontypool followed the fashion in silver design and current fashions in china for its decoration. On black, tortoiseshell, dark blue, crimson, green, orange or yellow backgrounds were painted—as fashions dictated—flowers, linear designs, chinoiserie and large floral sprays and, at order, coats of arms. There was much gilding, and where applied decoration was required in the classical and neo-classical taste—paw feet on a tray, an acorn finial for the lid of a hot chestnut holder, lion and ring masks on an urn-shaped vase—they were made of lead or brass (sometimes of silver) and japanned.

When the Hon. John Byng visited Chepstow in 1781, he vastly admired the fine handsome women with their 'fair skins, long eyes and noses'. No face, in his opinion, could be beautiful without 'long eyes and a nose'—a rather baffling statement one feels, since most faces always have noses. He also greatly esteemed Pontypool ware and notes 'I bought a Pontypool snuff box, a beautiful and dear ware and much to be admired'.[25] Indeed, Pontypool ware was not cheap, a quite uncomplicated, oval tray could cost as much as fifteen guineas—a good price for something which was neither silver nor Sheffield plate.

But two other metals, both cheap enough, were introduced in the Georgian era. The earliest, discovered in 1732 by a London clockmaker, Christopher Pinchbeck the younger, still bears his name. The eponymous Pinchbeck, who also invented a patent candle snuffer, found that when brass, which is chiefly copper with a touch of zinc, contains about 15 per cent of the latter, it takes on a rich golden colour and is very easily worked. This made a good imitation gold and was much used for small things like jewellery and for mounting snuff and patch boxes. Curiously enough 'pinchbeck' does not seem to have become a word of derogation until the nineteenth century. Perhaps Thomas Carlyle is responsible for this, when, writing in the time of William IV, he refers to the eighteenth-century charlatan, Count Cagliostro, as 'a pinchbeck counterfeit of all that is golden'.[26]

But if pinchbeck was mock gold, there were those who were intent on discovering mock silver and this was found at last around 1770. Called by its earliest producers in Sheffield 'White Metal', the best quality was made of nine parts tin to one part antimony and was of a silvery white colour with a blueish tinge. An even cheaper quality containing a minute amount of copper had a faint yellowish cast. This White Metal, known from around 1797 as Britannia Metal was also an English invention, and it competed with both Sheffield plate and pewter.

Pewter in this century certainly went into a decline, due to various things; the smugness of the Pewterers' company, the addition of too much lead to pewter, the great growth of the pottery and glass industries were all contributing factors. By comparison with the new, bright-burnished Britannia Metal, pewter was dull, uninteresting and expensive. Good sadware and hollow-ware were still to be found, polished and shining brightly in farmhouses throughout the country. But this farmhouse pewter had probably been handed down from generation to generation and was therefore the high quality, beautiful pewter produced in the previous century. It was also still much used—bright and old or new and dull—in inns and taverns, as it still is. It was to be found also in the kitchens of the rich, chiefly in the shape of those highly complicated and intricate moulds with many detachable parts with which the Georgians created the monumental jellies which served as centre and conversation pieces at sophisticated dinner parties. Such was the 'centre dish' which so astonished and pleased the guests of the Norfolk Squire Custance and his wife, it being 'a very pretty Pyramid of Jelly . . . a Landscape appearing through the jelly, a new Device and brought from London'.[27] But even here, Britannia Metal ousted pewter and it is probable this 'new Device' from London was made of this equally new metal.

Britannia Metal also took over at tea tables of those who could not afford Sheffield plate, even though Sheffield was one-third the price of silver. In truth, even those who could afford silver or Sheffield plate liked the new metal so well that they bought it as an addition to the plate they already had, for the Georgians were very keen on polished metals of all sorts, and metals had improved wonderfully. Sir Walter Scott had a tea service of Britannia Metal, and probably every house, rich or poor, had Britannia Metal spoons, as a flood of cheap spoons was produced. These replaced silver spoons for non-special occasions in grand houses, and tin spoons in poorer homes. So, metaphorically speaking, babies in the Georgian era could be born with one of a variety of metal spoons in their mouths—silver, Sheffield, Britannia Metal, pewter or tin. It is to be feared that the vast majority of infants were born into the tin-spoon category.

This love for polished metal led to a much greater use of burnished steel for grates and fireplace furniture. Probably the most beautiful of all are those of the Adam period when fire baskets with a pierced apron, pierced fenders and fire shovels were common. The anthemion motif in piercing was very popular and often the relief carvings of a carved pine or Coade stone mantelpiece match the piercing of apron and fender. But burnished steel

Polished steel grate, *circa* 1780

in the home had to be kept burnished and to this end the first
duty of the housemaid upon her crack-of-dawn rising was to rub
the fireplace furniture first 'with Oil, then with Emery, till clear
and bright, and next with Scouring Paper'.[28] This tedious daily
task had to be carried out on hearths and 'chimney sides' too, if
they were of polished steel. In summer some people had poker,
tongs, and shovel rubbed thickly with mutton fat or goose grease,
wrapped in paper and laid by until winter. Mr Byng complains
bitterly of this practice in late May 1791 when dining at a friend's
house. It was abysmally cold even for May, and he found that
'the grates were burnished up, the tongs and poker laid up for the
summer and the windows open'.[29] Dinner was very late. The
conversation like the wine was 'poor and sour'. Altogether it was
an unpropitious prelude to his forthcoming tour into Lincolnshire. For each year the Hon. John toured some part of England
and kept, as so many people—tourists or stay-at-homes—a
voluminous journal of daily events.

The Georgian era is so cram-full of journals, diaries, letters
that one forgets, sometimes, that everything was written by hand.
Millions of quills plucked from geese, swans, peacocks, crows and
turkeys; ton upon ton of paper, positive Atlantics of ink must have
gone into the personal records kept by our Georgian ancestors.
How did they find the time, the energy, the patience?—particularly as the point of a quill pen had to be resharpened or cut with a
penknife each time it was used.

It was after sharpening a quill for a friend that Lord Clive of
Plassey went quietly into an adjoining room and slit his throat
with the same penknife. And history unhappily repeated itself
in 1822 when Lord Londonderry, better known to us as Viscount
Castlereagh, did the same thing. But there were some metal
pens too. Dr Johnson (and doubtless others) had an exact replica
of a quill pen in silver given him by David Garrick, but it does
not look to have been much used.* That 'atheist' as Parson
Woodforde calls one of the most brilliant men of his time, Dr

* It can be seen at Dr Johnson's birth-place at Lichfield.

Joseph Priestley, was driven nearly demented by quill pens. But as early as 1780 a split-ring manufacturer in Birmingham, one S. Harrison, produced a metallic pen. It was too hard and difficult to use and it was not until after much experimenting by various people that in 1809 Joseph Bramah (1748–1814) eased the burden by patenting a machine for cutting goose feathers into three or four nibs to be used with a separate penholder.* This, however, was of no service to Dr Priestley who had died the year before in Northumberland, Pennsylvania, whither he had gone in 1794 in search of greater freedom for his political and religious opinions. Even James Watt in retirement turned his attention from steam engines to the pen-nib and attempted to improve it by gilding in 1818. But it was not until the year of George IV's death that Perry and Mason, of Birmingham, patented a machine for producing steel nibs of such flexibility that they could compete with quill nibs.

So the steel pen-nib was born in Birmingham in the very last year of the Georgian era. Like the button it is a very little thing of very great importance.

* A very inferior fountain pen was known and is described in Chambers's *Cyclopaedia* (1738). The parent of the modern fountain pen was invented by an Englishman, John Joseph Parker, in 1832.

CHAPTER FIVE

Of Food, Farming, and Famine

The 'Depraved Taste in Food', according to Robert Campbell, was not confined to the palates of the *ton*; it had become 'epidemical'. The poor no less than the rich observed 'A Regimen of Diet calculated not to supply the Wants of Nature, but to oppress her Faculties, disturb her Operations, and load her with, 'till now, unheard of Maladies'.[1] In short, we were as intent as ever on digging our graves with our deplorable teeth.

The reason Robert was in such a pet was that by the middle of George II's reign the fashion for French cuisine had reached what he felt to be unprecedented depths. Alas, how sadly things had changed since the time of Queen Elizabeth! Then, 'Roast beef was the Englishman's food'; English cookery was neither 'a Science or a Mistery' and 'required no Conjuration to please the Palates of our Greatest Men'. Cookery in those good old days had been 'as plain and simple as our manners'. This statement leads us to suspect that Robert either knew nothing about Elizabethan cooks or manners, or was deliberately suppressing evidence which might have weakened his case against 'Meats and Drinks dressed after the French fashion'—a mode which meant 'the natural taste of flesh and fish' had become nauseous 'to the fashionable stomach'.[2]

Nothing, it seemed, appeared in its 'native Properties'. Everything was disguised by sauces, relishes and goodness knew what other foreign nonsense. Fish, for example, when dealt with by a *French* cook, no longer resembled fish in taste, smell or look 'it and everything else is dressed in Masquerade, seasoned with slow

Poisons, and every dish [is] pregnant with . . . the Seeds of Diseases both Chronic and Acute'.[3]

This is hardly fair comment. Most fish, even when not tarted up by a French recipe, could not have tasted, smelled or looked very much like fish; at any rate not by the time it reached inland areas in warm weather. Quite beyond the aid of disguise, foreign or native, was that received by Henry Purefoy one spring day. It came from 'Mr James ffisher a ffishmonger' of Newgate market, London, and after several days on the road it understandably 'stank and could not be eat'.[4] A barrel of oysters—they cost from three shillings to three and sixpence in those days—was no better. Seasoned with a quick and natural poison, it arrived, one half 'as black as ink' and 'the other half . , . poisoned with the stench'.[5] Henry, sensibly, did not eat them.

Less fortunate was Mr Henry Carrington of Worsborough, who, dining with his friend Mr Hawksworth of Barnsley, Yorks, and 'eating of a barrell of oysters' fell into 'a fit of the stone and stranguary' complicated by a great 'feaver'.[6] He died a fortnight later. As this happened in February, the oysters were probably

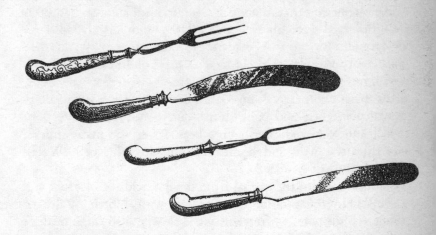

Knives and forks, with three and two prongs; ivory and silver handles, *circa* 1770

fresh enough but the fever suggests typhoid—oysters were notable typhoid carriers.

Even in London fish was often so dear and so stale that during the 1740s a certain Mr Blake proposed to set up a new market for fish at Broadway (Westminster) and supply it with fresh fish by a system of specially designed and very speedy land carriages. His ostensible reason for the market and speedy carriages was to break the ring of fishmongers. They had speedy carriages too, but were thought to be given to the horrid practice of resale price maintenance . . . even of stale fish! Blake received the enthusiastic support of the *Society of Arts and Commerce* and, later, of the Government. Prematurely grateful, the Society presented him with a gold medal inscribed 'Fish Monopoly Restrained'. This, unhappily, was untrue. The scheme failed. It appears to have benefited no one but its originator. He, rumour ran, appropriated the funds.

Blake may or may not have been a scoundrel but, as fish could neither walk nor be driven to market, his idea underlines the very real and increasing difficulty of supplying food, rapidly and in sufficient quantity, to early Georgian cities and towns.* The nub of the matter was that in previous centuries urban areas had been so small they were able to live off the immediately adjacent countryside. But now they were expanding so rapidly this was no longer possible. Although most of London's meat came regularly from remote districts, it came perforce on the hoof. It was fresh upon arrival, no matter how rancid it became afterwards in markets and cook-shops, but it must also have been tough and exhausted after having been driven too many miles a day from the wild and beautiful mountains of North Wales, Cumberland and Scotland.

Poultry came to the capital from the flat fields of Norfolk and Suffolk. No great distance compared with North Wales or Scotland; but poultry, frequently and slowly, also came on foot —webbed or otherwise. Poultry had become more of a status

* In later Georgian times canals, improved roads and transport partially solved this problem which was only really solved by the advent of the railways.

symbol than ever, so great numbers of hens, hitherto fed on free range or in runs, were fattened in coops by a vile method better described by Dr Tobias Smollett in *Humphry Clinker* than here. The coop system was new and was to the Georgians rather what the battery broiler system is to us. It is very probable that other kinds of fowl were fattened in the same way; chickens, geese, ducks and turkeys in prodigious number appear constantly as adjuncts to the vast meals eaten by the rich and the middling sort. The poor (pace Robert Campbell) probably never tasted poultry of any kind and, during the reigns of the last two Georges, they were lucky if they got a taste of bacon once a week and a bit of beef at Christmas.

We do not know from what remote corners of England Thomas Rundle, a notable cleric and a member of the *Society for Promoting Primitive Christianity*,* obtained supplies for the anything but primitive dinners he so often gave to those who could promote his career in the church. But wherever the food came from he went on to become a very rich Bishop of Derry. Unlike Robert Campbell, he did not believe that roast beef was the Englishman's food. He called 'a sir-loin of beef clumsy plenty'[7] or so a disgruntled brother clergyman notes in 1740. 'Bishop Rundle' the diarist says with, one feels, just a touch of malice and envy 'is famous for candyed carrots, pea-capons, peeper pye i.e. young new hatched turkeys put into a pye, taken out by spoonfulls' and 'Veal burrs† stuffed with ropes of 50 wood-cocks'. This does not sound as if the Bishop employed a French cook, but it is perhaps just a thought on the side of 'Depraved Taste'. Nevertheless, 'by this means he treated himself into £4,000 p.a̅n̅n̅.'[8]

If fish, flesh and fowl came from a distance, London and other

---

* Founded by William Whiston, 1715, Newton's successor as Lucasian professor of Mathematics at Cambridge. Whiston confirmed the story of Genesis on Newtonian grounds; believed the Tartars to be the lost Tribes; wrote much on mathematics and religion. His translation of Josephus, 1737, became the standard version.

† Burrs are sweetbreads; ropes are, strictly, intestines, but here it probably means liver, heart and gizzard.

big towns still drew vegetables and fruit from productive green belts of market-gardens surrounding them. Londoners rich enough to pay for the best vegetables and fruit did so at Covent Garden. Others bought from barrows in the streets. Foreigners, always unimpressed by our vegetables and what we did to them, found that 'Cabbage, radishes and spinnage' which grew about London were so impregnated with 'the smoke of sea-coal which fills the atmosphere' that 'they had a very disagreeable taste'.[9] Only asparagus was exempt. Fortunately it was so cheap and plentiful it was even used in stews.

Milk, when it came from nearby farms, was not too bad, although it must have been nearly always sour in summer but when it came from town cows it was an appallingly dangerous food. Town cows were kept in such dark, overcrowded, filthy conditions that their byres outrivalled the habitations of the poor. Milkmaids carrying open cans of milk on their heads vended it

Milk woman. Mid-eighteenth century

from door to door. The open cans protected their heads from the too frequent deluge of slops thrown out of windows. And, often, straight from stables which would have overtaxed the ingenuity of Hercules, cows were driven and milk sold directly from the source. This must have been useful, particularly to those who preferred that perennial favourite 'a fine syllabub from the cow'[10] rather than one made with artificially warmed milk. 'We have had . . . a syllabub under the cow'[11] Horace Walpole writes gleefully from Strawberry Hill, and an under-the-cow syllabub must have guaranteed fresh and unwatered milk—which country milk often was not. But whether supplied by cow or milkmaid, all milk, since it is the most easily contaminated of all foodstuffs, must have been a superb breeding ground for T.B. and coliform bacilli. But, of course, no one knew this.

London's best butter, which came by sea from East Anglia and Yorkshire, sold for an average of ninepence a pound. Cheaper butter sold for less, simply because it was rancid. 'A tallowy rancid mass . . . manufactured with candle grease and kitchen stuff'[12] is the way Matthew Bramble describes London butter to Dr Lewis. In country districts such horrors were not so evident. On the best farms and in dairies attached to manor houses growing attention was being paid to the cleanliness of the cows, the dairy, the dairy-maid and the utensils used for making cream, butter and cheese.

Cheese, bread and tea were by mid-Georgian times the staple diet of the poor—especially in southern England—just as 200 years before, beef, bread and beer had been. Cheese bulks largely if in insufficient amounts in the diet of the inhabitants of parish workhouses and in the domestic accounts of labourers so painstakingly gathered by Sir Frederic Eden. But cheese was a classless food, and if it was often the sole, inadequate source of protein for the poor, it was also a tasty addition to the high animal-protein diet of the rich. So many of the rich were by now city dwellers that cheese, formerly a local product locally known, quite literally went to town and was sold for the first time in its history by the name of its place of origin. By the end of the eighteenth century cheeses had a brand name—Cheshire, Gloucester, Wilt-shire, Cheddar, Stilton and so on—and cheese making, tradition-ally the duty of the farmer's wife, became a profitable sideline of farming. It is claimed, how rightly I cannot say, that one of our most famous cheeses was invented by a woman at the beginning of the eighteenth century. She was a Mrs Paulet of Wymondham, near Melton in Leicestershire, but as this cheese was first sold at a public house at Stilton (Huntingdonshire) it became known as Stilton. Women continued to be the cheese producers of England until the factories took over, but one wonders how so much cheese was produced when a really good country cow yielded only four gallons of milk a day;* or how much profit can have been made on milk at a penny a quart, or on cheese at 4*d* the pound.

Yet, despite difficulties of supply and the inferior quality of much food, the Georgians, or rather the richer ones, went in for the enormous meals which two centuries of prosperity and

* A good cow today yields eight or nine gallons.

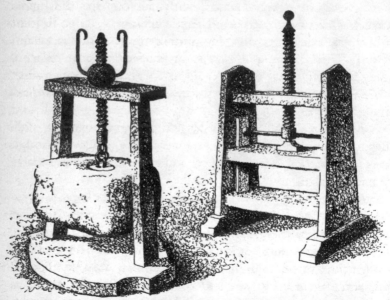

Stone cheese press, early eighteenth century. Screw-type cheese press, mid-eighteenth century

gluttony had made habitual. So habitual, so much a part of life, that when Mary Stukeley died in 1748, her sorrowing father had this affecting verse inscribed on her grave stone:

> Life is a journey of a winter's day,
> Where many breakfast and then pass away.
> Some few stay dinner, and depart full fed,
> Fewer that sup before they go to bed.

There is more, but it is kinder to leave it at that. Life is but a day was a well worn cliché even then; but a day seen only in terms of eating seems typical of one aspect of the Georgian era.

Nevertheless, certain refinements—perhaps changes is the better word—took place in meals, mealtimes, and in table manners. It was still customary to serve two courses, each course consisting of from three to nine meat dishes and an equal number of side dishes. It was still usual for women to do the carving, but now there were carving schools where they were taught this useful art. If no school were handy books, complete with diagrams, gave instructions on how to cope with the ordinary 20 to 30 lb joint of beef, the side of mutton, the quarter of veal, the giant ham. Women were also taught how to unbrace a mallard; unlace a coney; cut up a turkey, a bustard, a capon; how to rear a goose; thigh a woodcock, a curlew, a plover, a snipe; or to wing a quail or partridge. Pheasants were allayed, herns dismembered, and swans lifted with the greatest aplomb. Strangely enough, such quaint, old-fashioned carving terms were still in use, even though new-fangled 'Promiscuous seating'[13] began to creep in shortly after mid-century.

Promiscuous seating was as yet favoured only by the ultra-smart rich who, as all decent and envious people knew, were as low on the moral scale as they were high in the social or economic one. And promiscuous seating meant nothing less than men and women sitting next to each other, alternately, at table! For all that, strict precedence was still observed and guests were, as always, served in order of rank. Even with this safeguard who could tell to what depths of depravity the mixing of men and women at table might not lead? Far, far better to stick to the usual custom—and most did—where the women filed into the dining room in a crocodile, highest ranking lady first, hostess last, followed by a string of gentlemen also according to rank. Then, at the side of the table, the hostess took her place with the female guests, observing the same order of degree, to right and left; on the other side sat the host similarly surrounded. And even when promiscuous seating *was* indulged in, this old order of precedence was followed—no gentleman would have dreamt of offering a lady his arm.

It is odd, in an age which glorified good taste in other spheres, that prolific writer, the Rev. Dr John Trusler, who was so rude about William Blake's illustrations for one of his books, should find it necessary to advise young people just what constituted good table manners. Perhaps his book on the subject was designed for those who had not been born or bred into good taste, but were now economically in a position to achieve and even, perhaps, enjoy it. Those who wished to shed the 'characteristics of the vulgar' had to learn that it was bad manners to put one's nose in one's plate, to eat too quickly or too slowly; while 'to smell the meat on your fork before putting it into your mouth'[14] was anathema. It was also simply not done to scratch, spit, or blow the nose at table; if the latter were unavoidable the head must be turned away. Nor must the neophyte sit too far from the board, lean his elbows upon it, or pick his teeth *before* the dishes were removed. If, unhappily, the learner had to leave 'from any necessity of nature',[15] it was good taste to steal from the room and re-enter it as unobtrusively as possible. Gentlemen, in particular, were warned not to 'advertise' where they had been, either by adjusting their dress or replacing their watches as they returned. Further, and rather surprisingly, young women were told that eating a great deal 'is now deemed indelicate in a lady, for her character should be rather divine than sensual'.[16] The silly affection of the delicate appetite for the Romantic Movement lady of 'sensibility' was already creeping in along with promiscuous seating.

The time of dinner also changed considerably during the era. Richard Steele, who died in 1729, noted that during his own lifetime the dinner hour had moved slowly from midday to three o'clock. By 1740 the fashionable hour was four; and by 1780 any time between three and five appears to have been usual. Probably five was more fashionable because by the 1790s some were dining as late as seven o'clock. Horace Walpole, writing in 1789, says 'I am so antiquated as still to dine at four when I can, though frequently prevented as many are so good as to call on me at that hour because it is too soon for them to go home and dress so early in the morning'.[17]

'Dinner', says the young François de la Rochefoucauld in 1784, 'is the most wearisome of English experience, lasting as it does from four to five hours. The first two are spent in eating and you are compelled to exercise your stomach to the full to please your host'.[18] Little did François know that it had once been quite usual for us to linger seven hours over dinner. Added cause for dismay was that the dishes, to him, seemed to consist chiefly of boiled or roast meats, and, although the courses were much the same as in France, rarely did one see a ragout, while 'the use of sauce is unknown'.[19] Possibly the English interpretation of French food was unrecognizable to a Frenchman; certainly there were those in England, even at this date, who also disapproved of it. Parson Woodforde, a notable trencherman, for one: dining with Mr Townshend at Honingham in 1783, he tells us that there were two courses of nine dishes each 'but most of the things spoiled by being so frenchified in dressing'.[20]

On the other hand cookery books of the whole era presented many French recipes—and certainly there were 'ragoos' aplenty. 'The Turks', says Lady Mary Wortley Montagu as early as 1717, 'have at least as great a variety of ragouts as we have.'[21] But whether a ragout of cucumbers and onions, of asparagus, of peas or even of 'hogs feet and ears'[22] would have pleased a visiting Frenchman's palate is open to question. The same probably applies to sauces. But then it has always been very French, even among the English, to shudder at the mere thought of an English sauce.

Yet we did make and use sauces and in greater variety than ever before. In the most popular and best selling 'receipt' book of the time there are more than thirty recipes for sauces alone, including a time-saver for fish. Once made, this sauce kept a whole year. It contained twenty-four anchovies chopped, bones and all, shallots, horse-radish, lemon, spices, a quart of white wine and a pint of water. Two 'spoon fulls' with a pound of melted butter made an excellent fish sauce, and the mixture also had the dubious advantage of being 'a pretty sauce for boiled fowl, veal &c'. By 'lowering it with water' and thickening it with butter rolled in flour it could 'serve in the room of gravy'[23] as well. This particular sauce is specifically recommended to the attention of 'Captains of Ships', but one must remember that in those days passengers, too, had to provide their own food on a sea voyage. Still, this obviously all-purpose and long lasting sauce which would have disguised the taste of anything was probably just as popular with stay-at-homes. It may well be the condiment which caused Voltaire to remark 'the English have a hundred religions but only one sauce'.

A singular sauce and a deficiency of ragouts may have astonished the French, but what happened 'after the sweets' astounded them. 'Water in small bowls of very clean glass' made its appearance in order that mouths might be rinsed. This habit struck the nineteen-year-old de la Rochefoucauld as 'very unfortunate'. It was true 'the more fashionable folk' did not rinse, they had a good wash instead, so the water became 'dirty and quite disgusting'.[24] This suggests that fingers were used quite as frequently as forks. After this clean up, the cloth was removed, wine brought in, the ladies took one glass and left the room to the gentlemen who settled down to drink and talk. Conversation was very free: 'everyone expresses his political opinions with much frankness', something foreigners could certainly do in their own countries if prepared to risk exile or gaol. Often freedom became licence and then conversation ran upon 'highly indecent topics' and things were mentioned 'which would be in the grossest taste in France'.[25] Nor did the young visitor approve of the chamber-pots concealed in the sideboard. In view of all these barbarisms it might well be thought that this hapless visitor, either through ignorance or misfortune, was dining with the vulgar, whose manners were so deplored by the Rev. Dr Trusler. Not a bit of it. He was, in fact, the guest of the Duke of Grafton at Euston in Norfolk.

When the symposium finished at about half past eight, the gentlemen joined the ladies for tea, coffee, cakes, conversation, cards and music. By ten or eleven o'clock the whole party was more than ready for supper. On ordinary days and *en famille*, this was a simple collation of cold meats, fruit and wine. But when guests were present splendid hot dishes were added plus 'pretty little side dishes'[26] like goose pie; or 'genteel' ones such as 'boiled soals' plus a sweet. This, perhaps in the shape of a hedgehog made from cream, eggs, sugar, orange-flower water, canary and hartshorn, was moulded and stuck with almond quills. With its currant eyes it made a good 'middle dish' for suppers and could be further elaborated by means of other fanciful moulds into a really

Sheffield plate, tea urn, *circa* 1795. Silver jug, *circa* 1775

'grand desert'. So, all told, the dinner guest partook of two very large meals separated by a small one in the space of from six to eight hours.

Overeating at night was offset by not much for breakfast. During nearly the whole of the century breakfast was a light meal of bread, or toast and butter with tea, coffee or chocolate. It took place, commonly, at ten o'clock* and ended around eleven, although it could go on until one if friends dropped in, as they often did. By the first years of the nineteenth century, breakfast began to improve. The hour became earlier and good solid food such as meat, fish, and eggs were introduced. Back in 1726 when the Rev. Dr Stukeley called upon Sir Isaac Newton, he found the great man breakfasting on 'orange peel boiled in water . . . & bread and butter'.[27] The orange peel drink was a fad of Newton, he believed it 'dissolved Flegm'. But in 1816 when Messrs Foster, Escot, Jenkinson and the Rev. Dr Gaster stopped for breakfast at a coaching inn, they were given 'not only . . . the ordinary comforts of tea, and toast but . . . a delicious supply of new-laid eggs, and a magnificent round of beef'.[28]

As the gap between an earlier breakfast and a later dinner grew, it became necessary to fill this and the one in the stomach with a little snack. This snack became luncheon, first favoured by women who 'sit down to a substantial lunch about three or four'.[29] Maria Edgeworth certainly ate a most substantial one in July 1823 when she and two of her many half-sisters stopped at Moulinan while visiting Sir Walter Scott. The first course, cold, consisted of 'two roast chickens, better never were; a ham, finer never seen even at my mother's luncheons; pickled salmon, and a cold boiled round'.[30] The second, a hot course, provided river trout, potatoes, fresh greens, toast, poached eggs, and to finish, a 'custard pudding, a goose berry tart and plenty of Highland cream'. This luncheon cost six shillings.†

---

* Country people, farmers, apprentices, etc., breakfasted much earlier.

† Miss Edgeworth's brother William, may also have been with the party which would reduce the price to 1/6 per person.

Six shillings seems little enough for such a feast but six shillings, at that point in our history, would have kept a rural labourer and his family on an insufficiency of bread for a week. On a weekly wage of 8s to 12s—roughly £20 to £30 pound a year—his annual expenses for himself, wife and three children were estimated at £28. Of this £20 was spent on food. Wages had risen about 2s per week since the time of George I but the price of bread had trebled.

Almost exactly 100 years before Maria Edgeworth's sustaining luncheon at Moulinan, Daniel Defoe on a tour of Wiltshire wrote that it was 'exceedingly prosperous' and 'provisions of all sorts are very cheap, the quantity very great, and a great deal of over plus sent to London every day'. This rural area was then 'one of the most important counties in England . . . that is . . . to the publick wealth of the kingdom. The bare product in itself is prodigious great; the downs are an inexhausted store-house of wooll, and of corn, and the valley or low part of it is the like for cheese and bacon'.[31]

In 1821, a year after the accession of George IV, William Cobbett was also in Wiltshire, 'a horrible county', and on November 7th notes that he had never seen 'human wretched-ness' to equal that found at Cricklade 'no, not even amongst the free negroes in America'.[32]

Midway between Defoe and Cobbett we have the comments of the Hon John Byng who, in 1788, writes: 'How wretched do the miseries of the cottagers appear, want of food, want of fuel, want of clothing! Children perishing of an ague! and an unhappy mother unable to attend to or relieve their wants, or assuage their pains . . . whilst the worn-down melancholy father . . . pinch'd by cold and pining with despair, returns at evening close, to a hut devoid of comfort, or the smallest renovation of hope.'[33] Already the accelerated rate of enclosures and the new impetus in industry were, for good and for ill, doing their work. England was rapidly becoming what Disraeli was, later, to call 'the Two Nations'.

Yet enclosures were an economic necessity and the miscalled

industrial revolution was inevitable, simply because men are inventive animals. The first real step in the mechanization of agriculture came about because Jethro Tull (1674–1741) a musical gentleman-farmer whose hobby was playing the organ, saw that the tongue in the organ mechanism could be adapted to make the first really workable seed-drill—this was in 1701. In 1733 Tull wrote a book, *Horse-Hoeing Husbandry*, in which he explained the drill and also his own new method of pulverizing the soil with a horse-drawn hoe. He was so convinced his inventions, his methods, would save waste and time and increase crop yields that he called his own Berkshire farm 'Prosperous'.

In the year Tull's book was published, John Kay invented the fly or spring shuttle. This meant one man instead of two could now weave the broadest cloth. It meant increased production and increased prosperity. By 1753 it also meant rioting and the burning of Kay's home at Bury, Lancashire, as a protest. Increased production had certainly meant increased prosperity, but not for the weavers, nor for Kay. He died in poverty in 1764. Weaving had been speeded up by the new shuttle but not enough yarn could be spun to supply the looms.*

Had Tull stuck to the hand-hoe; and Kay been content with the traditional shuttle; had Charles, 2nd Viscount Townshend, remained in politics and Richard Arkwright stayed barber; had Robert Bakewell and 'Coke of Norfolk' never improved strains of sheep, cattle, horses, pigs; had James Hargreaves and Samuel Crompton not perfected the jenny and the mule, doubtless England would have continued to look like Defoe's England. But only for a bit. Stasis is apparent, it is never real, and time is a synonym for change. Even Defoe with his vivid, and for us, nostalgic picture of a still largely rural England, notes with pleasure and pride the growth of cities and the increase in trade, as well as the flourishing state of agriculture.

Undoubtedly, the first half of the eighteenth century was a

* This was overcome in 1775 by Arkwright's invention whereby the whole process of spinning yarn was performed by one machine. This led to even worse rioting.

more prosperous time for the labouring classes than the last half of the previous century had been. But it is a mistake to think of it as a golden age save for those who already had gold. As early as 1688 Gregory King had calculated, how accurately we do not know, that more than half the population was 'decreasing the wealth of the kingdom'. Out of an estimated five and a half million people, 2,795,000 were living below the subsistence level and, unable to earn enough to keep themselves, were dependent upon Poor Relief and other charities for a regular part of their livelihood. King called these 'the unprofitable majority'. The eighteenth century called them 'the labouring poor'. In addition, there were some 150,000 very small farming families with an average income of £44 and an annual expenditure of £42. These farmers were often less well off than rural labourers because they bore the risks and had no capital to tide them over bad years or to use on land improvement, even had they known how to improve. But at least they had land, and this meant they could make their own cheese, eat their own bacon, kill the occasional ancient hen. They did not contribute to the national wealth, they were not well fed, but they were not starving.

Similarly, in unenclosed parishes, cottagers, husbandmen and labourers who held various rights in the common land had the possibility of grazing a cow on the waste where the squatters built their terrible hovels. They could gather wood and furze for fuel, while a poached pigeon or partridge added to their diet, as did a garden. Wives and children could earn a bit extra at harvest time, or by weeding in the fields, or by setting beans. If the village had an industry or was near one, the family could earn by making gloves, knitting stockings or spinning yarn. Life was harsh and bitter, but there were opportunities—albeit very limited ones—for a small farmer or cottager to improve his lot occasionally. These opportunities, meagre though they were, petered out and died—along with hope—with the speeding up of the rate of enclosure after the accession of George III.

Many of these little and humble people were dispossessed by great landowners; others by rich merchants who wanted to turn

Seed drill, *circa* 1730. Jethro Tull

themselves into country gentlemen. Both kinds of landowner were usually enormously interested in farming. They turned waste into productive soil, drained marshes, enriched sandy soil with marl, followed the new, four-crop rotation system, and overwintered cattle on roots so that for the first time in our history fresh meat was available all the year round. They could afford to pay 1,000 guineas for the let of one of Robert Bakewell's breeding rams, which when Robert began his experiments were let for only fifteen shillings or a pound. They prospered, even if famous Robert Bakewell went bankrupt because he so lavishly entertained the European celebrities who came to see his sheep. They could afford to experiment with new methods and machinery, which the cottager and small farmer never could have done. They also devised new methods and improved machines themselves. They did much good. Farming was a passion, almost a craze. Crop yields increased. So did the population.

Of the dispossessed, the *déraciné*, some managed to find accommodation in still open parishes, others ended in the parish workhouse, where if meals were monotonous and inadequate they

Combined plough and seed drill, *circa* 1770

were at least regular. Many sought employment in towns and cities; women and children flooded into the cities too and, since no one had ever thought it wrong for women and small children to work on the land or at cottage industries, few thought it wrong they should find employment in factories. Their wages had always been low, their hours long. No need to alter this simply because they were being employed in mills and mines. And when natural dearth or the exigencies of war pushed food prices up, or when trade slumped, most people were glad of any work no matter what the pay, how long the hours, how dreadful the conditions.

To those living in the last quarter of the century who could look back to a youth spent in the time of George I or even George II, England must have seemed a paradise. Horace Walpole remembered it with palpable nostalgia for the lost glories of his father's house. The labouring poor remembered it as a time when, if they were poor and hungry, at least they had had roots. They had belonged to a village, a parish. They were part of a unit, a community. Now they were poorer, hungrier, and rootless.

Conditions of the poor in the always more heavily populated south and in the quickly expanding midlands were worse by the

time George III came to the throne and, inevitably, worsened
during the sixty years of his reign. In the north, the labourer could
still sometimes keep a cow on, or gather wood, turf and furze,
from still unenclosed waste. He had learned the value of the potato
in his daily diet and as a protection against dearth of corn. He
rarely ate wheat bread, he relied on oatmeal. But in the south,
grazing was so expensive that even if a labourer had a cow he
couldn't afford to keep it. Fuel was so scarce and dear that he
could not longer afford to bake his own bread. Often, because of
this, he boiled his kettle or cooked his stew at another's fire, and
paid a penny for doing so. He had not learned the value of the
potato, although rich Londoners had. He refused all but white
bread and when, to relieve want, the government in 1796
allowed rice to come in from Carolina free of duty, he refused to
buy it. Possibly because he, or rather his wife, did not know how
to use it.*

This unsuccessful attempt to introduce a wheat substitute was
made necessary by two disastrous harvests and the new French
war. When this war began in 1793 prices rose steeply. Wheat
soared from 43s to 75s 2d between 1793 and 1794. Many of the
poor were reduced to famine level and there were riots in Birmingham, Coventry, Nottingham, parts of Sussex and elsewhere.
On October 29th 1795 King George III, en route to and from the
House of Lords in his State Coach drawn by 'eight fine Cream-
Coloured Horses in Red Morocco Harnesses',[34] was attacked
by an angry and hungry mob in St James's Park. The coach
windows were broken and the mob, some 200,000 strong, shouted
'No King, No War' and 'Give us Peace and Bread'. Both were a
long time coming. The dearness and scarcity of bread brought
thousands to a state of pauperism.

In the year King George was rough-handled by the mob, a
certain labourer of Streatley, Berks, with a wife and four children,
had a total income from all sources (including an intermittent
sixpence or so his wife earned weeding) of about £46 per

* In 1795 in an attempt to find a substitute for wheat, the government imported
maize. This too was unpopular. Food taboos are always very strong.

annum. Of this he spent £36 8s 0d on bread alone. All other food-stuffs—cheese, butter, bacon, tea, sugar, old milk and a very small quantity of oatmeal came to £16 4s 4d. His food cost him roughly £6 more per year than he earned. This family ate neither fresh meat nor potatoes for 'that cheap and nutritious root, the potato' was 'very little cultivated or used'.[35] At least not by the poor in southern England.

In the north, life was a bit better. Oat cakes, porridge, frumenty, hasty pudding and potatoes took the place of wheaten bread. At Kendal, Westmorland, a calico weaver with a wife, who could earn nothing as she had 'an ulcer in her breast'[36] and six children (four of whom earned a bit by weaving or by knitting stockings) had a total income from all sources of £48 2s 0d. Not a farthing was spent on bread. The family consumed about a ton of oatmeal instead, at a cost of £17 per year. Potatoes for forty weeks came to £3 10s 0d. These substitutes or replacements for wheat cost £20 10s 0d, not including the cost of fuel for cooking. This is considerably less than the amount spent by the Berkshire labourer with a smaller family. The Kendal family also used tea and sugar, in smaller quantities, but they consumed more butter and milk. They also had a bit of butcher's meat and some fresh fish from time to time. They even managed a gallon of beer a week at 4d a gallon—and stayed within their income!

But not all misery was due to economic conditions. In 1795 in the thriving town of Leicester—population 15,000—where work was plentiful, a wool-comber, his wife and son, all working, managed to earn only £35 15s 0d per annum. Bread cost them £18 4s 0d; they ate ten pounds of butcher's meat a week at 3d a pound; they also had tea, sugar, ale, beer and a few potatoes; but they lived nowhere near their income. In fact they never laid by sixpence for a rainy day.[37] It is not easy to see how on this income, sixpence could have been saved. Regrettably, the wool-carder had a bad reputation; wages were high in Leicester and he could have earned more than he did (9s per week) by working every day. Unfortunately, he preferred to spend several days a week in the alehouses 'lamenting the hardness of the times'.[38]

Some foreigners thought, as some still think, it is a part of the Englishness of the English never to work unless and until they run out of money.

Happily, there is Richard Walker to speak for the other side. Richard, a thirty-six-year-old rural labourer lived at Rode, Northamptonshire with his wife, a daughter of nine, three boys aged seven, six and three and a one-year-old infant of unspecified sex. His income was £20 per year but he got breakfast and beer free. Three of his children were at school and, after paying for their education and 'thread', they each earned about 6d a week. Richard was honest and industrious. By ringing the church bell twice daily he earned another £1 6s 0d a year. He also picked up a bit as a barber and by digging graves 'at the dissenting chapel'.[39] These attentions to living and dead brought in another welcome pound annually. At harvest the whole family, bar the baby, collected corn worth about £3 10s 0d. Thus the grand annual total of all their industry and effort was £26 8s 0d. Even so, Richard's expenses came to £27 16s 2d not including fuel at 50s. His rent at 8s a year is the lowest item in his budget and is far lower than the rents paid by the other three men. It is pleasant to note that his landlord was Augustus Henry Fitzroy, 3rd Duke of Grafton, at whose country house the young de la Rochefoucauld had found dinner 'the most wearisome of English experiences'.

The labouring poor in their millions found hunger so wearisome an experience that towards the end of the eighteenth century and in the early years of the nineteenth century there were hunger riots, particularly after the passing of the iniquitous corn laws of 1815. Yet there were a number of people who believed hunger to be basically the fault of the hungry.* No one need starve unless he were idle and improvident (an old Puritan concept this). Furthermore, the poor had got above themselves in many ways and had even become finicky about food. No one, it is true, said 'Why

---

* There were also many like Eden, Hannah More, Count Rumford, Robert Owen, Feargus O'Connor, Arthur Young, Cobbett, John Wesley, John Howard and others, whose deep concern for the poor and wretched led them to spend their lives trying to ameliorate their condition.

Farmer's grinding mill, *circa* 1775

don't they eat brioche?' but Josiah Tucker expressed the sentiments of many when he wrote 'The Palates of the Poor are become Nice and Sickly' unable to buy 'Dainties' they refused to touch what was 'coarse and ordinary'.[40] This is on a par with Robert Campbell's earlier accusation that the poor, no less than the rich were guilty of 'Depraved Taste'.

Yet where Campbell says that food is 'seasoned with slow poisons' he is very near the truth, but for quite the wrong reasons. Apart from the normal kind of food poisoning—and 'I was poisoned by a meat-pye',[41] or an equivalent remark, is a constant note in diaries—our Georgian ancestors ran other and equally deadly risks in eating and drinking. Sometimes these risks were due to sheer ignorance; often they were due to the chicanery and avarice of unscrupulous food vendors. The deliberate sophistication of food is by no means new to the century, but the scale

upon which it was practised was. This was one of the consequences of the increased demand for food in rapidly growing
cities. Oceans of bogus vinegar made from oil of vitriol (which is
concentrated sulphuric acid) and water coloured either with
burnt sugar or an infusion of oak chips, flooded a pickle-conscious
country. And since there was 'a prodigious consumption of
Pickles in the Navy'[42] as well as in civilian life, wholesalers,
lacking the touch of Olivia Primrose which gave pickles their
'peculiar green',[43] did their pickling with fake vinegar in copper
vessels—despite 'an outcry against the poisonous quality of brass
and copper'.[44] Copper turned pickles a glorious green because the
action of acid on copper produces 'Verdigrease, a rank caustic
Salt; in Plain Terms, a poison'.[45] What with vitriol and verdigris
it is astonishing the Navy had any stomach at all for the sea
battles in which it was so often engaged.

Admittedly pickles are not a staple, although we might
reasonably suppose they were from the countless recipes in
cookery books on how to pickle everything from ox palates to
'elder shoots in imitation of bamboo'[46]—obviously a Chinese
Chippendale touch here. But bread *is* a staple and with the public
demand for nothing but white bread, stupid and extravagant
though it was, certain bakers, ever eager to turn a dishonest penny,
took to adding foreign substances to the flour. One of the
favourite adulterants seems to have been alum, which whitens
flour and gives extra size to a loaf; there was a notable increase in
the sales of alum, particularly in years of dearth. Whiting and
lime, it is said, were also used as well as white lead! This was bad
enough, but it was by no means all. There was yet another
adulterant 'more shocking to the heart, and, if posible, more
hurtful to the health', or so a pamphlet entitled *Poison Detected
or Frightful Truths and Alarming to the Metropolis** claimed. This
ingredient was bone-ash—so useful in china making—yet it can
hardly stun the heart and is surely less injurious than white lead.
But the really X certificate thing about this particular bone-meal
was 'that the charnel houses of the dead' were 'raked to add

* Published 1757 and possibly written by Dr Peter Markham.

filthiness to the food of the living'. The bakers' slogan wasn't 'Fee Fie Foh Fumme' but many believed it might well have been. 'The bread I eat in London', says Matthew Bramble, 'is a deleterious paste, mixed up with chalk, alum, and bone-ashes; insipid to the taste and destructive to the constitution.'[47] Even when it was pointed out that bone-ash (and there'd have been no need to use other than animal bones), whiting and chalk* would be too easy to detect and, in actual practice, would effectively reduce the size and impair the texture of bread, few believed it. Perhaps in a gothick novel way they preferred to sup full with horrors. So the controversy over the sophistication of bread went on for another half a century.

Beer, and the era saw the rise of the great brewing houses, could poison more easily and rapidly than gaudy green pickles or beastly bread. Dishonest brewers, faced by the competition of tea, kept their prices down by watering beer. But as weak beer is unpopular and easily detected they gave the diluted brew a good bitter flavour and a tremendous wallop by means of the Coculus India Berry; the neutral principle of which is picro-toxin. This explains the wallop. Picro-toxin stupifies, paralyses, causes convulsions, gastro-enteritis and over-stimulation of the respiratory system which could, not surprisingly, lead to death.

Even completely honest brewers like Mr Thrale,† who died in 1781 of an apoplexy due to chronic over-eating, added balls to the brew in a laudable effort to prevent beer from going ropy or acid. The best balls were made of calcined, powdered alabaster, oyster shells, horse-bean flour, chalk, red saunders, orris root, coriander seed, grains of paradise, cloves, hops, isinglass and molasses. They were harmless, but made the beer flat. To overcome flatness, 'headings' were—or was—added and 'headings' of copperas or green vitriol were not so harmless. Few knew that vitriol in its various forms could be harmful; it had been long

* Today by government regulation, 14oz. of chalk are added to every 280 lb. of flour to increase the calcium content of bread.
† Mr Thrale's Brewery was bought by Mr Barclay, whose partner was Mr Perkins.

used in food, drink, medicine and even as a complexion clearer. Cider drinkers, however, escaped the effects of picro-toxin and vitriol, they were merely done in by the sugar of lead used to sweeten cider. Cider was also the ingredient of a fake port, drunk just as much with a meal as after it and known to Eton boys as 'black-strap'. Six gallons of rectified spirit, 3 of brandy, 12 of port and 42 of cider, made 63 gallons of 'port'.[48] Bottled with a pinch of powdered catechu, which made a fine crust in a matter of minutes, it could be sold at 18s the dozen. Other wines required different ingredients, but given a thin solution of spirits of wine almost any type of wine could be simulated. As early as the reign of George I, a large factory near Cupids Gardens was doing a thriving trade in wine made principally from fermented raisins. By the beginning of the nineteenth century the adulteration of wine, of all foodstuffs, was so flagrant that virtually nothing edible escaped.*

Tea, beer's rival, was often mixed with dust and dried leaves—blackberry leaves were best. This was not a new idea either, the real innovation lay in giving the adulterated tea a nice even colour. This was obtained through the agency of that universal favourite, vitriol. Although ferrous sulphate is undoubtedly useful in tanning, dyeing and in making ink, to metamorphose one's stomach into a black leather bag cannot have been particularly desirable. Doubtless the poor escaped the worst effects of artificially coloured tea because they used the same leaves over and over again, and often bought spent leaves from rich kitchens where the selling of used tea-leaves was one of the perks of the servants. The spectacular increase in tea drinking is best illustrated by the import figures for tea. At the beginning of the eighteenth century about 20,000 lbs were imported annually; by the end, 20 million tons. That is, consumption rose from a few leaves per person to two pounds per head of a doubled population. Yet these

---

* Despite the work done by F. Accum (1820) in exposing adulteration and adulterators (for which he was persecuted). Nothing was done to stop swindling and poisoning until 1850 when an Analytical and Sanitary Commission was appointed to inquire into the quality of food and drink.

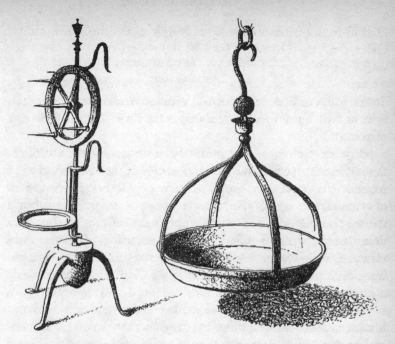

Open-fire meat toaster and iron frying-pan. George I and II

figures represent only tea upon which duty was paid. How much was smuggled in we do not know, but we do not know that smuggling was really big business and some authorities believe that as much 'illegal' as legal tea came into the country.

Bohea was still a favourite, as it had been in Queen Anne's day, but Hyson soon became the luxury tea of the well-to-do. As early as 1738, Henry Purefoy's mother, Elizabeth, in one of her firm letters to her London agent writes: 'When Mrs Robotham comes, I desire she will bring me two pounds of new roasted coffee beans and half a pound of Hyson tea.' In the next breath she asks for 'a fashionable hoop from Long's warehouse ... for one who is not half an Ell in ye wast'.[49] Thirty-five years later a posse of Bostonians, not very adequately disguised as Mohawks, dumped cargoes of Hyson tea into Boston Harbour and

> The waters in the rebel bay
> Have kept their tea-leaf savour.
> Our old North Enders in their spray
> Still taste a Hyson flavour.

Or so Oliver Wendell Holmes claimed some years after an incident which was greatly deplored at the time—even by George Washington.

Far more deplorable and infinitely more deadly than adulterants in food and drink was the terrible rise in the consumption of cheap spirits, especially gin, in London, in other ports and in industrial areas. It was illegal to sell beer or cider in any but a licensed house, but for some supremely idiotic reason this prohibition did not apply to the sale of spirits. In 1700 only 500,000 gallons of gin were imported, by 1735 the total of legal gin was 5 million gallons with duty at 2d a gallon. Much more came in as contraband and much more was produced at home from any old scraps plus the inevitable oil of vitriol and salt of tartar. Innumerable gin shops sprang up everywhere in squalid cellars and holes in the wall and, by 1780, it was estimated that in the worse London slums, such as St Giles, gin was sold at every fifth house. 'Gin', says Henry Fielding, 'is the principal sustenance (if it may be so called) of more than 100 thousand people', and in London 'many swallowed pints of this poison in twenty-four hours'.[50] As a magistrate, Fielding saw the effects of gin in increased crime, yet the urban poor cannot be blamed for taking to cheap gin. It, not religion, was the opium of the people. It killed them, either of itself or upon the gallows. It drove them mad or to suicide. It starved and abandoned their children. It beggared them . . . if beggars can be beggared. But before it did these things, it kept them warm in winter, was cheaper than food, allayed hunger and pain, and offered escape from a life without hope. In the early nineteenth century, due to low wages and high prices of ale and spirits, the taking of opium, which was cheap, became a habit among many workers in Manchester and doubtless elsewhere. Thomas de Quincey believed that after experiencing its 'divine luxuries'[51] no one would return to alcohol. I think this a bit of special pleading. Opium taken orally is of use in certain stomach conditions and by inhibiting peristaltic action also controls the pangs of hunger.

Temperance was not a notable virtue of the Georgians no matter what their social status. The rich drank much wine, brandy, punch, rum, arrack and cordials. It is a commonplace to think of the century as being full of three and four bottle men, with the three and four bottles being full of port—Dr John Campbell boasted he had drunk thirteen bottles of port at one sitting, 'solid orthodox man'[52] though he was. But burgundy was as well loved as port, both with and after dinner, and there always had been claret fanciers, although one hears more of claret at the beginning of the era than at the end. Thus when the Mayor of Newcastle upon Tyne celebrated the third anniversary of the accession of George I he gave his dinner guests 'the best wine, Margou, that ever mayor treated with'.[53] But Dr Johnson thought claret 'poor stuff' and the 'liquor for boys'.[54]

If the horrors and miseries depicted by Hogarth's 'Gin Lane' were not so evident among the rich, many men spent their lives 'half glazed', and many women were often, like Queen Dollalolla, 'half seas over' on 'arrack-punch'.[55] There were no half measures for Mrs Jenny Lambton of Harraton who 'hastened her end' by 'an over-indulgence in strong liquors'.[56] Mrs Lambton would, possibly, have done better to stick to lemonade, although even this is doubtful as at least one mid-century recipe for lemonade calls for equal parts of brandy, white wine and water, plus half a lemon. Parson Woodforde, who bought and drank licit wine, also bought a fine quantity of rum, brandy and gin every year from his local blacksmith and smuggler, John Buck, known as 'Moonshine' Buck. 'I bottled a Tub of Moonshine',[57] is a by no means uncommon entry in his diary. And on one terrible occasion—September 17th 1792—he had to spend the whole morning trying to find a place to hide the Tub as revenue officers were abroad.

But how useful it must have been to know there was nothing so 'servicable after a Debauch of Strong Liquors', or even after a quiet evening of lemonade, as coffee. William Ellis recommends this, and also roasting the beans oneself on a fire shovel which, one feels, might be a rather dangerous occupation for the badly hungover. But to many, unable to enjoy the amenities of town life with its food shops, brewers, bakers and pastry cooks there can have been nothing more 'servicable' than Mr Ellis's book. Printed in 1750, its bang-on title was *The Country House-wife's Family Companion, or Profitable Directions for whatever relates to the Management and good Œconomy of the Domestic Concerns of a Country Life. According to the Present Practice of the Country Gentleman's, the Yeoman's, the Farmers and Wives in the Counties of Hertford, Bucks and other parts of England, shewing How great Savings may be made in Housekeeping.*

Indeed, Mr Ellis, farmer, seller of agricultural machinery, trees, grass seed, pheasants, patent medicines and 'receipts . . . for preventing Rats, weasles and Polecats' (send only 1s for the latter) is indefatigable if fatiguing. Nothing escapes his plagiarizing pen —for he is nothing if not unoriginal. Cookery, bread-making, dairying, pickling, brewing, do-it-yourself home doctoring; everything is dealt with, from 'How to Preserve Naked Sausages' to how to preserve life from the ravages of consumption, plague and jaundice. Oddly, Mr Ellis, versatile at borrowing though he is, seems obsessed with pancakes. 'How commodiously Pancakes answer the Farmers' the Yeoman's, the Gentlemen's Interest', he sings. Cheap, serviceable, suitable for breakfast, dinner or supper and 'so conveniently portable', they are a boon to all. He gives fifteen recipes for pancakes ranging from those 'made for the Rich' to those 'Made by the Poor'. The poor he defines as 'poor day-labouring men's wives'. The rich, who need no defining, wolfed their pancakes made from lashings of butter, cream, eggs, sugar, sack and rose water with 'sufficient flour' as 'the finishing part of a dinner'. Pancakes for the poor were quite different. They were made of flour and water, and eaten without sugar. These, Mr Ellis says optimistically, 'provide a full meal'.

It is perhaps interesting to note that the word 'portable' used in connection with food seems new to the century. There is a 'portable soop' made from fifty pounds of beef and, even, a 'pocket soop' which 'you may carry in your pocket without getting any harm'.[58] This requires a leg of veal and it is the 'veal glew' of the previous century, renamed. And, somewhere along the way, the word Pick-Nick came to be used to denote a fashionable party frequently, but not always, held in the open air. 'I like the description of your *picnic*',[59] Lord Chesterfield writes to his son in 1748. This kind of al fresco meal was not new but the name for it was, and in late Georgian times Pick-Nicks became a rage. 'We are going to have a Pick Nick Dinner Party in the Grounds',*[60] Muzzy Capel writes to her grandmother, the Dowager Countess of Uxbridge, virtually on the eve of Waterloo. Even the pretentious 'abigails' of Lady Dashfort's party went to an Irish Inn and lunched on 'what they brought with them . . . a *pick-nick* lunch with madeira and champagne to wash it down'.[61] Madeira was the new, popular drink of the early nineteenth century. The French wars had seriously affected the importation of port and French wines.

But to return to that fraud Mr Ellis. What one notices from mid-Georgian days on, is the enormous increase in books of the Ellis genre written by those who had (or claimed to have had) practical experience, for the benefit of those who had not. These last might be people who were economically and socially on the way up, or they might be those who wanted places as servants. Some cookery books such as *Every Young Woman's Companion* compiled by, one, Madam Johnson who 'out of her benevolence fixed the price at 1s 6d bound'[62] even contained sections on 'Spelling, Reading, Writing and Arithmetick' as well as 'Bills of Fare for every month in the year', plus an 'Estimate of the necessary charges of a family in the middling station of Life, consisting of a Man, his Wife, Four children and one Maid Servant'.[63] Total £390 per annum including 4s a week pocket money for the 'Master'.

The rich and royal could, and did, import notable continental cooks. The Prince Regent lured Antonin Câreme to London;

* of the Château Walsheuse near Brussels.

Câreme hated the climate and returned, after two years, to France. But those in the middling station made do with a cook-general and paid her £4 10s 0d a year until she died of overwork.

Although the vastly rich Lord Mayor of London, William Beckford (*père*), could give a dinner for George III—the dessert a set piece twelve by seven foot 'composed in a triumphal chariot',[64] with Neptune, Amphitrite and attendants, to say nothing of pyramids, triumphal arches and palm trees above four foot tall, all done in sugar, marzipan and sweetmeats as well as in 'inedible' models—the middlings could only *épater* each other with fancifully shaped jellies and marchpane, everlasting syllabubs and large cakes. These cakes were iced with twenty-four egg whites and double refined sugar whisked together for a mere three hours with a birch twig whisk. The icing was applied with 'a bunch of feathers'.[65] Mrs Hannah Glasse's *The Compleat Confectioner* was indispensable for fancy sweets of all sorts, such as ice-creams (made in pewter 'basons') sugar puffs, hollow gumballs

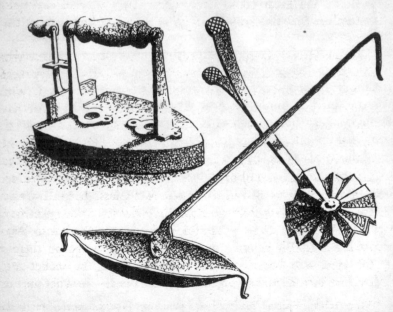

Iron candle-dipper and pastry marker. Mid-eighteenth century

and Whim-Wham (a sort of embryo trifle) but her *Art of Cookery Made Plain and Easy*, first published in 1747, made her name.*
It was avidly devoured by interested readers, ran into many editions, and was cheerfully plagiarized by any number of writers, including Mr Ellis and Madam Johnson, but it remained popular for half a century.

Mrs Glasse makes no bones about the audience she is addressing. It is an audience composed of those who do *not* go in for French taste—and waste. A French cook, says she, will use 'six pounds of butter to fry twelve eggs' when half a pound or less would do. 'But then it would not be French', she remarks acidly, and goes on to say that people are such fools 'they would rather be imposed upon by a French booby than give encouragement to a good English cook'. Her own stated intention is to instruct as simply and clearly as possible without any silly nonsense. 'If I have not wrote in the high polite stile'—and this apologia is a boast—'I hope I shall be forgiven for my intention is to instruct the lower sort . . . the great cooks have such a high way of expressing themselves that the poor girls are at a loss to know what they mean.'[66]

The modern reader, however, is often at a loss to know what Mrs Glasse means for, as usual with pre-nineteenth-century recipe books, ingredients and method are inextricably mixed, while quantities given are often so imprecise that results must have varied widely. Her 'French way of dressing partridges' for example—and she *does* give several French recipes despite her professed contempt—is so complicated and involved that one can scarce make beak or tail of it. It is also a trifle difficult to understand why it is included in the book; Mrs Glasse herself admits: 'This dish I do not recommend; for I think it is an odd jumble of trash.' And even she is not guiltless of putting dishes into 'Masquerade'. She has pigeons 'transmogrified' by wrapping them in puff paste and boiling them! She even tells the seeker after novelties how to make a pigeon look like a pear—to what purpose

* Many believe 'Hannah Glasse' to be a pseudonym for that man of many odd parts, John Hall.

it is not very easy to say. She gives exhausting instructions on how to make a hard boiled egg of a size which only a Roc could lay, and this was 'a grand dish for a second course'. She is expert in turning an eel skin stuffed with fish into something which looked exactly like 'a breast of veal collar'd' and which is infinitely more tiresome to prepare and cook than the real thing. This dish had to be carefully cooked in 'a tin oven before the fire'. In many ways the *Art of Cookery* is anything but Plain and far from Easy.

Better instructed were those who lived in Manchester where, by the late 1760s, the very first school of Cookery and Domestic Science in England, if not in the world, was established by Mrs Elizabeth Raffald, who had seen service in good country families. Her cookery book, first published in 1769, had thirteen legal and twenty-six pirated editions to its credit by 1806. In the intervals between running her school and writing books Mrs Raffald produced a large number of children. Fortunate Mancunians after 1772 could obtain servants from Mrs Raffald's Registry Office. This too was the first ever. Doubtless the servants were Raffald trained or had, at least, read Mrs Raffald's book.

But if recipes were lengthy, complicated and chaotic—which they were—the preparation and cooking of food was equally difficult. Lemons were painfully squeezed in large, hollowed out wooden nutcrackers, unless one were grand enough to have a French presser, a beautifully architectural affair on columnar legs. Frying pans, girdles and kettles swung from chains over the open fire. Meat was roasted before it on various kinds of spits, sometimes turned by a dog in a treadmill. Ovens were of two kinds, one built into the wall beside the fireplace—this had to be separately fired; the other, a tin boxlike affair which stood on a large trivet in front of the fire and presumably had to be turned round from time to time to cook evenly. A terrifying complicated machine on three legs toasted meat, so it must have been the greatest possible relief when, towards the end of the eighteenth century, the cast-iron kitchen range which provided cooking and baking facilities, as well as a boiler for heating water, made its first appearance.

Iron range with water heater. Late eighteenth century

The 'Rumford Stove' was one of these and it was 'a contrivance
. . . which immortalized its creator . . . in the annals of domestic
economy'.[67] The odious General Tilney had his old-fashioned
fireplace 'contracted to a Rumford'; curiously, this was the
fireplace in the 'common drawing room',[68] The Rumford was
invented by Benjamin Thompson, born 1753 at Woburn,
Massachusetts. He fought with George III's dragoons in America,
was probably a spy and counter spy, and was knighted in 1784.
The Elector of Bavaria thought so highly of Sir Benjamin's work
in laying out the English Gardens in Munich that he made him
Count von Rumford. The count was an opportunist, but he was
also a great social reformer and invented a number of things to
soften the rigours of domestic life. He also founded the Royal
Institution in 1799[*] and died at Auteuil in 1813. The Rumford

* His most famous paper, presented to the Royal Society, 1798, demonstrated that
heat was not a substance but was produced by the motion of particles.

stove may not have immortalized its creator, but it certainly revolutionized the actual methods of cooking and utilized heat to better advantage.

Another boon was the invention of matches, new to the era. Early ones consisted of a wax taper and a bit of phosphorous sealed in a glass tube. They, like 'Soop' were portable and could be carried in the pocket but were apt to do considerable harm as they were immensely fragile and ignited immediately on contact with air. In 1786 came an improvement in the shape of a glass bottle coated on the inside with sulphur from which matches were pulled out, but the bottle had to be carefully re-sealed after each match was pulled. Next, around 1810, came 'the Instantaneous Light Box' with its splinters of wood coated with chlorate of potash, sugar and gum arabic; just dip into a bottle of oil of vitriol and there you were—probably in great pain, because one drop carelessly spilt on hands or clothing burned a large hole in skin and cloth. In 1824 a Mr Berry, of London, invented the first safety match—a box containing all these ingredients, plus a spirit lamp, and a patent contrivance to prevent drips of acid. But all these early matches were expensive and were not in common use. In 1826 the complications and hazards of acid matches were eliminated by John Walker, an apothecary of Stockton-upon-Tees. He invented the first true friction match. One nipped the head in a fold of sandpaper, pulled hard and, with luck, the match lighted without nasty side effects. Finally, in the year before George IV exchanged this world for one where, many thought, sulphur was the chief element, John Walker's matches were being sold readily in London shops under the name of 'Lucifers'.

Curiously enough, another man, Dr William Kitchiner* (1775?–1827) revolutionized cookery itself. Aptly named, he was a noted epicure, who also wrote about music and optics, studied and practised cookery in his own kitchen, and his book *Aspicius Redivivus or The Cook's Oracle*, first published in 1817, was an immediate and well deserved success. This book is the first

* The name is also spelled Kitchener.

(at least to my knowledge) to state exact quantities in weight and by measure. The method is equally exact. And so the age-old muddle suddenly disappears. So keen was Dr Kitchiner on exactness that he even had graduated measures made for himself, a very novel idea, and advised his readers that these could be bought 'at Hancock's Warehouse in Cockspur Street'.[69] Cookery, like every other art, requires practice and care, he says, and he also forcibly impresses upon his feminine readers the absolute necessity for the mistress of a house to know about good and therefore economical housewifery. Accustomed as we now are to hearing much about Dr Kitchiner's exact contemporary, Brillat-Savarin (1775–1826), we forget that Kitchiner's *Cook's Oracle* appeared eight years before Brillat-Savarin's *Psychologie de Goût* and that Savarin is often indebted to Kitchiner.

'Wondrous, Admirable Kitchen Crichton',[70] Dr Kitchiner comes as a great relief after centuries of muddle and mess in cooking. Moreover, he is the first to be really good on vegetables —which most other experts of the time certainly were not. He rightly insists that vegetables are at their best when in full season and, like all true epicures, has small use for early forced and out-of-season vegetables which match expensiveness and tastelessness in equal proportion.

The Cook's Oracle is so plainly set out, says its author, that 'A small portion of the time which young ladies sacrifice, to torturing the strings of the Piano-Forte, employed in obtaining these domestic accomplishments, might not make them worse wives, or less agreeable companions to their Husbands'. This is rather doubtful as, by now, young ladies had a terrible facility for performing upon the pianoforte—so much improved by Mr Broadwood in 1780—or upon the harp. They were so talented at singing, drawing, painting in watercolour; so afflicted by 'sensibility', that the eating of food, let alone the preparation and cooking of it, was only for coarse and vulgar souls. It was for those who had never swooned away at the sublimities of nature or of poetry (the gloomier the better); and who had never wallowed in the despair of unrequited love as did

Marianne Dashwood, in fiction, and Harriet Capel in fact.

Such sensitive young ladies would certainly have fallen into a near fatal fit of lowness had they read *The Cook's Oracle* and found the 'sagacious gourmand' was enjoined to 'Masticate, denticate, chump, grind and swallow',[71] if unable to achieve this unaided, 'Patent Masticators' could be had 'of Mr Palmer, Cutler in St James's Street'.[72] No young lady could chump, grind, swallow or use a patent masticator and retain the sickly illusions of a debased romantic movement. And there were so many mundane things to be ignored by men and women affecting sensibility, or as we now call it, sentimentality. There were, for instance, the hordes of brute-like creatures who caused much trouble by rioting for food! Yet it must have been easy enough to ignore them for 'when the generous affections have become well nigh paralytic, we have the reign of Sentimentality' and 'the barrenest of all mortals is the Sentimentalist'.[73] Not only is he barren, he is also the most hard-hearted.

These dreadful, common, troublesome thousands were the poor, the unemployed, the hungry. They had far too little to chump, grind and swallow. In Waterloo year, there were riots in Norfolk, Suffolk, Cambridge and elsewhere with houses, barns and ricks fired. In 1817—the year the heiress to the throne, Princess Charlotte, died in childbed and her accoucheur Sir R. Croft blew out his ultra-conservative brains—500 people marched on Nottingham to protest about food, low wages and political rights. There was more to protest about in 1818 when a poor harvest brought hunger, and a high importation of cotton, silk and wool brought a glut and worse unemployment.

Then came 1819 and 'Peterloo'. This was also the year in which Edward Augustus, Duke of Kent, and Mary Louisa Victoria, daughter of the Duke of Saxe-Coburg-Saafeld, became the parents of their first and only child. In honour of Tsar Alexander of Russia, they named the baby Alexandrina. In honour of her mother, they added Victoria.

CHAPTER SIX

Of Medicine, orthodox and otherwise

The King had a pain in this thumb. Hardly a matter of grave concern, one thinks, but this monarch happened to be the second and 'viler' of the first two Georges. His temper, always fierce and ungovernable, went from its usual bad to a roaring worse. The royal physicians tried but could do nothing with thumb or temper. They owned themselves baffled. At this juncture a certain Dr Hemming suggested Dr Ward should be called in.

Clever, personable, ambitious Dr Ward had no medical qualifications whatsoever. He began his career as a dry salter and in 1717 entered Parliament as the member for Marlborough, Wiltshire. Unluckily for 'Spot' Ward (his real name was Joshua) it was soon discovered there had been a bit of hocus-pocus somewhere. In fact, the new member had not received one single vote. Corrupt though elections were, this was going too far and Ward fled to France. Here he hung about the Pretender's Court, winning friends and influencing people in highish places while living on the proceeds of certain remedies he had concocted. The best known were his 'drops and pills'. Pardoned in 1733, he returned to London, set up as a doctor and soon became the fashion among the nobility and those busy laying the foundations of future nobility by amassing fortunes. The summons to see George II was the final stage of Ward's devious climb. There could be no higher step.

To give Ward credit, he did trouble to find out beforehand all he could about the royal thumb. Then, arrived at the palace, he asked and was granted gracious permission to examine it. Holding the King's hand firmly in his own, he suddenly gave the thumb such a wrench that George, swearing violently, kicked him hard. This was one in the shins for Dr Ward. It was also one in the eye for the King's physicians. The pain had vanished! The King could move his thumb. He did so and pulled out several plums for Dr Ward; a carriage and pair, the privilege of driving through St James's Park; royal protection guaranteed against interference by the Royal College of Physicians; a room in the King's almonry where poor patients were treated and—most gratifying of all— a vote of thanks passed in the House of Commons.

There was no quackery about curing the King's thumb; it was probably dislocated and the clever jerk put it right. But Ward's famous drops, pills and other panaceas were another matter. The pills were antimony and dragon's blood. The drops were of two kinds; one, antimony dissolved in Malaga; the other—a special 'white' drop—an ammoniated solution of mercury. People swore by them. When the Princess Elizabeth Caroline, third daughter of George II, was ill, Lord Hervey persuaded her to take the pill which he says 'vomits, purges and sweats in a great degree'.[1] After four days of treatment she was almost free of pain, could get out of her chair and walk about without help. One cannot but feel that the drastic effect of the pill made this acutely necessary.

Had his lordship been able, doubtless he would have given Ward's pills to Queen Caroline when she lay dying. They could hardly have done more harm or good than the snake-root and brandy, Sir Walter Ralegh's Cordial (still going strong after 130 useless years), Daffy's Elixir,* usquebaugh, mint water, to say nothing of the bleeding and the glisters administered by a quartette of royal physicians. Sir Hans Sloane and Dr Hulse were called in—they ordered blisters and a purge. This could only

* Said to be the invention of Dr Thomas Daffy (c. 1660) It could be bought in London as lately as the 1930s and even then was 'as recommended by Dr King, Physician to King Charles II'.

Chemical laboratory. Early to mid-eighteenth century

have added to the intense pain of a stoppage due to a rupture at the navel. But the final attempts at surgery without benefit either of skill or anaesthetics must have been torment enough to make even the devil look merciful.

So it is really not surprising that the eighteenth century was the solid gold age for mountebanks as one remedy was as fatal as another. Quacks were innumerable and were in no way hampered by an ethical code. Further, they had an advantage in that usually they had a great deal more charm and personality than the average doctor while some, undoubtedly, had more skill. But to be a top quack, to make a fortune, one had to have the right patronage. Ward had that. Lord Chesterfield, Edward Gibbon, Henry Fielding and Horace Walpole thought highly of Ward's drops and pills—though Horace later put his faith in James's Powders.

Cynical and pain-wracked Alexander Pope held another opinion. 'See Ward by batt'red Beaus invited over'[2] (implying he cured V.D.); and, 'Ward tried on Puppies and the Poor, his Drop'[3] he gibes. Nor was Lady Mary Wortley Montagu, Pope's quondam friend, taken in by Ward or by quackery. 'If I find tar-water succeeded to Ward's drops' she writes to her husband, Edward, from Italy ' 'tis possible by this time, that some other quackery has taken the place of that; the English are easier than any other nation infatuated by the prospect of universal medicines, nor is there any country in the world where doctors raise such immense fortunes'.[4] This was a trifle unfair, but Lady Mary—a difficult woman of great intelligence, brilliant wit, and polished malice—was given to vigorous, outspoken opinions and prejudices. She remembered, possibly, only those stupid doctors who had been so against her campaign for 'ingrafting' against smallpox, forgetting that Doctors Maitland, Arbuthnot, Sloane, Jurin and Mead, all vastly eminent in their profession, had supported her.

Smallpox was now the scourge of Europe. Plague came and went in waves (it had died out in England after the Great Plague of 1665). Malaria could be controlled and cured by 'the bark', but smallpox was always with us. When endemic it was a good, steady, reliable killer. When epidemic, it ravaged whole areas. In England 'out of a hundred persons not more than two or three are exempted from it',[5] says Dr Tissot but this figure is probably too high. Eighty out of every 100 Europeans could be certain to contract smallpox at some time during their lives. They did not all die. Many had mild attacks and emerged unscathed. Others were blinded, disfigured or maimed for life. People lived in chronic fear and terror of it. Few, if any, diaries and journals of the time are free of the mention of smallpox. Sometimes it was almost a relief to get the disease and so be rid of this gnawing fear one way or another. Dudley Ryder, a future attorney-general, notes that his sister had smallpox, but they came out 'kindly'. Everyone was cheerful, even the patient, who is 'glad she has got them'.[6] Some people, like the Purefoys, made their servants sign guarantees that they already had had smallpox or if they had not would leave at once (for God knew where) if they contracted it. Sixty million Europeans died of smallpox in the eighteenth century alone.

Yet smallpox had its uses. In North America, during the Pontiac conspiracy of 1763–4, it was a cheap way of getting rid of troublesome Red Indians who, for some reason, disliked giving up their land. As they had had no contact with the disease they had developed no natural immunity. A pair of blankets and a handkerchief from a smallpox hospital ceremoniously presented to two Red Indian chiefs* and we could soon push the frontiers westward without having to waste time in negotiation or ammunition in killing these savages for 'a few months later the smallpox raged among the tribes of the Ohio'.⁷ Bacteriological warfare is not new to our century, it goes back to the age of enlightenment.

Smallpox had killed Lady Mary's brother and had left her with no eyelashes and a pitted skin. 'How am I chang'd! alas! how am I grown/A frightful spectre to myself unknown',⁸ she wrote bitterly in 1716. So when she found herself in Constantinople as the wife of the Ambassador to the Grand Porte she was, not unnaturally, enormously interested in the ways the Turks† prevented the disease. 'The small-pox, so fatal, and general amongst us', she writes to Miss Sarah Chiswell, 'is here entirely harmless by the invention of ingrafting, which is the term they give it.'⁹ Thousands were inoculated each September, she says, and people formed happy parties of fifteen or sixteen for the occasion. Indeed, the French Ambassador remarked that the Turks took their smallpox 'by way of diversion', just as Europeans took the waters, and the diversion was only briefly interrupted by the inoculator, an old woman carrying 'a nutshell of the matter of the best sort of smallpox'. After painlessly opening the veins of the

---

* According to Drs Stearn, Sir Jeffrey Amherst was responsible for suggesting this; and Col. H. Bouquet and Capt. Ecuyer carried it out.

† This method had been described in a paper to the Royal Society by Dr E. Timori, 1714. It differs from that which had been used for centuries in China.

inoculees with her needle she inserted 'as much venom as can lie upon the head of her needle', then bound a bit of hollow shell over the wound. Everyone remained perfectly well until the eighth day when a fever ensued and necessitated two or three days in bed. Another eight days and all were as well as ever— safe and unscarred. 'I am patriot enough . . . to bring this useful invention into fashion in to England',[10] Lady Mary concludes. Miss Chiswell cannot have been impressed. She died of smallpox in 1726.

Lady Mary had her own small son inoculated in Turkey and, after returning to England, her daughter Mary (who later married Lord Bute). She also won the support of Queen Caroline, then Princess of Wales. The first public test was made in 1721 on six condemned criminals in Newgate who were promised liberty if they survived. All won their freedom. The Princess then had the orphans of St James's parish successfully inoculated. Then two of her own daughters. Where royalty led, others followed and 'the growth and spreading of the inoculation' became 'almost a general practice'.[11]

This was not strictly true. Moreover, there had always been opposition to inoculation and, after several had died of it, opposition became more violent. Newspapers called Lady Mary an unnatural mother who had risked the lives of her unoffending children (her son certainly gave great offence to many later). Some of the clergy—mostly high church—with predictable idiocy thundered that it was wicked to take such matters out of the hands of Providence; it was defying God's will. Certain doctors foresaw dire and disastrous results. One, William Wagstaffe, wrote 'Posterity . . . will scarcely be brought to believe that an Experiment practiced only by a few Ignorent Women among Illiterate and Un-thinking people [meaning the Turks] . . . should so far obtain in one of the Politest Nations in the world [meaning us] as to be received in the *Royal Palace*'.[12] What posterity can scarcely credit is that this physician of St Bartholomew's Hospital should have been such a crass fool as to believe this type of nonsense a valid argument.

Nevertheless it was Lady Mary who pioneered the idea of preventive medicine in England, and she should share the honours with the Gloucestershire doctor, Edward Jenner, who in 1796 performed the first successful vaccination in the world, using cowpox rather than smallpox as the vehicle. Dr Jenner—a pupil of John Hunter—spent twenty years brooding over the relationship, if any, between non-fatal cow-pox and too often fatal smallpox. During that time he was often threatened with expulsion from the Convivio-Medical Club because he bored his fellow members rigid with his endless talk on the subject. In 1798 he published the result of his broodings and findings in *An Inquiry into the Cause and Effect of the Variolae Vaccinae*. This became available to the whole world which, grown wiser, hailed him as a saviour. By 1808 the National Vaccination Establishment was founded and vaccination centres set up all over the country (in 1853 vaccination was made compulsory). The Tsar of Russia, the King of Prussia were among the famous who sought interviews with this mild little country doctor who hated London.

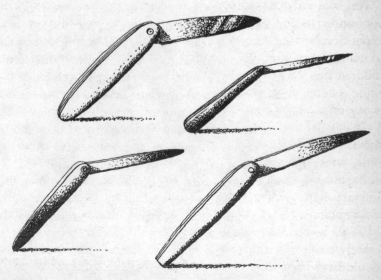

Edward Jenner's lancets used for vaccination

Honours from every country—including the Five Nations—were heaped upon him. Indeed, the spokesman for the Five Nations said, on November 7th 1807: 'We shall not fail to teach our children to speak the name of Jenner; and to thank the Great Spirit for bestowing upon him so much wisdom and so much benevolence.'[13] The Five—that is the federated tribes* of Mohawk, Oneida, Onondaga, Cayuga and Seneca Indians—had recently received, through the agency of the Lieut.-Governor of Upper Canada, Dr Jenner's book. In gratitude these 'savages' ceremoniously presented Dr Jenner with a belt and a string of wampum.

Lady Mary never saw the triumph of her pioneer work. Her old age overlapped Dr Jenner's boyhood in mid-century, and seventy-five years separated the first 'inoculation' in England from the first 'vaccination'. But it is entirely within the Georgian era that 'the most terrible of all the ministers of death'[14] was vanquished. This was the greatest medical achievement of the age. It was also the starting point for what our own century has developed into the science of immunology.

Yet this great achievement came late in the day, whereas the spirit of philosophical enquiry—without which it could not have been accomplished—began early. True philosophical enquiry (now called scientific research) had received its impetus, first, from Francis Bacon's dictum that the only way to arrive at a truth was to observe and state the observed correlations of facts; and second, from the brilliant work done by those natural philosophers of the second half of the seventeenth century who accepted this dictum, this new tool, this *novum organum* as the only valid means of discovering the secrets of nature. Thus, in 'science' the alchemy of the Middle Ages, thanks to Robert Boyle, was transmuted into chemistry. In medicine, due to the work of William Harvey, the liver ceased to be considered the central blood organ and the seat of most illnesses. But most startling of all, and this completely

---

* The league was traditionally founded by Hiawatha (Mohawk) and Dekanwida (Huron?) *c.* 1570. Some modern authorities doubt if Hiawatha ever existed other than as a purely legendary figure.

revolutionized man's approach to the physical world, was the great scientific generalization made by Isaac Newton (1642–1727) that the force which held the planets in place was exactly the same force which caused an apple—his favourite fruit—to drop to earth. Here, Newton was stating a formula which expressed observed correlations of observed facts, and this really was, and is, the first rule of all scientific method. What was so amazing—it excited some as much as it frightened others—was that Newton's discovery meant that a single law ran through heaven and earth and this law was a natural not a spiritual law. The earth was therefore not special, individual, or under a separate dispensation of Providence. It was part of a far greater whole, the Universe. And the Universe, obeying this natural law, was seen to have a new order; a new pattern. So it was here, at this point, the followers of Newton began to realize that the laws of nature are neither mysterious nor arbitrary. They are statements of facts from which, by a series of comparative and cumulative observations, a pattern, a regularity of sequence, is seen to emerge and persist. So men began to look for new patterns and order; to try to find the right tools to work with, just as Newton had created the Method of Fluxions (differential calculus) to prove his great theory.

Hardly less startling was what Newton had done to white light. White light, ordinary daylight, was not white. It was, he proved, composed of the whole spectrum of colours, each having its own degree of refrangibility. Were there not other things which could be broken down into their component parts? Robert Boyle had had something to say on this too—only the other way round. 'From the resolution of compound bodies,' he said, 'there may result mixts of an altogether new kind, by the coalition of elements never perhaps convened before.'[15]

And so in the white light of this new conception of natural law, the Georgians set to work on the great, but not very showy, task of re-examining, arranging, classifying, testing, assimilating, correlating, comparing, and trying to coordinate the vast accumulation of knowledge built up over the centuries. Observe, observe,

observe—does a pattern emerge? If so, there must be a law or principle which can be stated. What, for instance, are 'true' elements? The old belief was that there were only four—air, earth, fire and water—and since Aristotle's day this was the very last word 'hermetic philosophers' (physicists) and 'spagyrists' (chemists) had had to say on the structure of materials which composed the world and everything in it.

Although Boyle himself had worked with air, he certainly never suspected that there were other 'airs' (we call them gases) distinct from the stuff one breathes. It was not until 1754 that Joseph Black (1728–99) discovered that what he called 'fixed air' (carbon dioxide) was entirely different from everyday breathing air. Exactly twenty years later, Joseph Priestley (1733–1804) discovered 'dephlogisticated air' (oxygen) and in between these two discoveries that most eccentric philosopher, Lord Henry Cavendish discovered 'inflammable air' (hydrogen). In 1784 when

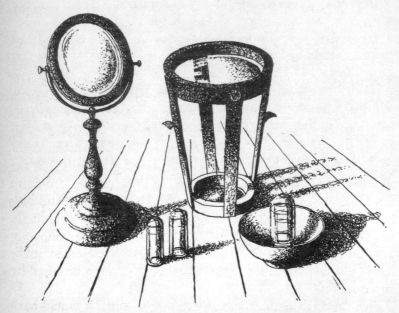

Joseph Priestley's apparatus used in the discovery of 'dephlogisticated air'

Cavendish proved that the sole result of the combustion of 'inflammable' and 'dephlogisticated' air was water, the old idea that water was a true element was completely discredited.

It all sounds so simple to us now. Carbon dioxide which helps make aerated drinks; oxygen which saves lives; hydrogen the first (and probably our last) element; H_2O the first chemical formula every child learns at school. But thirty years of unremitting work lay between the discoveries of carbon dioxide and the compound nature of water. This was only one of the things of the new Newtonian universe upon which 'natural philosophers' were working. But it took a very long time to learn how to apply such discoveries to science, to medicine and to industry. It is one thing to isolate carbon dioxide, it is another to know what to do with it, although a Swiss gentleman living in London, a Mr Schweppe made good use of it in the 1790s. Mr Priestley's oxygen then saved none suffering from asthma or congestion of the lungs. And certainly no newspaper blared forth in its vulgar way 'Peer's Grandson Makes Water'. These were not 'human interest' stories.

What newspapers did blare out, what excited everyone, was that a certain Joanna Stephens had discovered a cure for the stone, one of the most common and most painful afflictions of the day. It was probably in 1736 that Joanna first started advertising her cure and, like 'Spot' Ward, she quickly ingratiated herself with the aristocracy and influential politicians who always seemed to be absolute pushovers for quacks. Joanna received handsome testimonials—and fees—from her rich and famous patients, but she was shrewd enough to realize that this money-spinner could not last for ever. Either a new panacea would be invented and oust hers, or perhaps the cured would not stay cured. Accordingly in *The Gentleman's Magazine* for April 1738, the following advertisement appeared: 'Mrs Stephens has proposed to make her Medicine public on Consideration of £5,000 to be raised by contribution'.

Five thousand pounds was an astronomic sum. It would have taken a Methuselah of an agricultural labourer from Chaucer's day to Dr Johnson's to earn that much. But money did not flow in at all quickly so letters began to appear in various papers and journals appealing to the charity and benevolence of the rich, urging them to subscribe so that this medical blessing might be acquired for the good of everyone. The rich and charitable responded. The Bishops of Oxford and Gloucester; the Dukes of Richmond and of Leeds; the Earls of Pembroke, Clarendon and Godolphin; the Duchess of Richmond and the Countess Deloraine were among the well-known contributors. Alas, the total realized was not above £1,367. Undismayed, Joanna simply got her influential friends to apply to Parliament to grant the required amount. Parliament did so! And on June 19th 1737, the great boon was made known through the columns of *The London Gazette*. It turned out to be a tripartite remedy 'a Powder, a Decoction and Pills'. The powder was made of egg shells and snails 'calcined'; the decoction, herbs boiled with soap and burned swines-cress; the pills, snails, wild carrot and burdock seeds, 'ashen keys', hips, haws, honey and a good dollop of 'Alicante' soap.

This is what Parliament paid for—a trifle recklessly perhaps— but Parliament was acting in what it believed to be the best interests of all classes, and it may be that in the decision to purchase Mrs Stephens' remedy lies the first faint stirring of the National Health Service. Certainly, Sir Robert Walpole believed in the soap cure. He took one ounce of Alicante soap in three pints of lime water daily. When he died it was calculated that he had eaten about 180 lb of soap and drunk 1,200 gallons of lime water. It was also discovered at the autopsy, performed by Sir Caesar Hawkins, Sir Robert had so many bladder stones that his son Horace believed his father had been killed by a 'lithotriptic' medicine.

Caesar Hawkins (1711–86), of St George's Hospital, who invented the cutting gorget, was a member of the commission of enquiry the government set up to investigate the efficacy of Joanna's remedy. This was admirable—only the enquiry took place after, not before, the purchase. Other commission members,

St George's Hospital, London, 1736

in addition to well-known peers, were Samuel Sharp of Guy's whose book on surgical operations became the handbook of the day and William Cheselden. The commission expressed itself well satisfied with the 'efficacy, utility and dissolving power' of Joanna's remedy.

What really is extraordinary is that Cheselden, of all people, should have been satisfied. William Cheselden (1688–1752), of St Thomas's and Chelsea, was a friend of Newton and was with him when he died. He was the most famous surgeon of the early Georgian era and his speciality was operating for the stone. Until Cheselden, this had been a long and excruciatingly painful operation with a high mortality rate, but Cheselden, as early as 1727, with a technique as brilliant as it was rapid, had perfected a method of lateral lithotomy at which he was so expert he could do the operation in fifty-four seconds flat and the death-rate, due to haemorrhage, shock and infection, was reduced to 17 per cent. Still, less than a minute of unanaestheticised surgery must have seemed a lifetime to the patient, and it is no wonder people took almost any remedy rather than submit even to Cheselden's swift knife. Besides, his fee was £500, though he did treat the poor free. Cheselden also seems to have been the first to perform a successful iridectomy; he invented a method of draining the antrums, helped to create the Surgeons' Company and, generally, brought surgeons and surgery a prestige which had never been enjoyed before. Surgeons were becoming gentlemen and vice versa.

In the year when Joanna Stephens began to be famous (1736), a certain Sarah Wallen, bone-setter, married a footman with the delightful name, Hill Mapp. Unfortunately, only the name was a delight as one week after the wedding the bridegroom absconded with £100 and other portable property belonging to his spouse. It may be that Hill Mapp married Sally solely for this purpose as she was an enormously fat, enormously strong woman with hamlike hands, a hefty jaw and rather badly crossed eyes. Sally did not grieve over her faithless footman, she settled at Epsom and soon became the most famous bone-setter of the time. People came from all over the country to see her, and each week she drove up to London—in a coach with four horses plus liveried outriders and footmen—and saw patients at the Grecian Coffee House. Sally seems to have had an extraordinary gift for bone setting (her father was a bone-setter) and the fashionable physician Sir Hans Sloane had a high opinion of her. She cured his niece of a curvature of the spine and, more remarkably, a man who had had to wear a shoe with a six-inch lift. When Sally finished with him, his lame leg was 'brought even with the other'. Finally, her practice grew so that she moved to London and set up in Pall Mall. She was so famous that a popular song about her ran:

> You surgeons of London who puzzle your pates
> To ride in your coaches and purchase estates,
> Give over for shame, for your pride has a fall
> And the Doct'ress of Epsom has out-done you all

—which, very likely she had. She was certainly very well known but, perhaps, not quite so famous in the Old Kent Road as elsewhere. One day while driving there, a not very amiable crowd mistook her for the grossly obese Lady Darlington,* a 'widowed' mistress of George I. Sally was outraged: 'Damn your bloods', she shouted. 'Don't you know me? I'm Mrs Mapp, the bone-setter.'

The Old Kent Road had not seen the last of famous bone-setters. One freezing morning, twenty years after Sally became Mrs Mapp, Old Kent Roadians saw a horse slip and throw its rider— a small, spare, bewigged man. Spectators rushed to help and ordered a coach; but the madman refused to be moved. He just lay there and told them to fetch two chairmen from Westminster, minus their chairs but bringing with them their long chairpoles. He next bought the door of a nearby house, had it stripped from its hinges and nailed to the chairmen's poles. Only then would he allow himself to be moved on to this stretcher and gently carried home.

This eccentric creature was Dr Percivall Pott (1714–88) and he knew that in falling he had suffered a compound fracture of the tibia. For this, the usual remedy was to saw off the leg, which his colleagues advised at once. But Pott sent for his old teacher, the anatomist and bone-man, Dr Edward Nourse. Nourse, seeing the wound was a good few inches away from the fracture, felt there would be less danger of infection spreading from wound to bone once the leg was set. Pott agreed. The fracture was set, splinted and left strictly alone. Most doctors thought Pott would die. He didn't. He lay quite still and wrote the first of his many books, *A Treatise on Ruptures*. Here he refuted, on strict anatomical grounds, many old theories on the cause and treatment of ruptures. He recorded the cases he had dealt with, and urged early operation in cases of that notable killer, strangulated hernia, which he described and defined.

Perhaps it was his own fractured tibia which led him to become interested in fractures; over a period of thirty years he observed and noted every detail of the fractures he treated. In

* Her daughter by the King married Earl Howe.

1768 he published his treatise *On Fractures and Dislocations* where he pointed out the urgent need to set a fracture immediately (often fractures were treated with ointments and salves and were not set for weeks), and the equal necessity for relaxation of muscle if the job were to be properly done. His book revolutionized the treatment of broken bones and was soon famous throughout the world. It had taken him a quarter of a century to accumulate and correlate sufficient data, to analyse and record it, but from then on far fewer people died. Fewer still were maimed for life because of a broken bone. Pott's detailed description of a break at the ankle is now called 'Pott's fracture'. His description of a curvature of the spine with a certain amount of paralysis of the legs due to tuberculous caries is known as 'Pott's disease' from which it now seems that Alexander Pope suffered. His treatment of this condition was simple and far less brutal than the screw chairs, iron neck bands and steel corsets then usual. He used plasters, poultices and a light support to save the spine from weight bearing. Children, who were very subject to this condition, must have suffered less because of Percivall Pott . . . Here one wonders, uneasily, what Mrs Parson's 'stays for girls that are crooked or inclined to be so either by falls, rickets, sickness'[16] were like. Some sort of modified Iron Maiden, one suspects. Pott was a great anatomist, a great teacher. He observed, defined, recorded, analysed, and collated after the new fashion of the century. He

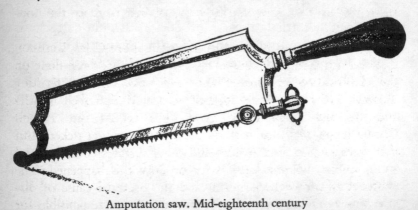

Amputation saw. Mid-eighteenth century

believed in simple methods and even redesigned many of the heavy cumbersome surgical instruments in use, so that they would better serve their purposes. The day before he died (of pneumonia) he said 'My lamp is almost extinguished. I hope it has burned for the benefit of others'.[17]

Needless to say, Dr Pott with his meticulous 'scientific' approach, had no use for Mrs Mapp, 'an ignorant, illiberal, drunken female savage' he called her. And indeed, poor Mrs Mapp did take to drink and died of it, and poverty, in the slums near Seven Dials. But Pott was unusual in his day because he had no use whatsoever for quacks, and even the best doctors made suspiciously ducklike noises from time to time. Sir Hans Sloane, president of the Royal College of Physicians, sold an eye ointment. Dr (later, Sir) Richard Mead concocted a remedy for smallpox, and also believed that earth vapours were good for one. You just removed a bit of turf and stood on, or were held over, the bare earth. Sir Charles Blicke (Dr Abernethy's master) thought there was nothing like 'Plunkett's Caustic' for curing cancer; and Richard Guy, founder of Guy's Hospital, is said to have bought the secret from Blicke and published it in *Lloyd's Evening Post* in 1754 for the benefit of humanity. It could not have cured, but also it might not have caused pain to any one with a malignant ulcer. Yet this mixture of white oxide of arsenic, sulphur and herbs could be agonizing on a non-malignant ulcer. In those days there was no means of knowing the malignant from the non-malignant.

There was no way of distinguishing one more or less common disease from another because very little work had been done on the classification of diseases and their specific characteristics. Thomas Sydenham (1624–89) had accurately described measles and had also distinguished gout from rheumatism. Francis Glisson (1597–1677) had written the classic work on rickets. But if it were known that measles and other diseases could be, and were, spread, no one knew why or how this happened. The existence of atmospheric germs and the bacterial cause of disease was as unknown as the dietary deficiency responsible for ever prevalent rickets. Many held rickets to be due to an hereditary taint—parents or grandparents were syphilitic or scrofulous.

And even if Sydenham had separated gout from rheumatism there was still a terrible muddle about gout. The purple-faced, pop-eyed, ill-tempered, bewigged squire with his huge padded foot on a gout stool, a bottle of port in one hand and a walking stick for hitting out with in the other, is suffering the kind of gout we suffer. But what was gout in the head? Gout in the stomach? And what, of all things was flying gout? All could be fatal, and it was a 'severe attack of gout'[18] that carried off that singular character, the 4th Earl of Bristol and Bishop of Derry.

As gout was supposed to be 'a defluxion of the humours', we are not much the wiser. Flying gout might have been pain and swelling which flew from one joint to the other; yet Dr Lightfoot's condition first termed 'flying gout' was later diagnosed as a burst blood vessel! Whatever it was it killed him. Head gout might have been anything from allergic rhinitis to a sinus infection, while stomach gout might have ranged from simple indigestion to a baleful ulcer. Venice treacle and gin taken on alternate days was good for stomach gout—which sounds rather improbable. But as nothing was known about the real processes of the digestive system, gout in the stomach, an understandably common complaint, must have been very difficult to cure.

Digestion, as everyone knew who had ever heard the rumblings of his own or anyone else's stomach, was obviously due to muscles working away and churning the 'putrefying' food into 'chyle'.* Chyle nourished the body either by circulating through the veins or through the hollow nerves. It was not until 1752, that a Frenchman, René Antoine de Réaumur (better known to us for his temperature scale) showed how the gastric juice of birds would dissolve food stuffs in a test-tube, and an Italian Abbé, Lazaro Spallanzani proved that although churning was a help

---

* Today 'chyme' is the word used to describe the pulp into which food is reduced in the stomach: chyle is chiefly a lymphatic fluid mixed with fats derived from the body.

it was not essential to digestion, that the old ideas began to break up. And it was an Englishman, William Prout (1785–1850), who first discovered, in 1823, the presence of free hydrochloric acid in the stomach.

But acid and alkali in the stomach due to foods producing acids and alkalis had been a favourite theory of doctors long before Prout's discovery. The idea originated because scurvy, 'a putrid fever', was believed to be caused by eating salt meat— and scurvy could be staved off or cured with fruit and vegetables. It had also been known for some time that there were salts other than the one used to salt meat and to flavour food. All salts were now held to be acid, alkaline or even volatile—as in 'sal volatile'. Meat when it goes bad gives off an alkaline substance (ammonia) therefore meat must be alkaline—or, to use the word most in use then, 'putrescent'. And, since vegetables and fruit cured scurvy caused by alkaline meat, then vegetables and fruit must be acid. So a new theory of how to maintain health was born. Maintain the proper alkali–acid balance in what you ate and you would be healthy. This quite discredited the old idea that health resulted from the perfect balance of the humours. Only old fogies could continue to believe with Mr Shandy that the whole secret of health depended upon 'the due contention for mastery between the radical heat and the radical moisture'.[19]

Nevertheless, good resulted from this new theory. As all sorts of diseases were held to be due to 'alkaline corruption', this meant people began to eat more fruit and vegetables than ever before. It was even beginning to be suspected that the rich ate too much. William Cullen (1710–90), a Scot, thought and said so. He found it amazing 'how voluptuous and lazy people of delicate constitutions should think themselves able to carry off such loads of high-seasoned food and inflammatory liquors without injury or pain'.[20] The great Dr Abernethy (1764–1831), the first to ligate the external iliae for aneurysm, believed that all diseases which were not external were due to digestive disturbances. His remedies were calomel and the blue pill. 'Go home, sir and never let me see your face again', he shouted—for he was a trifle abrupt

Lambeth Delft drug jar and feeding bottle

—at a farmer who had spent half an hour telling him that his complaint was a great thirst for a gallon and half of ale a day. 'Go home! Drink your ale and be damned.' Not perhaps a very good or helpful way of treating an alcoholic, but one does rather admire his telling a rich, over-fat, luxury-loving alderman 'Live on six-pence a day and earn it'.[21]

Much earlier than this, injury and pain in the form of heartburn, sleeplessness, nausea and gripings had so undermined Thomas Wood of Billericay, Essex, that in 1746 he decided to give up physicians and put himself on a diet. He chose one recommended by an Italian, Cornaro who seemed to have suffered the same complaint. It is true the Italian had suffered it two hundred years before Mr Wood, but he had managed to live a century on his diet, and in perfect health. So first Mr Wood gave up meat, and found himself improved. Then he gave up all alcohol and found even more improvement. Cheese went off the list next, and so on, until finally Mr Wood was living on a diet of sea-biscuit puddings, skimmed milk and eggs. He was completely cured. So it sounds very much as though Mr Wood's gouty stomach was an ulcerated one.

The year after Mr Wood went on his bland diet, another Scots doctor (and the eighteenth century is vastly indebted to Scots doctors), James Lind (1716–94), set out to prove that scurvy was *not* caused by salt meat. He took twelve seamen for his experiment and grouped them into six pairs. They all had the usual diet, but to the first pair he gave a quart of cider a day; to the second, 25 drops of oil of vitriol three times a day; to the third, two spoonsful of vinegar; to the fourth, a current remedy made of garlic, mustard seed, horse-radish, gum, myrrh and various other things. The sixth pair got two oranges and a lemon a day. In six days this pair was cured of scurvy. Those who had been given cider took longer; all other results were disappointing, though had there been large quantities of horse-radish in the made-up remedy the fifth pair might have been cured, too, as horse-radish is extraordinarily rich in Vitamin C. But to eat enough to cure scurvy would probably imperil the digestion. Nevertheless, Lind's experiment is the first record of a really controlled experiment I know of (which is not to say it *is* the first). In passing, it should be firmly recorded that the orange and lemon cure had been known to the Elizabethans, but the next century, believing the virtue of the cure to lie in the sour taste, thought that anything sour, like vinegar and vitriol, would have the same good result. It did not. Yet the old orange and lemon cure must have been remembered by some, or passed into folk medicine, for an early Georgian diarist records that he drank the juice of two Seville oranges 'in order to remove the scurvy which I believe I have got'.[22] He also thought orange juice would sweeten his breath and purify his stomach.

Lind published *A Treatise of the Scurvy* in 1753. It might be thought, since the proof was there, that the Admiralty would have leapt at it and supplied the navy with oranges and lemons. But no. Citrus fruits were much too expensive. Far cheaper to find something else and let thousands of sailors die. It was not until 1795, after endless argument and further proof from men like Captain Cook of the real efficacy of citrus juice, that the

Admiralty supplied lemon juice and sugar to its ships. By now we were again at war with France so we could not allow our sailors to die of anything other than French bullets. No doubt in 1806, when the Admiralty could not find a single case of scurvy in the naval hospital at Haslar (where there had been 2,000 down with it in 1760), it congratulated itself heartily on its remarkable foresight. So the Georgian era saw the end of scurvy too. But James Lind was dead before the Admiralty made up its mind about scurvy and, unlike Joanna Stephens, 'Spot' Ward or even Dr Jenner, Lind received neither money, honour nor thanks from the government.

In the year Lind's treatise was published the most fashionable physician of the day, Sir Hans Sloane, died. Sloane had been a pupil of Thomas Sydenham and was apparently a good doctor (and an extremely rich one), although the Rev. Dr Stukeley, one of Sir Hans's friends, did not think so. He thought that Sloane had only 'moderate parts and learning',[23] was a poor speaker and only bent on doubling his already great fortune—even though he had no male heir and his daughters were 'very richly married'.

Sloane's parts and learning may have been moderate, or even mean, but it is doubtful if he called in astrology to aid him in diagnosis and practice as many doctors still did and had done for centuries. Dr Stukeley himself was not only a clergyman and a doctor, he was also a very believing astrologer and related all the events of his life to his horoscope, which he cast himself. 'Under the following directions', he notes, giving five astrological signs which, alas, are meaningless to me, 'I studied physick under Dr Mead at London. Fell into a female scrape.'[24] This is all, and one wishes that either the stars or the doctor had been slightly more communicative. Even the great Sir Richard Mead believed the stars influenced health and wrote *A Treatise Concerning the Influence of the Sun and Moon on Human Bodies*. Stukeley was better known as an antiquary (with a positive passion for Druids) than as parson or physician. One cannot but think that Thomas Hearne, deprived of his librarianship at Bodley for being a non-juror, and an unamiable and rather spiteful scholar, was probably right in saying that Stukeley was 'a mighty conceited man', and 'though he be a Physician, yet I am informed he knows very little, or nothing of the matter'.[25] The Rev. Doctor, although a friend of Newton and other famous men, certainly seems to have had an antiquary's attitude toward medicine. One of the few bits of medical knowledge he gives us in his voluminous journals is that Lord Pembroke had got rid of a great wart on his hand by drawing a pin over it and posting the pin to the wife of a country clergyman. In a fortnight the wart was gone. Dr Bouchier's daughter, similarly afflicted—she had them all over her face—did the same thing and it worked! It very likely did. Even today doctors are puzzled to explain how some warts can be 'charmed' away.

Charms, spells, astrology and folk remedies still played a major part in medicine as they had done for centuries. A well tried bit of magic to cure jaundice made the sufferer hardboil an egg in his own urine, prick the shell all over with a pin, bury it in an ant hill and, as the egg wasted, so did the disease. If one preferred, which possibly one did not, jaundice would disappear if nine live lice were swallowed every morning. Nine is, of course, a magic number, but why lice? A less revolting but just as inefficacious treatment was to 'wear the leaves of celandine upon and under the feet'.[26] An application of hog's dung stopped bleeding—it had been horse's dung in the previous century—and probably gave the bleeder tetanus instead. A frog tied to the neck, or oil of vitriol rubbed upon the forehead, cured obstinate nose bleeds. But if bleeding from any part of the body stubbornly resisted all cures, gentlemen were advised to try 'soaking or washing the Testicles in the sharpest vinegar'.[27] In Sussex, passing a ruptured child through a young ash tree split down the middle cured the condition. The tree was bound together and for ever after the child's life was intimately connected with it. This magic cure remained in use until the second half of the nineteenth century, as did pills made of cobwebs. These were tranquillizers, recommended by reputable physicians as late as 1837 for the treatment of asthma and consumption.

I

Consumption was prevalent, so were remedies. John Wesley lists fifteen of them and particularly recommends 'sucking a healthy woman daily' because this cured his own father. A certain Mr Hume, when quite given over by Sir Hans Sloane, cured himself by drinking a liquid made of raw turnips and brown sugar candy, 'much to the surprise of the doctors and his friends'.[28] This sounds a more pleasant remedy than 'Snayle-Water' which called for a peck of garden snails roasted 'until they leave off making a noise',[29] beaten together with scoured, slit earth-worms and left to brew with ale, herbs and a dozen other ingredients. 'I use oil of earth-worms with opodeldoc* to disperse the lump';[30] Sir Anthony Westcomb, who had a lump on his hip, writes to Mrs Dewes. The same old, repellent ingredients seem almost as common in the early Georgian era as they had been in the previous century. Books on home doctoring and home surgery are as common and quite as horrifying.

Clever compilers or plagiarists were usually careful to give 'receipts' as used or recommended by famous doctors, plus others culled from ancient books, or taken from oral tradition. Such cures always worked after doctors had utterly failed. Mrs Caser, 'wife of the famous Surgeon-Apothecary and Man Midwife of Kent',[31] was cured of a tympany by a beggar woman who recommended camomile dipped in spirits of wine. The cure was such a lasting one that Mrs Caser outlived her husband.

Mr Ellis, whom we met in the previous chapter, is almost as exhaustive on home cures as he is on cookery but, one feels, less damage would result from his cookery than from his medicine. He, himself, had concocted a remedy, a special 'Balsamic Tincture', which, like his recipes for getting rid of moles and weasels, he would send on receipt of one shilling. This was certainly an all-purpose remedy. It cured bruises, strains, scalds, green wounds and also, 'which with Difficulty will be believed', stopped the most obstinate bleeding, even of arteries and veins 'without ligature'. This is indeed astonishing but it is a mere nothing for

* Probably a liniment with soap as its basis. The name 'opodeldoc' was first given to medicaments for local application by Paracelsus (1490–1541).

Mr Ellis and his Tincture. If the brain were wounded 'quit thro' either Length ways or Breadth ways', or if the pupil of the eye were pierced, or if tendons were 'cut quite asunder', the tincture was indispensable as it 'agglutinates the Parts and defends them from Corruption'. To have a cleft brain stuck together for a shilling was certainly inexpensive, not to say miraculous. But it was less easy to cure sore feet, although a raw egg in each shoe did wonders. This receipt to my certain knowledge was well known in Queen Elizabeth's day. It was recommended then for horses.

The space between head and foot might be troubled with thousands of horrid things with even more horrid names. There was the 'Hypochondriock Passion', a 'Mental as well as corporeall distemper',[32] which made poor Mr Hobson so ill in 1729, and also things like 'epoplectic fitts'. Up in Newcastle, Thomas Norris was carried off by one in September 1751 while dining with the Dean of Durham. No doubt this quite spoiled the meal. There was cramp in leg or arm caused by 'wind in the blood', but it could be coped with by tying an eel skin tightly about the affected part. But what the Moon Pall, the Marthambles, Hockogrocle and even the Strong Fives were I cannot say, but they sound perfectly appalling and had been discovered (or invented) by a quack called Tufts in the previous century. Very fortunately, Dr Tufts had discovered a sure cure for them. Worse than these must have been 'Rising of the Lights'. For this there was no better remedy than a paste of flour and water which, drunk frequently, 'will keep them down, else they are apt to rise and cause Fits'.[33]

One does not know how Hockogrocle or Rising Lights or other diseases with alarming names were diagnosed. But 'uroscopy' was still a favourite and quite bogus diagnostic method. The clever doctor needed no more than one look at a specimen to diagnose and foretell the exact course of a disease. The fate of John Gurney of Marston, Bucks, is clear evidence of this. John had a new and very weedy farm, which he laboured unceasingly to clear, cooling himself off from time to time with a draught of cold, small Beer. Presently John grew 'sickish', his appetite failed, he languished. Mrs Gurney, next door to desperate, finally consulted a Dr Crawley of Dunstable. Dr Crawley took a single look at the specimen Mrs Gurney had brought him, then asked, a shade brutally one feels, 'Woman are you willing to be a Widow?' Mrs Gurney was not. 'But I tell you you will be one', Dr Crawley roared, 'no Man can Cure him; for I find by his Water he has drank too much cold small Beer when he was hot, and so mixed his Grease with his Blood that there is no Remedy for him.'[34] This terrible admixture of grease and blood carried John off two or three years later and Mrs Gurney was left a most unwilling widow with five small children to support.

Although a mixture of blood and grease was incurable, and fatal, apparently a mixture of mercury and blood was not. Or rather it was not considered to be. Mercury and mercury water was a great cure-all. John Wesley says that three pounds of mercury swallowed ounce by ounce would untwist an intestinal knot,* and Mrs Delany recommends it for her nephew's worms. We, of course, would end up with mercury poisoning, our ancestors did not—or if they did, did not know it. The great advantage of mercury was that 'the particles . . . are so minutely divided globular and so smooth' they entered and passed into 'the Circulation thro' the imperceptible vascular system'. Mercury also 'pervaded all Capillaries even to the Pores of Perspiration', and so it cured sore eyes, leprosy, itch, rheumatism, the King's evil, scald head, scurvey, stone, gravel, and the Pox (it probably did help the latter). It was excellent for mange, for worms in humans and animals and, also for 'Bugs in Beds and Furniture'.

It is our tedious friend Mr Ellis who tells us about mercury, and he was just one of many who turned a dangerously dishonest penny by presenting to the reading public a gallimaufry of cures; some seem to go back to the dark ages and all are certainly completely unproven by any controlled test. And this in an age so desperately bent on sifting evidence and trying to arrive at least at an approximation of truth, when medicine and science were

---

* In the early editions of *Primitive Physic*. In later editions he does not consider mercury to be the panacea he formerly thought it.

beginning to link hands. One wonders who those who took to home-doctoring—and many did—survived.

One of those who did—and survived until the age of eighty-four—was the famous Sarah Churchill (1660–1744), Duchess of Marlborough, who distrusted all doctors. She had her own collection of cures and remedies and her advice was much sought by friends and relatives. 'Your Grace is such an excellent Physician',[35] Arthur Maynwaring writes, and on another occasion he says that the moon 'if her power is so eminent as 'tis thought to be in distempers & all cases of sickness . . . ought . . . to take particular care of so famous a Physician.' Yet all Sarah's skill could not save her only surviving son, John or her beloved (if odious) grandson 'Willigo'.[36] John died of smallpox in 1703; Willigo of drink in 1731.

Perhaps the run of professional men of the day knew little more than the lay compilers of medical books. In which case country people who could not read, or could not afford a doctor, were more fortunate than others. There were 'good receipts' in private

Traveller's medicine chest, early eighteenth century

hands but 'doctors decried them'.[37] So country people stuck to traditional folk medicine. Some of it was pure nonsense but probably less dangerous nonsense than the stuff found in the 'how-to-kill-yourself-at-home' compendiums.

Mrs Delany, whose letters are full of what to do for this or that ailment, recommends 'a spider put into a goose quill'[38] worn round the neck as an infallible ague preventive. This remedy goes straight back to Dioscorides, a doctor in Nero's army, and was still being used as late as 1837. On the other hand, in Shropshire they had been using the purple foxglove to cure dropsy for several centuries, perhaps even longer. William Withering, (1741–99) who had been born there, remembered this when he became a doctor in Birmingham. Withering belonged to the classifying, arranging, testing type of doctor. He was also an amateur and amatory botanist who first started collecting plants for an attractive woman patient. By the time he married her he had become a notable 'professional' botanist. Like Jenner, Withering also knew a bit about folk medicine— for it was a Gloucestershire folk belief that those who had had cow-pox wouldn't get smallpox—and he began to wonder, as he went about his practice or stayed home and played the German flute (which he did neatly), what caused dropsy. He came to the conclusion that a heart condition might be responsible. So, knowing about foxglove tea, he began experimenting with fox-glove. He discovered that when used carefully and discontinued if it caused nausea it was of great use in dropsy. In 1785 he put forward his findings in *An Account of the Foxglove*. So we cannot laugh at all folk remedies since here was the birth of digitalis, one of the most useful of all drugs in cardiac conditions. Here, too, a bit of 'unorthodox' medicine becomes orthodox.

One of the conditions in which digitalis can be useful is angina pectoris, and the classic* description of this disease was given by William Heberden, the Elder (1710–1801). Heberden also described the fingers in arthritis deformans and the knobbly bits

---

* The first unclassic but immediately recognizable description, was given by the great Earl of Clarendon, whose father died of it.

are still known as 'Heberden's nodules'. Early in his career he also published a tract against two well-known remedies, Mithridate and Theriac (Venice treacle);* the latter contained viper's fat among its many ingredients. This exploded the reputation of these fantastic remedies among medical men, but not among home curers!

Although that Druid fancier, Dr Stukeley, was now dead he had noted at least thirty years before Withering's book that one of the three chief reasons the Druids venerated the purple foxglove was because of its great medicinal virtues. This information could only have been based on oral tradition but it is a remote possibility that the Druids may have used foxgloves for dropsy. If so, this may suggest why the tradition persisted only along the Welsh border.

Another bit of regional folk-medicine, hitherto 'very little known in any county except Lancashire',[39] also achieved orthodoxy. This was 'the cod or ling liver oil' long used by fisherfolk on the north-west coast to cure rheumatic complaints. It is possible the idea first came to this country via Icelandic fishermen, who had always believed that a nauseous mixture of mutton fat and fish liver oils was an essential to health. By some 'accidental circumstances'[40] this folk remedy came to the attention of the doctors of the Manchester Infirmary in the early 1770s and they tried it out on chronic rheumatic cases with such success that the Infirmary was shortly ordering 50 to 60 gallons of the brew a year. Those who could stand the taste and smell of the stuff, for the oil was extracted chiefly by allowing the livers to rot, showed improvement where everything else had failed. So here, in this century, is the first record of cod liver oil being used internally and clinically. It may not have cured chronic rheumatism—we still do not know how to do that—but in cases where rickets was confused with rheumatism the results may have been dramatic and more beneficial than crawling through a hole in a large stone, which was the cure for rickets in Cornwall.

The incidence of rickets, known abroad as 'the English Disease',

* See *The Jacobeans at Home*, Chapter VI, for description of ingredients.

was still appalling. In London, Westminster and their suburbs alone, Sir John Fordyce estimated in 1773 that there were 'nearly twenty thousand children . . . ill at this moment of the Hectic Fever, attended with *tun-bellies, swelled wrists and ancles or crooked limbs*'⁴¹ (my italics). This description powerfully suggests rickets, and Fordyce puts the condition down to dark, overcrowded living conditions, and a bad diet. He was quite right. But who was to know that sunlight lay hidden in a cod's liver, of all improbable places, or that thousands of wretched, rickety, overworked, undernourished and poverty-stricken children could have been saved by a Lancashire folk remedy?

The mortality rate among infants and children was, as usual, shockingly high. If a child survived birth and its first year it quite frequently died before its third or fifth year of some quite simple thing which we today would not dream of allowing a child to die of. Ten or twelve children of whom three or four survived was a quite usual family pattern; King George III and Queen Charlotte had fifteen children. To breed like a rabbit was, metaphorically speaking, the common lot of woman. To do so, literally, was not.

It therefore created an immense sensation when Mary Toft, of Godalming, gave birth to her first rabbit in November 1726. As she achieved this feat in the presence of a reputable Guildford surgeon, Mr John Howard, it could hardly be a fraud. Further, as Mary continued to produce rabbits, torrents of pamphlets appeared about her and people streamed from London and the countryside to see this prodigy (for a fee). Even that dullard, George I, was astonished and sent his physician, Nathanael St André, to investigate. Mr St André arrived just in time to deliver a rabbit himself. Sceptics might jeer at the whole thing but was it likely that the king's own physician could be deceived by an illiterate country woman? It was very likely indeed; and by the time Mary had produced her seventeenth rabbit (more than double the number a real rabbit would produce) the king sent the most famous man-midwife of the day, Sir Richard Manningham (1690–1759) to make a thorough examination. Determined to arrive at the truth and to separate Mary from any possible accomplices, Sir Richard moved her to London 'and lodged her at Mr Lacy's Bagnio in Leicester Fields'.[42] Here he sat up with her all night and although she certainly appeared to be in labour and 'many Persons of Distinction' came to witness the birth, Mary failed to produce a single rabbit. Dr James Douglas, another eminent physician, was called in. He too suspected fraud—but it simply could not be proved. It was only by threatening poor Mary with 'a terrible operation'[43]—and operations rivalled the tortures of the Inquisition—she was brought to confess that the idea of breeding rabbits herself, was suggested by a woman accomplice 'as a way of getting a good livelihood'. Mary was imprisoned, but not for long. Mr Howard and Mr St André's reputations were ruined (St André lost favour at court and disappeared), but Sir Richard Manningham's reputation was considerably enhanced, as it deserved to be. His book *Artis Obstetricariae Compendium* (1740) opened—and high time—a new chapter in midwifery, and he was the first to institute lying-in wards in hospitals.

But the greatest man-midwife of the century was the Scot, William Smellie (1697–1763), who came to London in 1739. His *Treatise on Midwifery* appeared in 1752 and in it he gave a perfectly clear account of the mechanism of labour (he had attended

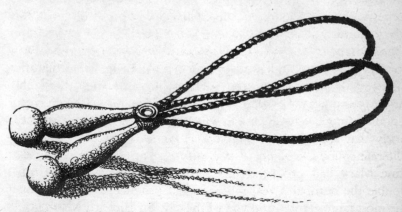

William Smellie's long leather-wrapped obstetric forceps. Mid-eighteenth century

1,150 cases himself), laid down good rules for practice, and corrected a good many ancient errors. Fortunately for women and children, Smellie was an excellent teacher; about 900 students passed through his hands and learned his technique. This must have been a great boon to women who were perpetually pregnant and who so often died in childbed either from puerperal fever or the brutal methods of delivery. Smellie altered these methods and, though he did not invent forceps nor advocate their general use, he was among the first to use them and he improved them so vastly that when used correctly they damaged neither mother nor child. No longer was there any excuse for an accoucheur* like Dr Slop† to disfigure a child with the 'new-invented'[44] forceps of the seventeenth century.

Smellie's most famous pupil was another Scot, William Hunter (1718–83), onetime assistant to Dr James Douglas, and surgeon-accoucheur who did much to improve midwifery. Delicate, painted and fashionable, he was also a 'dissector' or anatomist. But at this he was surpassed by his younger brother, John (1728–93), a pupil of Cheselden and Pott, whose life, like Dr Jenner's, is too well known to need detailing here. What is, perhaps, not so well known is that Natural History Museums all over the world owe a debt to John Hunter whose own museum, illustrating the development of life from the primitive to the highest form, was the model for all others. One catches a glimpse of what this 'teaching museum' was like in a letter from Hunter to his pupil Edward Jenner. 'I have a great scheme', he writes, probably in 1775, 'to teach natural history, in which will be included anatomy both human and comparative.'[45] Again, one gets the whole measure of his approach in another letter to Jenner concerning an experiment Jenner made on a hedgehog. 'I think your solution just', he says, 'but why think—why not try the experiment?'[46]

This sums up John Hunter's attitude and also the attitude of many other medical men of the time. Among them were men

* The word 'accoucheur' began to replace 'man-midwife' in the 1750s. The word 'obstetrician' did not come in until the end of George IV's reign.
† Dr Slop is a caricature of Dr Burton of York.

like Sir Charles Bell, another Scot who came to London. Bell wrote 'the first textbook of modern neurology'[47] in 1830 and had previously demonstrated that there were two great classes of nerves, motor and sensory. We laymen are more likely to remember him because he described and defined 'Bell's palsy' (peripheral paralysis of the facial nerve). There was James Parkinson who in 1815 identified the condition, paralysis agitans, 'Parkinson's disease'. There was Richard Bright who first described nephritis, 'Bright's disease', in 1827; and much, much earlier, Sir John Pringle (also a Scot), an army surgeon who in 1752 used the word 'antiseptic'[48] for the first time in history. Sir John has long been forgotten but his father-in-law, Dr William Oliver of Bath, has not. He is still famous as the inventor of the 'Bath Oliver'.

So, despite false starts, mistakes, blunders and blind alleys, true medical knowledge grew slowly but steadily between the accession of George I and the death of George IV. More was known about the functions of the body, more about the nature of disease, and many more diseases and disfunctions had been carefully observed and described. Even so, the rich and fashionable often found it very dull indeed to listen to a doctor's advice, and positively deadly to act upon it, particularly if advised to go on a diet, or to give up drink, or get more sleep, or live in the country merely because one suffered a loss of 'vital spirit' or from the 'vapours', gout, old age—or boredom. Many doctors, but by no means all, were now less prone to push panaceas, although Dr James spent his life pushing his powder. Instant diagnosis by uroscopy, with a favourable or a fatal prognosis, had had its day and this naturally slowed things down, while very few reputable medical men now took the stars into consultation. Doctors, in general, had become rather more cautious—and caution is never glamorous or very interesting. So it is not surprising that many doctors failed to fall upon Luigi Galvani's discovery, made in 1791, that muscular contraction could be produced by electrical action. It was the quacks who took this up and made a fortune. By the end of the eighteenth century and the beginning of the nineteenth, galvanism had become the rage. Not only was it new but it certainly provided a sensation both in the literal and figurative sense of the word. The vital spirits were positively galvanized into action, diseases were driven out and health was maintained by continued treatment.

It is often claimed that out of this bogus 'galvanism' the modern science of electrotherapy developed. This may well be true, yet it is curious to note that some sort of electromedical treatment was being used in England long before Galvani's discovery. 'Electricity . . . comes nearest an universal medicine, of any yet known in the world',[49] was John Wesley's view in 1760. Even earlier, on September 2nd 1752—that is on the day before we finally became European enough to adopt the Gregorian calendar—Thomas Gyll of Durham writes in his diary: 'My cousin Hunter (i.e. Thomas Hunter of Medomsley) was electrified on his lips and cheek by Mr Dixon, a surgeon of Barnard Castle, and by that means and a little instruction he was able to speak some words, which he had not been able to do ever since he was deprived of the use of his tongue by a fit of palsy, on the 19th May 1751.'[50] The words Thomas Hunter was able to say, were 'law, saw, no, yes, as, was, me', a not very encouraging list but Gyll hoped that 'by the means of electricity he will be restored to the use of his speech'.

Unfortunately Gyll tells us nothing as to the means or instrument used by Dr Dixon. Perhaps it was so well known that he felt no need to go into details. Here I can only suggest—or rather hazard a guess: Dr Dixon may have used some type of frictional electricity machine, perhaps a modification of the one invented by Hauksbee in 1709. Or he may have touched his patient on the lips or tongue with a glass rod rubbed with a piece of silk. Or have made use of the 'Leyden' jar, discovered in 1745 and improved upon by William Watson in 1746. But I cannot even guess whether Thomas Hunter did fully recover his speech; we hear no more about him from Cousin Gyll save that he died of a fit of apoplexy 'when taking the air on June 24 1756'.[51] Yet this shows electrotherapy, as such, certainly began in England in the

Leyden jars. Late eighteenth century

early not in the late Georgian period. And it certainly began in America around mid-century too, for in the very year Thomas Hunter was 'electrified', Benjamin Franklin (1706–90) discovered the identity of lightning and electricity. He then provided himself with a static generator, sent to him from England it is said, and opened a clinic in Green Street, Philadelphia, for the medical use of electricity. Just in case anyone should feel inclined to argue over which country was first in this electromedical field it should be noted, promptly, that very probably the earliest use of electrotherapy was suggested by Largus (Scribonius) court physician to the Emperor Claudius (*c.* A.D. 47). He recommended the constant application of the electric ray fish in cases of headache and facial neuralgia.

Nevertheless, one of the really great pieces of mechanical quackery to enliven the late eighteenth century *did* come from America. This was 'Perkins Patent Tractors' and they had nothing at all to do with agricultural machinery. Elisha Perkins, a medical practitioner of Norwich, Connecticut, believed that metals had a great influence if applied externally, and he invented an appliance called at first 'Mettalic Tractors'. It consisted of two rods each about three inches long, shaped like a half round of moulding, with a pointed end and a round end. One rod was of copper, zinc and gold; the other of iron, platinum and silver. Drawn downward over the body they attracted and drew out whatever it was that ailed one. The Medical Society of Connecticut was decidedly sceptical, so Elisha went off to Philadelphia (then the capital) and had a great success. Congress believed in Perkins, so did General Washington, who bought a pair of tractors (patented 1796) for his family. Even with this testimonial the medical men of Norwich were not satisfied. 'Delusive quackery' they called it, and expelled Perkins. When the popularity of the tractors started to wane, Elisha bethought him of England and sent his son, Benjamin Charles, over to introduce them into this country. Benjamin settled in a house once occupied by John Hunter and published a book about his father's wonderful discovery. As usual, we were eager and willing to be taken in. Even the Royal Society accepted the book as well as a pair of Tractors. Soon young Perkins was importing tractors in lots of 200 and selling them for five guineas a pair. Soon remarkable cures were reported from all over the country. Soon a *Perkinean Institute* was founded, with Lord Rivers at its head, to treat the poor, who could not possibly afford rods of gold and silver (as it happened the gold rod was pure brass and the silver one plain iron). Here, all disorders were cured, including such varied things as red noses, windy bowels, broken legs and hump-back.

But not everyone believed in the Tractors. Popular ballads—often more sceptical than sentimental—were circulated and sung. 'Armed with twin skewers, see Perkins by main force/Drag the foul fiend from Christian and from horse' one ran. Dr John Haygarth of Bath was sceptical also, and decided to try an experiment. He made up a pair of tractors of wood, painted them to resemble the 'real' thing, and with them out-Perkined Perkins with his cures. Then he and another doctor sent out dozens of pairs of these imitation tractors to other physicians—they too reported astonishing results. The two doctors published the results of their own 'experiments' and that was the end of Perkins Patent Tractors, though not of Benjamin Charles. He returned home the richer by £10,000. As Lord Byron puts it.

What varied wonders tempt us as they pass!
The Cow-Pox, Tractors, Galvanism and Gas,
In turns appear, to make the vulgar stare,
Till the swoll'n bubble bursts—and all is air.[52]

But the vulgar and not-so-vulgar had been staring—and will continue to stare—for centuries. One of the greatest late century sights—if one could afford it—was Dr James Graham's Temple of Health, which he opened in the Adelphi in 1778. Graham, a Scot, was an oculist, had travelled in America, and in Philadelphia had learned of Franklin's work with electricity. So his temple of health was full of electromedical appliances. Here too he had his consulting rooms where he peddled his own nostrums such as 'the Elixir of Life' (said to have sold for £1,000), his 'Imperial Pills', 'Electrical Aether', and something called the 'Nervous Aetherial'. The vaulted hall of his temple offered ample proof of his cures, it was ornamented with crutches, walking sticks, ear trumpets, eye glasses, trusses and so on, all left behind by cured patients. It was also full of great globes, fire-breathing sphinxes, marble statues, paintings—and very soft couches. But all this was as nothing to the 'Great Appollo Apartment' within which was the 'Templum Aesculapius Sacrum'.[53] Here odes were sung to organ music, and Graham—for a fee—lectured on subjects such as 'The Preservation and Exaltation of Loveliness'. Here, also, he displayed his Magnetic Throne in which patients could be treated. The Temple and sundry other apartments, including those containing his Celestial Beds, were presided over by a blacksmith's daughter known as 'Hebe Vestinia', goddess of Health. She is better known to us as Lady Hamilton. These early celestial beds cured all sorts of ailments and in them, Graham claimed, children of the most celestial beauty could be begotten. So successful was he that in 1781 he moved into Schomberg House, Pall Mall, (still standing) which he fitted up even more lavishly as 'the Temple of Health and Hymen'. This contained the greatest bed of all, 'the Celestial State Bed' (it is not clear whether 'celestial' modifies State or Bed). It stood on forty glass pillars and was filled with magnets which, surprisingly, gave 'a sweet, undulating, tittulating, vibratory, soul-dissolving, marrow-melting motion'[54]—so useful, he explained, on certain critical and important occasions. The fee (one provided one's own partner) was £100 per night.

But Graham failed. Possibly his expensive beds did not after all produce ravishing children; and if one were going to produce perfectly plain little babies one could do so at home, or elsewhere, for very much less than £100. Pursued by creditors, Graham left London and spent some time in gaol in Edinburgh before returning and deciding that religion was as good a paying proposition as sex (he obviously knew his Sassenach). He proposed to establish a new religion, and a new, true Christian Church. But as the field was, by now, rather overcrowded, his new religion was not a success. Furthermore, it was now clear that Graham was mad. He was confined, in Edinburgh, as a lunatic and died in 1794. He was only forty-nine and had clearly forgotten to take his own expensive Elixir, which prolonged life to the age of 150.

Graham's madness was said to be due to, or aggravated by, his habit of sniffing ether. One cannot but suspect, since 'ether frolics' were popular, that his various aetherial medicines must have contained ether—even a tiny amount taken by mouth has the most intoxicating effect (it is also highly dangerous because it leads to rapid addiction). What seems odd, now, is that although pharmaceutical ether (di-ethyl ether) had been known, probably as early as the thirteenth century and in 1730 had first received the name we now know it by, 'spiritus aetherius' (also called vini vitriolatus), no one seems to have suspected its uses as an anaesthetic. Further, the first suggestion that laughing gas (nitrous oxide) might be used as an anaesthetic was made by Sir Humphry Davy, who invented the safety lamp for miners as early as 1800, but nothing came of it. People just had to go on enduring agonies of unanaesthetized surgery for another forty-odd years.*

Nor had the treatment of madness improved greatly over the centuries. For the most part the demented were imprisoned and chained like criminals. At Bedlam they were still exhibited like—and as—wild beasts for the amusement of the public. There were, of course, private asylums for the lunatic rich where treatment was possibly better than that given to the psychotic poor: but of this we know very little. Obviously, the best known and best documented case of insanity during this period is that of George III.

In the autumn of 1788—the year in which Lord Byron was born—the King appeared to be greatly agitated and flurried. His physician diagnosed that useful all embracing disease 'gout' and recommended a course of the waters at Cheltenham. This caused some temporary improvement, but in October the King grew much worse so his physician, Sir George Baker, gave him a series of such violent purges that they had to be followed by sedatives.

---

* In 1842 the American C. W. Long used ether for a minor operation. In 1845 H. Wells used gas for the same purpose. In 1846 the American W. T. G. Morton carried out the first major operation using ether—and the science of anaesthetics was born.

Silver bleeding bowl, mid-eighteenth century

The results were appalling and Baker soon told the Prime Minister, the younger Pitt, that his majesty was now in a state bordering on delirium.* About this time Fanny Burney, lurking in the passages at Windsor, was stopped by the King who talked to her for half an hour about his health, 'still with that extreme quickness of speech and manner that belongs to fever',[55] she says, 'and he hardly sleeps . . . one minute all night. . . . He is all agitation, all emotion, yet all benevolence and goodness, even to a degree that makes it touching to hear him speak. He assures everybody of his health; he seems only fearful to give uneasiness to others.'

The wretched King went on talking non-stop sometimes for nineteen hours on end. He talked himself voiceless. His eyes reminded his terrified Queen of 'blackcurrant jelly'.[56] His face was red, the veins corded. Sir George applied agonizing blisters to his majesty's head to draw out the poisons in the brain. Dr William Heberden and various others were called in. They tried other painful and useless treatments. So it can hardly be called a symptom of his disease that the King had 'a rooted aversion to physicians'.[57] On November 5th, the Prince of Wales arrived from Brighthelmston. The two events may not be related but at dinner that day the King went raving mad. The Queen fell into 'violent hysterics'.[58] All the princesses were 'in misery'. The Prince of Wales burst into tears and sent at once for Dr Warren —a supporter of the Prince and of the Whigs. Dr Warren was extremely gloomy. He believed there was absolutely no hope of recovery—which suited the opposition and the Prince. It did not suit Queen Charlotte, or Mr Pitt. One month later the Queen sent for the Rev. Dr Francis Willis, a parson-doctor, rector of Wapping and head of a private asylum in Lincolnshire. Dr Willis and his son, Dr John Willis, were both encouraging.

In the meantime Sir George Baker had been threatened by a mob for not curing the King who was in high favour at the moment. But that 'first Gentleman of Europe', the Prince of Wales, an excellent mimic, drew great applause from his cronies

---

* The King had a mild touch of madness as early as 1765.

at Brooks's by mimicking his father's ravings. Other Whig gentlemen, addicted to gambling at the same club, found it infinitely witty to refer to the court card as 'The Lunatic';[59] and fashionable Whig ladies took to wearing Regency caps. Soon the Prince would be Regent with full sovereign powers and then— out with Pitt, in with Fox! Pitt, however, played for time* and backed Willis, *père et fils*, rather than Warren.

He was right to do so. In March the King recovered. London turned out joyfully to see the fireworks and the illuminations. George III's picture and the Royal Crown were everywhere. His popularity might, and did, wax and wane in London but he was always popular in the provinces. When he went to Weymouth to convalesce, all along the route he received the wildest welcome. Triumphal arches of flowers were set up bearing inscriptions such as 'The King Restored' and 'Long Live the King'. Everywhere he went 'the acclamation with which the King was received . . . was a rapture past description'.[60]

How had Dr Willis and his son 'restored' the King? It seems they tried a new method of treatment devised, developed and used by themselves. Firmness, kindness, cheerfulness and affection were its keynotes. Although when violent the King had to be confined in a strait jacket or strapped in a chair—his Coronation Chair, he called it (this is much more sadly revealing than humorous)—the two doctors treated him as a human being. They tried to understand him as well as his illness. They encouraged him to play backgammon, chess, picquet and the flute, for he loved music, and Handel above all other composers. They tried to draw him into rational conversation which the other physicians had not attempted, and although they enforced discipline they seem to have treated him, as far as possible, as if he were sane. They were simple, unaffected, unambitious men themselves and, at bottom, so was the King. In short, the doctors Willis used the elements of modern psychiatry before there was such a term as psychiatry.

---

* Ultimately he offered only a limited Regency Bill where the Regent would be under the control of parliament.

Although it is usual to consider the King to have been manic depressive, recent exhaustive medical research into contemporary medical documents certainly seem to cast doubt upon this diagnosis of his mental state.* Nevertheless, he certainly did have recurrent bouts of madness from which he recovered, and perhaps he might not have done so if repeated, blistering, purging and harsh treatment had continued. It may have been this success with the King which led to a more understanding treatment of the

* In January, 1966, Dr Ida Macalpine and Dr Richard Hunter on further examination of the medical reports of the king's madness, suggested that he suffered from a 'classic case of porphyria'—a genetically determined metabolic disturbance transmitted as a Mendelian dominant. For a full and beautifully documented account see *The British Medical Journal* No. 5479, January 8th 1966, p. 65 *et. seq.*

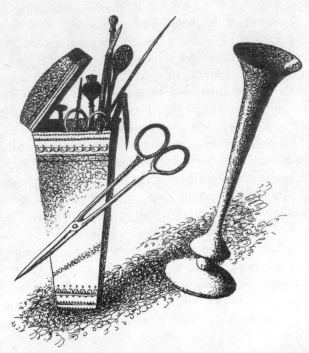

Pocket surgical instrument case, mid-eighteenth century, and monaural stethoscope, *circa* 1805

insane, and there was a good deal of insanity in the period. Although William Tuke, who had a private mental hospital in York in 1794, is usually credited with inaugurating humane treatment, the Rev. Dr Francis Willis and his son John, were earlier by half a century.

In 1810 the King went finally and hopelessly insane. 'An old, mad, blind, despised, and dying king',[61] Mr Shelley called him. One is saddened at this particular piece of man's inhumanity to man, even from a youthful republican poet. Lear too was 'a poor, infirm, weak, and despis'd old man'.[62] But Lear had had Shakespeare to speak for him.

CHAPTER SEVEN

Of Diversions and Amusements

Grumpy old Uncle Matthew elected to go by coach, his niece and nephew by boat; thus, at nine o'clock on a deceptively fine May evening around the year 1770, Miss Lydia Melford, her brother and two others embarked in a 'light and slender' wherry at Ranelagh for Vauxhall. Arrived there, Lydia was 'completely dazzled and confounded' by the beauty of the place. 'Imagine', she writes her friend, Miss Loetitia Willis, buried alive in dreary old Gloucester, 'a spacious garden, part laid out in delightful walks, bounded with high hedges and trees, and paved with gravel; part exhibiting a most wonderful assemblage of the most picturesque and striking objects, pavilions, lodges, groves, grottoes, lawns, temples, and cascades; porticoes, colonnades and rotundos; adorned with pillars, statues, and painting; the whole illuminated with an infinite number of lamps, disposed in different figures of suns, stars and constellations; the place crowded with the gayest company, ranging through the blissful shades, or supping in different lodges on cold collations, enlivened with mirth, freedom and good humour, and animated by an excellent band of music.' Here Lydia heard a celebrated soprano 'whose voice was so loud and shrill' that it made her head 'ake through excess pleasure'.[1] The only flaw in a wonderful evening was that it soon began to rain which made Uncle Matthew more peevish than ever. Unlike James Boswell, who thought the gardens 'an excellent place of public amusement . . . particularly adapted to the taste of the English Nation',[2] Uncle Matthew found Vauxhall 'a composition of baubles . . . contrived to dazzle the eye and divert the imagination of the vulgar'.[3]

Some twenty years before this, on a fine evening in June, the eyes and the imagination of a great concourse of the vulgar were dazzled and diverted by a party occupying one of the booths near the orchestra. To gape at the antics of the beau monde out for an evening's fun was one of the pleasures of Vauxhall. On this evening the occupants of the booth were 'gloriously jolly and handsome', Lady Caroline Petersham 'with the vizor of her hat erect',[4] Lord Orford and his witty, younger brother, the Hon Horatio Walpole, little Miss Ashe, affectionately known as 'Pollard', Harry Vane and a Mr Whitehed; Lord March (better known to us later as 'Old Q'), the 2nd Duke of Kingston,* nephew to that 'she-meteor'[5] Lady Mary Wortley Montagu; Lord Granby, undeniably drunk, and 'a very pretty Miss Beau-clerc and a very foolish Miss Sparre'.[6] All were busily engaged in cutting up seven chickens into a china dish which 'with three pats of butter and a flagon of water'[7] plus a lamp were being turned into what must have been a rather messy mince. Lady Caroline had brought Betty, the fruit woman from St James's Street, with her and there were hampers of strawberries and cherries to be eaten, and plenty of wine to be drunk. So the party went merrily on and on while the vulgar stared and gaped from ten until past one o'clock.

Vauxhall Gardens, occupying about twelve acres across the Thames from Westminster Abbey, was the oldest† of London's pleasure gardens. Originally known as Spring Gardens, it had alternately flourished and declined ever since the Restoration. But in 1730 it took a new lease on life when Mr Jonathan Tyers bought, enlarged and reopened it with a *ridotto al fresco*. Since few had ever heard of this species of entertainment before, every-

---

* He married the notorious Elizabeth Chudleigh in 1769.

† The next oldest of celebrated gardens was 'Cupid's' or Cuper's, founded in 1691 by Boyder Cuper. It stood near the southern approach to Waterloo Bridge and Waterloo Road now passes over the centre of it. It closed in 1759.

Vauxhall Gardens. Triumphal arches, *circa* 1752

one, including Frederick Prince of Wales, flocked to see what it was and the new Vauxhall was assured of success. Tyers went on improving the place. He added an organ to the orchestra—this he ultimately housed in a Gothic structure which wore a dome surmounted by a plume! The walks were much improved and through triumphal arches one could see paintings of the ruins of Palmyra and other scenes. On the 'Rural Downs' a clump of 'Musical Bushes' emitted music, due to a band concealed in a nearby hole in the ground. But this so often filled with water that it had to be abandoned, the orchestra preferring to play 'Water Music' on the dry stage of the Rotunda where concerts of songs, sonate, concerti lasting four hours were frequently given. There was something for everyone at Vauxhall, and those with the price of the entrance—one shilling—went there as often as possible, while those who could afford to paid a guinea for a silver season ticket. And, of course, Vauxhall drew visitors; it was one of the sights, although foreigners seem to have been less impressed with it than natives. 'A much vaunted pleasure garden', says a Swedish visitor, but also full of 'ruffians . . . who rob'.[8] It was not, he thought, a good place for young men and women to spend an evening, because it led them to become 'used to doing no work.' and to squandering money. Another and later visitor was positively astonished by 'the boldness of the women of the town; who along with their pimps' often rushed into booths 'by half dozens; and in the most shameless manner importuned . . . for wine for themselves and their followers'.[9] What foreigners, no doubt, could not and did not understand was that Vauxhall was a place of public amusement, open to all. Class distinctions did not apply. Ruffians, pimps and prostitutes on one hand, the *ton* on the other made it dangerous and glamorous—the combination is irresistible. For those who were neither *haut* nor *bas* Vauxhall was an excitement and a gaze.

This was more or less true of all London pleasure gardens.* There was Ranelagh, up the river and up the social scale where, as Walpole put it, 'you can't set your foot without treading on a Prince or Duke of Cumberland'.[10] Its large wooden rotunda was thought by contemporaries to compare favourably with the Pantheon at Rome. Inside was the orchestra, an organ, boxes, recesses, for supper, and a large pillared and arched structure to support the olive green ceiling painted with a rainbow. This structure originally held the orchestra, but was later turned into a very necessary open fireplace. Around it, the company promenaded to see and be seen. Coarse, vulgar, uneducated and unprincipled Mme Duval was shocked to see 'ladies come to so genteel a place with hats on'. Nothing so 'monstrous vulgar'[11] as hatted women were to be seen in places of public entertainment in Paris! Yet upon Dr Johnson, Ranelagh produced 'an expansion and gay sensation' such as he 'never experienced any where else'.[12] It must also have been an unique experience

---

* There were between sixty and seventy pleasure gardens in London during the eighteenth century, many short-lived and many only tea gardens or taverns with perhaps a bowling green.

when on June 29th 1764, the child prodigy, eight-year-old Wolfgang Amadeus Mozart, gave a concert there where he played his own compositions upon the harpsichord and organ. But all the large pleasure gardens gave concerts of excellent music as well as those of the more ephemeral kind. One cannot use the word 'pop' in connection with the latter for both the excellent and the ephemeral seem to have been equally popular.

Newer than Vauxhall or Ranelagh was Marybone Gardens,* particularly noted for its fireworks displays. We were as mad as ever about fireworks and almost the only engaging thing about George II is that he loved fireworks and was an authority on the designing of set pieces. Marybone fireworks went beyond set pieces, rockets, pumps with stars, and swarms when in the 1770s a French artist, M. Torré, introduced 'pantomimical spectacles'[13] with plenty of stage machinery and scenery. *The Forge of Vulcan* and *The Descent of Orpheus into Hades* lent themselves splendidly to pyrotechnical story-telling, even though there were mishaps— but mishaps with fireworks had been endured for centuries.† On one occasion, at the very moment when Orpheus gave Eurydice 'the fatal look which separated them for ever', there was 'such an explosion of fire and so horrid a noise' that 'everyone fled hastily fearing mischief from the innumerable sparks'.[14] Mischief for the fleeing Evelina Belmont came from quite other kinds of sparks, 'bold and unfeeling' men who constantly addressed her, so that in a panic she sought the protection of two strange women. They turned out to be tarts. Marybone like all other gardens attracted all kinds of people.

But London, itself the great centre of pleasure, was made up of and attracted all sorts and conditions of men and women. Those with any pretensions to *ton* who were unfortunate enough to be incarcerated in the country, 'with demi-human, demi-brutal

---

* It had existed but under other names since the end of the seventeenth century. It was renamed Marybone in 1738 and was then run (until 1763) by John Trusler, father of the Rev. John Trusler, By 1800 the eight acre garden had disappeared under buildings.

† At a great display in Green Park, 1749, rocket sparks caused grave accidents and many women had their clothing set alight.

boobies'[15] for neighbours, lived only for a London season. Who, indeed, could 'live in one of those temples of dullness called country seats, where yawns are the form of worship?'[16] The answer was, a great many could and did. Some even managed to enjoy it. Many also lived in or near expanding provincial towns. Many lived in still remote rural areas, and they lived, according to their means and occupations, in small houses, on tiny farms, in cottages. They comprised all but about fifteen per cent of the population. But by mid-Georgian times most of the larger provincial towns had their own Assembly rooms for cards, ridottos, routs, 'hops', concerts and 'come as you fancy' dress parties. Small towns and villages made do with a local inn or tavern for dancing, music, drums, masquerades or card parties held at seemly intervals.

The theatre had also come to the provinces. Provincial theatres were being built, slowly from the time of the first George and more rapidly after 1750. Where there was no local theatre, bands of strolling players performed, sometimes in the court house, sometimes in a large barn—hence 'barn-stormers'. The great increase in the number of theatres all over the country was a phenomenon of the Georgian era. In the previous century there had been but two theatres in London and none in the provinces. Further, from about the last quarter of the eighteenth century reputable London actors decided it was no longer beneath them (it could also be profitable) to tour the provinces for a summer season and Mrs Siddons was among the first to go on tour. Yet the puritanical prejudice against actors and the theatre was not yet dead. When Mrs Siddons was engaged to appear at the Theatre Royal, Sheffield, 'She wanted to put up at the Angel Inn but they would not take her in'.[17] The proprietor of the Angel was not going to have Mrs Siddons in his hostelry, not even if she had appeared at Windsor Castle to read *The Provok'd Wife* and part of Catherine of Aragon's speech from *Henry VIII* before King George III, Queen Charlotte, assorted Royal princesses, and select guests. 'I am an enthusiast for her', the king cried on an earlier occasion. 'I think there was never any player in my time so excellent—not Garrick himself; I owne it!'[18]

Walnut spinet. Early eighteenth century

Less happy in its visiting players was Alnwick where, in December 1787, Mr Strickland's company of comedians appeared. The actors 'were very indifferent', had been 'collected from all quarters' and were 'in no wise fit for a theatre'.[19] Or so that Alnwick attorney, coroner for Northumberland and devotee of cock-fighting, Nicholas Brown, informs us. He obviously preferred the performing pig exhibited publicly at Alnwick the previous February. This, he thought, truly 'remarkable'. Perhaps this was the same well-educated pig which Miss Seward saw in Nottingham in 1785, the tale of which so greatly amused the dying Dr Johnson.

Music was a provincial no less than a capital pleasure. The opera in London was particularly fashionable throughout the whole era. People had their favourite singers—usually Italian—as well as composers and grew so heated over their respective merits that great tracasseries ensued. Politics entered into music too. George

II was a devotee of Handel (as was George III) so his son, Frederick, supported Bononcini. It was at the Prince of Wales's house at Cliveden that *Alfred* was first performed, in 1740, with music by the celebrated but not very pleasant Dr Arne. Here the audience heard, with great fervour and for the first time, *Rule Britannia*. Thus broadly, one might say, a Walpolian type of Whig stuck to Handel. Others who favoured the Prince's politics (the elder Pitt among them) were stuck with Bononcini and, probably *Rule Britannia*—to say nothing of Frederick himself, who played the violoncello rather well. But the Hanoverian sovereigns were musical, played various instruments, and even George IV had a very pleasing baritone.

In the provinces, fortunately, music was a less complicated watch-your-step affair. Most towns had their own local bands,

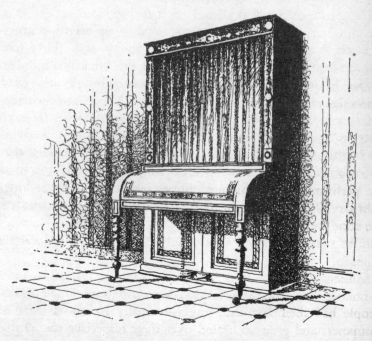

Broadwood cabinet pianoforte, *circa* 1810

orchestras, bell ringers, glee clubs, a fiddler or two, and plenty of talented or untalented amateurs willing and eager to perform upon harpsichord, spinet or, later, upon the new pianoforte. But professional musicians, like actors, also went on tour. Parson Woodforde (he played the spinet) and some friends had a feast of music when they attended a 'Miscellaneous Concert' in St Andrew's Hall, Norwich, in 1788 (tickets 7s 6d) where, he says, 'Madame Mara* the famous singer, sung delightfully. I never heard so fine a voice—Her Notes so high.'[20] A good sharp, shrill soprano seems to have been uncommonly pleasant to the English ear. But Parson Woodforde was equally pleased with 'the Kettle Drums from Westminster Abbey'. They 'sounded charmingly, beat by a Mr Ashbridge'. As no other percussion instruments were then used orchestrally, and the diarist speaks of 'drums' we can infer that Mr Ashbridge sustained the harmony with two of them; one tonic the other dominant.

The orchestra itself consisted of 'near 100 performers',[21] a circumstance well worth noting as the eighteenth-century orchestra usually numbered between thirty and thirty-five members except on special occasions like this when the number was trebled. On one even more special occasion in 1785 at a grand concert of Handel's works in Westminster Abbey, the orchestra numbered 600 members. So our own over-sized orchestras have their roots in the Georgian era. It would be interesting to know if the mammoth orchestra Parson Woodforde heard included that beautiful, new-to-the-century woodwind, the clarinet,† and if the string section made use of the elegant new balanced bow, invented around 1775 by François Tourte, instead of the centuries-

---

* Mme Mara (née Elizabeth Gertrude Schmeling) 1749–1833 a German soprano, appeared first in Dresden Court Opera in 1771 and in London in 1784. She was in great demand, sang at Ranelagh and the Pantheon and is said to have earned 3,000 guineas a year.

† In the early eighteenth century, woodwinds were little better than six fingered primitive pipes; but keys were added and the range extended. The brasswind section of any orchestra was then without trombones, tubas, valved trumpets or valved horns, none of which came in until the nineteenth century. Nor was the harp used orchestrally until then.

Glass 'Armonica', treadle-operated, mid to late eighteenth century

old arc shaped one, but the parson does not tell us. What he does say is that on the following evening they all went to hear Handel's *Judas Maccabaeus*, at St Peter's Church, which was 'very fine', although one of the party, Mrs Davy, obviously overcome 'made some little disturbance, fainting away, but she soon came to herself again'.[22]

Here it might not be amiss to note that new and necessarily ephemeral musical instruments were developed by the early Georgians. These were of glass and had become possible when methods of toughening Ravenscroft's resonant flint glass were discovered. Tapping out simple tunes and hymns on goblets filled with water to the correct scale-tone level was relatively common by 1730. By 1743 touring musicians were giving performances on larger and louder glasses and, in 1746, Gluck played a concerto in London which he had specially composed for twenty-six glasses and orchestra. These glasses produced their notes when flicked with a fingernail or rubbed round the rim with the finger. Benjamin Franklin, in London in 1762, constructed or improved upon an instrument which he first called 'the glassy chord' and later the 'armonica'* (not to be confused with harmonica). Playing upon musical glasses of various sorts soon became a favourite home entertainment. No one seemed to mind the shrill, piercing sound. But the shrill sound was considerably softened when emitted by the 'Sticcardo pastorale' made 'of several long pieces of glass and is played in the middle parts . . . by two little sticks with Nobbs'. It was a very small instrument 'and looks when covered like a working Box for ladies'.[23] Mrs Custance played upon this baby, glass, xylophone for Parson Woodforde in 1788, to his great pleasure.

Among less sophisticated or less cultural pleasures of country life were the far more simple rustic amusements and sports, in some of which the gentry participated. According to the novels written during the period, the chief sport of the young country gentleman was the seduction of female servants, a pastime which often seems to have been enjoyed as much by the quarry as by the hunter. But there were the Squire Westerns too, who cared only for the hunting of any animal which could be hunted, drink, and the damnation of 'a parcel of . . . Hanover rats' who threatened 'to eat up all our corn' and leave us 'nothing but turneps to feed upon'.[24] A most diverting sort of lazy hunting remained popular until around 1770; this was duck hunting, much practised in rural districts about London. It was an inexpensive sport requiring only a dog and a duck. The dog was set upon the duck and kept it diving until the bird was exhausted. An even more amusing variation was to tie an owl to the duck's back. The duck dived to shake off the owl. The half-drowned owl upon emerging hooted mournfully which frightened the duck into diving again. This went on until the wretched owl was dead. Sometimes the duck died too.

Bear, bull, and badger-baiting, and cock-fighting, were also enormously popular with all classes in both urban and country districts. But for sheer spectacle there was nothing to beat a

* This was made of glass bowls fitted concentrically and horizontally into a long harpsichord-like case. There is an armonica in the museum of the Royal College of Music.

hanging. This type of entertainment increased fivefold during the eighteenth century. At the beginning there were no more than fifty capital offences; by the end there were nearly two hundred and fifty. In London convivial parties of bucks would breakfast together and then go on to Tyburn to see victims hanged. George Selwyn, the noted wit, is said to have taken a particular pleasure in watching executions.

Other long-loved sports and recreations, however, declined in popularity. We hear less about skull-bashing cudgel play—although Parson Adams was a neat hand with a cudgel in self defence. Wrestling, once immensely popular, was now chiefly confined to the lower orders and, curiously enough, the once almost national pastime, bowling on the green or in open alleys, became almost exclusively a country sport. London had taken up the new form of long-bowling or Dutch rubbers, played in a long, narrow enclosure with a frame set at the far end to hold nine small pins. Quoits were still a diversion, but country people used a horse-shoe instead of a ring quoit. Prisoners' Base was still played by both adults and children, as it had been since the time of Edward III; although chiefly a rural sport as late as 1770 a great match for high stakes was played, in the fields where the British Museum now stands, between twelve gentlemen of Cheshire against twelve from Derbyshire.

Cricket, once a boy's game and a country sport, became very fashionable and was 'much countenanced by the nobility* and gentry'. 'Went and played Crickett, being the first time of our Clubbs meeting', writes a young Oxford undergraduate in April 1760; 'N.B. we play'd in Port Meadow.'[26] Next month his club beat Eton. Cricket clubs, at first confined to London and the Weald, now sprang up everywhere but there were no fixed rules. Rules varied according to agreement by both sides. Single wicket cricket required five players, double eleven; but this number too could be varied according to pleasure. Heavy stake money and heavy side bets contributed to the sport and to much rowdy behaviour—betting was one of our besetting sins. In London the

---

* Frederick, Prince of Wales was an enthusiastic supporter of Surrey.

most famous cricket ground was the Artillery Ground, Finsbury, where the Honourable Artillery Company still play, and here on June 18th 1744, the historic Kent versus All England match was played. It was the first game in which a full score was recorded. and preserved for posterity. But it was not until 1787 that Thomas Lord, of impoverished Yorkshire family, and ground bowler to White's Conduit Club, opened his first cricket ground in rural Dorset Square, just in time for the two-day match between Middlesex and Essex. This was not sacred ground; it was often used for pigeon shooting, hopping races and athletic meetings. Lord's, as we know it, was not established on its present site in St John's Wood* until the year before that battle reputedly won on the playing fields of Eton—and surely Harrow, too, as the first Eton–Harrow match was played in 1805 with Lord Byron on the Harrow side.

Gowf, goff or golf, originally a Dutch game and in its early days (thirteenth century) seemingly played as often upon the ice as upon the earth, began to snail its way from Scotland into the northern counties.† As 'goff-lengths', or the distance between first and last holes, were often over two miles the game remained rural and 'was rarely seen in the vicinity of the metropolis'.[27] The number of holes was optional and the game seems to have been played with a single 'bat', a straight ash-handled affair about 4½ feet long. The striking end was curved, faced with horn and backed with lead to give it necessary weight. The ball was small, very hard, made of leather tightly packed with feathers. But golf did not become popular in the southern half of England until well on in the nineteenth century. Tennis (not lawn tennis) once so popular with the rich, languished; particularly after the Prince of Wales died, due, it was thought, to having been hit in the side with a tennis ball. Since Frederick died after eating a piece of bread and butter it is surprising that this was not ac-

* The first Lord's in that district was opened in 1809 and was nearer Regent's Park Canal. Lord had the backing of the Earl of Winchelsea and the 4th Duke of Richmond.
† But Charles I had played golf while a prisoner of the Scots at Newcastle.

counted the death-bringer. In fact, he had a violent and ill-treated infection of the lungs.

More bucolic were the pleasures of the hard-working, small country folk. On age-old feast days—Whit Monday, Sheep Shearing or Harvest Home*—and also at country fairs, organized games, sports and competitions were held, wagers laid and prizes awarded; 'plowing for a pair of Breeches, running for a Shift, Raffling for a Gown'[28] were some of the excitements of a rural Whit Monday. Strong young men showed their prowess at running, leaping, vaulting and jumping to kick at an inflated bladder suspended from a tall stake. If the competitor were good enough he could go on a tour of country fairs and might even end up showing off in London, as a certain Ireland did. This six-foot Yorkshire youth leaped over nine horses standing side by side with a man seated on the middle horse and, we are told, he also 'jumped over a garter held fourteen feet high'.[29] As the record high jump in the last Olympic games (1964) was only 7 ft 1¾ inches (winner V. Bramel, U.S.S.R.) it is possible that Ireland may have been pole vaulting. Even so, the record is excellent as the last Olympic champion (F. Hansen, U.S.A.) cleared the bar at 16 ft 9 inches.

Less competitive athletic amusements were such sports as hunting-the-pig where the objective was to catch the pig by its docked, greased tail. Sack races were very popular, so were wheelbarrow races, but for this amusement competitors were blindfolded. What fun it was to see some one run down and, if lucky, really injured by a wheelbarrow. Smoking matches to discover who could smoke a pipe the fastest or keep it alight the longest, were events chiefly for elderly males, but anyone of either sex could join in a grinning competition. With heads thrust through horse-collars, contestants sported their ivories, as widely and for as long as possible, while spectators fell into stitches. Eating and drinking competitions were also great sport, as practically everyone in England was a gifted amateur in this line;

* By the end of the eighteenth century this festival with its traditional customs had degenerated into a dinner party.

certain refinements were introduced such as a time limit, or confining the competition to just one particular food or liquid. Hot Hasty Pudding Eaters, for example, were a great draw at county fairs where spectators, nibbling slabs of fair ground gingerbread, urged wager-backed favourites to win or bust. The winner doubtless did.

Overeating and drinking were, as we know, a daily diversion of the rich and middling for which the penalty was a disordered digestion, the shakes, or a liver indistinguishable from that of a Strasbourg goose. The cure—and preventive—was to take the waters at any of the innumerable spas. This the grand and the near-grand did in their thousands. Bath was still top of the spas. Its waters cured everything from Cold Humours to Hypondriacal Flatulence and, in addition, it was a place for pleasure and amusement.

> Of all the gay places the world can afford,
> By gentle and simple for pastime ador'd,
> Fine balls, and fine concerts, fine buildings and springs,
> Fine walks, and fine views, and a thousand fine things,
> (Not to mention the sweet situation and air)
> What place, my dear mother, with Bath can compare?[30]

Bath with its beautiful Assembly Rooms, its balls, concerts, ridottos, theatre and gaming tables attracted the ill, the not ill, and a good many rogues. The latter were generally suffering from that most degrading of all Georgian ailments, lack of money, and sought to repair their ill-fortune at Bath either by gambling or by marrying a rich heiress. But there were also, by now, perhaps two hundred other spas noted for cures of specific diseases where those who disliked Bath, or who couldn't afford it, could seek health, wealth and unhappiness.

But now, and for the first time, the older spa towns had rivals in tiny fishing villages because sea bathing—preferably before breakfast on a chill morning—had become a fashionable cure. Various fishing villages were suddenly transformed into fashionable watering places. Brighthelmstone, a small, dirty, unattractive spot, became fashionable and beautiful Brighton in the space of about thirty years, a metamorphosis almost entirely due to Dr Richard Russell, whose book, *The Uses of Sea-Water in Diseases of the Glands,** was an immoderate success. It brought almost as many people to Brighton as did the presence of the Prince Regent in later Georgian times.

Seaside villages began to prosper shortly after mid-century. Before then, 'prudent grand-mammas' and 'modern belles' had been

> Content with Bristol, Bath, and Tunbridge Wells,
> When health requir'd it would consent to roam,
> Else more attached to pleasures found at home—

but from the 1750s on

> . . . alike gay widow, virgin, wife,
> Ingenious to diversify dull life,
> In coaches, chaises, caravans, and hoys,
> Fly to the coast for daily, nightly joys,
> And all, impatient of dry land, agree
> With one consent to rush into the sea—[31]

Fortunate, indeed, were those villages with a spring *and* a sea front. Such was Scarborough with its mineral waters, its bathing machines,† its varied entertainments. It was civilization in a remote, rural setting. It provided the pleasures of town and country combined; the best of both worlds—if one wanted both worlds. Some did not. Lord Foppington, that 'ornamental pillar' of the state, was one. He simply could not endure the 'fatigue of country life'.[32] Foppington, at Scarborough to repair his fortune by marrying a local heiress, is a caricature of the fashionable, town bred, coxcomb.‡ Nevertheless, he is so wittily and accurately drawn that he is little, if any, larger than life. In town he says, he lives in 'a perpetual stream of pleasure . . . with a

---

* First published in Latin 1749, in English 1753.
† Bathing machines were invented by a Mr Beale of Margate. They were immediately popular, but Beale died in poverty.
‡ The play is Vanburgh's *The Relapse* brought up to date by Sheridan in 1777, the same year as his *The School for Scandal*. It was first performed at Drury Lane on Feb. 24th with the then almost unknown Mrs Robinson (Perdita) as Amanda.

variety of entertainment'. He rose at twelve, drank his chocolate, was dressed by two in order to ride in the park. Returned home to dress, dine and 'lounge, perhaps to the opera' where, perfectly unmindful of the music, he occupied himself ogling the ladies. This busy day concluded at one or two in the morning at 'one or other of the clubs'. Not that he ever played deep, he assures Amanda and Berenthia, for he had been for some years 'tied up from losing above five thousand paunds at a sitting'.³³

This is not an exaggeration. Deep play was one of the major pleasures—and disasters—of the time, for those who could and could not afford it. In 1731 Miss Fanny Braddock, sister to General Braddock, 'gamed away her little fortune' and hanged herself. 'Poor Fanny', said her brother, 'I always knew she would play until she would be forced to *tuck herself up.*'³⁴ Sir John Bland squandered his vast estates, which included the whole city of Manchester and environs, at the gaming tables and shot himself in 1755. Much later Georgiana, the beautiful Duchess of Devonshire, a compulsive gambler, ran up such enormous debts that no one quite knows what they amounted to. Her friend, the strange, brilliant and preternaturally charming Charles James Fox had lost £140,000 before the age of twenty-five, and his gambling debts remained monumental throughout his life. He would often play for nearly twenty-four hours at a sitting, losing £500 an hour. Had he stuck to whist, which he played excellently well, he could have made a comfortable annual income. But his real passion was for Pharo (faro) purely a game of chance requiring no skill. Fox may have inherited his love of gaming from his great-great-grandmother Louise de Kérroualle, he certainly did not get it from his great-great-grandfather Charles II—although that is perhaps where his quite staggering charm came from—for King Charles did not number gambling among his faults. Fox, however, like his royal ancestor was also a racing enthusiast, but as he carried politics on to the race course and backed only Whig horses he often lost considerable sums. Yet, like so many men of his era, 'every form of sport, every branch of knowledge made its appeal to him, as well as every species of luxury'.³⁵ He played cricket, tennis, was a not very good shot and, in his youth, was much given to amateur theatricals.

Fox's royal opponent, George III, had also appeared in private theatricals when young. 'Went to Leicester House to see Jane Grey acted by the Prince's children',[36] Bubb Dodington notes in his dull way in 1750.* The future king was then twelve years old and one wonders how this shy, retiring, withdrawn boy liked play-acting. Possibly it was good for him as he had few companions of his own age because 'young people of quality were so ill-educated and so very vicious'[37] they quite frightened his mother. Further, George 'did not take particularly to any body about him, but his brother Edward',[38] and even Prince Edward complained of George's 'lack of spirit'.[39]

Private theatricals had a continuing and increasing popularity during the eighteenth century, and between 1780 and 1800 the vogue reached its peak. Many of the noble and rich—the terms were quite often synonymous then—had beautiful private theatres on their estates where, with talented friends and an occasional professional actor, they put on performances nearly always rated by the invited audience, no less than by certain servile newspapers, as far surpassing anything yet seen on the legitimate stage. Lady Craven, later Margravine of Anspach, was famous for her magnificent productions at no less famous Brandenburg House. She wrote, translated and acted in various plays, but a nasty sarcastic little poem says that she 'Of all inglorious rivals makes a riddance/ And shines at once a Centlivre and Siddons'.[40] Earl Barrymore and his brother were such enthusiasts that they had private theatres at Richmond, Savile Row and Wargrave. The Dukes of Marlborough, of Richmond, of Ancaster; the Earl of Sandwich—who it was said had ingratiated himself with the Duke of Bedford by 'intrigues, cricket matches and acting plays'[41]—all had private theatres. The less grand, no less mad about private theatricals, had to make do with a stage run up by the local carpenter in some largish room, such as the billiard room at Mansfield Park, where

---

* The celebrated actor, Quin, instructed the royal children and young George had already appeared as Portius in Addison's *Cato*.

rehearsals for *Lover's Vows** were ended so abruptly by the unexpected return of Sir Thomas Bertram from Antigua.

But to return to the professional theatre. All the Hanoverian
sovereigns were devotees of the stage although drama, as such,
can not be said to have flourished during the reigns of the first two
Georges. Drama, in fact, had been almost totally eclipsed by
variety.† Rope dancers, performing animals, jugglers, fire eaters,
'ballettes', spectacles and startling stage effects—from real water
falls to erupting volcanoes—were what people wanted. The
Smithfield Muses reigned supreme. Audiences which included
'persons of the first quality in England'⁴² loved to see

> All sudden, gorgons hiss, and dragons glare,
> And ten-horned fiends and giants rush to war.
> Hell rises, Heav'n descends, and dance on earth,
> Gods, imps, and monsters, music, rage, and mirth,
> A fire, a jig, a battle, and a ball,
> Till one, wide Conflagration swallows all.⁴³

John Rich,‡ actor-manager and mimic, gave them all this and
something new when, in 1716, he presented the first English
Pantomime. This was Rich's own extremely successful invention,
and his pantomimes consisted of two parts. First, a tale from Ovid
or some other fabulous writer where gods, goddesses, nymphs
and shepherds were assisted by splendid costumes, scenery,
ballets and music. Next, between the acts, a second part which
consisted of episodes from the age-old comedy of Harlequin and
Columbine. The chief delight of the second part was the trans-
formation scene, invented by Rich, where Harlequin's wand
metamorphosed living men into monkeys, wheelbarrows, joint

---

* This, one of the most popular plays of the era, was an adaptation by Mrs
Elizabeth Inchbald of Kotzebue's *Das Kind der Liebe*.

† Probably the one notable play of this period was George Lillo's *The London
Merchant* (1731). Audiences who came to jeer remained to weep, and the play
became a stock piece. As a domestic tragedy of middle-class life, the subject matter
was unusual for the time. It had great influence on the continent.

‡ Rich, whose stage name was Lun, was a brilliant Harlequin. He produced an
annual pantomime until the year of his death in 1761. Each production ran for
between forty and fifty performances, a very long run in those days.

stools; and inanimate objects into ostriches and serpents. Trees became houses; palaces and temples, hovels; colonnades became flower beds, and sausage shops turned into Indian encampments.

Pantomime very soon became a favourite outdoor entertainment too, particularly at great fairs, and by 1731 one of our modern favourites was being advertised as an attraction at 'Lee and Harpers Great Theatrical Booth' at Southwark Fair. This was the already old favourite *The True and Antient History of Dick Whittington*, complete with cat but with a new 'Variety of Singing and Dancing by the best Masters' and 'entirely New . . . Cloaths and Scenes'.[44] But pantomime was to sound the death knell of the hitherto vastly popular puppet shows, although at Smithfield they remained almost a ritual performance at Bartholomew-tide. Here for many years a most spectacular *Old Creation of the World* was produced. It had an overpowering last act where the sun rose promisingly over Noah's Ark while the Noah family, human, animal and feathered, emerged to the accompaniment of angels ringing the inevitable bells and, for reasons utterly unknown to me, Dives rose from Hell, Lazarus was seen in Abraham's bosom, and various figures merrily danced jigs, sarabandes and country dances. Small wonder that Partridge says to Tom Jones, 'I love a puppet show of all pastimes upon earth'.[45] But even by then, for the story is set at the time of the '45, puppet shows had changed and 'good scriptural stories' where 'wicked people were carried away by the devil' were as unfashionable as belief in the devil himself. Puppet masters held that by 'throwing out Punch and his wife Joan and such idle trumpery'[46] and substituting adulterated Restoration plays, puppet shows had at last become 'rational entertainment'.

It was also in 1745, in February, that the aged actor, poet laureate and 'hero' of Pope's *Dunciad*, Colley Cibber, emboldened by the young Pretender's threatened invasion, produced *Papal Tyranny*. This was his own botched and mangled version of *King John*.* It had an immediate and undeserved success and netted

---

* The most fearful travesties of Shakespeare's plays were produced. Perhaps the worst was Lord Lansdowne's version of *The Merchant of Venice* with Shylock as a

Cibber a profit of £400. A few days later, a former pupil of Dr Johnson and the future composer of *Heart of Oak*, David Garrick, who had made his first appearance in London in 1741, opened at Drury Lane in the real thing, and with actor-manager-playwright Garrick (1717–79) the legitimate theatre, although not drama itself, revives.

Strangely, although the Georgian era produced a galaxy of great actors and actresses,* the only Georgian playwrights remembered today are R. B. Sheridan (1751–1816) and Oliver Goldsmith (1728–74). Yet there were well over 500 playwrights turning out plays between 1750 and 1800, and thousands of straight plays, comic operas, pantomimes, burlettas and melodramas were produced. Since long runs were still unknown, the Georgian theatre, particularly after mid-century, gobbled up plays with the avidity of present-day television and with much the same results for 'the great mass of late eighteenth-century plays make today but dull reading . . . countless are the artificial and absurd comic operas . . . weary tragedies . . . lachrymose comedies'.[47] The reason may lie partly in the rise of what we now call the 'star system'. The play was no longer the thing; the players were. Audiences did not go to see Shakespeare's *Hamlet*, they went to see Garrick's Hamlet, or Quin's Falstaff, or Macklin's Shylock.

But a great change took place in the theatre itself. In the first decade of George III's reign, seats and boxes were at last removed from the stage, so the audience, for the first time, was confined entirely to the auditorium. Auditoria were much enlarged to accommodate larger audiences but this, plus inadequate

---

low-comedy character, though Nahum Tate's *Lear* with a happy ending ran it a close second. Although Garrick did much to revive Shakespeare even he 'improved' upon the original text. But it is always better to see Shakespeare (since he cannot be wholly rewritten) than not to see him, and the Georgians certainly saw Shakespeare.

* It is impossible to list them all but among the greatest were Betterton, Booth, Quin, Spranger Barry, Garrick, Macklin, Henderson, Palmer, J. P. Kemble, Edmund Kean; Mrs Pritchard, Mrs Porter, Mrs Woffington, Mrs Cibber, Mrs Abingdon, Miss Farren, Mrs Jordan and the greatest actress of all, Sarah Siddons.

Drury Lane Theatre by Henry Holland. Built 1791, destroyed 1809

lighting, forced actors to exaggerate voice and gesture to gain effect, thus subtlety was lost and ranting came in. It was Garrick who improved lighting and made it 'invisible' by fixing strips of candle-holders behind the proscenium arch. A large brass chandelier with curving branches no longer rivalled the moon and threatened Romeo's head in the balcony scene. Nor were Barnwell's lines, 'Either the sun has slipped behind a cloud, or journeys down the west of heaven with more than common speed',[48] belied by rings of candles suspended in mid-air.

A further improvement came later with the disappearance of side wings and the adoption of the box-set. Players no longer had to sidle on and off through the lateral wings of a supposed room. The box set could be, and was, a real room with doors—although an actor, as always, still moved down stage after his entrance to speak his opening lines on the much smaller apron. Ideas about scenery and costume changed too. Flats were replaced by more realistic, three-dimensional and, even, dioramic scenes which became more and more complicated and splendid. Much greater attention was paid to getting historical detail right, both in setting and costume. Although Garrick, who did not depend upon costume for effect, always wore a tie-wig, even in Shakespearean roles, Spranger Barry as Othello went further. He appeared in gold-laced, scarlet knee-breeches with his gouty legs bulging in silk stockings, and wearing upon his wig a very small cocked hat. It was Macklin who, in 1773, dared to produce *Macbeth* in Scots dress instead of the usual contemporary costume, and by 1788 John Philip Kemble was adamant in insisting on accuracy in dress. Yet it was not until 1814 that Edmund Kean was brave enough to discard the red wig which from the time of Burbage had distinguished Shylock.* George Stephen Kemble was remarkable for playing Falstaff without 'stuffing' but this was due to nature, not art. His sister, Mrs Siddons (1755–1831), believing that airy gauzy garments in fashionable styles were not suited to tragedy, took to plain, sombre garments thus flying in the face of convention, as most actresses resolutely refused to appear in costume until near the end of the eighteenth century. No woman, least of all an actress, wanted to be seen looking a positive frump in the antediluvian styles of a bygone era. So the satin gown with fichu, sleeve frills, the powdered wig and plumed 'Gainsborough' hat of a Volumnia must have contrasted oddly with the correct toga of a Coriolanus.

Plays were popular reading too, for reading then seems to have been one of the major pleasures of life, and plays were published in quantity. It is perhaps a little surprising to learn that cheap editions are not new; they flourished in Georgian England. 'The English national authors are in all hands, and read by all people',[49] says a Swiss visitor, 'my land lady who is only a taylor's widow, reads her Milton', and he adds that her husband fell in love with

* Perhaps a red-haired Shylock was thought correct because, traditionally, Judas had red hair.

her because she read it with 'such proper emphasis'. He also conversed with several 'of the lower class . . . who all knew their national authors' and 'who have read many, if not all'. This is obviously greatly exaggerated, but the visitor does make the very important point that the sale of classical authors in England was greatly promoted by cheap, convenient, pocket volumes which were moderately priced 'so they come more within the reach of people'.

Certainly from the accession of George I to the death of George IV there was no lack of reading matter nor of interest in reading. Alexander Pope, Jonathan Swift and Daniel Defoe, at the height of their powers in 1714, continued writing into the reign of George II,* while George IV out-lived Byron, Shelley and Keats. An era which has Pope at one end and Byron at the other, which contains the Augustan Age and the Romantic Revival can hardly be other than interesting. As it happens, it was electrifying. A glance at fiction alone—and here one can deal only with the 'classics'—shows why. The first novel of character, imagination and analysis,† in fact the first modern novel, Samuel Richardson's *Pamela* appeared in 1740. The first novel to give a true and terrible picture of naval life, Tobias Smollett's *Roderick Random*, came out in 1745. What may be the greatest novel in the English language, *Tom Jones* by Henry Fielding was published in 1749. In 1759 Dr Johnson's only novel, *Rasselas*, appeared—one of the saddest and wisest books ever written—and, between 1759 and 1767 the first novel to play tricks with time, typography and words took London by storm. This was *Tristram Shandy* by Laurence Sterne—but many disapproved of it too. Dean Delany refused to have the book in his house and Horace Walpole thought little of it. Of less importance was the first Gothic novel, *The Castle of Otranto* (1764) by Horace Walpole, yet each of these books in its own way forms one of the mainsprings of English novel writing. In short, the whole of English fiction can be traced

* Defoe d. 1731; Pope d. 1744; Swift d. 1745.
† As opposed to Defoe's novels which are factual reportage. Defoe is interested in surfaces not in what really makes people tick. His characters are lively but flat.

back, very clearly, to the mid-Georgians for, like it or not, there has been nothing very new since then.*

What is so surprising is that this brand-new form developed in such an incredibly short time. Nineteen years only lie between *Pamela* and the first volume of *Tristram Shandy*. Even more astonishing is that there was nothing very much leading up to this great breakthrough. There were virtually no English novels in the seventeenth century,† yet the eighteenth is full of them, good, bad, indifferent—and superb. How exciting, how stimulating it must have been for reader and writer. Sir Joshua Reynolds sat up all night to read *Evelina*, while self-exiled Lady Mary Wortley Montagu, although she could not abide *Pamela* and despised Richardson (he wrote the book in two months) sobbed over *Clarissa* 'as being very resembling to my maiden days'.⁵⁰ It did in a way resemble Lady Mary's girlhood, but she was certainly no Clarissa, so here, undoubtedly, is reader identification. But for the majority of readers identification began with *Pamela*.

For the average reader, now a member of a much enlarged and prosperous middle class, was not interested in the endless, boring, artificial French romances which had been so popular with the upper classes in the previous century. They were all about silly foreigners with unpronounceable names, having impossible adventures. He cared not a button for satire, for moral tracts, for philosophical treatises—and there were plenty of these. He could hardly see himself as, say, Lemuel Gulliver or Jonathan Wild.‡ The *Fifteen Sermons* of that very great theologian, Joseph Butler, were not entertaining. As for philosophy! Well, Bishop Berke-

---

* The first 'North American' novel, *Emily Montague* by Frances Brooke appeared in 1769. Mrs Brooke lived in Quebec from 1763–68 when Canada had just recently been won by General Wolfe and the thirteen American Colonies were still British. The book, half of which is set in Canada, is still fascinating and amusing reading.

† See *The Jacobeans at Home*, Chapter VIII.

‡ *The Life of Mr Jonathan Wild the Great* (1743) by Fielding, a savage satire on power, corruption and Sir Robert Walpole was based on fact. Wild was a corrupt magistrate and leader of a gang. He was caught and hanged in 1725. It may be interesting to note that during the Napoleonic wars the Duke of Wellington used to refer to Napoleon as Jonathan Wild.

ley's name was certainly a household word, but only because he had written an essay zealously advocating the use of tar water as a universal panacea, not because his real concern lay with *The Principles of Human Knowledge*.

This large and flourishing middle class was ready and waiting to read about people. But about people who lived in an England they knew; people who possessed the vices and virtues common to human nature. It wanted distinctive stories of contemporary life with recognizable 'real' (if romantic) characters. And this is just what it got. First from a prosperous London printer, Samuel Richardson (1689–1761). Then from a Bow-street magistrate, Henry Fielding (1707–54), from a Yorkshire parson, Laurence Sterne (1713–68) and from a splenetic sailor-doctor, the Hogarth of the pen, Tobias Smollett (1721–71), as well as from a host of lesser novelists who sprang up about these giants and helped to meet the constantly increasing needs of the circulating libraries, those 'ever green trees of diabolical knowledge',[51] which were flourishing, particularly at spas and resorts. 'I don't believe there's a circulating library in Bath I haven't been at', Lucy tells Lydia Languish and pulls six books from under her cloak. They included *Peregrine Pickle*, *The Tears of Sensibility*, *Humphry Clinker* and the second volume of *The Sentimental Journey*—none of which was considered suitable reading for young females. But Lydia, as Mrs Malaprop said, was an 'intricate hussy', which Sir Anthony believed to be 'the natural consequence of teaching girls to read'.[52]

Girls, however, just went on reading. So did everyone else. Magazines and periodicals of all sorts and kinds sprang up to satisfy what seemed an unappeasable appetite. The number of newspapers—a bare handful at the beginning of the century—increased so greatly that by the 1790s one newsvendor alone was offering twelve daily papers, ten tri-weeklies, two bi-weeklies, and a dozen weeklies, to say nothing of specialized papers like *Lloyd's List*, a bi-weekly; or the daily *List of Exports and Imports*. These, if half-yearly subscriptions were taken out, were sent to country districts post free. Reading had become one of the most common of pleasures and many people even continued to read and enjoy poetry. After all, there were poets long before there were novelists or newspapers. Reading poetry aloud was once part of the Englishness of the English—even foreigners remarked upon it.

But now the admiration for Pope's wonderful, polished couplets, his brilliant, satirical and often profoundly wise poems began to give way to the 'sensibility' of newer poets, such as Pope's contemporary, James Thomson (1700–48). His *The Seasons*, written in pseudo-Miltonic blank verse, chiefly concerns God and nature, but his feeling for nature is genuine and pure. Nature is not merely a literary or stage prop. Dr Johnson, although admiring the poem, thought 'the great defect of *The Seasons* is want of method'[53]—and if we had no Academy like the French, we *did* have Dr Johnson. Then there was Edward Young (1683–1765) with, among other things, his glum, self-pitying *The Complaint, or Night Thoughts on Life, Death and Immortality*. Young was probably the first of the graveyard poets and began a long-lasting vogue for melancholy meditations in verse and for elegies composed in country churchyards,* as well as for other morbid pieces which set women and strong men a-weeping. *Night Thoughts* remained immensely popular throughout the century. But not with the Rev. Dr Samuel Salter. He found it 'affectedly laboured into obscurity . . . the sentiments . . . pompous, trifling and magnificently common place'.[54] Sensibility was, in fact, already becoming sentimentality.

Then there was William Cowper (1731–1800) a tender, affectionate man, given to religious melancholy and, like both Collins and Smart, afflicted with madness. Yet he managed to write one of the happiest poems ever, *The Task*, filled with enchanting miniatures of contemporary English landscapes. And, belonging to no school, fitting into no category; unique in his own or any other age; influenced by Swedenborg no less than by the Druidical revival (a revival fathered by the Rev. Dr

---

* Gray's famous *Elegy* (1751), not much liked by Dr Johnson, was once disliked by many a school child in Canada where it was a 'set poem', chiefly I feel because General Wolfe recited it to his men whilst crossing the St Lawrence to scale the heights of Quebec.

Stukeley) is William Blake (1757–1827). Blake who 'saw a treeful of angels at Peckham Rye' and whose 'hands could lay hold on the tiger's terrible heart',[55] was not popular either as a poet or as an illustrator. Although he did illustrations for an edition of *Night Thoughts*, his drawings for one of the many insignificant books written by the undistinguished Dr Trusler were turned down by that clerical gentleman with the words 'Your fancy . . . accords not with my Intentions'.[56]

Blake's near-contemporary George Crabbe (1754–1832), whose work was much admired by the Austen sisters, is one of the lesser poets, but he served as a link between the old poetry and the new. He often expressed very plain truths indeed about life, nature and the rural scene in the elegant eighteenth-century couplets perfected by Pope. Crabbe appealed almost equally to an older generation and a younger one, and was praised by the Augustan Johnson no less than by the Romantic (and ironic) Byron. By the time Crabbe died, revolutionary (in two senses) William Wordsworth (1770–1850) had done his best work, so had the father of the historical novel Sir Walter Scott (1771–1832) for whom the Regent gave 'snug' little dinners. So had S. T. Coleridge (1772–1834) and Robert Southey (1774–1843). The great Romantics, Byron (1788–1824) Shelley (1792–1822) and Keats (1795–1821) were all dead. So were Edward Gibbon (1737–94), supreme among English historians; and Jane Austen (1775–1817), supreme among women writers.

And women in the Georgian era took to the pen as never before. They had begun writing in the late seventeenth century and they continued with increasing fervour in the eighteenth. Writing, in fact, was the one profession, other than the oldest, open to women. Only a few can be mentioned here, such as Mrs Elizabeth Montagu (1720–1800), first of the blue-stockings,* a leader of society who held literary salons in her Portman Square

---

* It is said this appellation derives from the blue worsted stockings worn by Edward Stillingfleet (grandson of the famous Bishop of Worcester) when he attended Mrs Montagu's salons. He was so impoverished and impecunious that he could not afford the correct black silk stockings.

home, designed by Athenian Stuart. She was visited by most of the literary lights of the day and wrote an essay upon Shakespeare which many thought remarkable—for a woman. The redoubtable Dowager Countess Gower was not among the many. 'Mrs Montague has comenc'd author, in vindication of Shakespeare, who wants none', she writes. '. . . I'll have yt because I can throw yt aside wn I'm tired.'⁵⁷ But few were throwing away the gothic terror novels of Mrs Anne Radcliffe (1764–1823) and her followers, some of whom, like Mary Shelley with her Frankenstein, went one better—or worse. Fanny Burney (1752–1840) with fresh and charming *Evelina* became a lion over night—and the ill-paid second keeper of the Queen's Robes. And if Horace Walpole, rightly, thought little of Miss Burney's later work, the rather over-written and pompous *Camilla*, he praised, unwisely perhaps, Hannah More's poetry,* and thought her a saint—which she more or less was. Maria Edgeworth, whose novels depicting Irish peasant life influenced the work of Scott and, strange to say, Turgenev, was born in the year the last volume of *Tristram Shandy* appeared (1767) and died in the year of the first instalment of *David Copperfield* (1849). And then there was Jane Austen of whom one need say nothing for she is probably more read now than then and even better loved.

Jane Austen, Walter Savage Landor and Charles Lamb were all born in the same year. The year in which Mrs Siddons made her appearance in London as Portia, and failed. The year in which the battle of Breed's Hill—commonly known as Bunker Hill—was fought. The year in which the eighteenth century and Mrs Delany celebrated their seventy-fifth birthdays. And with Mrs Delany, whose life covers a good deal of the Georgian period, we get another and rather different picture of the pleasures and pastimes of that age. She and her greatest friend, the Duchess of Portland, like many other well born, well bred women, were not interested in fashionable frivolities of the *ton*. They were not

---

* The philanthropist Hannah More whose work among children is well known wrote a number of plays before she came to believe playgoing wrong. She also wrote a number of moral stories which were highly popular.

stuffy, they just had other interests. They read, discussed books, wrote innumerable, excellent and often amusing letters; went to the theatre, attended concerts and also had a variety of diversions and hobbies which depended entirely upon their own efforts and talents. They collected shells and did beautiful shell work (shell work was very popular). They collected and arranged mosses and mineral specimens. 'I have been sorting my mosses and ores', Mrs Delany writes her sister, 'my painting has lain dormant some time. . . . Shakespeare and the harpsichord fill up the evenings.'[58] They went on botanizing expeditions—on one the Duchess was accompanied by the French exile, J. J. Rousseau who was also interested in wild plants. They gardened, did japan work and when the Duchess, who also had a menagerie and aviary at Bulstrode, took to collecting and studying fungi, all the tables, chairs and couches in her breakfast room were covered with 'sieves, pans, platters', so it was 'a little difficult to find a seat'.[59]

While Mrs Delany painted pictures and produced exquisite needlework, the Duchess busied herself with turning in wood, ivory, amber and ebony. At this she seems to have been a dab, for among other charming objects she made 'an ear of barley; the corns amber, the stalk ivory, the beards tortoise shell'.[60] But it was to Mrs Delany that fame came in 1774, and almost by accident. One day, having a piece of bright scarlet Chinese paper beside her, and noting it was the same shade as a nearby geranium, she took up her scissors and amused herself by cutting out each floweret, by eye alone, in the paper.* She then laid them out on black paper and was so pleased with the result that she cut out calyx, stem and leaves in green papers. So her celebrated 'Paper Mosaick Flowers' were born. She produced nearly a thousand separate flowers before her eyesight failed in 1784, and her failing eyesight is not to be wondered at, since the delicate shading, the tiny veins in leaves, the minute variations of tint in the petals of

---

* Cutting paper into patterns had long been an amusement. The Baroness Schulenberg (Duchess of Kendal) kept that not very bright monarch George I entertained for hours on end by cutting odd shapes in paper; and Alexander Pope wrote verses *On the Countess of Burlington Cutting Paper*.

each flower were produced by separate cuttings in the right shades of paper, overlaid and pasted on the basic cut out. Sir Joshua Reynolds thought her work unrivalled (she had many imitators). Horace Walpole believed she had founded a new art; Sir Joseph Banks, the naturalist, said her flowers were 'the only imitations of nature that he had ever seen from which he could venture to describe, botanically, any plant, without the least fear of committing an error'.[61]

The flower mosaics brought Mrs Delany the friendship of King George III and Queen Charlotte. A true friendship which later found a practical expression. When Mrs Delany was old (she lived to 88) and in narrow circumstances, the King gave her a house at Windsor, had it altered according to her wishes, filled the larder and provided her with £300 per annum. It was all done with the greatest tact and kindness. The King and Queen seemed to be almost unable to do without Mrs Delany's company —but this must have been rather tiring for a very old lady.

Mrs Delany's *Hortus Siccus*, as she ultimately called her collection, is housed in the British Museum,* and the British Museum was first opened to the public on Monday, January 15th 1759 in Montagu House, Russell Street, Bloomsbury. It was not our first public museum, that honour belongs to Oxford's Ashmolean (1683), but its roots lie deep in the seventeenth century when collecting 'curiosities'—hence our word 'curio'—became a rage among virtuosi and others. The nucleus of the British Museum was the great collection made by the physician-virtuoso, Sir Hans Sloane† (1660–1753). It numbered 80,000 objects of all sorts (exclusive of books) some of them real treasures—medals, coins, cameos, intaglios, corals, crystals, mineral ores, semi-precious stones, butterflies, albums of plants from all over the world. Others were of rather more doubtful value like the split cane hat

---

* Not all are there, some were given away by Mrs Delany. One, to Sir Joseph Banks, fetched 3 guineas at the sale of his effects in 1820. Those who have seen the collection will certainly agree with Walpole.

† Created a baronet in 1716 by George I, he was the first medical practitioner in our history to be given an hereditary title.

of 'the Patriarch of China' and the bones of a mammoth, then thought to be those of a Roman elephant.

Sloane, who died at ninety-three, had suggested to his trustees that this collection in its entirety be offered to the King or to Parliament for the nominal sum of £20,000. He wished the collection kept together because he believed everything in it—presumably even the Patriarch's hat—was a manifestion, at first, second or third hand, of the manifold and various works of the Lord, and, as such, should be displayed so that it could be seen by as many people as possible. The purchase money was raised by public lottery,* but it was not all that easy for the many to see and praise 'all ye works of the Lord'. Admission was free but tickets had to be applied for, in writing, often two weeks beforehand. Open days were limited—so were visitors—and guides hurried parties of them through the unguarded rooms and up the broad staircase where they had the pleasure of seeing a bust of Shakespeare by Roubillac and a pair of enormous giraffes. So in its early days the British Museum was part treasure-house, part natural history museum and part sideshow. By the end of the Georgian era the story was different. Exhibits were reorganized in a more orderly fashion. The neo-classical movement brought to the Museum the treasures of Greece and Rome. The Egyptian antiquities—including the Rosetta stone—collected by Napoleon's experts on his ill-fated Egyptian campaign became 'ours' by treaty, in 1801, when George III gave them to the Museum; and the Elgin Marbles were acquired for £35,000 in 1816.

The British Museum was not London's only museum—for we have always loved to stop and stare at odd, unusual and even morbid objects throughout our history. There were still a good many private museums. There was John Hunter's anatomical collection (now belonging to the Royal College of Surgeons). There was Bedlam, where one could go and gawp at the antics of the insane—an old favourite pastime. There was Cox's

---

* Scandalously conducted, it none the less made a profit of £95,000 for the Museum, thus enabling the trustees to purchase the Cottonian Library and the Harleian Collection of MSS as well.

Museum, which terrible tempered Captain Mirvan thought was 'all kickshaw work'[62] and where there were all sorts of mechanical wonders—it was a great age for clockwork machines—including a pre-Fabergé pineapple which opened to disclose a nest of singing birds. There was Don Saltero's, out Chelsea way, still flourishing in 1778, as it had done since the time of Queen Anne, with its odd collection of some very dubious curiosities indeed.* And, though not for long, there was Dr van Buchell. This was, literally a one woman show. The one woman was the doctor's wife. She had died in 1775 and van Buchell—he was a dentist—had had her carefully embalmed by Dr Hunter. Dead, she was an excellent advertisement for van Buchell for she sat fully clothed, glass-eyed and bolt upright in a chair in the withdrawing room, receiving a steady stream of curious visitors to whom she was introduced as 'the dear departed'. This might have gone on being one of the sights of London indefinitely, as Katherine of Valois's body was in Westminster Abbey,† but the dentist remarried and his new wife, possibly motivated by jealousy, objected so strongly to the old one sitting about doing nothing that 'the dear departed' had to be laid away.

There were other and decidedly more pleasant things to be viewed. New to the era was the Royal Academy founded in 1768, with the great and fashionable portrait painter Sir Joshua Reynolds (1723–92) as its first president. The first show of 136 exhibits was held in premises in Pall Mall in 1739. It attracted many visitors for art was fashionable—looking at prints and drawings, visiting artists' studios, seeing the famous private collections of paintings in great houses were among the pleasures of the time. Drawing or painting, the latter with brushes made from the hair of a squirrel's tail (the best came from Russia), were also considered necessary accomplishments in a young lady. By 1780 the Academy had moved into its new premises the Strand block of Somerset House, as

* See *The Jacobeans at Home*, Chapter VIII.
† The remains of Henry V's Queen were kept in a chest to be viewed by anyone. The body was ordered to be interred in 1776 but this may not have taken place until 1793. The interested reader with a strong stomach may care to consult Pepys's *Diary*, Feb. 23rd 1669.

Somerset House, the first permanent home of the Royal Academy

rebuilt by Sir William Chambers, and in the show of 1787 exhibits totalled 666.* We know from contemporary prints that these shows must have been a sight: pictures were hung haphazardly to ceiling height with frames touching; full-length portraits hung 'on the line' brought the sitters' feet to spectators' eye level and there were such hordes of viewers—men, women, children, and even dogs—that it is probable the exhibits could not be seen any way.

But it was really in the eighteenth century that a true English school of painting developed. Seventeenth-century paintings, with but few exceptions had been chiefly the work of foreign artists, some of whom settled here and became naturalized like Sir Godfrey Kneller (1646–1723), whose best work was done by 1717 and who attracted a drove of the drabbest imitators. In fact, 'we are now arrived at the period in which the arts were sunk

* Exhibits today run to over 1,300. They are selected from about 10,000 entries.

to the lowest ebb in Britain' and 'we were fallen into a loose . . .
and *dissolute* form of painting',[63] or so one of the first trustees
of the British Museum, Horace Walpole, said, for the first Hanoverian sovereign was 'devoid of taste'[64] and the second was not
much better.

Yet the reigns of George I and George II were what might be
called a formative period for English painting and, dreary though
it was, it included such painters as William Hogarth (1697–1764),
who is not typical, and the charming Joseph Highmore (1692–
1780), who illustrated Richardson's *Pamela*.* Conversation pieces
(they were not called that) became fashionable and to these easy,
informal pictures of families and friends we owe much of our
knowledge of the details of middle and upper class life, indoors
and out, just as we owe much of our knowledge of the more
brutal aspects of this not always elegant or reasonable century to
Hogarth, James Gillray (1757–1815) and Thomas Rowlandson
(1757–1827).

The first three decades of the reign of George III might be
called the neo-classical period in painting (as in architecture) just
as from about 1790 on we have the Romantic period. Reynolds,
the supreme portrait painter of the neo-classical period, harks
back in feeling to the splendours of paintings of the High Renaissance in Italy, which is not to say he was not original. His is the
grand style, unmannered and full of human values. Thomas
Gainsborough also seems typical of the late Georgian period, and
it comes perhaps as a shock to realize that J. M. W. Turner was
born in 1775 and John Constable a year later. Turner first exhibited at the Royal Academy in 1790 and Constable in 1802.
Constable, who founded the true English school of landscape
painting, was not popular in his own era. One may hazard a guess
at the reason. A cultural 'must' among late Georgians was the
appreciation of mountain scenery, the wilder the better, and if it

---

* Some of the painters born in the first half of the Georgian era are: Allan Ramsay
(1713–84); Richard Wilson (1713–82); George Stubbs (1724–1806); Paul Sandby
(1725–1809); Thomas Gainsborough (1727–88); Henry Fuseli (1741–1824, not
native born); all these became Royal Academicians.

included a ruined castle or a decayed tower or two it was highly prized. There was nothing like mountain scenery either as personally viewed in Switzerland or Italy, or as described by Mrs Radcliffe in *The Mysteries of Udolpho*, or as painted by almost anyone—even one's sadly untalented sister—to lift the soul to the agonies of the sublime. John Constable's 'scenery' was usually the flat, quiet English countryside of East Anglia and Essex. He did not even paint Welsh mountains, as Richard Wilson did. Nevertheless even Wilson died in poverty.

In addition to a laudable craze for native portraits and a perhaps not so discriminating one for the wilder and more rugged bits of nature, was the passion of those with sufficient money for paintings by great foreign masters of the past, particularly those of central and northern Italy, and thus many of our finest private collections were formed.

Here, in passing, it may be noted that up to the very end of the eighteenth century few virtuosi or collectors ever left the well beaten track. What was 'good taste' in art, and who were its great masters had been laid down in 1550 by Vasari, with a few later additions by Barri and others. Art was of course, chiefly Italian—but the Italian primitives came nowhere; its infancy ran from Cimabue and Giotto to Lorenzo di Bicci; its adolescence, or experimental period, ended with Signorelli; its maturity began with Leonardo, who was surpassed by Raphael in colour, and ended with Vasari's friend Michaelangelo. Few collectors were going to risk collecting infant or adolescent art—though they did add, with received authority, other later painters such as Poussin, Claude, Guido Reni, Salvator Rosa, Annibale Carracci and even a Venetian painter or two, including Titian. But for the most part the virtuoso, or Grand Tour collector, contented himself with comparing and describing in threadbare clichés, in unmeaning or pretentious adjectives, and in neat little ready-made labels what was already well known, established and accepted as Art. Botticelli, for example, was stiff and awkward, and if any collector thought of Fra Filippo Lippi it was probably to remember that he had run off with a nun.

Those who could not own originals, either because they were already owned by someone else, or because they had not the money, went in for the next best thing, copies. Copyists were kept busy here and on the continent producing pictures to meet the demand—those by Salvator Rosa were particular favourites. Arthur Young, visiting Northumberland House in 1772 and noting its paintings, is full of admiration for the taste of the collector as 'rather than furnish . . . with such originals as are to be procured at present . . . [he] ordered copies of some capital ones of the greatest painters'.⁶⁵ So a contempt for contemporary art was born and is only now dying out.

Other exhibitions were of a less exalted nature. Crowds would collect in any street to watch boys boxing, or a gentleman at fisticuffs with a porter whom he thought had overcharged him, or to see a man (for a ha'penny) take vipers and snakes out of a bag, play with them and even stuff one into his mouth. Or there were prodigies like that 'wonderful Phoenomena' which James Woodforde and others saw for a shilling—a three-year-old heifer with 'two distinct heads'. Each head perfectly fitted with the right number of eyes, ears, horns and mouths. 'It chewed the Cud in both Mouths and eat with both at the same Time.'⁶⁶ Was it difficult for the parson to decide whether to use 'phenomenon' or 'phenomena' in describing this two-headed beast, one wonders?

Then there were the first balloon ascents. Little Miss Port of Illam, Mrs Delany's great-niece, went to see Lunardi's beautiful balloon in 1785. It had been on view at the Lyceum in the Strand where 20,000 visitors inspected it. The gallery was decorated in white and pink satin with a gold fringe, and thirteen-year-old Miss Port wanted to ascend with Lunardi as there was 'no danger in the world'.⁶⁷ Lunardi, who might be called the first to introduce 'aerostation' into England,* soared into the smoky air of London from the Artillery Ground on September 15th 1784 in the presence of a notable company, including the future George IV. The French, however, had already beaten us to it with the

* The first attempt in Britain was made in Edinburgh on April 27th 1784 by J. Tytler, in a fire balloon of his own making. It was unsuccessful.

Lunardi's second balloon inflated in St George's Fields, 1785

first aerial voyage since Daedalus, made in November of the previous year: a voyage which led President Washington to comment that his French friends might soon come flying through the air to America rather than 'ploughing' the ocean. Benjamin Franklin argued that balloons would outlaw war because of the threat of invasion by air. Horace Walpole took the opposite view. Although he pretended to care not a rap about balloons and could not foresee 'with what airy vehicles the atmosphere would be peopled' two hundred years or so after his death, he at least presumed that the four corners of the earth would be 'more expeditiously . . . ravaged and butchered, than they have been by the old-fashioned and clumsy method of navigation'.[68] In 1785 J. P. Blanchard and an American, John Jeffries, flew the channel. This was the beginning of the end of that 'moat defensive to a house'.[69]

Then there was the Tower, always one of the sights of London, beloved by natives and visitors alike. Here one could see the Mint, of which earlier in the century Sir Isaac Newton had been Master. And the Armoury, where among other things was the 'sword used to decapitate Anne Boleyn'. Behind the sword was a green curtain which was raised to show 'a picture' of Anne's daughter, Elizabeth, standing 'next to the stuffed horse ridden by her, when once she, herself, commanded her army'.[70] There was, too the old Tower Zoo with its 'monstracious lion, with teeth half a quarter long'[71] as Win Jenkins, with pardonable exaggeration, says. But the animals by late century were kept in large, light cages—lions, leopards, tigers, wolves, hyenas and two kinds of bear, black and white, to say nothing of monkeys (also sold as pets in numerous shops), and captive eagles, creanced to the branching arms of trees.

But as the eighteenth century settled into the nineteenth, as London grew, as the City became more congested and the bustle in the streets worsened, the age-old Tower Zoo became *démodé*. Further, there were those who felt that zoology was of just as much interest and importance as botany, and that a society should be formed to serve this interest and amuse the public too. One of the earliest enthusiasts was Sir Stamford Raffles (1781–1826) who, among other achievements, persuaded the East India Company to acquire the island Singapore in 1819, and who made immense zoological and botanical collections whilst in the Far East.* Sir Stamford and Sir Joseph Banks (1743–1820), it is said, put their heads together as early as 1817 to try to form a society which would provide a 'zoological collection which should interest and amuse the public'.[72] Its larger purpose was that the society's collection of animals should bear 'the same relation to Zoology as a science that the Horticultural Society does to Botany'.[73]

* His splendid collections and papers never reached England. The ship on which they were embarked caught fire and everything was destroyed.

The Society finally came into being in 1826, with Sir Stamford as first chairman and Sir Humphry Davy (1778–1829) as an enthusiastic co-founder, for Sir Joseph Banks was dead. The press largely ignored or was amused by this event 'The Zoological or Noah's Ark Society' was what the *Literary Gazette* called it. Then came all the bother and fuss of acquiring five acres in Regent's Park, of having gardens and buildings designed by Decimus Burton (he had recently redesigned Hyde Park), of what to do with the exotic animals given by kind donors while gardens and accommodation were being built. Fortunately, the keepers of the old Tower Zoo and Exeter 'Change took them in and gave them board and lodging until they could be moved to their new and much more suitable surroundings. So, on April 27th 1828,* the new Zoological Gardens were opened to amuse a new, elegant and, strangely enough after the first novelty had worn off, not all that interested public.

* Incorporated by Royal Charter in 1829.

CHAPTER EIGHT

Of Paint, Powder, and Allied Artifices

Slim as a girl, exquisitely dressed, painted and wearing the 'finest set of Egyptian pebble teeth'[1] the Duchess of Portland had ever seen, John, Lord Hervey, Vice-Chancellor to Queen Caroline, was the envy of some, the sport of many. Married to the beautiful Mary Lepell by whom he had eight children, he also played box and cox with Frederick, Prince of Wales, for the favours of Miss Vane. In addition he had a number of intimate male friends including Stephen Fox and Count Algarotti—the latter a wildly ambitious young ambivert who preferred the embraces of the Crown Prince of Prussia (later Frederick the Great) to those of either Lord Hervey or Lady Mary Wortley Montagu.

That Hervey was slim in an age noted for grossly fat men was due to a rigorous diet which he believed helped control the fits* to which he was subject; and it is charitable to suppose that he painted to hide his pallor. But many men painted, as they had done for centuries and would continue to do right up to the 1850s. Lord Hervey's use of cosmetics was not unusual; yet, when combined with his known prediliction for delicate silks and young men, it branded him as effeminate. The 'Lady of the Lords' he was called when he took his seat in that not so august House in 1735. And Alexander Pope, 'at open war with Lord Hervey',[2] pillories him as Sporus.

---

* These were probably epileptic although, from the description given in the *Memoirs*, they may have been due to severe abdominal migraine.

Let Sporus tremble—What? that Thing of silk,
Sporus, that mere white Curd of Ass's milk?
Satire or Sense, alas! can Sporus feel?
Who breaks a Butterfly upon a Wheel?
Yet let me flap this Bug with gilded wings,
This painted Child of Dirt, that stinks and stings; . . .
Eternal Smiles his emptiness betray,
As shallow streams run dimpling all the way. . . .
His Wit all see-saw, between *that* and *this*
Now high, now low, now Master up, now Miss,
And he himself one vile Antithesis. . . .
Fop at the Toilet, Flatt'rer at the board,
Now trips a Lady, and now struts a Lord.[3]

The reference to Sporus,[*] one of Nero's fancy boys, cannot
have been lost upon an age when education was primarily
classical. Even less could Hervey himself have missed it. After
falling out with the Prince of Wales, perhaps over Miss Vane, he
drew upon Suetonius for a sort of 'Parallel Lives' of Nero and
Frederick which he included in his Memoirs.[†] But it was Lady
Mary Wortley Montagu a great friend of Hervey's who said, and
meant it one thinks as a compliment, that there were three sexes,
'men, women and Herveys'.[4] Still, whatever the sex, those who
painted were unaware, or more probably unmindful, of the fact
that poisons could be absorbed by the cutaneous route.[‡] They
whitened the skin with mercury water and so besmeared themselves with ceruse containing white lead that they ruined their
skins, their hair fell out, they developed appalling gastric disturbances, got the shakes, and sometimes even died like Kitty
Fisher (1741–67). Kitty, a charming intelligent and highly
successful courtesan who sat for Reynolds and with whom Lord
John Hervey's second son, Augustus (later 3rd Earl of Bristol)

[*] The interested reader may care to consult *The Twelve Caesars*. Nero VI. 28, in
Robert Graves's translation.
[†] See Lord Hervey's *Memoirs*, ed. R. Sedgwick, III, p. 858 *et. seq.*
[‡] It was certainly recognized at the time that arsenic and arsenical fumes were
poisonous and that mercury could be caustic.

'got in with',[5] as he so nonchalantly puts it, died 'a victim to cosmetics'. While 'that pretty young woman, Lady Fortrose, Lady Harrington's eldest daughter', was 'at the point of death', Horace Walpole says, 'killed like Lady Coventry and others by white lead of which nothing could break her'.[6]

Lady Coventry was the beautiful Maria Gunning, daughter of a poor Irish squire who with her younger sister, Elizabeth, came to England in 1751, seeking a fortune through an advantageous marriage. Both girls were wildly successful. Elizabeth became a double duchess; first, of Hamilton and next—death not divorce—of Argyll. Together the sisters were declared 'the handsomest women alive' and when they arrived in London not only were they surrounded by a satisfactory horde of highly eligible young men, they could not even 'walk in the Park or go to Vauxhall but such mobs follow them that they are generally driven away'.[7] Mobs also crowded about their door daily to see them get into their chairs, and when Elizabeth appeared at court after her first marriage 'even the noble mob in the Drawing-room clambered upon chairs and tables to look at her'.[8] When she travelled north 'seven hundred people sat up all night in and about an inn in Yorkshire to see her get into her post-chaise next morning'.[9]

Maria, more beautiful but less intelligent, married the young Earl of Coventry and received equally enthusiastic tributes to her beauty; 'a shoe-maker at Worcester made two guineas and a half'[10] simply by exhibiting a shoe he was making for the young Countess at a penny a peep. So more than six hundred people—probably about ten per cent of Worcester's population were willing to part with a penny merely to see Maria's shoe. The age had no film stars, no Beatles, but it had the Gunning girls. Elizabeth stayed with it until 1791, but poor Maria departed in 1760. Despite the fact that her 'dear Cov' was one of those men who disapproved strongly of painting, and suffered Maria 'to wear neither red or powder', what must have been their first recorded marital passage-at-arms took place in a rather ill-bred fashion on their wedding trip to Paris. At a dinner party given by Sir John Bland where Maria appeared *en grande tenue*, the Earl suspecting,

Ladies' hats, 1750–70

rightly, that his bride was painted 'coursed' her 'round the table
. . . seized her . . . and scrubbed it off by force with a napkin,
and then told her that since she had deceived him and broke her
promise, he would carry her back directly to England'.[11] Needless to say he did not. Perhaps he even gave up the struggle
against Maria's paint. In any event, eight years later at the age of
twenty-seven Maria was dead. Another victim to cosmetics, said
the disapproving. Others, more kindly and more accurately, said
it was consumption. While 'the mob who never quitted curiosity
about her went to the number of ten thousand only to see her
coffin'.[12]

But if some men preferred 'the changeable rose' and found
'nothing on earth so impudent as an everlasting blush',[13] few
women, no matter how young or pretty, would have dreamt of
appearing in public with an undressed face. And, as a woman
grew older (old age began around thirty), the dressing usually
became heavier. When Horace Walpole met Lady Mary Wortley

Montagu in Florence in 1740 (she had pursued Algarotti to Italy to no purpose) she was then fifty-one, and he describes this once beautiful woman and toast of the Kit Kat Club as wearing 'a foul mob, that does not cover her greasy black locks, that hang loose, never combed or curled; an old mazarine blue wrapper, that gapes open and discovers a canvas petticoat', and, he adds, 'her face is swelled violently on one side with the remains of a — —, partly covered with a plaister! and partly with white paint, which for cheapness she has bought so coarse, that you would not use it to wash a chimney'.[14] This pitiless picture is no doubt accurate—but it is also malicious. Horace is insinuating that the sore on Lady Mary's cheek was a gumma due to syphilis,* whereas it might have been caused by a too frequent use of a strong mercury wash or, since arsenic is a carcinogen, to the coarse white paint. It is very probable that Lady Mary, like many another woman, used coarse white so heavily to fill up the horrible pitts in her skin which were the aftermath of smallpox.

Lady Oldborough, perhaps more successful in trying to 'stifle the truth of her age . . . her faded, sallow complexion, the retreat of her eyes inwards and the funeral stamp of the crow's foot on their corners', also used 'such notoriously false witnesses as ceruse, carmine, powder, and the rest of the *fourberie* of the toilette'. She took enormous pains with 'plaistering up her ruins' and 'exhausted all the powers of paint, powder, laces and jewels to forge herself a face and figure'. Even so, 'the spurious glaze of varnish, presenting nearly the disagreeable shine of coarse enamel' was no substitute for the 'inimitable roseate' colours 'of nature'.[15]

But what could a woman do? If she were fool enough to stop painting to please husband or lover, other women noticed at once and made the most disobliging remarks. The Duchess of Grafton 'having left red and white quite off' was 'one of the coursest brown women'[16] Lady Sarah Bunbury had ever seen. Lady Sarah,

---

* Gummata very rarely appear on the face and there is no evidence that Lady Mary suffered from syphilis. This libel probably originated from Pope's satire in which he refers to Lady Mary as Sappho and says 'Pox'd by her Love, or libell'd by her Hate' (*Imitation of the First Satire of the Second Book of Horace*, line 84).

née Lennox, was famous for her lovely complexion, and so enchanted the youthful George III that he seems to have wanted to marry her. His mother and Lady Mary Wortley Montagu's son-in-law, Lord Bute, had other ideas, so George dutifully married Charlotte of Mecklenburg-Strelitz. Lady Sarah consoled herself for the loss of a crown by nursing a pet squirrel which subsequently died.* As for the Duchess of Grafton? Coarse and brown she may have looked but she and the Duke parted,† and she subsequently married the Earl of Upper Ossory.

Curiously enough, there seem to be no cases on record of men becoming victims of cosmetics. This may be because fewer men painted and those who did painted less heavily than women. Also, the amount of skin exposed to public gaze in a man was only from chin to wig line, whereas feminine fashions from the time of Charles II, no matter how much they changed in design, detail or fabric, always insisted on a very low *décolletage*. Face, neck, chest and a good part of the bosom 'incontestably the least platonic of all female charms'[17] had to be painted, to say nothing of the arms. As girls started to paint, often at the age of fourteen, while boys were still in school, not only was the area for painting much greater but women began at an earlier age. Contact dermatitis and allergic reactions must have been responsible for many very unbeautiful and painful skin conditions.

Beauty and/or money were, it seems, the only things required of a Georgian woman. If she had the first she usually managed to marry the second. If she had the second she did not need the first. No matter how ill-favoured, there was small chance of a rich woman 'leading apes in Hell'—the unenviable lot of spinsters in the after-life. The practical Irish, it is said, even issued a list of Englishwomen of fashion from Duchesses down to untitled rich nobodies 'for the benefit of Irish fortune hunters'.[18] A plain girl,

---

* By a later marriage, she became the mother of the famous and heroic Napier brothers.

† Her marriage to the Duke—one of our notably unsuccessful prime ministers—was most unhappy. He divorced her and she married her lover, the Earl, and retired from Society.

even a downright ugly one, were she the daughter of a rich business man or merchant, might end up a duchess, while the beautiful (and even not-so-beautiful) daughter of an impoverished duke could become the rich wife—and preferably widow—of a non-aristocratic money maker. Alliances between sons and daughters of noble families when both families were rich were of course preferable and frequent, but impoverished noble families and rich city families entered into marriage treaties or contracts to their mutual benefit. Since this is what governments do and always have done on a much larger scale, it would be folly to regard it as outrageous, immoral or even just another example of eighteenth-century materialism. In reality, it was probably a very good thing. It certainly meant that our very complicated class structure had not hardened into a caste system, had not become rigid and inflexible as in France; and it also meant, in many instances, a healthy intermingling of blood. All that was required of a woman born or married into the aristocracy was that she provide her husband with a male heir; after fulfilling this function she was more or less free to go her own way. If she were beautiful, she often did. If she were not, she could at least earn the reputation of being a faithful and devoted wife. But as it is hardly a compliment to remain faithful simply because no male has ever tempted one not to be, beauty aids were probably more sought after by those whom nature had failed or totally forgotten, than by those who wished to improve upon or maintain nature's gift of beauty. In either case, lovely and not-so-lovely women were equally certain to be troubled with 'blemishes and imperfections' which fortinately could be 'remedied or concealed'.[19] Spots, freckles, scarlet faces, red eyes, cracked lips and countless other minor afflictions are no respecters of beauty.

To conceal a few spots and pimples was relatively simple because patching by both sexes remained fashionable until about 1790. But a face quite covered by tiny black polka dots to hide a superfluity of real spots cannot have been particularly enchanting. Hence there are innumerable ointments, salves, pomatums and washes guaranteed to do away with multiple maculations. Sophisticated city dwellers could buy many different wonder working aids from those who dealt in secret remedies of all kinds and who, by now, had branched out into equally secret beauty products. Or they could be bought from bogus doctors like that 'old illiterate German quack', Mr Keypstick. He began as a corn-cutter to the quality then 'sold cosmetic washes to the ladies, together with teeth powders, hair-dyeing liquors, prolific elixirs, and tinctures to sweeten the breath' and finally so ingratiated himself with the fashionable that he was able to set up a school 'with five and twenty boys of the best families'.[20]

The unsophisticated and less rich city or country dweller could, and often did, make her own beauty aids. Certainly there were enough recipe books to tell her how to do so. For the most part the recipes seem harmless enough and require little beyond herbs, flowers, vegetables, fat, brandy, spring water and considerable patience. One favourite spot remover contained a pound of veal minced fine, but this, though it doubtless became a trifle odorous in time, cannot have been so dangerous as a patent, secret ointment on sale guaranteed not only to wear away smallpox scars but to cure a red face. It is not all that easy to see upon what principle this unguent worked, unless it quite simply removed the skin and left the anointed to grow a new one. It may have contained 'salt of saturn' which, from its name, was very probably lead sulphate. This is mordantly caustic.

Complexion clearers are too numerous to mention and vary from birch-sap, which was recommended for the same purpose in the time of Queen Elizabeth, through various herbal washes to the more harmful mercurial ones. A quite late Georgian recipe, absolutely guaranteed to preserve the complexion, calls for a good many white flowers, cucumber water and lemon juice plus 'seven or eight White Pigeons',[21] plucked, beheaded, minced fine and digested in an alembic for eighteen days before use. This is interesting because so many of the ingredients, including the pigeons, are white; so the recipe even at this late date falls into what might be called the imitative magic class of cosmetic.

Freckles were rather more easily coped with than spots or a

muddy or sallow complexion. Women were advised to avoid the sun, which they did often with the aid of masks and/or straw hats. If these small sun spots did appear, a recipe of 1719 recommends 'six oak apples' and a few elder leaves steeped in 'wine vinegar'[22] as a sure banisher. A less innocuous recipe of 1784 calls for fresh wood ashes boiled in water and used repeatedly as a wash. Since this liquid would be a mild lye it might indeed remove freckles along with the stratum corneum. By the 1820s, such things as crushed strawberries, green grape juice, asses (and even human) milk are recommended as freckle removers. None can have lived up to the claims made for it.

Red eyes have never been considered beautiful in any age, and the Georgian age seems to have been full of them. A dietary deficiency is less likely to be the cause in this period than in previous centuries, as the rich now ate butter in quantity and no longer despised it as the food of barbarous races or the native

Parasols, mid-eighteenth century

poor. Lady Mary Campbell reputedly cried 'her red eyes to scarlet'[23] upon learning she was to be married off to Viscount Coke, who had already been offered to 'all the great lumps of gold in the city'.[24] Judging from Coke's treatment of poor red-eyed Lady Mary,* the lumpy rich girls were quite right not to have him. But this kind of thing cannot have been a very typical cause of red eyes. Much redness and soreness must have been due to the chronic irritation caused by the powder men used on their wigs, and from the hair powder women used from about 1760, to say nothing of the things they smeared on their faces and eyes. If Turkish women used 'a black tincture around the eyes which Lady Mary Wortley Montagu fancied 'many of our ladies would be overjoyed to know the secret',[25] Englishwomen were at this time making do with messy old lamp black, or the residue of burnt ivory shavings. No matter how attractive the result, a shaky hand meant soot in the eye as well as on lashes or lid. Eyebrows could be 'turned a beautiful black' by first washing them in a 'decoction of Gall water'[26] then brushing them over with a solution of green vitriol and gum arabic. Small wonder that remedies for sore eyes are almost as chronic as the condition.

A most frightful sounding 'Ophthalmic Lotion' calls for an ounce each of 'White Vitriol and Bay Salt' and the instructions for preparing it begin, ominously enough, with 'decrepitate them together and when the detonation is over, pour on them . . . a pint of boiling water or Rose water'.[27] Presumably one poured if one had not been blinded by the detonation. Still, there were many cures for blindness, which was a comfort. A mixture of scraped white copperas, white salt and spring water often cured blindness and was a certain remedy for redness, soreness, pearls, and rheums . . . or so John Wesley says as late as 1792. White copperas couldn't have cured blindness, but if by white copperas the Rev. Mr Wesley meant zinc sulphate, then his lotion would be

---

* She subsequently separated from her husband, son of Thomas Coke, Lord Leicester, and had an affair with Edward, Duke of York, brother of George III, to whom she wished people to think she was secretly married. She became notably eccentric and died in 1811. Horace Walpole dedicated his *Castle of Otranto* to her.

very useful. Wesley also, with much more sense than was usual for the day, warns that 'If it makes the eyes smart, add more water to it'.[28] Twenty years later a book on beauty advises its readers to remove 'superficial specks with a weak caustic, such as vitriol'.[29] One does not care much for this advice.

Chapped lips are almost as unpleasant to own as they are to kiss, and many and varied are the lip salves recommended, some coloured red with alkanet root. A highly recommended and quite obviously 'home' recipe of the time of George I advises 'take your own Watter, boyle it to a Syrrup with sum Duble Refine Lofe Sugar'.[30] Unlike the sugar, this linament may not sound all that refined to us, but this is because we tend to read history backwards. To a generation whose parents (if not themselves when young) had been treated with medicines in which animal excrement figured prominently, this recipe can have occasioned few if any qualms.

Apart from things to rub in, anoint, wash or cover the skin, there were other beauty aids of a mechanical nature which repaired 'the Wastes of Fatigue' and averted 'the Marks of Age'.[31] Forehead pieces of leather lined with linen which, if strapped on overnight, did away with furrowed brows were partnered with night vizards which did the same for wrinkled cheeks. There were women specializing in what we now call beauty culture who shaped eyebrows 'without pain' or provided false ones which sometimes rather embarrassingly fell off. A low forehead could be raised as high as one pleased and as women's hair styles began to move up off the forehead around 1750, a low forehead was a definite disadvantage. So the low brow became a high brow by plucking the hair line—a trick which had been indulged in by Italian Renaissance women some 300 years before. Optimistic mamas even had their children's foreheads rubbed with oil of walnuts 'to prevent hair growing on that part'.[32] As oil from a fresh walnut will successfully disguise a scratch on mahogany, a walnut-coloured high brow must have been considered rather better than a low, hairy one. A forehead bandage 'dipped in vinegar in which cats' dung has been steeped'[33] also prevented a low hair line. This repulsive recipe, obviously a very old one, is being recommended as late as the time of George IV.

There were also other special 'plaisters' advertised to remove hair permanently from any part of the body. What such plaisters contained was a trade secret, but it is probable that one of the ingredients was quick lime, because most home-made depilatories contained it. Several—still in use in the nineteenth century—even call for ants' eggs as well. The test of a really good home-made depilatory was to dip a feather or quill into the brew; if the feathery bits fell away from the central rib then the mix was strong enough, and when applied to the body unwanted hair immediately dropped off. There is no reason to suppose that it did not. Many women must have suffered miseries trying to get rid of superfluous hair and to little purpose. Even if, as rumoured, the Duke of Newcastle * had paid a French barber £400 to rid his wife of this affliction it apparently did little good, for upon the duke's temporary retirement from politics in 1756 a contemporary writes, 'The Duke of Newcastle is retired . . . and will let his beard grow as long as his Duchess's'.34

But if, in an era when plastic surgery and hormonal treatments were unknown, the 'Marks of Age and Decline'35 stubbornly refused to yield to external applications or mechanical aids, they might yet give way to an elixir of some sort. The search for the philosopher's stone had been given up by most philosophers and alchemists, but the quest for an elixir of life and youth went on just as feverishly as it always had, and still does. To this end 'the Countess of Thanet's mother, fed a man with the design it is supposed to kill him and distill him to give to her husband—to make him live long'.36 Whether this Medea-like story had any basis in fact I am unable to say; the tale may be contemporary or legendary gossip. The odd thing about it, at least to our way of thinking, is that it was carefully noted down in the journal of a north country parson.

Fortunately for all concerned, there were many less drastic and

---

* Thomas Pelham-Holles, 1st Duke of Newcastle-upon-Tyne and the master of eighteenth-century political corruption.

difficult ways of procuring elixirs and preservers of life. There was a patent one, which appeared around 1760, called the 'Balsamic Corroborant' or 'Restorer of Nature' much advertised as being highly praised by royal and noble personages (names wisely not given). In 1765 Lady Sophia Thomas is busy staving off old age by requesting our Ambassador in Paris, the Earl of Hertford, to send her 'twelve little bottles of le Baume de Vie composé par le Sieur Liévre, apoticaire distillateur du Roi'.[37] Those unable to make use of an Ambassador or to afford the Balsamic Corroborant, could always fall back on the older 'Syrup for the Preservation of Long Life',[38] which could be run up at home. The recipe, it is said, was first discovered in Barbary by an English officer serving in the armies of Charles V (1500–58). By some unexpected means, the Englishman got the recipe out of a sprightly old gentleman of 132, used it himself for years and then, at the age of ninety-two, decided that for the good of the Commonwealth, he ought to make the secret known. Accordingly, and rather mystifyingly, he confided it to a prebendary of Canterbury, Peter Du Moulin, (d. 1684). Dr Du Moulin, in turn, gave the recipe to the Countess of Feversham and from there it got into the beauty books of the day. The Recipe itself is as long and complicated as its history. It had to be prepared 'in the Moone of May', which indicates it had magical or astrological properties, and it called for 8 pounds of the juice of 'mercurial' (which in this instance probably means the plant, dog's mercury) 2 pounds of borage juice, 12 of clarified honey, all boiled together and strained. To this was added 3 pints of white wine, $\frac{1}{4}$ of a pound of gentian root, $\frac{1}{2}$ a pound of Irish (? orris) root or 'blew Flower de Lis' which had been infused together for twenty-four hours. Then the whole lot was reduced to a syrup by slow boiling. Taken each morning, fasting, the syrup prolonged life prodigiously. This elixir may have been rather a bother to prepare but it was certainly less expensive than, and probably just as efficacious as, Dr Graham's famous Elixir of Life.

Almost exactly contemporaneous with Dr Graham (1745–94) was Sicilian born, Giuseppe Balsamo (1743–95) who was 'by profession, healer of diseases, abolisher of wrinkles . . . spirit

summoner . . . and thaumaturgic moralist and swindler'.[39]
Better known to his own era and to ours by his assumed name
and title, Count Alessandro Cagliostro, this arch-rogue, quack,
probable hypnotist, dabbler in the occult, and founder of a most
peculiar Egyptian Masonic Lodge, numbered among his other
accomplishments a knowledge of drugs and cosmetics. He came
to England several times; first, perhaps in 1771, when he worked
as a house painter; next, in 1776 when, complete with assumed
name, he set up in Whitcombe Street as a seller of paint and beauty
aids for both men and women. His handsome wife, the Countess
Seraphina (her real name was Lorenza), was an excellent advertisement for his products. Women went wild about the count,
flocked to him for advice and to buy his wonderful cosmetics,
love philtres and, in particular, his famous 'Beautifying Water',
guaranteed to iron out wrinkles and restore even the most elderly
and faded complexion to youthful freshness. For faded or jaded
gentlemen there was a provocative look at Seraphina and a
precious and expensive 'Wine of Egypt' which probably contained nothing newer than that old favourite, cantharides (later
Cagliostro, too, produced an Elixir of Life). In trouble with the
law over fake lottery tickets, the count, after a spell in prison,
returned to the continent and did not come back to England until
ten years later after an even longer stretch in the Bastille. He
seems to have had only a very moderate success on this third
visit. His 'Egyptian Pills' which sold in Paris at 'thirty shillings a
dram'[40] (that would be perhaps £30 in today's money) were not
popular enough to bring visitors to 'one of London's outermost
suburbs',[41] viz. Sloane Street, Knightsbridge, where he now lived
almost as a recluse with his 'pretty, virtuous and ever-smiling
wife'[42]—still the same one and still famous for her whiter than
white 'breast, neck and hands'. Here, on September 11th and
12th 1786, the Count was called upon by a curious German
visitor to London, the sentimental German novelist, Sophie v. la
Roche (she met the infamous Lord George Gordon there) who
notes in her journal, rather to our astonishment, that although
Cagliostro's 'medicaments' for a long life and a gay one were

inevitably popular in Paris, 'the English do not believe in such tonics'. In support of this odd statement she says: 'The numerous suicides from trifling causes, the cool unimpassioned way young thieves are watched dying on the gallows, seems to indicate the cause lies in the national character . . . little store is laid by life'.[43]

This is just plain Germanic theoretical nonsense. To commit suicide * over trifles, to regard hanging as a form of entertainment, are certainly most melancholy signs that something is very much amiss, but do not necessarily mean that we, as a people, set no store by life. What is more to the point is that many, then as now, equated youth with life and by the time Sophie came to London, Cagliostro's nostrums were thought very *vieux chapeau*. We were, at this stage in our history, deferring the 'melancholy arrival of frigid age'[44] by being electrified, taking shudderingly cold sea baths, resorting to newer quacks and, ever hopeful, using newer cosmetics and beauty aids.

It need not be thought that men were not at it too. They were. Some were open about it. Others, like rheumaticky old Lord Ogle, spurned such things as the famous Cosmetique Royale—which took away 'all heats, pimps, frecks . . . and wrinques of old age'[45] and secretly took to wearing 'a faint tincture of rose' to overcome pallor and give 'a delicate spirit to the eyes'. Still others were, doubtless, like Mr Du Quesne who, at seventy-five and dim sighted, refused to wear age-making spectacles and could not bear 'to appear old, but must be as young in anything as the youngest person'.[46] No matter how poorly Mr Du Quesne looked or felt he just could not help 'talking young'. This he did to everyone's annoyance until the day of his death in 1793.

This was the year in which France declared war on us—no novelty in the eighteenth century—but a novelty fashion in the *mauvais*-est possible *goût* made its first appearance in England that year, after Louis XVI, Marie Antoinette and much of the French aristocracy were guillotined. The fashion was to wear a thin

---

* In fairness, it must be said that most foreigners found us much given to suicide 'an act of despair so frequent' that even Smollett in his *History* comments on it (1812 edn., vol. II: bk, II: ch. V. sect. 1).

crimson ribbon around the neck and a tousled, unkempt hair style called, engagingly, *la victime coiffeur*. But this was probably the last excess in a period noted for excessive hair styles; certainly until the 1790s this was the century par excellence for fabulous and fantastic hair styles for both sexes. Equally certainly, in the early Georgian era it was men who led the fashionable way.

Men were now wholly clean shaven, having quite given up the minute lip beard and moustache favoured in the last quarter of the previous century; all hair emphasis was on the head. The curled, full-bottomed, high, peaked wig remained in favour until about 1720, and for a decade after that was worn by elderly and professional men. But young men had taken to the tye-wig where the hair was drawn back into a queue and tied with a ribbon or allowed to fall in loose curls down the back. The tye-wig in its various permutations was the basis of men's hair styles until the end of the century. Similar to the tye, were the ramillie wig—worn by Uncle Toby when he set out to woo the Widow Wadman—and the pigtail. The ramillie, named after the battle of Ramillies (1706) and a great favourite in the army, had the back hair plaited into a queue and tied at nape and nether end by black bows. The pigtail was no different save that the plait was encased in a long, rectangular black silk sheath, rather like an umbrella case, with the ends of the hair curling out below the lower bow. A variation was the bag wig which when first worn by some outré person was not considered to be at all genteel by Society, perhaps because it was said to have originated among servants to protect the hair while working or, alternately, to have come from the stables where the horses' tails were always bagged in the stalls. One can credit the first objection but the second sounds most un-English. By the 1730s the bag wig, with the hair enclosed in a case of 'gummed' (stiffened with gum) black taffeta and drawn tight with a string, the string itself concealed by a black rosette or bow, was moving in the best circles. Sometimes the ribbon ends of the bag or tye were brought round the neck and tied with a bow ornamented with a jewelled pin—the beginning of the black silk tie; this variation was called the Solitaire. Jerry Melford's new valet, Mr Dutton, was 'an exceeding cox-comb' and, says his young master, wore 'a solitaire, uses paint, and takes rapee with all the grimaces of a French Marquis'.[47] The bag wig became much larger during the 1740s and protected the coat a little from hair powder and grease. These, then, were the chief masculine modes until around 1760, although they naturally persisted long after that date, and there were innumerable minor variations on these themes; bushy 'pigeon's wings' (over the ears) the cauliflower, the comet, the royal bird, the stair case, the rose, the long bob, the short bob and, strangest of all, the she-dragon!

Throughout this period powder was used, and more and more lavishly as time went on. Men discovered long before women that grey or white hair flattered the face, made the eyes look brighter and eliminated one of the signs of age—grey or white hair. Grey powder was used until about 1720, although white had

Tie wig, grey powdered, black ribbon solitaire, *circa* 1730. Horse-shoe toupet wig, Cadogan puffs, *circa* 1770

been worn by the pace setters before then it did not become general until *c.* 1725. 'Uncle found fault with my wig, for being so light, said I should have a darker one',[48] complains the Rev. John Tomlinson in 1718. Uncle was also a vicar and probably stuck to an old-fashioned grey or even brown powdered wig. Rice or wheat meal was the favourite powder, and the wig had to be liberally greased to make the powder stick. Yet wig wearing was by no means confined to the rich, the professional or middling classes. When Pehr Kalm visited us in 1748 he notes with astonishment that everyone in England wore a peruque, from boys hardly breeched to grandfathers. Farmers 'farm servants, clod hoppers, day labourers . . . all labouring folk'[49] working in the fields or anywhere else wore wigs. Since the cheapest wigs sold for a guinea, and agricultural and labourers' wages were what they were, many of these wigs must have been bought second, third or even fourth hand from Slop-shops and were probably made of wool or tow, as human hair cost 17s 6d a pound. At the other end of the scale was Lady Mary Wortley Montagu's mad son, Edward, whose expensive clothing startled even Horace Walpole. 'He diamonds himself even to distinct shoe buckles for a frock; and has more snuff boxes than would suffice a Chinese idol with an hundred noses', he writes, and then adds, 'But the most curious part of his dress, which he has brought from Paris, is an Iron wig; you literally would not know it from hair'.[50] Attracted perhaps by the iron wig, Miss Elizabeth Ashe—the one known as Pollard —who had a bad reputation even for good society, married Edward. It was Edward's third, and trigamous marriage, and was performed suitably enough by an unfrocked clergyman.*

In contrast to all this fuss with men's hair, women's hair styles during the first half of the period seem simplicity itself. The hair was dressed close to the head with a small top-knot invariably covered with a minute, flounced or lace-edged cap with lappets.

---

* Edward and his wife soon returned to Paris where he became involved in a nasty affair of gambling and robbery; was caught and imprisoned in the Châtelet, where he remained for eleven days before the English Ambassador could bail him out.

Small, demure, artificial flowers, blonde lace, striped ribbons and aigrets were used as hair ornaments. When the cap was worn outdoors, as it always was, it was covered by a hood. By mid-century, however, there were presages of things to come when the small head silhouette began to enlarge. The front hair or 'toupet' was now drawn up off the forehead over a pad and shaped into flat ringlets held in place by a messy mixture of pomatum and flour. As height and width increased, as it did if the hair, due either to niggardly nature or thievish time, proved insufficient in quantity to meet the increasing demands, false hair was used. This was bolstered up and out with a good greasy wool. Powdering came into fashion; greys, blue, light blonde or brown powders were favourites, often delicately dusted over with white which gave the confection a slightly frosted look. The higher and wider silhouette, which went on climbing up and spreading out until it reached a peak or high plateau in the 1780s, was known as 'Frenched' hair, for French fashions in hair and dress for both sexes were avidly followed until the French Revolutionary period.* Those unfortunate enough to be unable to go to Paris to see fashions at their source were kept *au courant* by French 'fashion babies' (or 'pattern dressed dolls') which were sent regularly from Paris to London.

But if English fashions were always just a step behind French modes they were at least in advance of fashion as interpreted in Mecklenburg-Strelitz, that tiny Duchy which one could find on the map only with the aid of a magnifying glass. When Charlotte of Mecklenburg-Strelitz, a 'remarkably genteel' girl of seventeen, arrived in England to marry George III, the English ladies sent to meet her—one was the beautiful Duchess of Hamilton—were rather contemptuous of her old-fashioned hair style and urged her to 'curl her toupet'.[51] Just how this was to be accomplished (apparently in a coach) en route to London one does not know, but Charlotte in her sensible, plain fashion replied that 'she thought it looked as well as that of any of the ladies sent to fetch

* Similarly, in France there was a craze for English things. But it was not until the French Revolution that London became the centre for men's fashions.

her; if the king bid her she would wear a periwig, otherwise she would stay as she was.'⁵²

Queen Charlotte, who was plain, parsimonious, had a vile temper and an iron will, never did become a leader of fashion, as for example, Marie Antoinette was. Also, as George III's private life was as dull as the private lives of the first two Georges but, unlike theirs, morally impeccable, there were no English Pompadours or Du Barri's to be slavishly followed in matters of dress.

By 1766 Lady Sarah Lennox, the English girl who did not become Queen, was writing to her dear friend Lady Susan Fox Strangways* that the fashion of 'the common run of people' at Ranelagh and other public places 'is not to be described'⁵³ and English taste was appalling and vulgar. But she says, 'I think by degrees the French dress is coming into fashion (by this she means more generally into fashion) tho' 'tis almost impossible to make the ladies understand that heads bigger than one's body are ugly; it is growing the fashion to have the heads moutoné: I have cut off my hair & find it very convenient in the country without powder because my hair curls naturally, but it is horrid troublesome to have it well curled; if it is big it is frightful. I wear it very often with the rows of curls behind & the rest smooth with a furzed toupé & a cap, that is *en paresseuse*. . . . Ther is nobody but Ly Tavistock who does not dress French who is at all genteel, for if they are not French they are so ill-dressed its terrible. Almost everybody powders now & wears a little hoop; hats are vastly left off; the hair down on the forehead belongs to the short waist & is equally vulgar with poppons,† trimmings, beads, garnets, flying caps & false hair.' So to be perfectly 'genteel' one must dress thus: 'The hair must be powdered, curled with very small curls . . . and neat but it must be high before & give your head the look of a sugar loaf a little. The roots of the hair must be drawn straight up and

---

* By then Lady Susan O'Brien. She had run off with an actor and this infuriated her family, as O'Brien had neither money nor influence. This so-called mésalliance seemingly turned out to be an extraordinarily happy marriage.

† Perhaps pompons which, in those days, could be a top-knot, a tuft or a bunch of ribbons worn in the hair.

not fruzed at all for half an inch . . . you must wear no cap and only little, little flowers, dab'd in on the left side; the only feathers permitted is the black or white sultane perched up on the left side.'[54]

Hair *moutoné* was hardly new; it was a variation of a style which had been worn a good hundred years before and known then as 'à la mouton', but it led to a sad quarrel between Horace Walpole and Lady Harriot Vernon. When Lady Harriot's daughter, the newly married Lady Grosvenor, appeared at a party at Northumberland House with 'such a display of friz, that it literally spread beyond her shoulders',[55] Horace remarked to some one that 'it looked as if her parents had stinted her in hair before marriage and that she was determined to indulge her fancy now'. This remark got back to Lady Harriot, as such remarks always do even if they have to travel around the world to do so, and the offended mother was so angry with Mr Walpole that one suspects there must have been some truth in the remark.

During the 1770s and on into the 80s the fashionable coiffure went ever upward and became a ridiculous affectation. Many a woman looked as if she were divided into two equal parts, body and head separated or linked by a face. The head was a fantastic and often elegant minor architectural creation, lavishly powdered and loaded with ornaments. Over foundations of wire, cotton wool or a curly wig, the hair was built up and puffed out to fabulous proportions, augmented by false hair, curls and yet more puffs of various kinds and shapes each with its own name. Acres of tulle—newly invented in Nottingham in 1768—or gauze were used chiefly for the gigantic mob caps, (the *thérèse*). Lace, feathers and artificial flowers—the best flowers came from Italy—were the usual hair ornaments. Fresh flowers were also used and kept fresh in small, water-filled containers shaped to the head. On extremely grand occasions, models of coaches and horses, ships in full sail, windmills, battles, butterflies and other unlikely things, usually of blown glass, were perched on top of the snowy, decorated mountain. Enormously tall feathers were also worn—the fashion began in France—and these could be

Wig and bonnet dressing stand, late eighteenth century

highly dangerous when a feather caught fire in the flame of a chandelier.

Women, however, did not have it all their own way in the matter of high fantastic hair styles. In the 1770s a group of young men interested in extreme fashion formed the Macaroni Club. Although the nearly knee-length, slightly flared coat with fitted sleeves and wide cuffs common in the time of George II had, by the late 60s, grown a bit shorter, the Macaronis found this too dull and conventional for words, and introduced a plain, very much shorter coat, pleated and flared at the back, to be worn with a plain or horizontally striped waistcoat and plain or vertically striped breeches. This dazzling and outré costume, a forerunner of the slender silhouette for men, was topped by an exaggeratedly high, powdered wig. As the tricorne was still a favourite, and had been for seventy years or more, the Macaronis wore a miniature version perched precariously on top and at the front of the wig. It was called the Nivernois. Macaronis also painted, wore two watches and carried pretty nosegays. Young men who were not members of the Macaroni Club imitated those who were, and doubtless older men, apeing youth, did the same. But many elders thought all this really too absurd, if not downright hideous, a sad sign of degeneracy, and what *was* the country coming to! Non-macaronis were by now wearing the cadogan or club wig, but the bag and pigtail wigs were still popular, even if from about 1765 some men had discarded the wig altogether and wore their own hair, wig-style. This flouting of wigs so alarmed the periwig makers, they marched, wigless, to complain to George III that if this sort of thing went on they would be ruined. They need not have worried. Women were on the verge of taking to false hair and wigs on an unprecedented scale, and the complicated hair structures which went on ascending and distending until 1782 brought wig makers, as well as all hairdressers, undreamed of prosperity.

Such extraordinary styles took hours and hours to create and a rich woman could spend half a day with her hairdresser 'making a head' and surrounded by friends, male and female. The toilette was a time for social gossip while the hairdresser worked away and no doubt picked up enough tit-bits to enable him to engage in highly profitable blackmail, or to make him the human equivalent of a scandalous gossip column. Once the hair style was completed it remained so for, at the very least, a fortnight, and fashionable women slept propped up in bed. Nevertheless, the hair-do needed daily retouching and twice or thrice daily powdering. Powder rooms were, of course, a necessary adjunct to every dressing room, but there were other necessary accessories too; a glass or paper cone to be held over the face, powdering jackets, puffs, dredgers and even powdering machines were a part of the equipment. Bewigged men had used these things for years, but since most women made use of their own hair, at least as a basis for the hair style, it was very necessary for a woman to 'open the head', once a week at least, to work on the accumulated vermin with some special ointment or compound often of a poisonous nature. When desperate, however, a lady scratched with a slender hooked rod made of lignum vitae, ivory, silver or gold and often bejewelled at the handle. What with managing fan, handkerchief, snuff-box, patch box, perfume container, parasol, head scratcher, long cane, muff, and a full skirt, there can never have been any problem for a woman of fashion in knowing what to do with her hands.

All such accessories, with the exception of the parasol, were common to both sexes. All could be exquisitely beautiful and varied in design and material to suit different occasions. Although snuff taking by women began to decline and was favoured by the older generation—Queen Charlotte was always spotted with snuff—it was still very much the fashion with men, and the choice of the right snuff box for the right occasion was as important as choosing the correct dress. Many beaux had snuff boxes to complement every coat they possessed, others had a separate box for each day of the week, still others were most particular to have their boxes made in winter and summer weights. Such boxes no less than patch boxes, pocket combs, toothpick cases, and cosmetic boxes were bijou *objets d'art* and called for all the skill of goldsmith, silversmith, jeweller, miniature painter, enameller and workers in ivory, amber and alabaster.

Muffs, worn by both sexes, came in winter and summer weights too. Winter muffs were of fur often vastly beribboned; summer ones of swansdown or feathers. But muffs had considerably reduced in size since the time of Charles II, and by mid-century were little more than finger muffs.* 'I send you a decent smallish muff, that you may put in your pocket, and it cost but fourteen shillings',[56] Horace Walpole writes to George Montagu on Christmas Eve 1764. Men's coats had very large pockets but a woman, when her muff was not in use, often wore it pushed up her arm. Tall, silver, gold or amber topped canes, decorated with loops of ribbon and held halfway down the length were for

* They grew much larger again in the early nineteenth century.

Fans, variously decorated with paint and ivory

feminine wear; the unribboned sword stick was more usual for men, and every fashionable man had dozens of sticks—sword or otherwise. Sticks, like snuff boxes, in late century had to be matched to the dress, to the occasion, even to the time of day or mood. Some had toilet mirrors fitted into the tops, some had perfume containers, others had amorous pictures. Non-folding, gaily coloured silk parasols often replaced the feminine cane, but no gentleman until well after mid-century would have been caught dead with an umbrella.* It was not until the early nineteenth century that men wore umbrellas. Clumsy steel or silver framed, covered with fancy blue or green silk, they were aristocratically held firmly by the middle with the carved ivory, gold, silver or

---

* Jonas Hanway is said to have been the first man ever to appear in the London streets carrying an umbrella.

stag-horn handle pointing to the ground. Both men and women indulged in decorative handkerchiefs; small and inevitably lace-edged for women, large and expensively edged with gold and silver lace for men—valuable objects for pickpockets. Sometimes women filled in a too low neckline with a lace-edged handkerchief and this was called 'a bosom friend'. Fans were also worn by both sexes (men used them in summer) and these too were often works of art, beautifully painted on vellum, stretched on ivory sticks often overlaid or decorated with amorini, goddesses, shepherds, fruit, flowers and leaves in wrought gold.

Even the simplest of toilettes required an enormous variety of bits and pieces and *The New Bath Guide*, which first appeared in 1766, gives an humorous but nonetheless accurate picture of the kind of things found in any lady's band-box. Among them,

> Painted lawns and chequer'd shades
> Crape that's worn by love lorn maids,
> Water'd tabbies, flower'd brocades;
> Vi'lets, pinks, Italian posies,
> Myrtles, jessamines, and roses,
> Aprons caps and 'kerchiefs clean,
> Straw built hats, and bonnets green.
> Cat guts,* gauses, tippets, ruffs,
> Fans, and hoods and feather'd muffs.
> Stomachers and Paris nets,
> Ear-rings, necklaces, aigrets,
> Fringes, blondes and migionets;
> Fine vermillion for the cheek,
> Velvet patches, a *la grecque*.[57]

There is much more, but it is difficult to see how a band-box could contain even this amount and not get into a fearful state of chaos—vermilion on the clean aprons and caps, earrings tangled in the gauzes, necklaces inextricably ensnared in Paris nets, and ribbons more wrinkled than the oldest skin—but these wrinkles could be ironed out rather more successfully than those of age.

Yet no matter how well one managed to preserve the skin and

---

* A ribbed material used for stiffening.

the complexion, no matter how young one was, or looked, there were always teeth to make or mar beauty. Good white teeth were greatly admired and greatly desired, but few seem to have had them—

> Tis not that lovely range of teeth so white,
> As new-shorn sheep, equal and fair[58]

sings Frederick, Prince of Wales, in an interminable poem addressed to his bride, the Princess Augusta of Saxe-Gotha. We may find the simile a trifle forced, but at least it tells us that the mother of George III had fine white teeth. She had probably not ruined them by over-indulgence in sweets as we did, always had done and, seemingly, will continue to do.

Lord Hervey, as we know, by the age of thirty-nine was already wearing that very fine set of Egyptian pebble teeth and here, one wonders, if Egyptian pebble can possibly be that brown mottled jasper found in Egypt? Even so, Egyptian pebble would be more attractive than blackened stumps and probably did not differ much in colour from most people's teeth. Although Pierre Franchard, a Frenchman, was making false teeth of jeweller's enamel and gold plate as early as 1728—French dentistry was far more advanced than English—most false teeth were still made of bone or ivory and wired into place. Dentures were made with a base-plate of wood, the long bone of an ox or an ivory tusk, whittled away and worked at until it fitted, more or less, and into this the false teeth were set.* Spiral springs were often used to keep these dentures in place, but sometimes they were dubiously held by atmospheric pressure. The making of 'china teeth' seems also to have been first thought of by a French chemist, Du Château; while a French dentist, Nicolas Dubois de Chemant, exhibited baked porcelain dentures in 1788. It was not until 1793 that he was granted a patent to manufacture them in England, and by 1800 he was being supplied with the right kind of paste from the Wedgwood factory. One could not only eat off Wedgwood but with it.

* Metallic plates began to be used in the late eighteenth century.

Well over a half a century lies between Egyptian pebble and Wedgwood paste, and in that long interval people went on trying desperately to fasten in loose teeth and 'strengthen the roots' with all sorts of curious mixtures, patented or made at home. Most of the fastening-in preparations contained alum which would certainly shrink the gums, temporarily, but the prevalence of gum shrinkers suggests a great lack of vitamin C in the diet.

Tooth whiteners, too, indicate that discoloured teeth must have been so common that people bought various advertised tinctures, powders, and tooth sticks absolutely guaranteed to whiten the teeth, fasten them in, prevent decay and cure 'scurvy in the gums'. Failing these, there were preparations to be made at home which would do the trick. Lemon juice, mixed with burnt alum and salt, rubbed on with a clean rag wrapped around the end of a stick was one of them, 'be careful not to have too much liquid on the rag', the recipe warns, 'for fear it should excoriate the gums';[59] and further, the user is admonished not to use this liquid 'above once every two or three months'. This is wise advice. Lemon juice is a bleach but also an excellent remover of tooth enamel. By the time of George IV this fact seems to have been fairly well known for lemon, vinegar, cream of tartar and 'mineral acids' are all said to be bad. In spite of this, a mixture of charcoal, sugar candy, 'quinquina' (quinine) and the forbidden cream of tartar is recommended as the best whitening dentifrice.

Once teeth were decayed by any cause, including frequent scouring with highly abrasive tooth-sticks made of powdered coral, pumice and gum traganth, the remedy was to apply a mixture of honey, myrrh, juniper root and rock alum. Applying honey to a decayed tooth sounds positively maniacal. But toothache, one of the commonest complaints of the time, could also be cured by herbal washes, a magnet or by roasted turnip parings laid behind the ear, and also by soaking the feet in hot water and rubbing them in bran at bed time. A certain M. Rostan, about whom I regrettably know nothing, wrote a book engagingly entitled *Comparisons Between the Nourishment of Feathers, and that of Teeth*, in which he claims that toothache could be greatly relieved by 'fumigation with rosemary, sage, roses, mastic, paper, warm water, coffee and particularly wasps' nests'. One does not much fancy having to dig up a wasps' nest at any time, let alone when afflicted with a raging toothache. Yet this 'cure' which sounds as if it harked back to the seventeenth century was being recommended in the second decade of the nineteenth.

Even so, more was known about the care of teeth in Georgian times than in previous eras, and if dentistry was bad—which it was—and if one suffered tortures having a tooth drawn, or hand drilled and stopped with molten lead, or tin (and later gold)— which one did—at least, and at last, a few enlightened people were beginning to realize that daily care of the teeth from an early age was important. Lord Chesterfield, toothless at fifty-three, is urgent in advising his fifteen-year-old son on this point. 'Do you take care to keep your teeth very clean by washing them constantly every morning and after each meal?' he asks, and explains, 'This is very necessary both to preserve your teeth a great while, and to save a great deal of pain. Mine have plagued me long, and are now falling out, merely for want of care when I was your age'.[60] And, mincing no words, he writes again 'A dirty mouth has real ill consequences to the owner, for it infallibly causes the decay, as well as the intolerable pain of the teeth; and it is very offensive to his acquaintance, for it will most inevitably stink'.[61] George II observed of Bishop Hoadly that he had 'nasty rotten teeth',[62] while Lord Hervey tells us that Sir Horace Walpole's* plain wife was as 'offensive to the nose and ears as to the eye.'[63] Even earlier in the century a future Lord Chief Justice, Dudley Ryder, then in his early twenties, fears he has 'a stinking breath and it was perceived' which made him 'very uneasy in company'.[64] This is not surprising as he admits to having a very hollow tooth with the nerve exposed, but he had heard—one hopes correctly—that the nerve could be 'seared out' without pain!

From all this it may perhaps be concluded that the fan was a

* Brother of Sir Robert Walpole and uncle of Horace Walpole.

very necessary piece of equipment in those days. Apart from its normal fanning and flirtatious function, it could be used to hide a smile which displayed a squalid lot of teeth, or as a screen to protect the nose against mephitic breath. Foetid breath added nothing to the attractions of either sex, and must have been socially most unacceptable for, again, we find many breath sweetners being sold or made at home. A decoction of wine, bramble leaves, cinnamon, cloves, orange peel, gum lacque, burnt alum and honey infused in hot ashes and used as a 'rince' must have tasted and smelled very pleasant but it must also have been quite ineffective. For complete coverage it was necessary to suck constantly upon perfumed pastilles—musk was a favourite— and this no doubt sweetened the breath as effectively as it ruined the teeth.

> I cannot talk with civet in the room,
> A fine puss-gentleman that's all perfume;
> The sight's enough—no need to smell a beau—
> Who thrusts his nose into a raree show?[65]

This is all very well, but the unpalatable truth is that without a liberal use of civet, musk, ambergris and various strong essences, no room full of people was likely to remain habitable for long. 'At court last night, there was dice, dancing, crowding, sweating and stinking in abundance as usual',[66] Lord Hervey writes. This age of urbanity, of reason, of romance, of high fashion, of beautiful silks, satins, damasks, velvets,* was not notable for what we call personal cleanliness. Perfumes had to mask what a regular use of soap and water would have washed away; but a regular use of soap and water, even had it been thought advisable, was virtually impossible. Only the grandest houses had a built-in bath, although high-sided, portable, tin bathing tubs as well as less portable iron-bound wooden ones, were certainly known. Water supplies to those city dwellings with water 'laid on' were intermittent.

---

* Cleaning such textiles was a dreadfully involved process. Things did improve greatly when cottons were introduced; they were cheaper, more easily washed, they could be boiled and boiling at least killed lice.

Water flowed into the cistern for only a few hours on two or three days a week, and it was best to let it stand before use so that the sediment could settle. When water was not piped to houses it was fetched in buckets from the nearest local street or parish pump. Soap was taxed at 1*d* per lb in 1712; a hundred years later the tax was 3*d* per lb. Soap was quite out of reach of the poor, so was perfume. There were, of course, public baths (also out of reach of the poor), some of which were very old, like Queen Elizabeth's Bath at Charing Cross (it remained in use until 1831), and Queen Anne's Bath in Long Acre, so called because Queen Anne once used it. There was also the Royal Bagnio and the Floating Baths on the Thames, and other inadequate bathing facilities elsewhere. Then there were the 'hummums' or Turkish Baths in Covent Garden where, in 1765, it cost a rich man about six guineas to bathe, sup and sleep with any fashionable harlot. But none of this made for habitual personal cleanliness, as we

Round snuff boxes, *circa* 1752–1800. Heart-shaped patch box *circa* 1780

know it. To lose one's sense of smell must have been a blessing in the eighteenth century.

And so the century remained as highly perfumed as it was powdered, and for about the same length of time. Rooms were perfumed by pastilles smoking away in incense pots which, in design, reflected the changing tastes of the century, and great houses must have resembled, in a minor and less lavish way, the fourth palace of *Vathek*. Hair powder, unguents, skin washes, pomatums, snuff—everything which could be perfumed was. In addition, men and women carried with them flasks for liquid and boxes for solid perfumes made in glass, silver, china or enamel. Some flasks were in the shape of naked figures rather rudely designed to appeal to the schoolboy humour of those who remained schoolboys.

But throughout the century there were a few people eccentric enough to regard personal cleanliness as essential for both health and manners. Not surprisingly, Lord Chesterfield (1694–1773) was one of these and he continually stresses the point to his unfortunate son;* 'take care to be very clean', he writes in mid-century, 'a thorough cleanliness in your person is as necessary to your health as it is not to be offensive to other people'.[67] And, more precisely, 'Washing yourself, and rubbing your body and limbs frequently with a flesh brush, will conduce as much to health as cleanliness'.[68] It is more than probable this advice was taken to heart by some because Lord Chesterfield's *Letters* were an immediate success and went through five editions in the first year of publication (1774). His maxims were extracted and, handily arranged alphabetically for ready reference, were printed and became a useful manual of etiquette for young gentlemen (or those who wished to be thought gentlemen) as well as for those who wanted to get on in, or into, the superficial, fashionable world. And if Dr Johnson thought the *Letters* taught 'the morals of

---

* Philip Stanhope, his illegitimate son by Mlle du Bouchet. Lord Chesterfield married the Countess of Walsingham, an illegitimate daughter of George I, in 1733. It was a marriage of convenience and there were no children. A distant cousin and godson succeeded him as 5th Earl.

a whore and the manners of a dancing master',[69] the epigram is as clever as the judgment of Chesterfield is false. Chesterfield was no reformer. Rightly or wrongly he accepted his world as he found it, and laid down rules for living in it with a maximum of comfort and worldly success. As Lord Chesterfield was 'short, disproportioned, thick and clumsily made; had a broad, rough featured face . . . and a head big enough for Polyphemus',[70] he may have cultivated perfect manners, great courtesy, unostentatious perfection in dress, wit and urbanity, to compensate for those qualities of beauty and grace of form which he so conspicuously lacked.

Another who may have done much the same thing for similar reasons was Beau Brummell, whose friend and patron was, for a time, the Prince Regent. George Bryan Brummell (1778–1840), the son of a valet (some say pastry cook), Eton educated, acid tongued, and the supreme arbiter of men's fashions for a number of years, bathed three or four times a day. His fear of dirt was so ingrained he even had the soles of his boots polished—no doubt with that mixture of ordinary polish and champagne which he recommended to one young dandy. Brummell may have been trying to wash away and shake from his feet the 'dust' and 'dirt' of his humble origins. Nevertheless, whatever the cause, he succeeded in turning this neurotic obsession into high fashion. It soon became extremely *haut ton* to be scrupulously clean, to wear spotless linen, to drop with shame at a speck of dust on high boots, coat, or on the new, skin tight, light-coloured trousers men were wearing.

Trousers or pantaloons had begun, rather tentatively at first, to replace breeches as early as the 1790s. They seem to have been a much tightened and infinitely better cut version of the *sans culotte* pantaloons and until 1820 both breeches and trousers continued to be fashionable, although breeches were always worn at court and upon formal occasions. But when the Prince Regent became King in 1820, he gave a lead for adopting trousers for all occasions. These trousers were the skin tight ones, and in lightness of colour for day wear did their best to suggest the skin. For evening wear the correct colour was black. If nature had failed to provide, or sheer idleness had prevented, well developed muscles in the right places, padding and, where necessary, *fausse cuisses* easily overcame this defect. Aggressively cut shoulders to a frock coat, a pouter pigeon front, an impeccable cravat, a waist pinched in with stays if necessary, the better to display the rounded yet muscular thigh—all contributed to the now familiar lean male silhouette. And all in time also contributed to a dark and dreary era in men's clothes. It is curious to reflect that this revolution in men's dress, this switch over from gay, bright colours to dark coats—later to dark trousers and hats like truncated chimneys—took place almost simultaneously with the Industrial Revolution.

One of Brummell's decrees was that no gentleman should ever use perfume, but should send his linen to be washed and dried on Hampstead Heath. The French took this dictum so seriously that those who could afford it sent their linen to England to be laundered; today, of course, in England we have French cleaners! Yet despite Brummell's ban on perfumes, gentlemen, and others, continued to use them. In 1822 George IV's perfume bill for the year came to £263; six years later it was almost double at £500 17s 11d, but by then Brummell, a bankrupt, was living in great poverty at Calais.

Lighter perfumes were, by now, more fashionable for men and women than were heavier essences, and so 'sweet waters' not only retained but increased their popularity. Sweet, or perfumed, waters had a number of advantages over perfumes. Honey Water, a favourite, containing essence of musk, cloves, vanilla, benzoin, orange-flower water, ordinary water and alcohol, imparted a charming light perfume and was also excellent for smoothing the skin. Even better, due to the large quantity of pure spirit it contained, it was a most excellent pick-me-up. Imperial Water, made with frankincense, mastic, benzoin, cloves, pine-nut kernels and half a dozen other things, combined all the advantages of Honey Water with that of being a good mouth wash. Old favourites such as Rose Water, so beloved of the Elizabethans, and Hungary Water, a seventeenth century craze, were still steadily popular but were joined by a brand newcomer in the eighteenth

century, Eau de Cologne. This new sweet water is said to have
been invented by the Farina Brothers, Italians from Domo
d'Ossola, who settled in Cologne and started in a small way as
silk sellers. On the side they also sold their own remedial water
called by them Aqua Admirabilis. By the 1730s the brothers were
doing a brisk local trade in their sweet water, but success really
came as the result of the Seven Years War (1756–63) when
Cologne was packed with foreign troops quartered there. The
soldiers took to Aqua Admirabilis like ducks to any kind of water,
particularly the French soldiers. And the French took it, or its
reputation, back to France where it became known as Eau de
Cologne. Another story has it that Aqua Admirabilis was invented
by a Milanese who went to Cologne in 1690 and passed on his
secret formula to his nephew, Jean Antoine Farina, who began to
produce this admirable water in Paris. Either or neither of these
stories may be true, but points common to both are that Eau de
Cologne was invented by an Italian, first made in Germany, and
named in France. The original formula remained a secret, but
other perfumers soon produced their own versions—and kept
their formulae secret too—so that by the end of the Georgian era,
Eau de Cologne had become undisputedly the most famous sweet
water in all Europe, and it is very probable that by the early
nineteenth century it was used in much greater quantity by men
than by women—not always as a perfume. Sheridan's favourite
tipple, it is said, was a mixture of brandy, arquebusade* and Eau
de Cologne.

During the time masculine dress was undergoing that change
which turned London into the male fashion centre of the world,
women's dress changed too. The neo-classical movement no less
than the French Revolution were both influential. The Revolution
in its attempt to wipe out class—or since it happened in France
'caste' is perhaps more accurate—distinctions, wiped out differen-
tiation in dress. All ornament, all superfluities were banished. The
neo-classical revival had a rather similar effect, only it was all for a
beautiful simplicity. As everyone knew, Greek and Roman

* A spirituous lotion used for gun shot wounds (hence its name) and sprains.

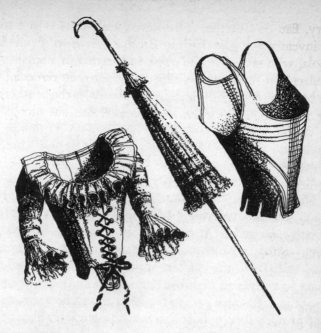

Corsets, *circa* 1760 and *circa* 1800. Parasol walking-stick, *circa* 1770

statues when not stark naked (and always excepting Pallas Athene) showed off their beauty of form by very scanty, clinging light garments. In men's wear, as we have seen, this took the form of skin tight pantaloons which in lightness of colour resembled the skin. George IV on his visit to Scotland donned the Royal Stuart Tartan over flesh coloured tights, preferring an imitation and, therefore, very probably a more beautiful nakedness to the real thing. Women did not lag behind. For formal wear they took to the most diaphanous, high-waisted dresses, often with a greek-key pattern embroidered at the hem. Soft pastel shades were now popular, but white was most fashionable of all. Women also, for a time, discarded corsets, and those with naturally good figures even dampened their wispy underslips to make them cling to their bodies and display the figure in greater detail. Rheumatism was not too dear a penalty to pay—it never has been. But, by 1810 a lighter boned waist-corset came in and by 1821 the heavier, fully whaleboned model, overaccentuating the figure, was back again and really tight lacing began. Men also continued to wear corsets, as they had done off and on since the fifteenth century, a twenty-six inch waist was considered infinitely desirable. 'They say the Prince has left off his stays', Lord Holland writes in 1817, 'and that Royalty divested of its usual supports makes a bad figure.'[71] It is doubtful if the Prince Regent left off his stays for any length of time, even though advised to by his physicians.

Naturally with the great changes in fashion, hair styles changed too. The wig, after a run of 140 odd years, was entirely given up by 1800, as was powdering.* Men now cut their hair short at the back and sides and let it cluster in Byronic curls in front (Lord Byron created a romantic, anti-Brummell fashion for open-necked shirts). Women, from around 1790 to 1805, adopted a Grecian hair style of artful artlessness—a chignon worn at the back of the head, curls on the forehead and all bound round with a band or fillet. Really short hair was also worn for about the first twenty years of the nineteenth century and then women's hair styles began to climb upward again—the ups and downs of female hair fashions seems to occur about every thirty years.

For both sexes these new, unpowdered and relatively uncomplicated coiffeurs must have been a great relief; so much easier to do, to manage; so much less prone to harbour undesirable aliens and, best of all, so much easier to wash. It therefore comes rather as a surprise to find, in a popular beauty book published as late as the 1820s, that, although frequent bathing of the whole body is recommended in a water temperature of 64–68 degrees in winter and 70 to 75 degrees in summer, to which 'a little soap may be added' as it 'cleanses the skin more perfectly',[72] washing the head is absolutely forbidden. It was a pernicious practice which brought on 'head-ache, ear-ache, tooth-ache and complaints of the eyes'. The reason it did so was that no matter how hard one tried it was impossible ever to get the hair really dry at the roots. This, quite obviously, kept the brain 'in a state of constant humidity'[73] and,

* Save for footmen and lackeys.

as all could see for themselves, the humidity had to escape somehow, hence 'watery eyes, a running nose, supperating ears, and frequent swelling of the gums'.[74] None of these added greatly either to beauty or health, therefore women best obey the old proverb 'wash the hands often, the feet seldom and the head never'. Combing the hair regularly, cleaning it from time to time with hair bran or ivory powder, was quite sufficient and, if the hair were thin, apply rich, nourishing unguents to the scalp. If thinness unhappily turned into baldness, fear not! A young lady whose hair fell out after an illness washed her egg-like head in a decoction of box with the most striking results. She grew a lovely thick head of long, glossy hair but, having carelessly wetted her face and neck with this puissant preparation, she grew the most lovely hair in those places too. Even the beauty book admits that the last state was worse than the first and wisely

Regency hat with ribbon and flower trimming

urges the greatest possible care to be taken when using a box-wash for baldness.

As for cosmetics and beauty aids? In the reign of the last George, home recipes and advice proliferate, but recipes are now less deadly, less crude. Art, or the art of beauty, is beginning to try to imitate not outdo nature. For women, bathing is highly recommended as it is now believed by many that to preserve the skin all over the body leads to the preservation of youth and beauty. All sorts of things, good and bad, can be absorbed from the atmosphere through the skin, women are told. Look at cooks, for example, urges the *Ladies Toilette*. They are nearly always fat and this is because they absorb the nourishment from the perpetually nourishing atmosphere in which they work. This piece of nonsense, when and if believed, must have stopped a few women using poisonous washes and cosmetics. Yet white lead is still advised by the book which makes this absorbing statement, although the safer Venetian talc is also advised, white vegetable rather than metallic dyes are said to be much safer for colouring cheeks and lips.

For beautifying the skin before applying paint, there are such things as Oil of Cacao, particularly good for dry skins, Oil of Talc, to make the skin white and clear and remove spots; Virgin Milk, a fancy name for preparations of various kinds whose chief ingredient seems to have been tincture of benzoin; a Wash of the Ladies of Denmark, which must be a very old recipe since it calls for bean flower and the 'four cold seeds', that is—pumpkin, melon, cucumber and gourd. There are the rather simpler things like Vine Water, Strawberry Water, Pimpernel Water, and then there is the highly complicated and extremely expensive Balm of Mecca. The real thing cost four guineas an ounce, but an imitation could be had for from 25s to 35s. And with the Balm of Mecca we find ourselves back once more in the early Georgian era. Or, more correctly, in Turkey with Lady Mary Wortley Montagu whose English friends had urged her to send them some of this famous and fabulous Balm. Lady Mary had used it herself and did not think much of it—it made her face swell and her skin turn red. She was probably allergic to one of its many ingredients for it contained, among other things, various resins, turpentines, and aromatic oils, and yet managed to give off a lemon scent. Nevertheless, Balm of Mecca was as highly esteemed by most women in 1822 as it had been in 1717.

As for men, they too continued to use cosmetics where necessary. George IV, a victim of the Guelph tendencies to overweight and a florid complexion, so admired a pale skin that he had leeches applied regularly in an attempt to achieve a fashionable pallor. But age, familial fat (of which he became morbidly sensitive) and self-indulgence, increasingly and inevitably betrayed him. In the end, the firmest stays could no longer disguise the gross corpulence of a monarch who so loved to appear in splendid uniform and impeccable, if bizarre, undress. Nor could the powder he used liberally on his face conceal a cherry brandy redness of complexion.

All the frills, the furbelows, the cosmetics, the pomades, washes and perfumes used between the birth of John, Lord Hervey in 1696, and the death of George IV in 1830, are now tucked away in the band-box of time. Yet the 'painted child' who began the century has left us memoirs of his own age and class which are surpassed only by those of the Duc de Saint-Simon; while to Florizel we owe many beautiful things—not the least of them the National Gallery. For George IV, in many ways an absurd figure, had great taste and was an excellent judge of painting. He made a wonderful collection of seventeenth century Dutch paintings in a period when most people preferred Italian. He also managed to persuade the Government to buy the Angerstein Collection for £300,000. It is this which is the nucleus of our National Gallery. No king since the days of Charles I—who wore lovelocks and lace, much to the horror of the Puritans—has done more for art in England than raddled George IV. And, sad to relate, no monarch since the last of the Hanoverian Georges has done nearly so much.

CHAPTER NINE

Of Gardens, Gardening, and Gardeners

In the year George III came to the throne, Mrs Delany visited Longleat and found its formal parterres and clipped alleys were no more. They had been replaced by 'a fine lawn, a serpentine river, wooded hills, gravel paths meandering round a shrubbery, all modernized by the ingenious and much sought after Mr Brown'.[1]

Twenty-three years later the ingenious and much sought after Mr Brown was dead. Soon after the news 'reached the royal ear' it is reported that King George went to Richmond garden and, 'in a tone of great satisfaction said to the under-gardener: "Brown is dead : now Mellicant [sic]* you and I can do here what we please"'.[2] But more than Capability Brown had happened to Richmond, to the royal parks, to great gardens like Longleat in the years between the accession of George I and the twenty-third year of the reign of his great-grandson. We had come a very long and winding way from the formal gardening which, based on French styles, followed upon the Restoration; had grown even more rigid and devitalized under the influence of Dutch William, and was finally ridiculed by Mr Addison in the time of Queen Anne and, later, by Mr Pope.

Both Addison and Pope, in their very different ways, expressed the opinion that a garden should copy or at least subtly co-operate with nature as far as possible. 'The works of Nature and Art

---

* Michael Milliken had come from Chatsworth in 1764 to be Brown's right-hand man at Richmond and Hampton Court.

Garden plan early eighteenth century, with ha-ha represented by dotted
line, top centre

mutually assist and compleat each other,'³ says Addison, while the
'artificial Rudeness' of continental gardens, particularly those of
Italy, were 'much more charming than that Neatness and Elegancy
with which we meet with in our own country'.⁴ Nature, in short,
did not depend upon set-squares, rulers and compasses to achieve
her effects; neither did she create vast, level, geometrically
patterned parterres, nor did her rivers and streams run straight as a
Roman road. And although she produced a multitude of trees and
shrubs of divers kinds and shapes, none resembled gladiators
fighting, peacocks with tails spread, bears dancing or heraldic
beasts. It was man who inflicted such horrid patterns on nature.
Nature gave contour to a landscape with valleys and hills. Man
often filled up the first in the interests of 'regularity' and frequently
removed or cut through the second for the sake of a distant 'view',
because a view—no matter of what*—was fashionable. A certain

* The modern cult of the picture window seems rather similar.

rich citizen of Hertfordshire spent above £5,000 to cut through a mountain so he could look out upon a singularly uninteresting plain. This gap provided a perfect tunnel for the north wind which froze him to the marrow and his parterres to death.

Obviously, then, it was far better to work with, not against, nature; to

> Consult the Genius of the Place in all;
> That tells the Waters or to rise, or fall,
> Or helps the ambitious Hill the heav'n to scale,
> Or scoops in circling theatres the Vale,
> Calls in the Country, catches opening glades,
> Joins willing woods, and varies shades from shades,
> Now breaks or now directs, th' intending Lines;
> Paints as you plant, and, as you work, designs.[5]

Here it will be noted that nature is regarded as a painter and designer, man merely as her assistant. Yet the painters who, according to our English taste, had best transferred nature to canvas were all foreigners, and dead ones at that. They were Salvator Rosa (1615–73), Gaspard Poussin (1613–75), and Claude Gellée of Lorrain (1600–82) whose paintings, or copies of them, were in great demand amongst rich virtuosi almost from the beginning of the eighteenth century.

Rosa, actor, poet, musician and painter, began first with historical and mythological subjects and later became the leader of the trend toward the romantic and picturesque. His grand, wild scenes with sinister trees and rushing cascades were particularly popular, had he lived a hundred years later he could have illustrated *The Mysteries of Udolpho* superbly. Poussin, who had come under the influence of Claude in Rome, devoted himself to quieter 'Claudian' landscapes. But it was Claude, himself, one of the greatest masters of classical landscape painting,* who really stirred us and suited us best. His pictures were quiet, filled with light, air and atmosphere; and if it is possible to say he had a formula, it was to paint an infinitely receding, luminous sky, with

* He had a great influence on Gainsborough, Constable and Turner.

half-tones in the middle distance and a dark mass of trees or buildings in the foreground. A few tiny legendary figures suggest the scale and he is the prime exponent of the classical—romantic in landscape painting. This, I feel, is what really spoke to our eyes and hearts. The classical—romantic feeling is, or was, part of the Englishness of the English. Sometimes the emphasis was on the one, sometimes on the other. Sometimes it tipped too far to one side. Sometimes, as in part of the Georgian era, it was perfectly balanced.

Thus in the eighteenth century, gardening became for the first time 'landscape gardening' (though the term was not in common use until Repton's day*), and the impulse or influences behind this new and freer style were primarily literary and artistic. Yet it is not easy to say who first began, in practice, to collaborate with nature. Possibly one of the earliest (and Dr Stukeley certainly thought so), was Stephen Switzer (1682?–1745), although by later standards he is a most timid assistant. Despite his name, Switzer was of English stock and well educated. He came from East Stratton, Hampshire; served under the famous gardeners to Queen Anne, London and Wise; became a seedsman in Westminster Hall; had a nursery garden at Millbank and was active in designing gardens, particularly in the north. He edited a monthly periodical, *The Practical Husbandman and Planter*, and most fiercely defended Virgil against those who dared attack the long dead Latin poet's agricultural methods as set out in the *Georgics*! He also wrote a number of books on gardening, among them, *Ichnographia Rustica or the Noblemen, Gentlemen and Gardeners Recreation* (1718), wherein he clearly acknowledges his debt to the thoughts of Addison, Pope, and many other poets and makes a strong plea for less 'exactness'.

The 'Dutch Taste' which had come in with the Revolution was, he says, 'almost universally followed' by people of 'the common

---

* But in 1764, in *Unconnected Thoughts on Gardening*, William Shenstone says: 'I have used the term landscape gardener because in accordance with present day taste, every good landscape painter is the proper designer of gardens.' This may be the first use of the word.

level of understanding'. Having thus flattered his readers that they are above the common level, he is sure they will appreciate his idea of introducing a method of gardening 'more agreeable to the Simplicity of unadorned Nature'. And if, perhaps, their understanding failed or was even greater than their fortunes, he cannily adds that his method was 'at the same time less expensive to the pocket'.[6]

Avoid, says he, 'Mathematical Exactness and crimping Stiffness'.[7] And if he did not actually disapprove of great, regular, stiff parterres as such, he remarks, ' 'tis a very wrong way of thinking to imagine Greatness consists in Size and Dimension' for it will be only 'a great many littlenesses put together'.[8] Nevertheless, he did not object to size when it came to the 'Great Terrace Walk' placed next to the house. It should be 100 feet wide, otherwise the house cannot be properly viewed. Neither did he object to 'exactness' here, for he gives the most precise instructions as to how the great walk should be laid out, in what sounds like alternating ribbons of gravel, or cockle shells, and grass all in specified widths.[9]

Yet certainly Switzer did not approve of those great, straight, boring avenues cut through regimented plantations and woods, or which radiated, star-shaped, from some central point—designs which had become so popular with the owners of great estates ever since the Restoration. More desirable was the occasional 'private or natural turn' in a wood with the little hills and dales left as they were. 'It is a mistake often made', he says, 'to esteem nothing . . . beautiful but what is regularly planted and distributed out.' It was equally erroneous to think that trees planted thick and close together 'as are our common Coppices' were beautiful. In fact, Switzer would much 'rather devise it (a coppice) to be mixed with Lawns, Vallies and rising Hills . . . in this place a Hillock of Oaks for Shade, in that a hollow or natural lawn with a Cave or Grott'.[10]

This tells us a bit more than is immediately apparent. Men plant oaks not to shade themselves but to shade their descendants, and when any generation feels it worth while to plant oaks and make great gardens which only its heirs will see in perfection it is a fairly sure sign that the country as a whole feels secure and prosperous. So the great Whig oligarcy, which for nearly forty years provided England with peace and prosperity, played its part in creating the eighteenth-century garden, just as it did in creating its great houses. Many of the grand, new gardens belonged to rich Whigs.* But whatever the politics, whatever the fortune of the owner, the designer 'ought to have a general idea of everything, that is Noble and Stately in the Production of Art, whether it appears in painting, or Statuary, in the great works of Architecture, which are in their present Glory, or in the Ruins of those which flourisht in a former Age'.[11]

Although Switzer's own designs and plans for gardens seem to us to show an almost mathematical regularity, with only a rather tentative and timid curving line apparent here and there, yet he does, in the above words, and indeed throughout the whole of the *Ichnographia*, sum up the new idea of a freer, more natural idea of gardening. An idea which in other hands was elaborated, changed and grew until English gardens became the envy of Europe.

A contemporary of Switzer was Charles Bridgeman who died in 1738. He appears never to have put himself down on paper as other gardeners did so we know very little about him, save that he was for a time a partner of Henry Wise and carried out Switzer's tenets far more boldly than their author. Switzer believed when creating a garden that 'all the adjacent country should be laid open to view and the eye should not be bounded by high walls' by which it is 'imprisoned and the feet fettered in the midst of the extensive charms of nature and the voluminous tracts of pleasant country'.[12] Whether he ever practised this effect in his own work seems doubtful. Bridgeman, on the other hand, very probably did achieve this for, if we can believe Horace Walpole, Bridgeman was the first gardener ever to release the eye and unfetter the feet by introducing the ha-ha or sunk fence into

* Capability Brown was a Whig, and this, it is said, is one of the reasons his appointment as Royal Gardener to George III was so long delayed.

Sectional view of eighteenth-century ha-ha

England. The ha-ha* kept out invaders such as cattle, sheep or deer, hitherto restrained by walls and fences. With the ha-ha the eye could rove unstopped beyond garden, and even park, to meadows, fields and cornlands. The countryside was thus incorporated into the scene; foreground, middle distance and distance melted 'naturally' into each other.

We also know that Bridgeman collaborated with Vanbrugh in laying out Bubb Dodington's gardens at Eastbury. That he, with Pope and Lord Bathurst, designed the garden at Marble Hill for the Countess of Suffolk. Pope, who was finishing his own enchanting garden at Twickenham, was a friend of both Bridgeman and William Kent. We also know that in 1723 Bridgeman was called in to improve the grounds of King's College, Cambridge—the first attempt to realize the potentialities of the Backs—and that in 1728 he became Royal Gardener and carried out various works for Queen Caroline at Richmond and Hyde Park.

* So called because one exclaimed with surprise 'aha' when one came upon it. It is not a fence, it is more like a fosse with one straight and one sloping side.

It may even be possible that the Serpentine is Bridgeman's work. Dr Dallaway writing in 1828 states that it is. Mr Miles Hadfield, writing in 1960, believes it to be the work of Charles Withers. Lysons, in volume III of his *Environs*, says, 'Kensington Gardens were originally only 26 acres; Queen Anne added 30 acres . . . but the principal addition was made by the late Queen (Caroline) who took near 300 acres out of Hyde Park, which were laid out by Bridgeman'. All we really know about Bridgeman is that in 1731 he certainly worked in Hyde Park where he made a ditch beside the Round Pond, and that in 1738, after his death, his widow, Sarah, petitioned the Lords of the Treasury for money due for 'making the Lamp Road . . . and the Lake in Hyde Park'.[13] But a lake is not a ditch and it is a fact that originally there were three squalid little ponds in Hyde Park, fed by the Westbourne. Queen Caroline is credited with suggesting the Westbourne be dammed and the trio of out-size mud puddles be turned into a lake. As Bridgeman was Royal Gardener it is possible the lake referred to by his widow may be the Serpentine. Since Hogarth had described the 'line of beauty' as a curving line, and the idea caught on, the lake was given the fashionable shape. This must have been around 1730, for by 1731 the *London Journal* informed its readers that two yachts were to be kept on the Serpentine 'for the diversion of the Royal Family'.[14] So the Serpentine seems always to have been called that, although it is no longer fed by the Westbourne. This river now spans Sloane Square station in a huge iron pipe.

Much earlier than this, in 1713, Bridgeman was at work at Stowe, where he assisted Sir Richard Temple, later 1st Viscount Cobham,* in modernizing the old, formal gardens. These old gardens were 'one below another with low breast walls and taress walks, and is replenished with all the curiosities or requisities for ornamental pleasure and use, beyond it are orchards and woods with rows of trees; on the other side you see the park rowes of trees'.[15] Although the idea of 'ornamental pleasure' is charming the description is not very adequate, but it does tell us that the old

---

* A Whig who broke with Walpole in 1733 and formed an independent Whig party called 'the boy patriots'. Pitt, the elder, was a member of this group.

garden was what we now call 'formal', with descending terraces, regular parterres, and trees laid out Roman phalanx fashion. Bridgeman did away with the terraces but stuck to the straight, although not narrow, by making double avenues of parallel rows of trees running from the house to the octagon lake. He cut longer rides through the woods, and as the entire village of Stowe, which lay about a mile south east of the house, sadly interfered with the 'prospect' as well as with the longer rides, it was entirely removed and the villagers resettled at Dodford two miles away. The only part of the village which could not be removed was the vulgar old fourteenth-century church of St Mary, and this ancient eyesore, like the stables and other outbuildings, was carefully screened by trees and shrubs.

As for other non-vulgar buildings especially constructed to enchant the eye, these were put up in the new classical style, and in time multiplied almost to excess. 'We went . . . into Oxfordshire; saw the uncomfortable glories of Stowe,* and its ridiculous temples,'[16] says an unappreciative visitor late in the century. The earlier buildings, by Vanbrugh, include the Boycott Pavilions, the Ionic Rotunda, the Temple of Bacchus (demolished to make room for the school chapel) and a pyramid 60 foot high set in an 'antient wood'. This last became Vanbrugh's monument. By 1724, so cleverly contrived were the original 28 acres, so many and varied the walks, that the acreage seemed trebled and Stowe attracted a stream of visitors, native and foreign. It continued to do so throughout the century.

Stowe, in a special sense, is a key garden of the first half of the Georgian era because in it three great gardeners of the time worked, Charles Bridgeman, William Kent and Lancelot— better known as Capability—Brown. Although it is now virtually impossible to solve the problem of who was responsible for what, Miss Dorothy Stroud suggests the answer to the conundrum may be that after Bridgeman's work in modernizing the old garden,

---

* Stowe is now a well-known public school. The gardens can be seen on certain days in August. Many of the buildings are in a most melancholy state of disrepair, though work is being done to preserve them.

'Kent produced the initial schemes for softening and breaking up Bridgeman's layout, and the execution of this work was left to Brown as resident gardener'.[17] Brown, already a practical gardener, had come to Stowe shortly after Bridgeman had quitted this demi-paradise for good. He was then twenty-three, had had experience as a gardener and had begun his career, humbly enough, in the kitchen gardens. But his talent no less than his charm soon brought him to the attention of Lord Cobham, and he was taken from the kitchen gardens and glasshouses to work on the great garden itself. William Kent, already famous as an architect, furniture designer, interior decorator and planner of gardens, had been working at Stowe from around 1732. His most famous garden, where he completely effaced Bridgeman's work, was designed for Colonel Dormer at Rousham, Oxon, and completed between 1720 and 1725. Rousham is, so far as I know, the only relatively intact Kent garden in England. At Rousham, Kent created a three-dimensional landscape painting, and he completed and constructed it as if he were working *inside* as well as outside the canvas. To walk through the garden of Rousham even today* gives one the delicious and exciting sense that one has, at last, achieved the satisfaction of that childhood longing to step *into* a painting and discover for oneself, all its internal aspects, the delights, the surprises, and even the terrors, which lie beyond the external.

Kent was, as we know, a painter and a not very good one. But if he could not get his feelings and thoughts down on canvas, what he could do was 'paint' a landscape with living material, and the Claudian influence in Kent is strong. Kent probably believed that he followed and imitated nature, but it was nature idealized. It was Elysium. It was that golden colophon of Antioch, Daphne, in little. Kent was 'painter enough to taste the charms of landscape, bold and opinionated enough to dare to dictate and born with a genius to strike out a great system from the twilight of imperfect essays', while 'the pencil of his imagination bestowed all the arts of landscape upon the scenes he handles'.[18] It is one thing to create

* Open to the public during the summer.

a living landscape which looks beautiful from a single vantage point, it is quite another to produce one which looks beautiful from any point without or within. This Kent did. 'The great principles on which he worked were perspective, light and shade. Groups of trees broke too uniform or too extensive a lawn; evergreens and woods were opposed to the glare of the champaign, and when the view was less fortunate, or so much exposed as to be beheld at once, he blotted out some parts by thick shade, to divide into variety, or to make the richest scenes more enchanting by reserving it to a further advance of the spectator's step. Thus selecting favourite objects, and veiling deformities by screens of planations, sometimes allowing the rude waste to add its foil to the richest theatre, he realized the compositions of the greatest masters of painting.'[19] So addicted to the natural was Kent that he even used dead trees among work carried out in Kensington Gardens, but he was 'laughed out of this excess', Horace Walpole tells us.

Kent also had a particular genius for managing water. Straight canals, circular basins and cascades tumbling down marble steps were not only highly unnatural but definitely démodé. So Kent taught the stream 'to serpentize, seemingly at its pleasure',[20] and where different levels made falls necessary he concealed them with thickets. As might be expected Kent's taste in the design of garden buildings, seats and other adjuncts and ornaments was superb, and some of the most superlative of the garden buildings at Stowe are his work. The south Doric Pavilion (now altered), the Temple of Venus, the Hermitage, the Temple of Ancient Virtue which led the eye away from the clump of trees screening that vulgar old church, the Temple of British Worthies (a very Italian idea this) and that of Concord and Victory (unfinished), as well as the Palladian Bridge, a replica of that at Wilton, are his. This work of redesigning and 'softening' the Bridgeman layout and the erection of garden buildings took much time, so Kent's work and, to a lesser extent, that of Bridgeman must have had a great influence on Brown. Sometime in the 1740s the stiff, octagon lake was suitably irregularized and the laying out of the Grecian Valley took place. 'We owe the restoration of Greece and the diffusion of architecture to his [Kent's] skill in landscape',[21] Horace Walpole remarks, rather obscurely for him, but one knows what he means even if the Grecian valley at Stowe bears scant resemblance to any real Greek valley. By mid-century both Bridgeman and Kent were dead. So was Lord Cobham. But the gardens were already so extensive, the buildings so numerous that in 1751 Walpole writes, 'I ran through the gardens at Stowe which I have seen before, and had only time to be charmed by the variety of scenes. I do like that Albano glut of buildings; let them be ever so much condemned',[22] which indicates that already some felt Stowe to be excessive and overloaded. In this same letter Walpole remarks, apropos of a visit to Warwick, 'the castle is enchanting . . . the river Avon tumbles down a cascade at the foot of it. It is well laid out by one Brown, who has set up on a few ideas of Kent and Mr Southcote.'* This appears to be the first extant reference to Brown in contemporary letters. What is odd is that Walpole does not mention him in connection with Stowe, but does recognize the influence of Kent on Brown's work. By this time, however, Brown had already set up for himself at Hammersmith, and perhaps it is as well, at this point, to stop and look not at great gardens but at the English countryside, at smaller gardens, at just a few of the 'florists' and botanists whose interests lay not so much in creating a Claude-like landscape but in gardens, flowers, shrubs and trees.

On February 4th 1748, with the temperature standing at 40·01°F, Pehr Kalm (1715–99), a Swedish professor of natural history and agriculture, arrived at Margate and next day sailed up the Thames to London. The countryside seen from the river delighted him, 'one of the prettiest I had hitherto seen',[23] he records—and he had seen much of Europe. He expresses great joy

---

* Philip Southcote bought Woburn Farm, some 150 acres, in 1735, and here commenced his *ferme ornée*. About 35 acres were turned into garden, but the theme of the garden was the pursuit of farming. Southcote was not attempting a classical landscape, he was creating a pastoral one. It was made for nymphs and shepherds not for gods and goddesses.

at the sight of green meadows at this time of year, the distant hills and the beautiful hedgerows which separated our fields. There were big brick houses and small ones of 'crossbeams covered with boards',[24] and these clapboard cottages were reed-thatched. The bare 'leaf woods' in particular pleased his eye, accustomed as it was to the pine woods of Sweden. And here, unconsciously, he tells us something which someone who has never lived out of England for a long period cannot know: the shapes of deciduous trees in this country, due to our curious climate, are, especially in winter, more beautiful than anywhere in the world. Kalm noted the lack of snow, the ploughed fields, the green pastures where sheep were safely grazing in February—things which do not happen anywhere else in northern Europe; he also comments upon the number of horses. Later, when touring the environs of London, he was most impressed with the earth walls, with a ditch on the outer side, which surrounded the small fields, meadows, and market gardens. These he thought practical and excellent. They were far cheaper than wood or stone, took little time or trouble to build and keep in repair, were broad bottomed and rose, often six foot, narrowing to a top where all sorts and bits of broken glass were set to keep out thieves. The broken glass he notes, in his thorough way, was sold for this purpose by 'inns and beershops'. Further, the sides of these earthen walls were sown with grass or plants to hinder depredations by frost and because their roots held the earth together. He especially admired the 'most beautiful grass growth' in pastures, as visiting foreigners still do.

In May he visited Chelsea: it was all orchards and market gardens with beautiful houses 'scattered among them'. Apple, plum, pear and cherry trees were in full flower,* as well as fields of Broad Windsor Beans. The great asparagus beds were thriving and he observed broken bottles placed over plants and shoots to bring them on in advance of the season. 'They know here in England how to make use of nearly everything, often such things

---

* This puzzles me, as nowadays the trees mentioned do not flower at the same time. One imagines this was, perhaps, due to the different varieties of fruit trees then grown, but one may be wrong.

as are regarded by us as useless',[25] he says. This is a welcome comment. Most foreign visitors thought us—as many still do—a rather thriftless, lazy people. At the Chelsea Physic or Botanic Garden, where the famous Philip Miller* (he sent the first cotton seeds to Georgia in 1732) was gardener, the cedars of Lebanon, first grown from seed,† were now as tall as Swedish fir trees, and the garden was already famous for its collection of American plants. Kalm also visited the great open spaces of Wimbledon Common and Putney Heath, and when he travelled into Kent he says, 'the country all around resembled a garden'[26] and one could see the whole of London from the hills. Kent, then as now, was one of our most densely populated areas.

On another journey, one is astonished to learn, he thought the countryside between Little Gaddesden and St Albans 'resembled that lying between Moscow and Tula'[27] (Tula, incidentally, is where Tsar Boris Godunuv had founded the first Russian gun factory in 1595). Kalm went to Little Gaddesden especially to meet Mr Ellis (whom we have already met in chapter Five), whose books on rural economy he had read. But Kalm very quickly discovered that Ellis was a fraud with little if any experience of farming. The machines which he 'invented' and advertised were, it is true, made locally and to his instructions, but he never used them himself. Nor did he use his fabulous and much advertised manure. Mr Ellis's real achievement had been to make two good marriages; these enabled him to buy a farm, let it go to ruin, sit back and write his books on farming. His agricultural books have no value as all are rewritten from the works of other authors and are not based on any experience or skills of his own. Ellis also smoked tobacco mixed with anise seed, which sounds vile, and every time the poor Swedish professor asked a question on

* Miller (1691–1771), a famous botanist and florist, specialized in rare plants. His chief work *The Gardener and Florist's Dictionary* was a standard work for years, and was translated into many languages. It was Miller who, in 1730, first discovered the method of flowering bulbous plants in bottles filled with water.
† Somewhere around 1683 four cedars of Lebanon, the first to bear cones, were planted at Chelsea and became the parents of the Lebanon cedars so much a feature of eighteenth century gardens. But see *The Jacobeans at Home*, Chapter X.

agriculture, the wretched fraud blandly referred him to his books! He did, however, vouchsafe the information, at no charge, that the fat of snakes and swine cured both snake bite and sore eyes.

Rather better was a visit to Mr Warner, who lived near Woodford, a place where sea kale* was being grown in large quantities. Mr Warner had an attractive garden and kept four seagulls, two imported from Newfoundland, as scavengers. Each bird had a wing clipped to prevent flight, and all would wander about the garden happily eating frogs, snails and caterpillars 'and so cleared the garden industriously . . . without doing harm to the plants'.[28] These natural pest destroyers were so tame that when Mr Warner cried 'Gull, gull' they came to him. Pests were as great a nuisance then as now and gardening books of the time are full of advice on how to deal with them. Mr Warner seems to have found an easy, pleasant and natural way of dealing with at least some of them.

Still later the Swedish visitor went to see Mr Peter Collinson's garden at Peckham, where the flower beds were bordered with 'the knuckle bones' of horses and oxen, 'rounded, curled ends uppermost'[29] just like the borders of the market gardens outside Moscow and, had he known it, just like a lot of our own borders in the early seventeenth century. Mr Collinson had ignored high fashion to such an extent that he not only grew quantities of flowers in beds, but had so clipped an elm 'that it with its twigs formed the roof of one of his summer houses'.[30] He had also done the same to a horse chestnut so that it spread a cool, green canopy over a garden seat. Both these innocent and charming little conceits might well have been frowned upon by Kent or Brown, but might have been approved by Mr Southcote.

Yet Peter Collinson (1694–1768) was as famous in his own way as Kent, Bridgeman or Brown. He was a Quaker, like his father, a merchant and haberdasher who expanded his business greatly by trade with the American colonies. He also had many influential friends, such as Lord Bute, a keen botanist, and the Duke of

---

* Sea kale is a native plant but there seems to be no record of when it first began to be cultivated. It is the only vegetable improved by forcing.

Argyll who laid out acres of trees. In America, Collinson corresponded with the Penns, Benjamin Franklin and America's first botanist, John Bartram (1699–1777); in China, with Fr d'Incarville and Père Herbestein. These men sent him seeds which he attempted, often very successfully, to raise here. In fact it is believed that Collinson introduced or cultivated more than 170 new species, including *monardia didyma* (1744) or the scarlet bergamot, commonly known in those days as Oswego tea, for it was used as such by the Oswego Indians. We must also thank Peter Collinson for the Tree of Heaven, with its white flowers and pinnate leaves, the Swamp Honeysuckle, the red or river birch with its strong, light brown wood which makes, in America at any rate, excellent furniture; the *abies canadenses*;* the Virginia snow-flower bush, to say nothing of the latifolia branch of the Kalmia family (the family is named for Pehr Kalm) which is beautiful but unfortunate in that its leaves are poisonous to cattle, so it would never do for a *ferme orneé*.

A year after Kalm's visit, Peter Collinson moved to Ridgeway House, Mill Hill,† where, though he avoided publicity, he could not escape fame. He was made a member of the Royal Societies of London, Berlin and Sweden, and it was at Mill Hill that he first really began an intense specialization in American plants, many of which he received from John Bartram‡ who was subsequently appointed 'Botanist Royal for America' by George III. A munificent £50 a year went with the post.

There was an enormous and increasing interest in botany and in rare plants throughout the era. Florists went on improving old varieties and welcoming new ones. Absolutely new to the period, and a unique phenomenon in flowers, was the green edge which

---

* This puzzles me. Abies, or true firs, include about forty species. Nine are native to North America and four occur in Canada. Three of these four are western species, the fourth is found on the Atlantic seaboard. As western Canada was not then opened up, I can only conclude that *abies canadensis* means the fourth, that is the balsam fir.

† The grounds are now part of Mill Hill School.

‡ Bartram set up his own house and gardens in 1728 a few miles outside Philadelphia, it is today part of the city and, I believe, the house still stands.

appeared on the English auriculas. This plant—also known as
Arthritica for its reputed medicinal properties—had been introduced in the fifteenth century, it pegged along during the six-
teenth century, but in the seventeenth we really began to work on
it so successfully that it became known abroad as the 'English'
auricula, to distinguish it from the Alpine strains being developed
in Germany, France and Holland. Despite the work done by
florists, the green edge was due entirely to a 'natural break',[31] and
English auriculas became more famous than ever. In addition to
work at home there were still great areas of the world unmapped,
and ships sent on voyages of scientific discovery usually numbered
a professional or amateur botanist among officers and crew. Thus
Joseph Banks and Dr Solander sailed with Captain Cook in the
*Endeavour** and 'it was upon account of the great quantity of plants
which Mr Banks and Dr Solander collected in this place that
Lieutenant Cook was induced to give it the name of Botany
Bay'.[32] Archibald Menzies went with Captain George Vancouver
and brought back, among other things (rather mistakenly I think),
the monkey puzzle. Later David Douglas (1798–1834)† made a
series of journeys exploring, charting virgin territories, and
collecting plants of great botanical interest. He reaped an enormous harvest on the west coast of America, and the subsequent
introduction of new, hardy evergreens, of which the Douglas Fir
is but one, completely altered our winter landscape.‡

The discovery of a new plant was, in fact, just as exciting, if not
more so, than the discovery of a new planet. Georgium Sidus,
better known to us as Uranus, discovered by the musician-
astronomer Sir William Herschel, could interest the scientific
world and those of the social world who, like Fanny Burney,
were able to see it through Herschel's great telescope. But no one

---

* Captain Cook also took with him a good many seeds and domestic animals to
give to the natives in places he discovered.

† Douglas met his death in Hawaii in 1834. He fell into a trap set by the islanders
to catch wild bulls and was trampled to death by a bull already caught.

‡ The Horticultural Society, formed in 1804 began to send out collectors to all
parts of the world, as the Royal Horticultural Society still does.

needed anything more than the naked eye to see and appreciate the hundreds of plants and flowers introduced during the era, from the shy South African *pelargonium pelatum*, first known in England in 1701, to that Victorian favourite, the aspidistra, which appeared first in 1822. How exciting it must have been to see the first alyssum (1710) dusted with gold; or the purple aubretia (1710); the tall phlox (1725) or the dicentra (1731) with its exquisitely deep-cut leaves and small, hanging, heart-shaped flowers. How intoxicating the perfume of the first sweet-scented stock (1731), and what strange delight lay in the crisp headed hydrangea (1736). Then in 1739, the tiny pink trumpets of the Diervilla, and, in 1754, the tall lily-like Alstromeria, named after the Swedish botanist Baron C. Alstromaer, who visited the Duchess of Portland at Bulstrode in 1788 and there met Mrs Delany. Then there was the South African corn-flag (1756), and the lovely golden lily, *lycoris* (1758). These, and dozens more, became known during the first half of the century; and after that there were more and more and more, most of which are garden commonplaces today—if there can be such a thing. Gallardias (1787), fuchsias (1788), and in the very last year of the century the graceful cosmos, so named because it was so beautiful. These, which constitute a very random and impossibly brief selection of just a few of the flowers we grow today, were all brand new to the Georgians, and it must have seemed to them as if a whole new and wonderful creation of growing things had suddenly come into being before their astonished eyes.

The new style in gardening, however, had very little influence on cottage gardens—new styles rarely have—and there were then, as now, far more cottage gardens than grand ones. Unlike great gardens, which follow fashion, no two cottage gardens are alike; they are not the work of a planner or professional and this is their charm. Gardening was and still is our true popular art and the cottage garden, if for no other reason than lack of space, had never followed the seventeenth-century formal style. Nor did it follow the fashions of the eighteenth century. The cottage gardener did not grub up old apples or pears, or the sweet provence rose, or tear out the old favourite martagons or the pinks which had come in with William the Conqueror from Normandy. He did not eschew gooseberries, cabbages, onions and such like in favour of an unproductive lawn surrounding his cottage with a skinny tree or two set somewhere artistic, or as a screen for the pigsty. And, uncouth wretch that he was, he did not even gothicize the pigsty. But he was glad enough to have new flowers and plants when he could get them, notably the china aster after it first came in, in 1731, and he probably got the occasional cast-out if he had a friend who had a friend who knew one of the gardener's boys at the nearby big estate. So cottage gardens went on being cottage gardens, expressive of the individuality and the needs of the owner, and of that deep love for flowers which is so much a part of the Englishness of the English that, sometimes, one wonders how Capability Brown managed to persuade so many owners of great estates to give up flowers in favour of lawns. Perhaps the answer is that the cottage gardener is the true amateur. He grew what he loved and loved what he grew.

But there were amateurs other than cottagers who preferred to design their own gardens according to their own ideas. One was that minor poet and indifferent painter, the shy, melancholy William Shenstone (1714–63). Another was Henry Hoare the younger. Shenstone turned the Leasowes,* a tiny farm of about thirty acres, into a *ferme ornée* which, since the acreage was so small and his income minute, was excessively improvident of him. Beginning around 1744, Shenstone created a garden, and it took his whole life to do it, in his own style. It was a pastoral garden complete with winding walks and thirty-nine different seats where the spectator could rest and admire a carefully contrived view against a backdrop of the Welsh mountains. One seat was a root house, another was set in a temple to rustic Pan, while more ordinary ones were gothic or set in 'natural' bowers. Paths were lined with urns and trophies suitably inscribed with mottoes. Fauns with pipes and other rustic denizens of Arcady were placed in the glades. All who visited the Leasowes were enchanted with

* Locally pronounced Lezzers.

Garden 'temple', Gothic style, after a design by Batty Langley, *circa* 1742

it, and it had an enormous effect on the planning of middling gardens well on into the nineteenth century. 'He made', Dr Johnson says of Shenstone, 'his little domain the envy of the great; a place to be visited by travellers and copied by designers.'[33] So great was Shenstone's passion for his garden that 'he spent his estate in adorning it',[34] and died not only impoverished but in debt. Yet he had enriched his own life, and hundreds of other gardens were indebted to the Leasowes for style and character.

Henry Hoare (1705–85), unlike Shenstone, belonged to an immensely rich family of goldsmith bankers but, like Shenstone, he had 'the good taste . . . and the good sense not to call in the assistance of a landscape gardener'.[35] Between 1742 and 1772 at Stourhead, Wilts, Hoare created, out of a bleak valley near Salisbury plain, what many consider to be the most perfect of all eighteenth-century gardens. As far as we now know, Stourhead is entirely Hoare's own design.* It is idyllic, classical/romantic, Italian, Claudian and at the same time unmistakably English. Doubtless it greatly influenced professional gardeners of the day, and certainly it became a 'must' for all travellers. Contemporary letters, diaries and journals are full of praises for its wonderful lake (created out of a series of deadly little fish ponds), its walks, its variety of trees, its exquisite and perfectly set garden buildings. The 'Temple of Hercules' alone must have cost £10,000, Parson Woodforde thought when he visited Stourhead in September 1763. He meant, of course, the lovely 'Pantheon' built by Henry Flitcroft in 1745. But all the buildings at Stourhead were, and are, beautiful and formed stations for the two main walks or circuits about the garden. On the inner walk leading around the lake are the Old Bristol Cross, the Temple of Flora, the Paradise Well, the Grotto, the Rustic Cottage, the Pantheon and the lovely miniature Temple of the Sun (based on that at Baalbec). All these can still be seen, but the Turkish Tent, the Chinese Parasol and the small, single-span Chinese bridge which Mrs Lybbe Powys and her friends found so frightening to cross, are now no more.

The outer circuit—a walk for the energetic, a ride for the enfeebled, aged or merely lazy—displayed a rustic convent, with some of its windows reputedly taken from Glastonbury Abbey (the century had its own kind of vandalism as we have ours), St Peter's Pump which, like the Old Cross, had been imported from Bristol, and the still famous landmark, Alfred's Tower, a triangular brick building rising 160 feet, built in 1772, reputedly upon the very spot where King Alfred, 'England's darling', set up his standard against the Scandinavian invaders. Since the tower stood, and still stands, upon an eminence 1,000 feet above sea-level, the panoramic view from the top was superb.† 'Mrs Leveson took the pains to mount to the top of the edifice (256

---

* The planting of trees did not then go to the water's edge, nor were there rhododendrons, azaleas and hydrangeas in the original garden.

† The tower is now (1965) unsafe and cannot be entered, but the view from the eminence upon which it stands is still superb on a clear day.

steps) but I contented myself visiting and admiring a very extensive prospect from its foot', Mrs Boscawen writes after a day spent at Stourhead. She was 'lucky in a fine day' and so could 'sit and tarry at the different stations' and admire what she calls, a trifle ineptly, 'the pretty opera scenes'.[36] Mrs Boscawen, however, seems to have preferred Longleat, the work of Capability Brown, to the work of Henry Hoare at Stourhead. She could not know then, as we do now, that Stourhead is probably the earliest example extant of that type of informal or so called 'natural' landscape which has become so closely associated with Brown's name. Yet Stourhead is at least a decade ahead of the earliest known plan by Brown and is the work not of a professional but of an amateur.

At Beaulieu Abbey the greatest professional, or amateur, of all seems to have been responsible for the landscape. There 'nature only is to be admired',[37] or so the Countess of Bute thought. Here the river wound 'under a bank of woods extending several miles, and growing down to the edge of the water'; on the opposite side was 'a range of meadows, as green as the plains of Arcadia, forming altogether (really) a pastoral scene, such as Mr Brown has attempted to make in many places at the expense of half the owner's fortune'.[38]

But Mr Brown, although he often certainly and expensively 'assisted' nature by levelling hills, or creating them; filling up hollows or digging valleys, scooping out lakes or making rivers wind according to his plan of what the landscape needed, is neither to be blamed nor congratulated for the passion and fashion for fields as green as the Arcadian plains. The Georgians had developed almost an obsession for great green stretches, or lawns, before Capability Brown came upon the scene. It is a little confusing for us to realize that a lawn originally meant nothing more than any piece of grass-covered or untilled ground and, in the eighteenth century, included such things as a deer park! But the lawn proper, that is the great spread of green turf covering anything up to eight acres and quite unencumbered by trees, shrubs, borders or beds, was a typically Georgian idea. Every good gardening book throughout the era—and there were many—dealt minimally or extensively with the subject of lawns. Great people were, it seems, willing to do away with almost anything—ancient oaks, old dower houses, balustraded terraces—in order to get an enormous lawn to surround the house. Sometimes an ancient house looked incongruous if not downright embarrassed sitting so nakedly on a vast green carpet; so the house was often altered or refaced to suit the new setting. Batty Langley—and Batty was naturally right there with a book on modern gardening—thought Hampton Court would be much improved if such trifling things as the yews and hollies were removed from the parterre garden and the whole turned into a nice green lawn. Langley in his book *New Principles of Gardening* shows various plans for gardens,* one of which consists of nothing but variously shaped lawns surrounded by either avenues or plantations of trees. This book was first printed in 1728; as Capability Brown was then only thirteen years old he can hardly be responsible for the yen for lawns.

Langley, like Sir Francis Bacon and Joseph Addison, despised topiary work. He favoured statues as garden ornaments including one of Runciana,† the goddess of weeding. Switzer too had had much to say on statues—they gave 'Grace and Majesty to a country seat'.[39] And he supports this with the argument that the Romans, ancient and modern, 'the greatest and politest people in the world', used statues and 'their gardens as well as those of France, abound so much in them that 'tis in that point they are still likely to out-do us'. We were likely to be outdone in statues for other reasons, too. In our unenlightened and enthusiastic way we tended to ignore the nature of the gods we dotted about our gardens. Jupiter, 'set perching upon a little Pedestal', was reduced

---

* Some of his ideas are far from new and hark back to Le Nôtre, with canals, cascades, cabinets, bowling greens and so on.

† I cannot trace this goddess and suspect, possibly unjustly, that she is a latter-day addition to the hierarchy. The name, however, must derive from the L. *runcator*—a person who clears a crop of extraneous herbiage or weeds, and *runco* is the word for a weeding hook. Certainly in England poor women were glad to earn a few extra pennies a day by weeding the fields—this was women's work, hence, possibly, 'Runciana'.

Eighteenth-century garden ornaments

to the status of a 'mere citizen'. Mars, pike in hand, looked no more than a common foot soldier; Neptune, set on dry land and holding his trident, resembled nothing more than a cart filler; little better was Neptune in his proper element trying to manage his sea-horses and Amphitrite at one and the same time; even worse was Mars embracing Venus in full armour; and if any one had such a 'Cruel Piece' as 'Andromeda fasten'd to a Rock', it should be set near water 'where she can weep and lament her fate'. Errors were made with minor deities too: Pan trampled the flower garden with his hoofs while poor Ceres and Flora languished in woods and groves. More shameful than our lack of knowledge, or our carelessness, about the true and correct habitat for gods, was statuary itself—a much neglected art. Switzer was all for setting up an Academy with 'Royal Patronage' where young men could be taught to draw and carve. Once taught, they could be 'distributed amongst the Nobility and Gentry', who stood greatly in need of 'noble Decorations of Statues', since all they had were 'a few Leaden Copies, abounding with all the incongruities I have before mentioned'.[40]

One does not know whether the statue of Flora given to the Rev. Dr Stukeley by the Duke of Montagu would have met with Switzer's approbation; but cetainly Stukeley—and he and Switzer were friends—cannot have paid the smallest attention to the plea to put the right statue in the right place. Stukeley made this unfortunate goddess a 'theatrical building' (i.e. round) with niched walls to hold 'statues and bustos'. Although this edifice had a roof 'with a cupola' the work, he says enthusiastically, 'is gothick . . . with pinacle work . . . foliage work . . . coats of arms', and 'pointed windows with painted glass'.[41] Somehow one cannot quite reconcile all that pinnacle work and painted windows with a cupola. Nor poor Flora set within a bastard gothic temple. According to Switzer, Flora, Ceres and Pomona were best for farms and rural work and, perhaps like Runciana, even for lawns which by mid-century were already acknowledged to be the finest in Europe, even by the French who did their foreign best to imitate them. But no country, fortunately or unfortunately, is possessed of our English climate which produces absolutely top quality bronchitis, rheumatism and grass.

Nevertheless, although we had the natural advantage of a suitable climate we took enormous pains to get the right seed or turves to make a lawn. Good hayseed was often used, but turves were thought to be much better and in those days could be bought for 1s or 1s 6d per hundred. All lawns were still cut by scythe, it was not until the last year of the reign of George IV that a patent was taken out for 'a machine for cropping or shearing the vegetable Surface of Lawns, Grass plots etc.'; and all lawns were carefully rolled. If great in area, horsedrawn rollers were used and the horses' hooves were carefully wrapped in woollen mufflers. Small lawns were hand rolled, for labour was cheap and rollers were not. But by the 1790s rollers had been greatly improved and Parson Woodforde sent Ben off in the cart to fetch his 'new Garden Roller of Cast Iron . . . a very clever Roller and is called the ballance Roller, as the handle never goes to the Ground'.[42] It also seems to have been as heavy as it was dear. The cast iron, presumably the operative bit, weighed above two hundredweight and was charged at 2½d per pound; total £2 17s 6d while the 'Hammer'd Iron', possibly the shaft, weighed 40 lb and cost, at 6¾d per pound, £1 2s 6d. So the new 'ballance Roller' worked out at £4, a good sum of money to spend on a garden implement in those days.*

But not everyone approved of vast lawns nor, indeed, as we have seen of the work of Capability Brown. Sir William Chambers, the famous architect, was a staunch disapprover. 'Whole woods', he writes, 'have been swept away to make room for a little grass and a few American weeds', and he thought gardens now differed little from common fields, because they were so closely copied from 'vulgar nature'. All this vulgarity could be traced back to the fact that 'peasants emerge from the melon ground to take the periwig and turn professor' and so 'this island is abandoned to kitchen gardeners well skilled in the production of salads'.[43]

Since one can always interrupt the long dead with small fear of reprisal, it can be said that kitchen gardens were at any rate infinitely better and more productive than ever before. Due to an enormous increase in professional as well as amateur gardening, kitchen gardens flourished. By now we were producing salads and vegetables which from the time of Elizabeth I, had been imported in quantity from Holland. We had learned, too, the secret of growing such exotics† as 'pines' (pineapples) in special 'pineries' (or rather the rich had), and we were still bent on growing melons which, perhaps, we grew more successfully then than now, but we continued to ask for seed from Italy as James I had done. The

---

* One should perhaps, multiply by twenty to approximate the cost in today's money. But with the value of money now so fluid it is almost pointless to suggest any multiple.

† The English interest in trying to produce fruit and flowers which cannot be naturalized is of long standing. Cardan advised Edward VI to grow olives ('of endless age', one wonders). He may or may not have done so, but in 1719 an olive tree against a wall at Campden House, Kensington, produced fruit. Oranges and lemons were a special effort of the Elizabethans and Jacobeans, and pomegranates certainly seem to have flowered, if they did not fruit, in seventeenth-century England.

melons produced by Thomas, 3rd Earl of Strafford (1672–1739), filled one visitor to his garden with 'wonder' not because of size or flavour, but because each melon had Lord Strafford's 'Arms, Coronet, Star and Garter naturally imprinted on them'.[44] This natural imprint the visitor subsequently discovered was really due to the ingenious and artful employment of a needle when the melons were 'in their infancy'. The design had then been pricked onto the tender skin and had enlarged with the fruit.

Such a pretty and ornamental conceit would have seemed a trifle naïve to Sir William Chambers who, when it came to gardens, was certainly all for strange conceits, but of a far more urbane and sophisticated kind. In fact he is probably far better known for his Chinese Pagoda at Kew than for Somerset House in the Strand. Chambers, who seems to have travelled to China, wrote *A Dissertation on Chinese Gardening* in 1772 and had planned and designed various buildings at Kew for the Dowager Princess of Wales (mother of George III) as early as 1763. But he was by no means the first to introduce into England what we believed to be the Chinese style in gardens. So called Chinese gardens had been popular as stage sets in the seventeenth century, and, in 1685, in his *Upon the Gardens of Epicurus*, Sir William Temple (not to be confused with Sir Richard Temple) had spoken of Chinese gardens and had advised against them; 'they are too hard of achievement for any common hands; and though there may be more honour if they succeed, yet there is more dishonour if they faile' which he adds glumly, ''tis twenty to one they will'.

But eighteenth-century hands were not common and twenty years before Chambers wrote his *Dissertation* 'Sir Harry Beaumont'* had translated the famous letter by Fr Attiret on the Emperor of China's magnificent gardens. Even in 1760 that charming character, Lieu Chi Altangi, is made to say, 'The English have not yet brought the art of gardening to the same perfection with the Chinese but have lately begun to imitate them'.[45] So Chambers is rather a late-comer with his book, for we had

---

* The pseudonym of the Rev. Joseph Spence, the anecdotist. He was a keen gardener and was drowned in 1768 when he fell into an ornamental canal.

Pagoda, Kew Gardens, *circa* 1761. Sir William Chambers

already been experimenting with our own ideas of Chinese styles for a number of years. There is indeed nothing very new in his remarks that the Chinese planted oaks, beeches and other types of deciduous trees to get variety in autumnal colouring, we had been doing it for years. Nor was it novel to suggest planting dead stumps and trees among the living for effect. William Kent had done this at least forty years before. To recommend that a garden should be enlivened with picturesque ruins, castles, deserted religious houses, seems to indicate that Chambers had no notion that in certain circles this sort of thing had been growing in fashion since the time of George I. There was some novelty, certainly, in the idea that in Chinese gardens, pavilions and walks were occupied by 'the fairest and most accomplished concubines'. One can hardly vizualize this happening in George III's gardens at Richmond or Kew, although it would not be out of place with the character of George IV. Yet London's pleasure gardens contained all three—pavilions and walks and concubines, though, admittedly the last were chiefly common prostitutes. As for introducing wolves, vultures, tigers, jackals and half-famished animals among the wilder wooded bits to add a titillation of terror to the beauty of the garden, we, in our timid way, preferred to have aviaries and menageries attached to ours. Many a noble lord had his own menagerie as well as his second *ménage*.

But gardening in China, as both Fr Attiret and Chambers pointed out, was an art; a fine art which had been developed over centuries. The Chinese gardener–artist had a long strict training in botany, philosophy and painting. As gardening was held to have a profound influence upon general culture, it was not to be undertaken lightly. Mistakes were unforgiveable since it might take a century to undo the error of an hour. Here Chambers is getting at Brown and his followers, who were busy cutting down ancient trees, making lakes, and so on, and altering the landscape into what a young American visitor once called 'just one big park'. And, indeed, parklike England, or what remains of it, is largely due to the ideas of Brown and his followers. For if they cut down trees, they also planted them in different situations, hence the accusation that Brown was given to clumping and belting.

Chambers is interesting on Chinese glasshouses which were built like temples and held rare trees, shrubs and flowers, with the woodwork of the glass frames cleverly disguised by figs, apricots, peaches and cherries. Apart from orangeries, our glasshouses were more for use than beauty, and one wonders if it were Chambers's description which so inspired the Rev. William Mason,* in one of the most painful of his many painful poems, to describe the fantastic glass house which Alcander put up for his beloved, unresponsive and pining Nerina as

---

* To be fair, Mason's biography of Gray, where he lets the poet speak for himself through his own letter, is the first biography of its kind and greatly influenced Boswell.

A glittering fane, where rare and alien plants
Might safely flourish. . . .
A proud rotunda; to its sides conjoin'd
Two proud piazas in theatric curve,
Ending in equal porticos sublime.
Glass roof'd the whole, and sidelong to the south
'Twixt every fluted column, lightly rear'd
It was pellucid. All within was day,
Was genial summer's day, for secret stoves
Through all the pile solstitial warmth convey'd.[46]

Despite solstitial warmth, which might have been expected to attract a girl who had arrived suddenly on these shores from Boston via a nasty shipwreck, Nerina would have none of it. She preferred to pine away and die in a gloomy, damp little bower of sweet woodbine.

Not that the Chinese were opposed to gloom in the right places. A touch of the gloomy added a proper sense of appreciation to the peace and beauty of the garden. Deep woods, dank caverns, contorted trees, sinister valleys, had as great a part to play as lakes, streams, exquisite buildings, pavilions, boats and bridges. The whole idea of the Chinese garden was to keep the spectator amused and interested by a variety of things to be seen on walks, which never deviated just for the sake of deviation (as ours often did), and by strange, enchanting and varied scenes— perhaps in modern jargon we should call them 'happenings'. A great turfed lawn, water in the distance, hills topped with a 'cushion of trees', and the whole vast area surrounded by a belt of green, as advocated and practised by Brown, was hardly a garden, in the view of Chambers and others. Surprisingly, the Chinese had no objection to the formal garden, they thought the regular, geometric figures beautiful in themselves. This particular Chinese idea we largely ignored. We could hardly do otherwise since we had been busy for half a century or more tearing up our own formal gardens. But we did go in for Chinese touches to a greater or lesser extent. Sophie von la Roche particularly comments on Osterley Park (then owned by Mrs Child) and its 'Chinese summer house, where all the furnishings come from China, arranged in the taste and custom of the Country'.⁴⁷ Others went in for pagodas, fishing pavilions, puzzle bridges, boats and various other Chinese notions, and the idea of adding Chinoiserie to gardens became a craze. Abroad, the curious yet somehow enchanting *mélange* which we had eclectically developed, became known as 'le jardin anglais'. It was envied, admired and copied, particularly in France. But English visitors thought the French imitation very poor indeed.

It must not be supposed for one moment that English gardens suddenly and overnight gave up the classical–romantic, or the romantic–picturesque, and dotted Chinese buildings and so on in a pure Claudian or Poussin landscape. As we know at Stourhead there were among the classical buildings, a Turkish Tent, a Chinese umbrella and bridge, a rustic cottage and a nunnery, to say nothing of Alfred's Tower. Throughout the era, despite purists, many English gardeners, amateur and professional, introduced highly unnatural and artfully contrived effects into their so-called 'natural' gardens. They often mixed the architecture of garden buildings with surprising and enchanting results. Here, of course, we were like the Chinese, but even more like ourselves. There is nothing we cannot absorb, if we wish to, and then turn it into something which becomes 'typically English'.

We have always had summer houses, banqueting houses and bowers in our earlier gardens, and in the seventeenth century, inspired by Italy and France, we took to grottoes. By the eighteenth century, they had become the rage and continued so throughout the era. Although highly artificial they also occurred naturally since nature does produce grottoes though perhaps not very lavishly in England. Pope's grotto was famous and remained so long after his death. 'Composed of marble, spars, gems, ores and minerals',⁴⁸ it was finished in 1725 and, like his small and carefully designed garden, was the delight of his life. It still exists much altered by various hands, a pallid shadow of its former self. No longer does it sparkle with ores from Mexico, Peru, Germany and Cornwall; crystals and even humming-birds. It had real stalactites too, though they were not formed *in situ*, they were shot down in the Wookey Hole and cemented into place. Pope's grotto cost him 'above a thousand pounds'.[49] Lord Shaftesbury's, built in 1751, cost him £10,000—which is not surprising as many of the oyster shells used in its decoration were complete with pearls. At Clifton near Bristol, Thomas Goldeney* began his famous grotto at the end of an already completed subterranean passage. It had a lion's den within, but Mrs Delany does not mention this when she saw it, barely half finished, in 1756. Incomplete though it was, it was yet 'one of the few things that answer expectations',[50] but difficult to describe. Nevertheless, she attempts description: 'a rocky cave . . . four pillars to support the dome . . . a river god . . . a cascade . . . walls, richly irregular and very boldly adorned with everything the earth and sea can produce proper for the purpose . . . pillars covered with spar' which 'look as if they were set with as many jewels as old Grognon's cask'.[51] Mrs Delany knew a great deal about grottoes and had designed and made several herself. 'I am making a grotto in Sir John Stanley's garden at North End' (Fulham), she writes to Jonathan Swift on September 2nd 1736, 'chiefly composed of shells I had from Ireland'. So great was the passion for shell work, indoors and out, and for collecting shells that such collections fetched enormous prices. A Mrs Kennon, a midwife who died in 1750, had a collection worth £2,500.

The second wife of Sir Robert Walpole also made herself a grotto much despised by the Duchess of Portland. 'It is a *shellery*', she says, 'for *grotto* I will not call it'.[52] The regularity was 'abominable'. Besides all the red coral was painted! That ebullient and eccentric antiquary, the Rev. Dr Stukeley, also planned a shell grotto† where, a trifle unusually one feels, 'Cherubims of oak as

---

* Defoe's *Guide*, 1778 edition, refers to him as Gabriel Goldney.

† Shell grottoes are older than fashionable gardens would lead us to suspect. They are probably a relic of the old shell grottoes erected to St James of Compostella for the benefit of those too poor to pay a visit to his shrine. In the last century 'Pray remember the grotto' was still occasionally said by small boys begging for pennies on St James's Day (July 25th).

big as life' from Croyland,* would, caryatid-like, support the '4 corners of the arch of the grot'.⁵³ Unfortunately one of the cherubims turned out to be cross-legged. Obviously then, there was a great diversity in style, shape and conception of grottoes, but some of them, notably that at Stourhead were, and are, exquisitely beautiful. Grottoes diminished in size, beauty and fashion in the nineteenth century and have, perhaps, become the rock gardens of our own era.

When Arthur Young visited Mr Goldeney's garden and grotto in 1772 he was certainly not so impressed with it as Mrs Delany had been, and particularly disliked the sculptured lion in its den. He also notes that 'This gentleman at one end of his terras has a summer house with *gothic* battlements and windows encompassed by a colonade on *tuscan* pillars . . . and in his garden other curious strokes'.⁵⁴ What these curious strokes were he does not tell us, but he manifestly objects to the combination of gothic with tuscan architecture and would no doubt have had a very curious stroke himself had he seen Dr Stukeley's Temple of Flora. Yet this mixture of styles was by no means uncommon, and if it seems absurd it is really no more absurd than the craze for garden buildings designed like hermitages, convents, monks' cells or carefully built ruins. 'I'll only show his lordship my ruins and the cascade and the Chinese bridge before breakfast', says Mr Stirling, and explains that the ruins are 'reckoned very fine ones too. You would think them ready to tumble on your head. It has just cost me a hundred and fifty pounds to put my ruins in thorough repair.'⁵⁵

Young, himself, particularly admired the 'Hermitage' with its dark entrance room and Hermit's parlour (unoccupied, though many did keep ornamental hermits) in 'Mr Hamilton's† orna-

---

* This must be Crowland's Abbey since Stukeley remarks he has 'two of St Guthlake's (St Guthlac) devils in stone'. This saint, an eighth-century Mercian noble, is usually represented either as scourging demons, or being consoled by angels while demons torment him.

† The Hon. Charles Hamilton, youngest son of the Earl of Abercorn, had a famous garden at Painshill, also a must for travellers. It was sold in 1775.

Neo–classical Orangery and sham Gothic ruin. Late eighteenth century

mented park at Cobham',[56] though perhaps he really preferred
that statue of Venus 'with fine haunches' which stood in the
Temple of Bacchus. That most fantastic of all Gothic revival
buildings, Fonthill, began as an idea in Beckford's mind for a
ruined convent built as a garden folly.

Follies of all sorts, but especially of the gothic kind, were typical
of the era. Charming though they are no one can claim they are
not absurd, for absurdity is their chief charm. Dr Stukeley, not
unexpectedly, planned a 'Temple of the Druids' in 1728, with 'an
antient apple tree ore grown with sacred mistletoe'[57] as its central
feature. Queen Caroline went even further with Merlin's Cave
which she had built for her at Richmond, New Lodge,* around
1735. In June of that year *The Gentleman's Magazine* reports 'A

* The grounds of this now form a large part of Kew Gardens.

381

subterraneous building is, by her Majesty's Order, carrying on in the Royal Gardens at Richmond, which is to be called Merlin's Cave, adorned with Astronomical Figures and Characters'. The magazine was inaccurate. The building was not subterranean despite its name; it was a three-roomed building based on a design by William Kent, and stood well above ground. In style it was an excessively odd mixture of classical and gothic with an ogee doorway; its three, steep-pitched roofs thatched and shaped like conical hay stacks. Every bit as odd was the mixture inside where wax figures of Merlin, Queen Elizabeth, Minerva, Melissa and other personages, real or mythological, stood or sat in various attitudes. The cave also contained a choice collection of English books provided by the Queen who appointed Stephen Duck,* 'the Thresher Poet,' as keeper of the cave and library. Inevitably the pond near the cave, which would have swamped it had the cave been underground, became known as the Duck Pond. George II, naturally, thought the whole thing extravagant nonsense, which it doubtless was. But it was a good deal less extravagant and far more diverting and amusing than the King's utterly dreary mistresses.

Bridgeman was very possibly concerned with Merlin's Cave because at that time he was Royal Gardener, and it is odd and a little sad to record that when Brown took over the job, he did away with much of Bridgeman's work, including Merlin's Cave. In an *Heroic Epistle*, no less painful than *The English Garden*, Mason mourns the destruction thus:

> To Richmond come; for see untutor'd Brown
> Destroys those wonders that were once thy own;
> Lo! from his melon ground the peasant slave
> Has rudely rush'd, and levell'd Merlin's Cave,
> Knocked down the waxen wizard, seiz'd his wand,
> Transformed to lawn what late was fairlyland

* Stephen Duck (1705–56) agricultural labourer, self-educated, and a great reader of *Paradise Lost*, turned poet and came under the patronage of Queen Caroline in 1733; became rector of Byfleet in 1752 and drowned himself during a fit of melancholy in the Thames near Reading.

And marr'd with impious hands each sweet design
Of Stephen Duck and good Queen Caroline.

Since this poem, a sharp satire on Chambers, was published in the same year as Chambers's *Dissertation*, it is not easy to determine who was first with the snide remarks about the peasant Brown rushing from the melon patch to wreak destruction upon the gardens of England.

Brown had many imitators during and after his life—some good, some decidedly inferior. But his true successor in the picturesque tradition* was Humphry Repton (1752–1818). 'I have adopted the term *Landscape Gardening*', Repton says, 'as most proper, because the art can only be perfected by the united powers of the *landscape painter* and the *practical gardener*.'[58] Although in time he became the target for as much abuse as Brown, no one could accuse him of having crept out of the melon patch. His father held a lucrative position as Collector of Excise in Bury St Edmunds and, determining that his son should become a merchant, sent him, after a grammar school education, to the Netherlands to learn how to be one. Three years later Humphry returned. He did not appear to have acquired much mercantile sense, but he had picked up many social graces, a well-developed ability to draw, and a knowledge of mathematics and botany. Once home, he turned his hand (unsuccessfully) to various mercantile ventures, married, and then retired to Susted, Norfolk, where he spent several years and enjoyed the patronage of William Windham† (1750–1810) of Felbrigg studying gardening, botany, entomology and the beauties of nature in general and particular. In 1783 when Windham became Chief Secretary to the Lord Lieutenant of Ireland, he took Repton with him as his own confidential

---

* Picturesque, for a great part of the century, when used in connection with gardening meant that this new type of gardening had its roots, or at least a good deal of its roots, in landscape painting. By the end of the century the meaning had shifted and picturesque meant producing in a country estate that kind of scenery which has strongly marked features and is a suitable subject for the landscape painter.
† Windham, a statesman, was a friend of Johnson and Burke, but readers of Mme d'Arblay's Diary will probably best remember him as one of the M.P.s charged with the impeachment of Warren Hastings.

secretary. Windham resigned after a month and Repton carried on alone for six weeks during which time, as he wrote to his wife, he made 'some very valuable aquaintances . . . and formed some connexion with the great'.[59]

Returned to England, he settled at Romford, took to gardening, lost money financing a fast-mail coach business and then, with an ever growing family, began to worry in earnest about his future. He had no real training, no business, no profession, but he had a number of talents. Carefully summing these up he decided these fitted him to become Brown's successor. For once he was right. He set up as a landscape gardener in 1788, wrote 'round to his influencial friends and valuable aquaintances' and was an immed-iate success.

We know a good deal more about Repton than about the other great gardeners of the period because he invariably put himself down on paper. Whenever called upon to 'landscape' an estate he wrote a carefully detailed report—'digest' he calls it—of what needed to be done and why. The report was usually accompanied by a Red Book, so called because it was bound in red morocco, and in the Red Book Repton gave his prospective employer a before and after look at the landscape. 'I invented the peculiar kind of slides to my sketches . . . ', he says, 'to show the proposed effects.' These slides were drawings which could be slotted into a basic drawing to show improvements and alterations. He also used more elaborate hinged overlays for the same purpose. This new type of visual aid so delighted people that Repton remarks, 'with some mortification', they were often 'the only part of my labours which the common observer has time or leisure to examine'.[60]

Repton does not hesitate to call Brown a genius. He points out that the chief faults in taste were made by Brown's imitators, 'who had the mistaken notion, that greatness of dimension would pro-duce greatness of character; hence proceeded the immeasurable extent of naked lawns; the tedious length of belts and drives; the useless breadth of meandering roads; the tiresome monotony of shrubberies and pleasure grounds; the naked expanse of waters, unaccompanied by trees; and all the unpicturesque features which disgrace modern gardening, and which have brought on Brown's system the opprobrious epithets of bare and bald'.[61] Brown, he says bluntly 'copied Nature, his illiterate followers copied him'.

Repton, though eclectic, was no mere imitator. What he aimed at was a complete unity, a harmony of all parts to make a perfect whole, and all parts included the house itself. He puts it this way: 'The fatal experience of some, who begin improvements by building a house too sumptuous for the grounds, has occasionally induced others to consider the grounds independent of the house; but this, I conceive, will unavoidably lead to error. It is not necessary that the house and grounds should correspond with each other in point of size, but the *characters* of each should be in strict harmony, since it is hardly less incongruous to see a palace by the side of a neglected common, than an ugly-designed mansion, whether large or small, in the midst of highly improved scenery; to every part of which it must be considered a disgrace.'[62]

If, say, the landscape were fantastic or irregular, then the house and its buildings should conform. This meant that houses often had to be improved or even built to suit the landscape and, as Repton had no training in the mechanics of architecture though he certainly had an eye for it and could draw, sometime in the mid 90s he was joined by John Nash, who provided the necessary architectural knowledge; they remained partners until around 1802. Perhaps the chief difference between Brown and Repton is that where Brown set a picturesque landscape around a house, Repton and Nash conceived the house and necessary buildings as a part of the picture; ideally, they should be designed together. 'Congruity of style, uniformity of character and harmony of parts with the whole', Repton writes, 'are different modes of expressing that *unity* without which no composition can be perfect; yet there are few principles in gardening which seem to be so little understood'; and, he adds, 'This essential unity has often been mistaken for symmetry or the correspondence of similar parts'.[63]

This, however, does not rule out symmetry and, quoting from Montesquieu's essay *On Taste*, he says, 'Things seen in succession

ought to have variety . . . those . . . that we see at one glance
ought to have symmetry: thus, at one glance we see the front of a
building, a parterre, a temple; in such things there is always a
symmetry which pleases the soul by the facility it gives her of
taking the whole object at once'.[64]

So in small flower gardens Repton advises symmetry—irregu-
larity would appear 'like affectations'. Symmetry was also
necessary near the front of a regular building, otherwise the house
would appear 'all twisted and awry'. But such symmetry should be
confined to the terrace (and he reintroduced terraces) a road, a
walk, an ornamental fence and should not be carried too far; it
should not extend to 'plantations, canals or over the natural shape
of the ground'.[65] He had, incidentally, no objection to avenues of
trees if and where they were a necessary part of picturesqueness.

Winter Orangery, convertible to summer 'Chiosk'. Designed by Humphrey
Repton, 1806

What he really held to be the greatest mistake in 'modern' gardening, was to set a large house bang in the centre of a huge naked lawn, with all necessary adjuncts—stables, dairy and kitchen gardens—banished to an inconvenient distance so house and garden could be surrounded, without interruption to the eye, by a park. Here he was at one with one of his detractors, Richard Payne Knight, in feeling that

> Where only grass and foliage we obtain
> To make a flat, insipid, waving plain;
> Which, wrapt all o'er in everlasting green
> Makes one dull, vapid, smooth and tranquil scene.*[66]

Repton had no objection to flower gardens. He even recommended them—a special one for American plants—and beds for roses.† He approved, when appropriate, of flowers 'in beds or baskets standing on the neatest mown grass'.[67] Tiny flowers, he believed 'should be lifted from the ground to meet the eye', while among the infinite variety of flowers now available some 'should be raised even above the eye'. In this category he includes 'the fuchsia, the American cowslip and other pendulous plants'.[68] Vases, statues, trellis work—all have their places in certain types of garden and, says he firmly, 'I am aware that this will cause some alarm to those who fancy all NATURE at variance with ART . . .', but 'I am not now describing a landscape but a garden, AND A GARDEN IS A WORK OF ART, USING THE MATERIALS OF NATURE'.[69]

He too, inevitably, had his detractors; among them Sir Uvedale Price, author of the famous *An Essay on the Picturesque*. There are funny caricatures of Repton and Price, disguised under the names

---

* Repton's memory played him a trick here. The lines do occur in Payne Knight's poem *The Landscape* (1744) but not in the order quoted by Repton. Correctly they are: 'Some features then, at least we should obtain/To mask this flat, insipid, waving plain' (Bk. II, ll. 13–14) and 'But wrapt all o'er in everlasting green/ Makes one dull, vapid, smooth and tranquil scene' which comes in Book I, ll. 271–72.

† He must have loved roses for he expressed a wish to be buried in a 'garden of roses' and selected a small enclosure on the south side of Aylsham Church for this purpose, so that his dust might give 'form and colour to the rose' (*Epitaph* on Tomb of H. Repton, written by himself.)

of Marmeduke Milestone Esq. and Sir Patrick O'Prism, in Peacock's *Headlong Hall*, published in 1816. Price did not care for Repton and his work while Peacock seems not to have cared for landscape 'improvements' at all, which was very unfashionable of him. Like his predecessor, Brown, Repton was also blamed for many things he did not do. He became, he tells us, 'the mark for envy and rivalship' and saw himself 'attacked in the public papers for blunders at places I had never visited, or for absurdities introduced before I visited them; and I heard opinions quoted as mine, which I had never advanced, and was blamed for errors which I had never advised'.[70]

Repton, who had 'improved' Brown's work at Longleat in 1803, died in 1818—exactly a hundred years after the publication of the first edition of Stephen Switzer's *Ichnographia Rustica*. During that hundred years much had happened. Queen Caroline had once said, in her forthright way, to her Vice Chancellor, 'I had lief be Elector of Hanover as King of England, if the government was the same. Who the devil would take you all, or think you worth the taking, that had anything else, if you had not your liberties? Your island might be a very pretty thing in that case for Bridgeman and Kent to cut out into gardens: but for the figure it would make in Europe, it would be of no more consequence here in the West than Madagascar in the East.'[71]

Our island was, indeed, still a very pretty thing when Repton died, for it had been 'cut into gardens' by a long line of great gardeners, professional and amateur. We had also, on the way, reformed the government, extended our liberties, fought various wars; lost a colony, gained an Empire, and were rapidly becoming the most powerful and richest nation in the world.

We may have lost or gained a great deal since then—it depends upon the point of view. But we still have our liberties—and our gardens.

Perhaps it is better to be envied for these than for other things.

BIBLIOGRAPHY

Adam, Robert and James, *Works in Architecture*, 3 vols, 1778, 1779, 1822; reprinted 1900–1.
Amherst, Alicia, *A History of Gardening in England*.
Amici, Domenico, *Vedute di Roma*, 1835.
Anon, *The Georgian Era*, 4 vols, 1832.
Anon, *The Ladies Toilette*, London 1822.
Anstey, Christopher, *The New Bath Guide*.

Baron, John, *The Life of Edward Jenner*, 2 vols, 1838.
Blenheim Archives, *Letters*, as noted in sources.
Bond, Donald F., ed., *The Spectator*, 5 vols, 1965.
Bonham Carter, Victor, *The English Village*.
Boswell, James, *Life of Dr Johnson*, Everyman edn, 2 vols.
Branch-Johnson, W., *The Carrington Diary*
Brown, Nicholas, *Diary*, Surtees Society Publication CXVIII.
Burton-Adams, G., *Constitutional History of England*.
Burton, Elizabeth, *The Jacobeans at Home*.
— *Here is England*.
Byng, John, *The Torrington Diaries*, ed. C. B. Andrews; abridg. F. Andrews.

Campbell, Colen, *Vitruvius Britannicus*, 2 vols, 1717, 1735.
Carlyle, Thomas, *Essays*, as noted in sources.
Chalmers Mitchell, P., *Centenary History of the Zoological Society of London*, Society Publication, 1929.
Chatsworth Settlement, various letters, accounts, etc., noted in sources.
Chenevix-Trench, C., *The Royal Malady*.
Chesterfield, Lord, *Letters to his Son*.
Chierici, Gino, *Palladio*, Milan, 1952.
Chippendale, Thomas, *The Gentleman and Cabinet Makers Directory*, 1st edn, 1754; 3rd edn, 1762.

Cowper, Mary, Countess, *Diary 1714–1740*.

Cowper, William (1st Earl), *Private Diary*, Roxburghe Club, vol. 49.

Creevey, Thomas, *Papers*, ed. Sir Herbert Maxwell.

D'Arblay, Mme (Fanny Burney), *Letters and Journals*, 8 vols, 1842.

Defoe, Daniel, *A Tour through England*, 1st edn, 3 vols, 1724–5–6.

— *A Tour etc.*, 8th edn, 4 vols, 1778.

Delany, Mary, *Autobiography and Correspondence*, Series I, 3 vols; Series II, 3 vols, ed. Lady Llanover.

Delves-Broughton, Mrs, ed., *The Court and Private Life of Mrs Papendieck*.

Dodington, George Bubb, *Diary*, ed. Wyndham, 1784.

Doran, John, *Lives of the Queens of England of the House of Hanover*, 1855, 2 vols.; rev. edn 1874.

Drummond, Sir J., and Wilbraham, A., *The Englishman's Food*, rev. by D. Hollingsworth, 1958.

Eden, Sir Frederic M., *The State of the Poor*, 3 vols, 1795–97.

Edwards, Ralph, *Hepplewhite Furniture Designs*.

Eland, G., ed., *The Purefoy Letters*, 2 vols.

Ellis, William, *The Country Housewife's Family Companion*, London, 1750.

Elville, E. M., *English and Irish Glass 1750–1950*.

Erskine, David, ed., *The Journals of the Hon. Augustus Hervey*.

Fastnedge, Ralph, *English Furniture Styles*.

Fiennes, Celia, *Journeys*, MSS Broughton Castle; also as ed. by Christopher Morris.

Filby, F. A., *A History of Food Adulteration*.

Fortescue, Sir J., *The Correspondence of George III*, 1927–8.

Fisher, H. A. L., *A History of Europe*.

Fretwell, James, *A Family History*, Surtees Society Publication LXV.

Fulford, Roger, *George the Fourth*.

Gell, Sir William, *Pompeii*, 2 vols, 1837.

George, D. M., *London Life in the Eighteenth Century*.

Glasse, Hannah, *The Compleat Confectioner*, 1770.

— *The Art of Cookery Made Plain and Easy*, 7th edn.

Goldsmith, Oliver, *The Citizen of the World*.

Bibliography

Graham, T. J., *Modern Domestic Medicine*, 7th edn., 1837.
Green, David B., *Gardener to Queen Anne*.
Green, J. R., *A Short History of the English People*.
Greig, James, ed., *Diary of a Duchess*.
Greville, Charles, *Diary*, ed. P. Whitwell Wilson, 2 vols.
Guthrie, Douglas, *A History of Medicine*.
Gyll, Thomas, *Diary*, Surtees Society Publication CXVIII.

Hadfield, Miles, *Gardening in Britain*.
Hare, Augustus J. C., *The Life and Letters of Maria Edgeworth*, 2 vols.
Halfpenny, Wm (Michael Hoare), *New Designs for Chinese and Gothic Architecture*, 1750.
Halsband, Robert, *The Life of Lady Mary Wortley Montagu*.
Hamilton, Lady Anne, *Epics of the Ton*, published anonymously, 2nd edn, 1807.
Hepplewhite, George, *Cabinet Makers and Upholsterers Guide*, 3rd edn, 1794.
Hervey, John, Lord, *Some Materials towards Memoirs of the Reign of King George II*, ed. Romney Sedgwick, 3 vols.
Hicks, George, *The Gentleman Instructed*, 10th edn, 1732.
Hobhouse, John Cam, *Recollections of a Long Life*, ed. Lady Dorchester, 6 vols.

Ilchester, the Earl of, *Lord Hervey and his Friends*.

Jackson, H., *An Essay on Bread*, 1758.
Jesse, J. H., *Memoirs of the Court of England from the Revolution in 1688 to the Death of George II*, vol. II, edn 1833; vol. III, edn 1891.
Johnson, Madam, *Every Young Woman's Companion in Useful and Universal Knowledge*, 3rd edn, 1765.
Jourdain, Margaret, *The Works of William Kent*.
Johnson, Samuel, *Lives of the English Poets*.
Jones, M. A., *The Charity School Movement*.

Kalm, Pehr, *An Account of his Visit to England on his way to America in 1748*, trans. and ed. Joseph Lucas.
Kimball, Fiske, and Donnell, Edna, *The Creators of the Chippendale Style*, Metropolitan Museum of Art Studies (o.p. photographic copy, courtesy of New York Public Library).
Kerr, S. P., *George Selwyn and the Wits*.
Knight, R. Payne, *The Landscape—a Didactic Poem*, 1794.

Lees-Milne, James, *The Age of Adam.*
Lecky, W. E. H., *A History of England in the Eighteenth Century*, vols I–VI, 2nd edn revised, 1879.
Lennox, Lady Sarah, *Life and Letters (1784–1826)*, ed. the Countess of Ilchester and Lord Stavordale.
'Longinus', *On Sublimity*, trans. D. A. Russell.
Lybbe Powys, Caroline, *Diary*, ed. Emily J. Climenson.
Lysons, Daniel, *The Environs of London*, 3 vols.

Macaulay, T. B., *Essays*, noted in sources.
Manningham, Sir Richard, *Diary Concerning Mary Toft the Pretended Rabbet Breeder*, 1726.
Marshall, Dorothy, *English People in the Eighteenth Century.*
— *Eighteenth Century England.*
Mason, William, *Collected Works*, 5 vols, 1811.
Morrice, Alexander, *A Treatise on Brewing*, 5th edn, 1815.
Moritz, C. P., *Travels Through Several Parts of England in 1782*, reprint of English trans. 1795. Introduction by P. E. Matheson.

Nardi, Famiano, *Roma Antica*, 2nd edn, 1704.
Neill, the Rt. Rev. S., *Anglicanism.*
Newington, Thomas, *The Butlers Receipt Book (1719)*, ed. Philip James.
Nicoll, Allardyce, *Eighteenth-Century Drama 1750–1800.*

Piesse, G. W. S., *The Art of Perfumery*, 1879.
Plumb, J. H., *The First Four Georges.*
Pollio, M. Vitruvius, *The Ten Books of Architecture*, trans. M. H. Morgan.
Price, Sir Uvedale, *Essays on the Picturesque as Compared with the Sublime*, 3 vols, 1810 edn.
Pyne, W. H., *Royal Residences.*

Raper, Elizabeth, *Receipt Book*, ed. Bartle Grant.
Rhode, E. S., *The Story of the Garden.*
Roche, Sophie v. la, *Diary 1786 (Sophie in London)*, trans. and ed. Clare Williams.

Rochefoucauld, François, de la, *Mélanges sur l'Angleterre, or A Frenchman in England*, ed. from MSS by Jean Marchand; trans. and notes S. C. Roberts.

Rogers, Thorold, *Six Centuries of Work and Wages*, short version and preface by G. D. H. Cole.

Ryder, Dudley, *Diary*, ed. William Matthews.

Repton, Humphry, *Collected Works*, 1840. Introduction and biographical note by J. C. Loudon.

Robinson, Victor, *The Story of Medicine*.

Saussure, César, de, *A Foreign View of England in the Reigns of George I and George II*, trans. and ed. by Mme v. Mayden.

Secker, the Rt. Rev. Dr T., *Visitation Returns* (1738), Oxfordshire Record Society XXXVIII.

Sheraton, Thomas, *Cabinet Directory*, 1803.

Singer, Charles, *A Short History of Medicine*.

— *A Short History of Scientific Ideas*.

Singer, S. W., ed, *Spence's Anecdotes*.

Smith, Preserved, *A History of Modern Culture*, vol. II.

Smollett, Tobias, *A History of England from the Revolution to the Death of George II*, 5 vols, revised 1812.

Steer, F. W., ed., *Farm and Cottage Inventories of Mid Essex 1635–1749*, Essex Record Office Publication 8.

Stroud, Dorothy, *Capability Brown*.

Strutt, Joseph, *The Sports and Pastimes of the People of England*, 1838.

Stukeley, W., *Family Memoirs*, 3 vols, Surtees Society Publications: LXXII; LXXVI; LXXX, numbered in sources as I, II, III.

Summerson, John, *Architecture in England 1530–1830*.

— *Georgian London*.

Swarbrick, John, *Robert Adam and his Brothers*.

Switzer, Stephen, *Ichnographia Rustica, or the Nobleman, Gentlemen, and Gardener's Recreation*, 3 vols, 2nd edn, 1742.

Thomlinson, J., *Diary*, Surtees Society Publication CXVIII.

Thompson, C. J. S., *Quacks of Old London*.

Trevelyan, G. M., *English Social History*.

Trusler, J., *The Honours of the Table for the Use of Young People*, 1787.

Venturi, A., *L'architettura del Cinquecento* (*Storia dell' arte italiana*), vol. III, Milan 1940.

Walpole, Horace, *Anecdotes of Painting in England*, ed. the Rev. Dr J. Dallaway 1828.
— *Letters*, ed. Mrs Paget Toynbee, 16 vols.
Watkin, E. I., *Roman Catholicism in England from the Reformation to 1950*.
Wesley, John, *Primitive Physic*, 24th edn, 1792.
Whatman, Susanna, *Housekeeping Book* (*c.* 1778), ed. Thomas Balston.
Wiley, Basil, *The Eighteenth-Century Background*.
Williams, E. M., ed., *The Eighteenth-Century Constitution*.
Wittkower, Rudolph, *Art and Architecture in Italy 1600–1750*.
Woodforde, J., *Diary*, ed. J. Beresford, 5 vols.
Wortley Montagu, Lady Mary, *Letters and Works*, ed. W. Moy Thomas, 2 vols.
Wright, Thomas, *Caricature History of the Georges*, 1868.
Wroth, W. and A. E., *London Pleasure Gardens of the Eighteenth Century*, 1896.

Young, Arthur, *A Six Months Tour Through the North of England*, 2nd edn, 1771.
— *A Six Weeks Tour Through the Southern Counties of England and Wales*, 3rd edn, 1772.

The Toilet of Flora, or a collection of the most simple and approved methods of Perfumery, Baths, Essences, Pomatums, Powders, Perfumes and Sweet Scented Waters, with Receipts for Cosmetics of every Kind, that can smooth and brighten the SKIN, give force to BEAUTY, and take off the Appearance of OLD AGE and Decay (this is almost a literal translation of *La Toilette de Flore* by P. J. Buc Hoz, with a supplement. First printed 1775. I have used the 1784 edition).
Pharmacopeia Officinalis & Extemporanea, or Quincey's English Dispensatory; printed for T. Longman and I. Shewell, 1743 (I have used the 2nd edn, 1765.)
    Also various relevant Journals of the Royal Horticultural Society; The Oxfordshire Record Society; *History Today, The Connoisseur, Country Life*.

SOURCES

CHAPTER I

1 Mary, Countess Cowper, *Diary*, October 20th 1714.
2 Lady Mary Wortley Montagu, *Court of George I*, ex. *Letters and Works*.
3 J. H. Jesse, *Memoirs of the Court*, etc., vol. II.
4 H.M. Patent Office, Patent No. 542, dated May 26th 1733.
5 Job, C 38: 31–2.
6 Daniel Defoe, *Tour through England and Wales*, 1st edn, Letter IX.
7 Defoe, *op. cit.*, Letter VIII.
8 Defoe, *ibid.*
9 Defoe, *op. cit.*, Letter X.
10 C. de Saussure, *A Foreign View of England*, Letter VII.
11 W. E. H. Lecky, *A History of England in the Eighteenth Century*, vol v., ch. 20.
12 Saussure, *op. cit.*, Letter II.
13 Saussure, *op. cit.*, Letter III.
14 Saussure, *op. cit.*, Letter II.
15 Pehr Kalm, *Visit to England*, etc.
16 Samuel Johnson, *London—a Poem* (1738), ll. 13–18.
17 C. Ryskamp and F. A. Pottle, *Boswell, The Ominous Years* (March 31st 1775).
18 Saussure, *op. cit.*, Letter V.
19 Saussure, *ibid.*
20 Daniel Lysons, *The Environs of London*, vol. III.
21 Saussure, *op. cit.*, Letter III.
22 Saussure, *ibid.*
23 Saussure, *ibid.*
24 Saussure, *op. cit.*, Letter II.
25 Saussure, *ibid.*
26 C. P. Moritz, *Travels Through . . . England.*

27 Moritz, *ibid.*
28 Saussure, *op. cit.*, Letter VI.
29 Moritz, *op. cit.*
30 Moritz, *op. cit.* From which all quotations in this paragraph are taken.
31 Horace Walpole, August 30th 1782, *Letters*, ed. Toynbee, Vol. XIV.
32 Lysons, *op. cit.*, Vol. III.
33 Lysons, *ibid.*
34 Defoe, *op. cit.*, 1st edn.
35 Defoe, *op. cit.*, 8th edn.
36 Defoe, *op. cit.*, 1st edn.
37 Defoe, *op. cit.*, 8th edn.
38 Defoe, *op. cit.*, 1st edn.
39 Defoe, *op. cit.*, 8th edn.
40 J. Copeland, in *Country Life*, April 19th 1962.
41 G. Eland, ed., *The Purefoy Letters*, vol. I as quoted.
42 Arthur Young, *Tour . . . North of England*, vol. I, Letter xli (author's abstract).
43 Young, *op. cit.*, vol. I, Letter xviii.
44 Young, *op. cit.*, vol. I, Letter i.
45 Young, *op. cit.*, vol. I, Letter xix.
46 Erasmus Darwin, *Steam Power—a Poem*, 1792.
47 Thomas Creevey, *The Creevey Papers*, September 19th 1830.
48 George Gordon, Lord Byron, *Don Juan*, Canto XI; stanza lxxxii.
49 D. M. George, *London Life in the 18th Century*.
50 A. Koestler and C. H. Rolph, *Hanged by the Neck*.
51 Sir F. M. Eden, *The State of the Poor*, preface.
52 Eden, *op. cit.*, vol. II.
53 Lecky, *op. cit.*, vol. III, ch. 10.
54 Eden, *op. cit.*, vol. II.
55 J. H. Plumb, *England in the 18th Century*.
56 Lecky, *op. cit.*, vol. V, ch. 19.
57 Lecky, *op. cit.*, vol. II, ch. 9; see also *Methodism* by R. E. Davies.
58 Lysons, *op. cit.*, vol. III.
59 Mrs Delany, Letter, January 3rd 1738/9, Series I, vol. I.
60 Sara Tytler, *The Countess of Huntingdon*; see also, 'The Queen of the Methodists', by David Mitchell in *History Today*, vol. 15.
61 Eustace Budgell, *The Spectator*, No 307, vol. III.
62 The Rt. Rev. S. Neill, *Anglicanism*.

63 M. A. Jones, *Charity Schools in the 18th Century*, Ch. 3.

64 Jones, *op. cit.*, Epilogue.

65 Mme d'Arblay, *Journals etc.*, July 14th 1788, vol. IV.

66 Charles Greville, *Diary*, November 9th 1829.

67 Lord Macaulay, *Edinburgh Review*, June 1831 (reviewing Moore's *Life of Byron*).

68 Jesse, *op. cit.*, vol. II.

69 J. Thomlinson, *Diary*, April 24th 1717.

70 Lady Elizabeth Finch, Letter, April (?) 1735, Chatsworth MSS 230.0.

71 Henry Pelham, Letter, September 27th 1739, Chatsworth MSS 249.3.

72 Andrew Stone, Letter, November 28th 1739, Chatsworth MSS 249.4

73 J. Grieg, ed., *Diary of a Duchess*, Thurs. November 18th, 1760.

74 Grieg, *op. cit.*, Tues. May 6th 1760.

75 F. Montagu, Letter, October 24th 1788, in Delany S. II; vol. 2.

76 John Cam Hobhouse (Lord Broughton), *Recollections, etc.*, vol. I; Ch. 3, May 27th 1812.

77 Hobhouse, *op. cit.*, June 2nd 1812.

78 Hobhouse, *op. cit.*, vol. IV; ch. 9.

79 Greville, *op. cit.*, July 16th 1830.

80 Hobhouse, *op. cit.*, vol. V, ch. 10, June 26th 1830.

CHAPTER II

1 F. A. Hervey, Letter, March 6th 1789, quoted from *The Two Duchesses* by Vere Foster.

2 Mme d'Arblay (F. Burney), *Diary*, August 20th 1791, vol. V.

3 Margaret Jourdain, *The Work of William Kent*, introduction by Christopher Hussey.

4 Arthur Young, *Tour . . . Southern Counties*, Letter I.

5 Mrs Lybbe Powys, *Diary*.

6 Humphrey Repton, *Theory and Practice of Gardening*.

7 Horace Walpole, *Anecdotes of Painting*.

8 John, Lord Hervey, Letter, July 14th 1741, quoted from *Lord Hervey and his Friends* by the Earl of Ilchester.

9 Lybbe Powys, *op. cit.*

10 Lybbe Powys, *op. cit.*

11 F. de la Rochefoucauld, *A Frenchman in England*, 1784, ed. J. Marchand, trans. S. C. Roberts.

12 John Hobson, *Journal*, as dated in text.

13 Horace Walpole, June 10th 1750, *Letters*, ed. Toynbee, vol. II.

14 John, Lord Hervey, *Memoirs etc.*, vol. III.

15 Defoe, *Tour etc.*, 1st edn.

16 Defoe, *op. cit.*, 8th edn.

17 Ralph Dutton, *The English Country House.*

18 D. Lysons, *Environs*, vol. III.

19 James Gibbs, *A Book of Architecture.*

20 Lybbe Powys, *op. cit.*

21 Walpole, September 13th 1741; *Letters*, vol. I.

22 J. H. Plumb, *England in the 18th Century.*

23 William Cobbett, *Rural Rides*, vol. II (Leicester, April 26th 1830).

24 Sir William Chambers, Report to the House of Commons, May 1st 1780, quoted in *The Homes of the Royal Academy*, by S. C. Hutchison.

25 Alexander Pope, *Moral Essays IV*, lines 25–8; 31–4.

26 W. H. Woodcock, *Encyclopaedia Britannica*, 1939 edn, vol. 5.

27 Lady Mary Wortley Montagu, Letter, January 20th 1758.

28 Horace Walpole, *Anecdotes of Painting.*

29 Walpole, September 17th 1785, *Letters*, vol. XIII.

30 Walpole, *ibid.*

31 Walpole, May 6th 1770, *Letters*, vol VII.

32 W. Stukeley, October 15th 1774, *Memoirs* I, S.S.P. LXXIII.

33 Horace Walpole, *Anecdotes of Painting.*

CHAPTER III

1 John Byng, *Diary*, June 14th 1792, in *Torrington Diaries*, ed. C. B. and F. Andrews.

2 Byng, *ibid.*

3 Byng, July 4th 1792.

4 Horace Walpole, *Anecdotes of Painting.*

5 Walpole, *op. cit.*

6 Mrs Lybbe Powys, *Diary.*

7 Arthur Young, *Tour . . . Southern Counties.*

8 Young, *op. cit.*

9 Lybbe Powys, *op. cit.*

10 Lybbe Powys, *op. cit.*

11 Lybbe Powys, *op. cit.*

12 *Purefoy Letters*, G. Eland, ed. October 7th 1739.

13 *Purefoy Letters*, January 6th 1739/40.

14 D. Lysons, *Environs etc.*, vol. III.

15 Pehr Kalm, *Visit to England*.

16 Essex Record Office, *Farm and Cottage Inventories*.

17 John Hobson, *Journal*, 1726.

18 *Purefoy Letters*, July 1738.

19 Mrs Delany, Letter, February 11th 1743, S. I; vol. 2.

20 Elizabeth Burton, *The Jacobeans at Home*.

21 Moss Harris and Sons, *The English Chair*.

22 Lybbe Powys, *op. cit.*

23 F. Kimball and E. Donnell, *The Creators of the Chippendale Style*.

24 R. and J. Adam, *Works in Architecture*, vol. I, Preface (B).

25 Adam, *ibid.*

26 Delany, Letter, September 16th 1774, S. II; vol. 2.

27 Delany, *ibid.*

28 Adam, *op. cit.*, text relating to Plate VII; vol. I.

29 John Swarbrick, *Robert Adam and his Brothers*, quoting letter to Lord Kames.

30 Madam Johnson, *Young Woman's Companion*, 3rd edn, 1765.

31 Johnson, *op. cit.*

32 Walpole, November 14th 1796, *Letters*, vol xv.

33 Walpole, November 20th 1796, *Letters*, vol. xv.

34 M. D. Mann, *The Roman Villa at Woodchester* (also author's notes on excavation 1963).

35 T. Balston, ed., *The Housekeeping Book of Susanna Whatman* (1778–1800).

36 William Cowper, *The Task*, Book I, l. 88.

37 Thomas Love Peacock, *Nightmare Abbey*.

38 Balston, *op. cit.*

39 George Hepplewhite, *Cabinet Makers and Upholsterer's . . . Guide*, 3rd edn, prefatory remarks.

40 Richard Cumberland, *The West Indian*, in Epilogue by David Garrick.

41 M. Johnson, *op. cit.*

42 Walpole, June 23rd 1752, *Letters*, vol. III.

43 Ralph Fastnedge, *English Furniture Styles.*
44 Walpole, September 17th 1785, *Letters*, vol. XIII.
45 *Nouveau Larousse Classique*, extract.
46 Maria Edgeworth, *The Absentee.*
47 Lybbe Powys, *op. cit.*

CHAPTER IV

1 John, Lord Hervey, *Memoirs* vol. I.
2 James Boswell, *The Life of Dr Johnson*, Everyman vol. II.
3 Essex Record Office, *Inventories etc.*, Publication 8.
4 Lady Elizabeth Finch, Letter, May 29th 1735, Chatsworth MSS 230–5.
5 G. Colman and D. Garrick, *The Clandestine Marriage*, Act I; sc. I.
6 Boswell, *op. cit.*, vol. II.
7 Mrs Delany, Letter, April 11th 1771, S. II; vol. I.
8 J. Woodforde, August 24th 1793, *Diary*, vol. IV.
9 Delany, Letter, June 7th 1774, S. II; vol. I.
10 *London Gazette*, April 6th 1714, Advertisement.
11 *Daily Post*, October 27th 1727, Advertisement.
12 *Daily Post*, November 14th 1738, extract.
13 Delany, Letter, March 4th 1728/9, S. I; vol. I.
14 Delany, *ibid.*
15 Chatsworth Settlement, notes, MSS 260–293 (extract).
16 *Purefoy Letters*, ed. G. Eland, March 15th 1739/40.
17 Tobias Smollett, *Peregrine Pickle.*
18 Daniel Defoe, *Tour . . . etc.*, 8th edn.
19 Defoe, *op. cit.*
20 Boswell, *op. cit.*, vol. I.
21 Woodforde, *Diary*, May 24th 1793, vol. IV.
22 *Journal of Mrs Papendiek*, ed. Mrs Delves Broughton.
23 Defoe, *op. cit.*
24 Christopher Anstey, *The New Bath Guide.*
25 John Byng, *Diary*, June 16th 1781.
26 Thomas Carlyle, 'Count Cagliostro', *Essays*, 1833.
27 Woodforde, *Diary*, March 28th 1782, vol. II.
28 Madam Johnson, *The Young Woman's Companion.*
29 Byng, *Diary*, May 24th 1791.

CHAPTER V

1 R. Campbell, *The London Tradesman*, as quoted by Drummond and Wilbraham.
2 Campbell, *op. cit.*
3 Campbell, *op. cit.*
4 *Purefoy Letters*, ed. G. Eland, May (1737).
5 *Purefoy Letters*, March 1739.
6 John Hobson, *Diary*, February 18th 1729/30.
7 W. Stukeley, *Memoirs . . .*, vol. I.
8 Stukeley, *ibid.*
9 Sir John Drummond and A. Wilbraham, *The Englishman's Food.*
10 Mrs Hannah Glasse, *The Art of Cookery*, 7th edn, 1760.
11 Horace Walpole, June 6th 1752, *Letters*, vol. III.
12 Tobias Smollett, Dr, *The Expedition of Humphry Clinker.*
13 J. Trusler, *The Honours of the Table.*
14 Trusler, *op. cit.*
15 Trusler, *op. cit.*
16 Trusler, *op. cit.*
17 Walpole, February 25th 1789, *Letters*, vol. XIV.
18 F. de la Rochefoucauld, *A Frenchman in England.*
19 Rochefoucauld, *op. cit.*
20 J. Woodforde, *Diary*, August 18th 1783, vol. II.
21 Lady Mary Wortley Montagu, Letter, April 18th 1717.
22 Glasse, *op. cit.*
23 Glasse, *op. cit.*
24 Rochefoucauld, *op. cit.*
25 Rochefoucauld, *op. cit.*
26 Glasse, *op. cit.*
27 Stukeley, *op. cit.*, vol. I.
28 Thomas Love Peacock, *Headlong Hall.*
29 Anon, *Real Life in London*, 1822.
30 Augustus J. C. Hare, *Life and Letters of Maria Edgeworth*, vol. II.
31 Daniel Defoe, *Tour . . . etc.*, 1st edn.
32 William Cobbett, *Rural Rides*, vol. I.
33 John Byng, *Diary*, August 28th 1788.
34 Woodforde, *Diary*, October 29th 1795, vol. IV.
35 Sir F. M. Eden, *The State of the Poor*, vol. II.
36 Eden, *op. cit.*, vol. III.

37 Eden, *op. cit.*, vol. II.

38 Eden, *op. cit.*, vol. II.

39 Eden, *op. cit.*, vol. III.

40 Josiah Tucker, *Tracts of Political and Commercial Subjects* (1776).

41 Dudley Ryder, *Diary*, June 13th 1715.

42 H. Jackson, *An Essay on Bread* (1758).

43 Oliver Goldsmith, *The Vicar of Wakefield*.

44 Mrs Delany, Letter, November 10th 1754, S. 1; vol. 3.

45 Anon, *Dangers Attending the Use of Copper Vessels* (1755), quoted by Drummond and Wilbraham.

46 Glasse, *op. cit.*

47 Smollett, *op. cit.*

48 T. Warner Allen, *A History of Wine*.

49 *Purefoy Letters*, ed. G. Eland, September 15th 1738.

50 Henry Fielding, *An Inquiry into the Late Increase in Robbers* (1751).

51 Thomas de Quincey, *Confessions of an English Opium Eater*, Preface to 1822 edn.

52 James Boswell, *Life of Dr Johnson*, vol. II.

53 John Thomlinson, *Diary*, August 1st 1717.

54 Boswell, *op. cit.*, vol. II.

55 Henry Fielding, *Tom Thumb the Great*.

56 Thomas Gyll, *Diary*, April 2nd 1757.

57 Woodforde, *Diary*, May 19th 1787.

58 Glasse, *op. cit.*

59 Lord Chesterfield, Letter, October 29th 1784.

60 The Marquess of Anglesey, *The Capel Letters 1814–1817*.

61 Maria Edgeworth, *The Absentee*.

62 Madam Johnson, *Companion, etc.*, Title page, 3rd edn, 1765.

63 Johnson, *op. cit.*

64 *The London Magazine*, 1762.

65 Johnson, *op. cit.*

66 Glasse, *op. cit.*, Introductory Remarks.

67 Anon, *The Georgian Era*, compilation 1832, vol. IV.

68 Jane Austen, *Northanger Abbey*.

69 W. Kitchiner, *The Cook's Oracle*.

70 Thomas Hood, *Ode to William Kitchener, M.D.*

71 Kitchiner, *op. cit.*

72 Kitchiner, *op. cit.*

73 Thomas Carlyle, 'Characteristics', *Essays*, 1831.

Sources

CHAPTER VI

1 John, Lord Hervey, *Memoirs, etc.*, vol. III.
2 Alexander Pope, *Imitations of Horace*, Ep. I; vi; l. 56.
3 Pope, *Imitations . . .* , Ep. II, i; l. 182.
4 Lady Mary Wortley Montagu, Letter, April 24th 1748.
5 Dr Tissot, *The Family Physician*.
6 Dudley Ryder, *Diary*, December 6th 1715.
7 E. W. and A. E. Stearn, *The Effect of Smallpox on the Destiny of the American Indian*, Boston, 1945.
8 Wortley Montagu, *Town Eclogues*, No. VI.
9 Wortley Montagu, Letter, April 1st 1717.
10 Wortley Montagu, *ibid*.
11 Wortley Montagu, Letter, April/May 1722.
12 Robert Halsband, *The Life of Lady Mary Wortley Montagu*.
13 John Baron, *The Life of Edward Jenner*.
14 Lord Macaulay, *History of England*, Ch. xx.
15 Robert Boyle, *The Sceptical Chymist*, The Fourth Part.
16 *The General Advertiser*, February 11th 1784, Advertisement.
17 Harvey Graham, *Surgeons All*.
18 *Gentleman's Magazine*, Obituary, 1803, p. 769.
19 Laurence Sterne, *Tristram Shandy*.
20 W. Cullen, *Lecture on Materia Medica* (1773), quoted by Drummond and Wilbraham.
21 Graham, *op. cit.*
22 Ryder, *Diary*, February 29 1715/16.
23 W. Stukeley, *Memoirs*, vol. I.
24 Stukeley, *op. cit.*, vol. I.
25 Philip Bliss, *Reliquiae Hernianae*, 1857.
26 John Wesley, *Primitive Physic*.
27 William Ellis, *The Country Housewife's Family Companion*.
28 Ellis, *op. cit.*
29 Thomas Newington, *The Butlers Receipt Book* (1719), ed. Philip James.
30 Mrs Delany, Letter, April 17th 1746, S. 1; vol. 2.
31 Ellis, *op. cit.*
32 John Hobson, *Journal*, April 15th 1729.
33 Ellis, *op. cit.*
34 Ellis, *op. cit.*

35 Arthur Maynwaring, undated letter [1709], Blenheim Archives (E. 27).

36 Maynwaring, undated letter [1709], Blenheim Archives (E. 29).

37 Ryder, *Diary*, April 16th 1716.

38 Delany, Letter, March 1st 1743/4, S. 1, vol. 2.

39 T. Percival, *Essays Medical Philosophical and Experimental* (1798), vol. II.

40 Percival, *op. cit.*

41 Sir William Fordyce, *A New Inquiry into the Causes . . . of Fevers* (1773), quoted by Drummond and Wilbraham.

42 Sir R. Manningham, *An Exact Diary Concerning Mary Toft the Pretended Rabbet Breeder* (1726).

43 Manningham, *op. cit.*

44 Sterne, *Tristram Shandy*.

45 John Hunter, Letter, May 24th 1775, quoted by Baron in *Jenner*.

46 Hunter, Letter, August 12th 1775, quoted by Baron.

47 Douglas Guthrie, *A History of Medicine*.

48 Guthrie, *op. cit.*

49 Wesley, *op. cit.*

50 Thomas Gyll, *Diary*, September 2nd 1752.

51 Gyll, *Diary*, June (?) 1756.

52 Lord Byron, *English Bards and Scotch Reviewers*, ll. 131–4.

53 C. J. S. Thomas, *Quacks of Old London*.

54 Lawrence Wright, *Warm and Snug*.

55 Mme d'Arblay, *Journal*, October 26th 1788, vol. IV.

56 C. Chenevix-Trench, *The Royal Malady*; also *History Today*, vol. XII, June 1962.

57 d'Arblay, *Journal*, November 3rd 1788, vol. IV.

58 d'Arblay, *Journal*, November 5th 1788, vol. V.

59 Chenevix-Trench, *op. cit.*

60 d'Arblay, *Journal*, June 30th 1789, vol. V.

61 P. B. Shelley, England in 1819 (sonnet).

62 W. Shakespeare, *King Lear*, Act III; sc.–2.

CHAPTER VII

1 Tobias Smollett, *The Expedition of Humphry Clinker*.

2 James Boswell, *Life of Dr Johnson*.

3 Smollett, *op. cit.*

4 Horace Walpole, June 23rd 1750, *Letters*, vol. II.

5 Walpole, July 31st 1740. *Letters*, vol. I.

6 Walpole, June 23rd 1750, *Letters*, vol. II.

7 Walpole, *ibid.*

8 Pehr Kalm, *Visit to England.*

9 C. P. Moritz, *Travels Through . . . England.*

10 Walpole, Letter, May 26th 1748, quoted by W. and A. E. Wroth, not in Toynbee.

11 Frances Burney, *Evelina.*

12 Boswell, *op. cit.*, vol. II.

13 Joseph Strutt, *The Sports and Pastimes of the People of England.*

14 Burney, *op. cit.*

15 John, Lord Hervey, Letter, November 29th 1733, quoted by the Earl of Ilchester in *Lord Hervey.*

16 John Cleland, *Memoirs of a Coxcomb.*

17 J. Byng, *Diary*, June 12th 1789.

18 Mme d'Arblay, *Journal*, December 3rd 1785, vol. III.

19 Nicholas Brown, *Diary*, December (?) 1787.

20 J. Woodforde, *Diary*, vol. III, September 25th 1788.

21 Woodforde, *ibid.*

22 Woodforde, *ibid.*

23 Woodforde, *ibid.*, September 9th 1788.

24 Henry Fielding, *Tom Jones.*

25 Strutt, *op. cit.*

26 Woodforde, *Diary*, April 29th 1760, vol. I.

27 Strutt, *op. cit.*

28 Woodforde, *Diary*, May 12th 1788, vol. III.

29 Strutt, *op. cit.*

30 Christopher Anstey, *The New Bath Guide.*

31 William Cowper, 'Retirement', ll. 516–24.

32 R. B. Sheridan, *A Trip to Scarborough*, Act II; sc. I.

33 Sheridan, *ibid.*

34 Walpole, August 21st 1755, *Letters*, vol. III.

35 Christopher Hobhouse, *Fox.*

36 George Bubb Dodington, *Diary*, January 11th 1749/50.

37 Dodington, *Diary*, October 15th 1752.

38 Dodington, *ibid.*

39 Dodington, *Diary*, December 18th 1753.

40 Lady Anne Hamilton, *Epics of the Ton.*

41 Horace Walpole, *Memoirs and Portraits*.

42 Alexander Pope, *The Dunciad*, note to line 229 (variorum).

43 Pope, *op. cit.*, Book III; ll. 231–6.

44 *The Grub Street Journal*, September 9th 1731, Advertisement.

45 Fielding, *op. cit.*

46 Fielding, *op. cit.*

47 Allardyce Nicoll, *Eighteenth-Century Drama (1750–1800)*.

48 George Lillo, *The London Merchant*, Sc. 5.

49 Moritz, *op. cit.*

50 Lady Mary Wortley Montagu, Letter, September 22nd 1755.

51 Sheridan, *The Rivals*, Act I; Sc. 2.

52 Sheridan, *ibid.*

53 Samuel Johnson, *Lives of the English Poets*.

54 The Rev. Dr Salter, Letter, September 11th 1744, in Delany. S. I;
   vol. 2.

55 William Rose Benét, *Mad Blake*.

56 William Blake, Letter to G. Cumberland, August 26th 1799.

57 Mrs Delany, Letter, August 30th 1756, S. II; vol. I.

58 Delany, Letter, October 22nd 1745, S. I; vol. 2.

59 Delany, Letter, September 3rd 1769, S. II; vol. I.

60 Delany, Letter, December 29th 1757, S. I; vol. 3.

61 Lady Llanover, ed., *Delany Letters*, etc., S. II; vol. 3, editor's note
   p. 95 *et seq.*

62 Burney, *op. cit.*

63 Walpole, *Anecdotes of Painting*.

64 Walpole, *ibid.*

65 Arthur Young, *Tour . . . Southern Counties*.

66 Woodforde, *Diary*, January 8th 1782, vol. II.

67 Delany, Letter, February 12th 1785, S. II, vol. 3.

68 Walpole, October 23rd 1784, *Letters*, vol. XIII.

69 W. Shakespeare, *Richard II*, Act II; sc. I.

70 Sophie v. la Roche, Diary, 1786, *Sophie in London*. trans. and ed.
   Clare Williams.

71 Smollett, *op. cit.*

72 P. Chalmers Mitchell, *Zoological Society Centenary History*.

73 Chalmers Mitchell, *op. cit.*

CHAPTER VIII

1 Duchess of Portland, Letter, December 1st 1735, in *Delany* S. I; vol. I.

Sources

2 Samuel Johnson, *Lives of the English Poets.*

3 Alexander Pope, *An Epistle to Dr Arbuthnot*, ll. 305–10; 314, 315; 323–5; 328, 329

4 Lady Mary Wortley Montagu, Letter to Carr, Lord Hervey, quoted by Robert Halsband in *Life of Lady Mary.*

5 David Erskine, ed., *Journal . . . Augustus Hervey.*

6 Horace Walpole, December 12th 1776, *Letters*, vol. VII.

7 Walpole, June 18th 1751, vol. III.

8 Walpole, March 23rd 1752, vol. III.

9 Walpole, May 13th 1752, vol. III.

10 Walpole, June 23rd 1752, vol. III.

11 Walpole, October 28th 1752, vol. III.

12 Walpole, November 1st 1760, vol. IV.

13 R. B. Sheridan, *St Patrick's Day*, Act I, sc. I.

14 Walpole, September 25th 1740, *Letters*, vol. I.

15 John Cleland, *Memoirs of a Coxcomb*, Part II.

16 Lady Sarah Lennox, Letter, December 24th 1762, quoted by the Countess of Ilchester and Lord Stavordale in *Life and Letters.*

17 Anon, *The Ladies Toilette* (1822).

18 Walpole, May 26th 1742, *Letters*, vol. I.

19 Anon, *The Toilet of Flora*, Advertisement prefacing 1784 edition.

20 Tobias Smollett, *Peregrine Pickle.*

21 Anon, *Flora* etc.

22 Thomas Newington, *The Butlers Receipt Book*, ed. Philip James.

23 Walpole, July 3rd 1746, *Letters*, vol. II.

24 Walpole, *ibid.*

25 Wortley Montagu, Letter, April 1st 1717.

26 Anon, *Flora*, 1784 and *Toilette*, 1822, quoted in both.

27 Anon, *Flora.*

28 J. Wesley, *Primitive Physic*, 1792 edn.

29 Anon, *The Ladies Toilette.*

30 Newington, *op. cit.*

31 Anon, *Flora*, Advertisement.

32 Anon, *Flora.*

33 Anon, *Toilette.*

34 Walpole, Letter, October 28th 1756, vol. IV.

35 Anon, *Flora.*

36 Thomlinson, *Diary*, August 7th 1717.

37 Walpole, Letter, February 12th 1765, vol. VI.

38 Newington, *op. cit.*

39 Thomas Carlyle, 'Count Cagliostro', *Essays*, 1828.

40 Carlyle, *ibid.*

41 Sophie v. la Roche, Diary, quoted by Clare Williams in *Sophie in London.*

42 v. la Roche, *op. cit.*

43 v. la Roche, *op. cit.*

44 Anon, *Toilette.*

45 G. Colman and D. Garrick, *The Clandestine Marriage*, Act II; sc. 1.

46 J. Woodforde, *Diary*, May 2nd 1793, vol. IV.

47 Smollett, *Humphry Clinker.*

48 Thomlinson, *Diary*, July 12th 1718.

49 Pehr Kalm, *Visit to England* (1748).

50 Walpole, February 9th 1751, *Letters*, vol. III.

51 Walpole, September 9th 1761, *Letters*, vol. V.

52 Walpole, *ibid.*

53 Lennox, *op. cit.*

54 Lennox, *op. cit.*

55 Walpole, February 12th 1765, *Letters*, vol. VI.

56 Walpole, December 24th, 1764, *Letters*, vol. VI.

57 Christopher Anstey, *The New Bath Guide.*

58 Anon, *The Georgian Era*, vol. I, 1832.

59 Anon, *Flora.*

60 Lord Chesterfield, Letter, July 30th 1747.

61 Chesterfield, Letter, November 12th 1750.

62 John, Lord Hervey, *Memoirs*, vol. II.

63 Hervey, *op. cit.*, vol. I.

64 Dudley Ryder, *Diary*, September 14th 1715.

65 William Cowper, 'Conversation', ll. 283–6.

66 Hervey, Letter, January 9th 1728/9, quoted by the Earl of Ilchester.

67 Chesterfield, Letter, July 30th 1747.

68 Chesterfield, Letter, July 6th 1749.

69 James Boswell, *Life of Dr Johnson*, vol. I.

70 Hervey, *Memoirs*, vol. I.

71 Lord Holland, Letter, no date, presumed to be 1817, in *Creevey Papers.*

72 Anon, *Toilette.*

73 *Ibid.*

74 *Ibid.*

Sources

CHAPTER IX

1 Mrs Delany, Letter, November 8th 1760, S. 1; vol. 3.
2 William Mason, Letter, May 31st 1783, quoted by Toynbee, in Walpole's *Letters*, vol. XIII; fn.
3 Joseph Addison, *The Spectator*, No. 415, ed. Donald F. Bond, vol. III.
4 Addison, *op. cit.*, No. 414, vol. III.
5 Alexander Pope, *Moral Essays, Epistle IV*; ll. 57–64.
6 Stephen Switzer, *Ichnographia Rustica*, (Prooemial Essay), vol. I, 2nd edn, 1742.
7 Switzer, *op. cit.*, Preface.
8 Switzer, *op. cit* (Prooemial Essay).
9 Switzer, *op. cit.*, vol. II.
10 Switzer, *op. cit.*, vol. III.
11 Switzer, *op. cit.*, vol. III.
12 Switzer, *op. cit.* (Prooemial Essay).
13 P.R.O., Treasury Books and Papers, ccxcix, No. 10, fols, 35–8.
14 *London Journal*, May 1st 1731.
15 Celia Fiennes, *Journeys*, ed. Christopher Morris; also MSS, Broughton Castle.
16 Frederick Montagu, Letter, August 5th 1782, in Delany, S. II; vol. 3.
17 Dorothy Stroud, *Capability Brown*.
18 Horace Walpole, *On Modern Gardening*, supplement to *Anecdotes of Painting*, ed. Dr Dallaway.
19 Walpole, *ibid*.
20 Walpole, *ibid*.
21 Walpole, *ibid*.
22 Walpole, July 22nd 1751, *Letters*, vol. III.
23 Pehr Kalm, *Visit to England*.
24 Kalm, *op. cit.*
25 Kalm, *op. cit.*
26 Kalm, *op. cit.*
27 Kalm, *op. cit.*
28 Kalm, *op. cit.*
29 Kalm, *op. cit.*
30 Kalm, *op. cit.*
31 C. O. Morton, *Journal of the Royal Horticultural Society*, vol. 99, Part 8, August 5th 1964.

32 A. Kippis, *A Narrative of the Voyages round the World performed by Captain James Cook*, 1788 edn.

33 Samuel Johnson, *Lives of the English Poets*.

34 Johnson, *ibid*.

35 National Trust, *Stourhead*, pamphlet quoting Sir Richard Colt Hoare.

36 Mrs Boscawen, Letter, September 22nd 1783, in Delany, S. II, vol. 3.

37 Countess of Bute, Letter, October 11th 1786, in Delany S. II, vol. 3.

38 Bute, *ibid*.

39 Switzer, *op. cit.*, vol. II.

40 Switzer, *op. cit.*, vol. II.

41 W. Stukeley, Letter, June 12th 1747, *Memoirs*, vol. I.

42 J. Woodforde, *Diary*, June 11th 1794, vol. IV.

43 Sir William Chambers, *A Dissertation on Oriental Gardens*.

44 R. Bruce, Letter to Lord Burlington, July 19th 1719, Chatsworth MSS, 1440.

45 Oliver Goldsmith, *The Citizen of the World*, Letter XXXI.

46 Mason, *The English Garden*, Book IV.

47 Sophie v. la Roche, *Diary*, ex. *Sophie in London*.

48 Alexander Pope, 'On His Grotto at Twickenham'.

49 Joseph Spence, *Anecdotes*, ed. Singer, Section V.

50 Delany, Letter, November 18th 1756, S. I; vol. 3.

51 Delany, *ibid*.

52 Duchess of Portland, Letter, June 21st 1737, in Delany S. I; vol. I.

53 Stukeley, Letter August 1st 1746, *Memoirs*, vol. I.

54 Arthur Young, *Six Weeks Tour . . . Southern Counties*.

55 G. Colman and D. Garrick, *The Clandestine Marriage*, Act II, sc. 1.

56 Young, *op. cit.*

57 Stukeley, Letter, October 14th 1728, *Memoirs*, vol. I.

58 H. Repton, *Sketches and Hints on Landscape Gardening* (1795), Introduction.

59 J. C. Loudon, 'Biographical Notice of the late Humphry Repton Esq.', in *Collected Works*, ed. Loudon, 1840.

60 Repton, *op. cit.*

61 Repton, *An Inquiry into the Changes of Taste in Landscape Gardening*, 1806.

62 Repton, *Sketches etc. . . . .*

63 Repton, *op. cit.*

64 Repton, *op. cit.*

65 Repton, *op. cit.*

66 Repton, *On the Theory and Practice of Gardening,* in *Collected Works,* Fragment XXXIII.

67 Repton, *ibid.,* Fragment XXV.

68 Repton, *ibid.*

69 Repton, *ibid.*

70 Loudon, *op. cit.*

71 John, Lord Hervey, *Memoirs,* vol. II.

INDEX

Index

Index

Sheffield Plate, 176–8
Shelley, Mary, 296
Shelley, Percy Bysshe, 267
Shenstone, William, 351 n, 366–7
Sheraton, Thomas, 28, 137 n, 140, 143–7
Sheridan, Richard Brinsley, 288, 342
Ships and shipping, 11–12, 34
Shops and shop signs, 10, 13, 14
Siddons, Mrs, 273, 296
Slavery, abolition of, 36
Sloane, Sir Hans, 226, 228, 238, 241, 246, 298–9
Slums, 20, 53, 86–7, 103
Smallpox, 228–9
Smeaton, John, 22
Smellie, William, 255–6
Smollett, Tobias, 291, 293, 322 n
Smuggling, 215
Snuff and snuff-boxes, 331
Soane, John, 100–1
Soap, 338
Social services, 40
Somerset House, London, 89, 300–1
Sophia Dorothea (wife of George I), 1
South Sea Bubble, 30, 53 n, 85 n
Southcote, Philip, 359 n
Southey, Robert, 295
Spas, 282–3
Speenhamland System, 35, 46 n
Spirits, 13, 212, 214–15
Sports and games, 278–81
Spranger, Barry, 290
Stanhope, James, 1st Earl, 27
Stately homes, 67–86, 105–8
Steam engines, 24–6, 34
Stephens, Joanna, 235–6
Stephenson, George, 25–6
Stearn, Laurence, 291, 293
Stillingfleet, Edward, 295
Stockton and Darlington Railway, 25
Stokes, Mrs (prize-fighter), 10
Stow, John, 17
Stowe, 355–7, 359
Street lighting and paving, 8, 40
Stuart, James, 90–1
Stubbs, George, 302 n

Stukeley, the Rev. Dr William, 104, 195, 200, 246–7, 253, 294–5, 351, 372, 379–80, 381
Sunday Schools, 16, 55–6
Surgery, 236–41
Surgical instruments, 240–1
Swift, Jonathan, 291
Switzer, Stephen, 351–3, 370
Sydenham, Thomas, 241–2, 246

Tassie, James, 165, 170
Taverns, 9
Taylor, Robert, 87–9
Taxation, 19, 36, 172
Tea-drinking, 155, 159, 193, 212–14
Teeth, care of the, 335–6
Telford, Thomas, 22
Test and Corporation Acts, 44–5
Textile industry, 2, 34
Thames, river, 11–12
Theatre, the, 273, 286–90
Theatres, 9, 273
Thompson, Sir Benjamin, 221
Thomson, James, 294
Toby jugs, 165–6
Tom Jones (Henry Fielding), 23
Toothache, treatments for, 335–6
Tower of London, 12, 306
Townshend, Charles, Viscount, 27 n
Traffic congestion, 12–13, 17
Transport, 17, 18, 19–26, 190 n, 304–6
Trevithick, Richard, 24–5
Trusler, the Rev. Dr John, 196, 199, 295
Tuke, William, 267
Tull, Jethro, 2, 202
Turner, J. M. W., 302, 350 n
Turner, Thomas, 160

Unemployment, 62 n

Vaccination, 231
Valois, Katherine of, 300
Vanbrugh, Sir John, 354
Vauxhall Gardens, 268–71
Victoria, Queen, 224
Villages, 10, 15–16, 17, 13 n, 282–3

**If you would like a complete list of Arrow books
please send a postcard to
P.O. Box 29, Douglas, Isle of Man, Great Britain.**